CLUSTER™

BOOM! STUDIOS

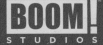

ROSS RICHIE *CEO & Founder*
MATT GAGNON *Editor-in-Chief*
FILIP SABLIK *President of Publishing & Marketing*
STEPHEN CHRISTY *President of Development*
LANCE KREITER *VP of Licensing & Merchandising*
PHIL BARBARO *VP of Finance*
BRYCE CARLSON *Managing Editor*
MEL CAYLO *Marketing Manager*
SCOTT NEWMAN *Production Design Manager*
IRENE BRADISH *Operations Manager*
CHRISTINE DINH *Brand Communications Manager*
SIERRA HAHN *Senior Editor*
DAFNA PLEBAN *Editor*
SHANNON WATTERS *Editor*
ERIC HARBURN *Editor*
WHITNEY LEOPARD *Associate Editor*
JASMINE AMIRI *Associate Editor*
CHRIS ROSA *Associate Editor*
ALEX GALER *Assistant Editor*
CAMERON CHITTOCK *Assistant Editor*
MARY GUMPORT *Assistant Editor*
KELSEY DIETERICH *Production Designer*
JILLIAN CRAB *Production Designer*
KARA LEOPARD *Production Designer*
MICHELLE ANKLEY *Production Design Assistant*
AARON FERRARA *Operations Coordinator*
ELIZABETH LOUGHRIDGE *Accounting Coordinator*
JOSÉ MEZA *Sales Assistant*
JAMES ARRIOLA *Mailroom Assistant*
STEPHANIE HOCUTT *Marketing Assistant*
SAM KUSEK *Direct Market Representative*
HILLARY LEVI *Executive Assistant*
KATE ALBIN *Administrative Assistant*

CLUSTER™

CREATED BY **ED BRISSON** & **DAMIAN COUCEIRO**

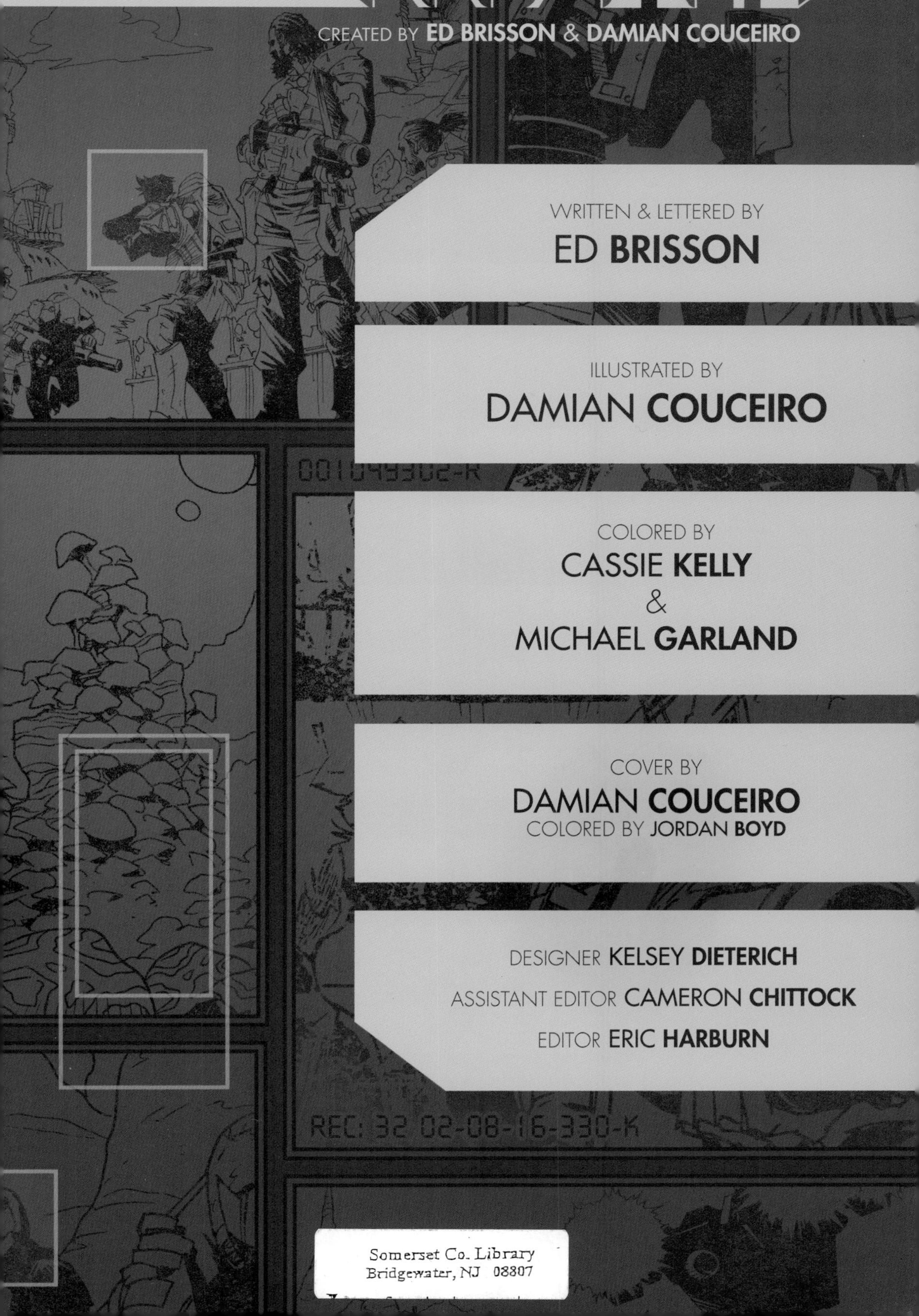
REC: 32 02-08-16-330-K

WRITTEN & LETTERED BY
ED **BRISSON**

ILLUSTRATED BY
DAMIAN **COUCEIRO**

COLORED BY
CASSIE **KELLY**
&
MICHAEL **GARLAND**

COVER BY
DAMIAN **COUCEIRO**
COLORED BY **JORDAN BOYD**

DESIGNER **KELSEY DIETERICH**
ASSISTANT EDITOR **CAMERON CHITTOCK**
EDITOR **ERIC HARBURN**

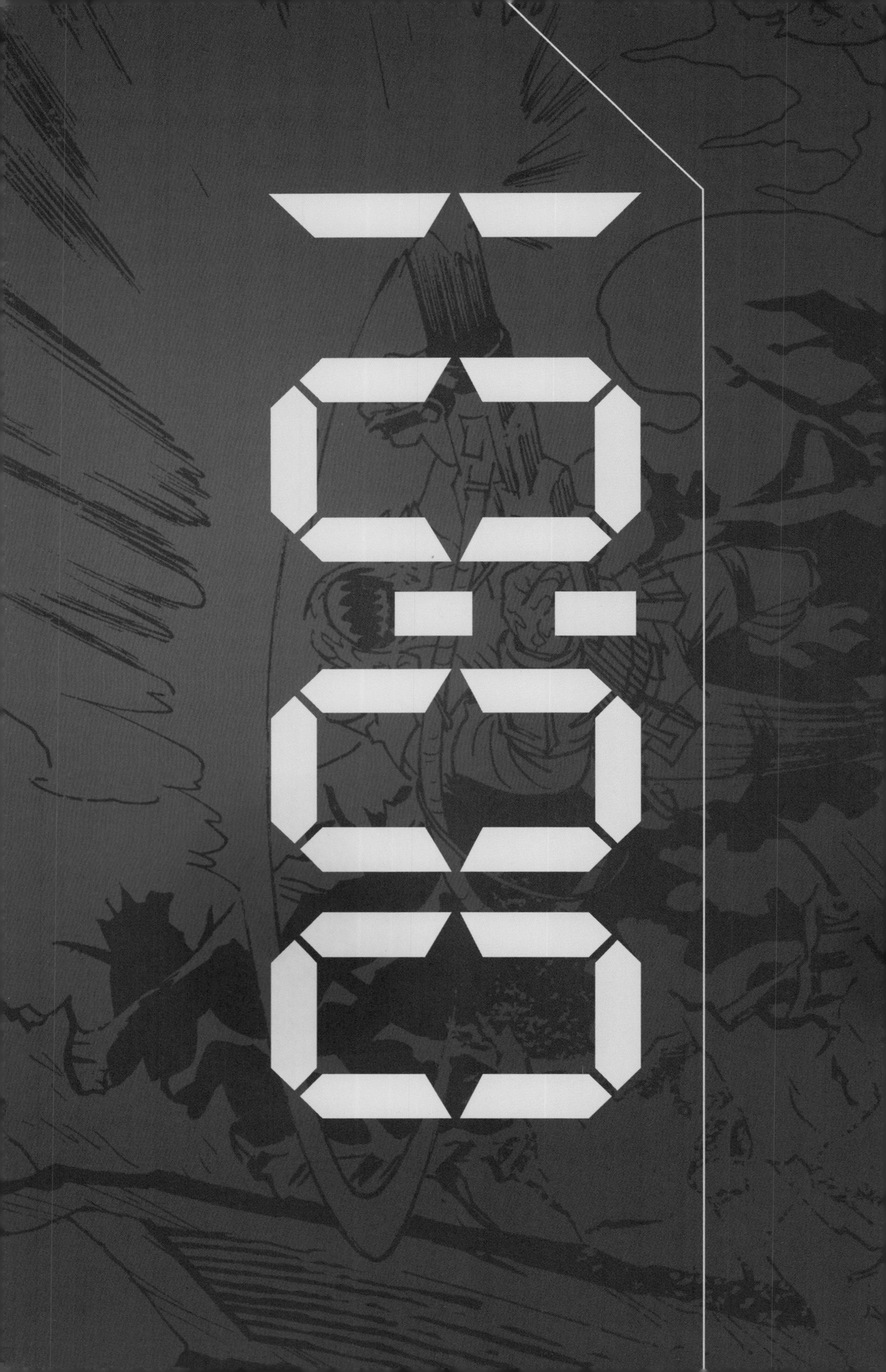
00:01

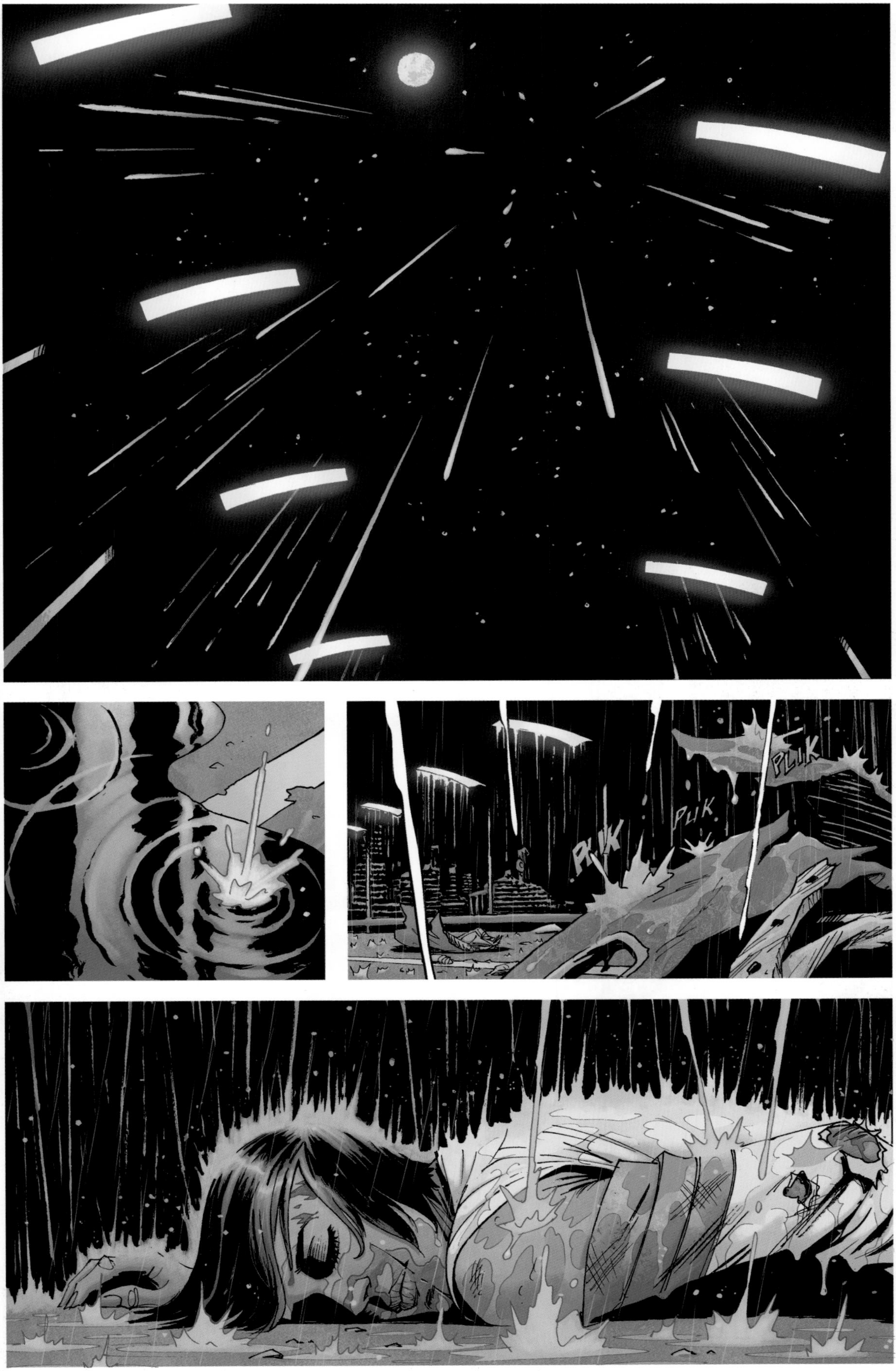
PLIK
PLIK
PLIK

UNGHHH
PLIK
PLIK
PLIK
PLIK
PLIK
PLIK
PLIK
NO.

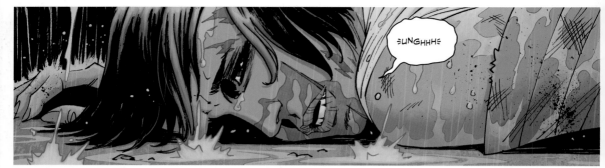

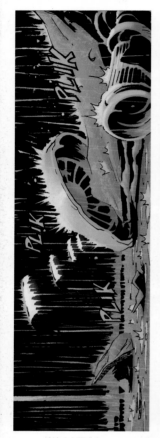

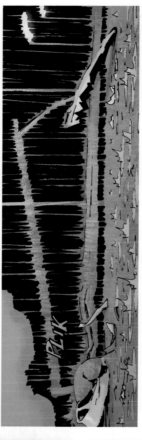

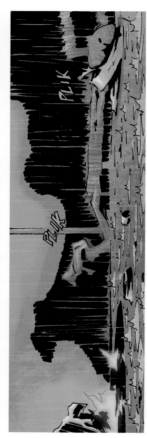

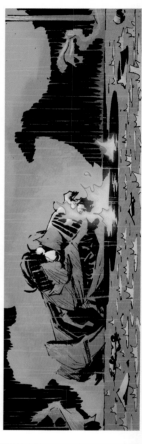

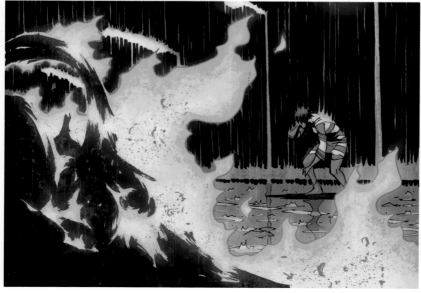

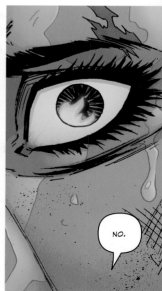

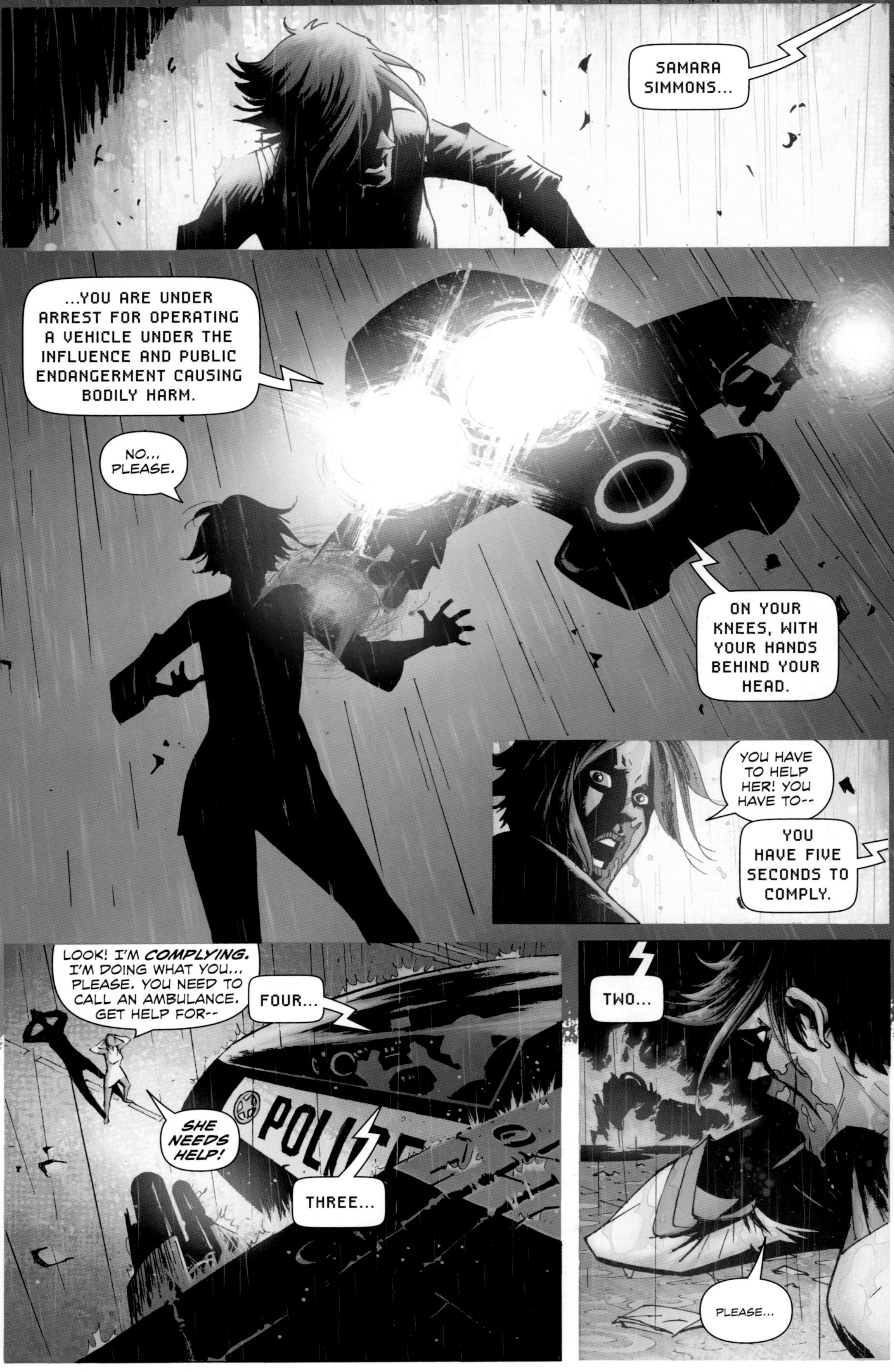
SAMARA SIMMONS...
...YOU ARE UNDER ARREST FOR OPERATING A VEHICLE UNDER THE INFLUENCE AND PUBLIC ENDANGERMENT CAUSING BODILY HARM.
NO... PLEASE.
ON YOUR KNEES, WITH YOUR HANDS BEHIND YOUR HEAD.
YOU HAVE TO HELP HER! YOU HAVE TO--
YOU HAVE FIVE SECONDS TO COMPLY.
LOOK! I'M COMPLYING. I'M DOING WHAT YOU... PLEASE. YOU NEED TO CALL AN AMBULANCE. GET HELP FOR--
FOUR...
SHE NEEDS HELP!
POLI
THREE...
TWO...
PLEASE...

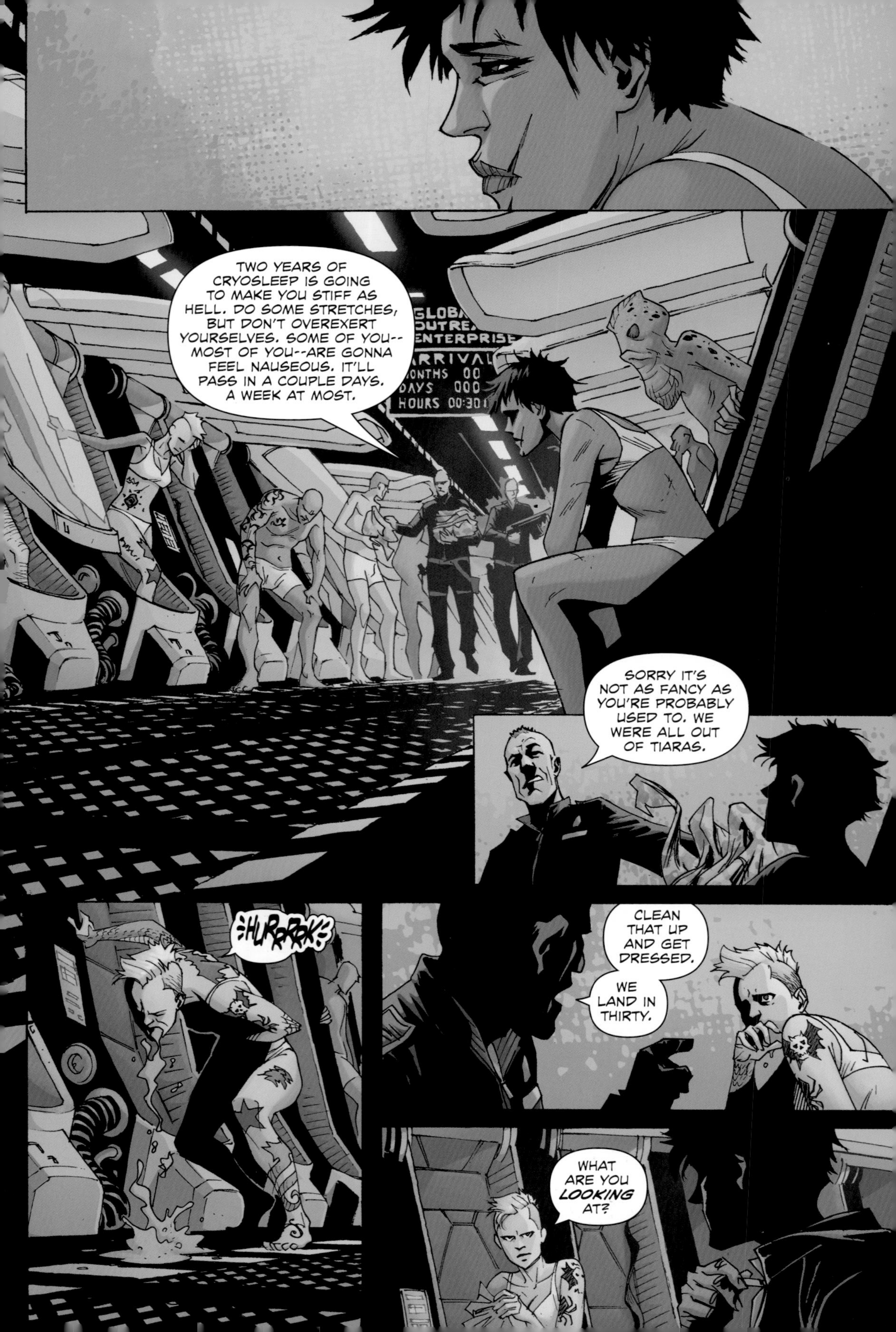
TWO YEARS OF CRYOSLEEP IS GOING TO MAKE YOU STIFF AS HELL. DO SOME STRETCHES, BUT DON'T OVEREXERT YOURSELVES. SOME OF YOU-- MOST OF YOU--ARE GONNA FEEL NAUSEOUS. IT'LL PASS IN A COUPLE DAYS. A WEEK AT MOST.
ENTERPRISE
ARRIVAL
DAYS 000
HOURS 00:30
SORRY IT'S NOT AS FANCY AS YOU'RE PROBABLY USED TO. WE WERE ALL OUT OF TIARAS.
HURRRRK!
CLEAN THAT UP AND GET DRESSED.
WE LAND IN THIRTY.
WHAT ARE YOU *LOOKING* AT?

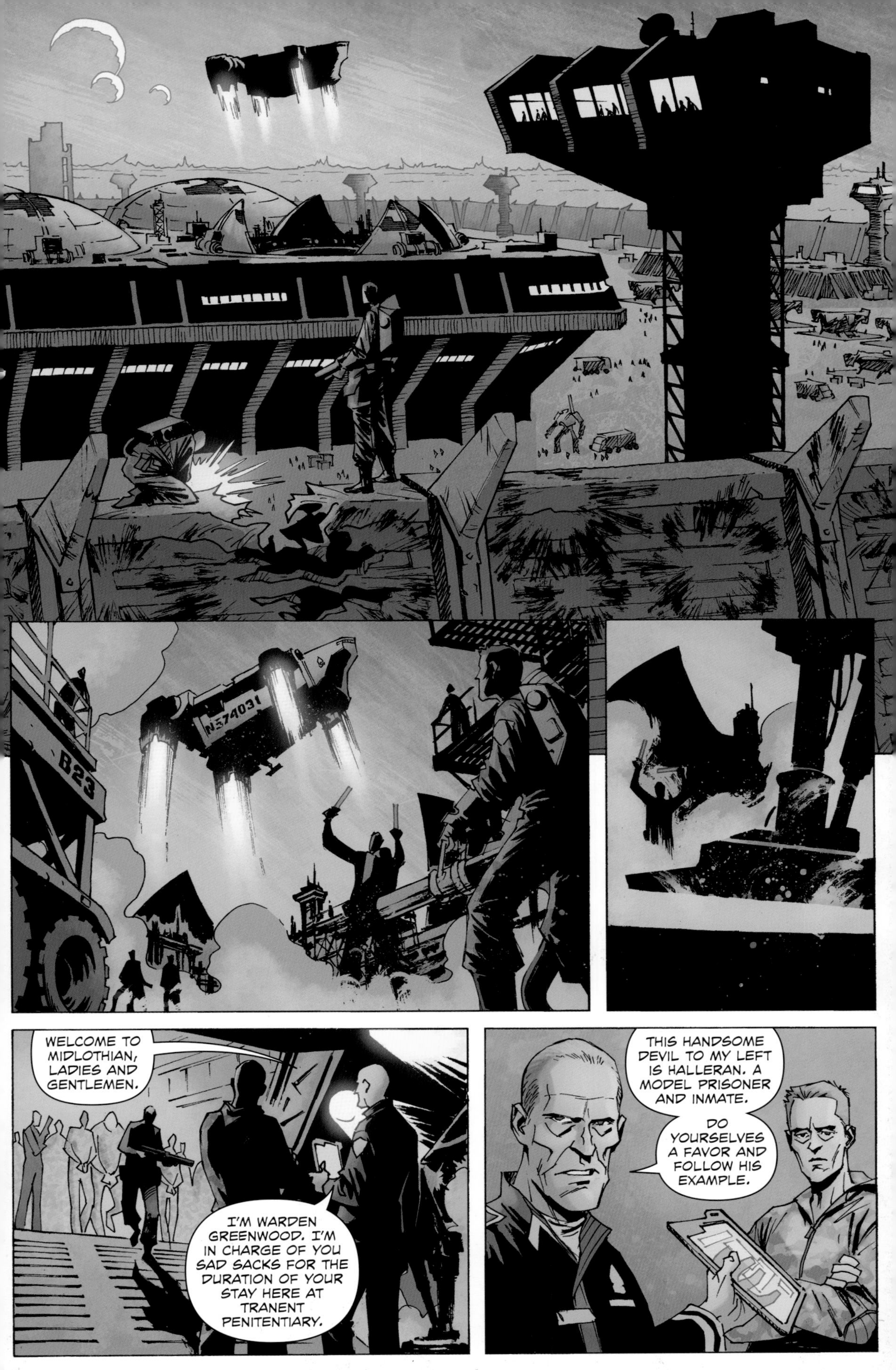
WELCOME TO MIDLOTHIAN, LADIES AND GENTLEMEN.
I'M WARDEN GREENWOOD. I'M IN CHARGE OF YOU SAD SACKS FOR THE DURATION OF YOUR STAY HERE AT TRANENT PENITENTIARY.
THIS HANDSOME DEVIL TO MY LEFT IS HALLERAN. A MODEL PRISONER AND INMATE.
DO YOURSELVES A FAVOR AND FOLLOW HIS EXAMPLE.

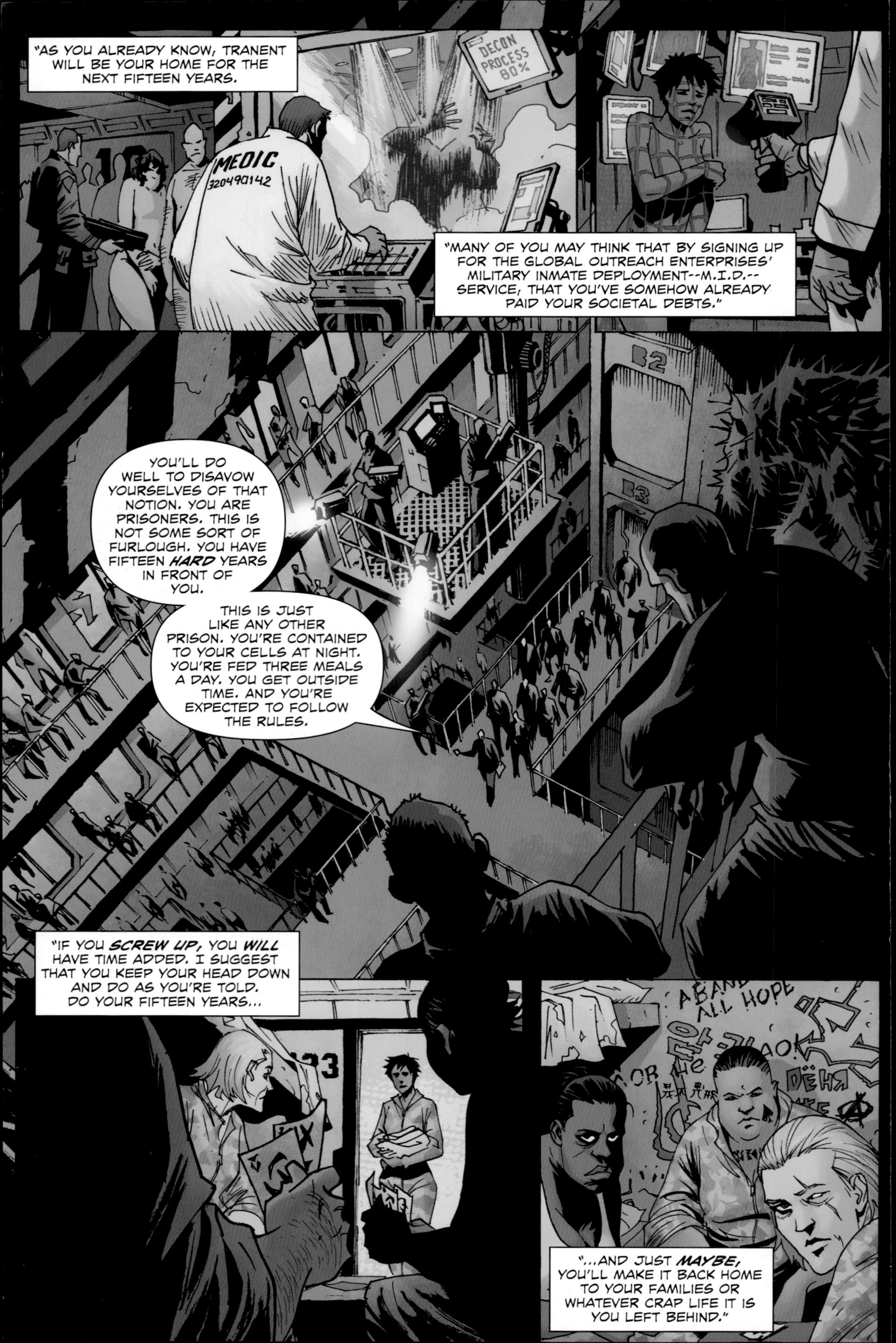
"AS YOU ALREADY KNOW, TRANENT WILL BE YOUR HOME FOR THE NEXT FIFTEEN YEARS.
DECON PROCESS 80%
MEDIC 320490142
"MANY OF YOU MAY THINK THAT BY SIGNING UP FOR THE GLOBAL OUTREACH ENTERPRISES' MILITARY INMATE DEPLOYMENT--M.I.D.--SERVICE, THAT YOU'VE SOMEHOW ALREADY PAID YOUR SOCIETAL DEBTS."
B2
B3
YOU'LL DO WELL TO DISAVOW YOURSELVES OF THAT NOTION. YOU ARE PRISONERS. THIS IS NOT SOME SORT OF FURLOUGH. YOU HAVE FIFTEEN *HARD* YEARS IN FRONT OF YOU.
THIS IS JUST LIKE ANY OTHER PRISON. YOU'RE CONTAINED TO YOUR CELLS AT NIGHT. YOU'RE FED THREE MEALS A DAY. YOU GET OUTSIDE TIME. AND YOU'RE EXPECTED TO FOLLOW THE RULES.
"IF YOU ***SCREW UP,*** YOU ***WILL*** HAVE TIME ADDED. I SUGGEST THAT YOU KEEP YOUR HEAD DOWN AND DO AS YOU'RE TOLD. DO YOUR FIFTEEN YEARS...
"...AND JUST ***MAYBE,*** YOU'LL MAKE IT BACK HOME TO YOUR FAMILIES OR WHATEVER CRAP LIFE IT IS YOU LEFT BEHIND."

WELCOME TO TRAINING DAY, FOLKS.

YOU MAY HAVE NOTICED THE LACK OF WALLS HERE ON THE TRAINING FIELD. DON'T LET THAT FOOL YOU.

EACH OF YOU HAS BEEN IMPLANTED WITH A SMALL DEVICE INSIDE YOUR CHEST CALLED A *"PUNCH."* IT'S TRANENT'S WAY OF KEEPING YOU ALL ON A SHORT LEASH.

WHEN YOU LEAVE THE COMPOUND, YOU'RE AUTOMATICALLY SCANNED AND "PUNCHED OUT" FOR TWENTY-FOUR HOURS.

G.O.E. HAS SUPPLIED YOU WITH A TIMER TO TRACK YOUR TIME AWAY.

KEEP A CLOSE EYE ON IT AT ALL TIMES.

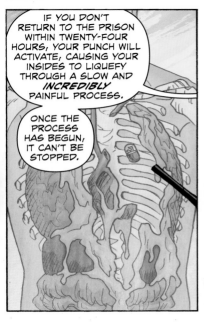

IF YOU DON'T RETURN TO THE PRISON WITHIN TWENTY-FOUR HOURS, YOUR PUNCH WILL ACTIVATE, CAUSING YOUR INSIDES TO LIQUEFY THROUGH A SLOW AND *INCREDIBLY* PAINFUL PROCESS.

ONCE THE PROCESS HAS BEGUN, IT CAN'T BE STOPPED.

TRYING TO ALTER OR REMOVE THE PUNCH WILL ALSO CAUSE IT TO ACTIVATE, SO DON'T GET ANY BRIGHT IDEAS.

MANY HAVE TRIED, NONE HAVE SUCCEEDED.

SO, PLEASE. FOR YOUR SAKE AND MINE, DON'T MESS WITH THE PUNCH.

I'VE SEEN THE PUNCH TAKE OUT MANY GOOD SOLDIERS. IT'S NOT SOMETHING YOU WANT TO SEE--LET ALONE EXPERIENCE.

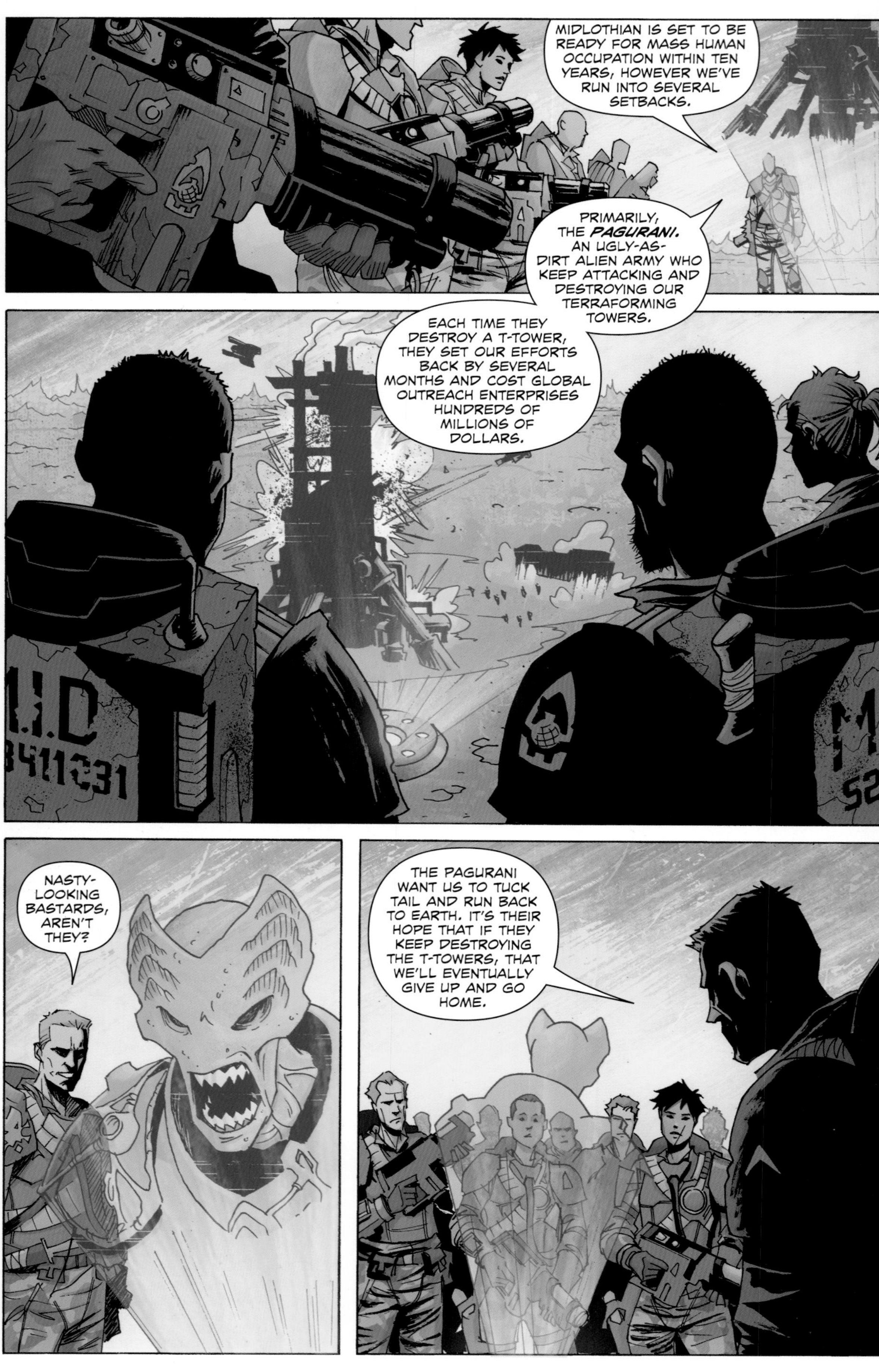
MIDLOTHIAN IS SET TO BE READY FOR MASS HUMAN OCCUPATION WITHIN TEN YEARS, HOWEVER WE'VE RUN INTO SEVERAL SETBACKS.
PRIMARILY, THE ***PAGURANI.*** AN UGLY-AS-DIRT ALIEN ARMY WHO KEEP ATTACKING AND DESTROYING OUR TERRAFORMING TOWERS.
EACH TIME THEY DESTROY A T-TOWER, THEY SET OUR EFFORTS BACK BY SEVERAL MONTHS AND COST GLOBAL OUTREACH ENTERPRISES HUNDREDS OF MILLIONS OF DOLLARS.
NASTY-LOOKING BASTARDS, AREN'T THEY?
THE PAGURANI WANT US TO TUCK TAIL AND RUN BACK TO EARTH. IT'S THEIR HOPE THAT IF THEY KEEP DESTROYING THE T-TOWERS, THAT WE'LL EVENTUALLY GIVE UP AND GO HOME.

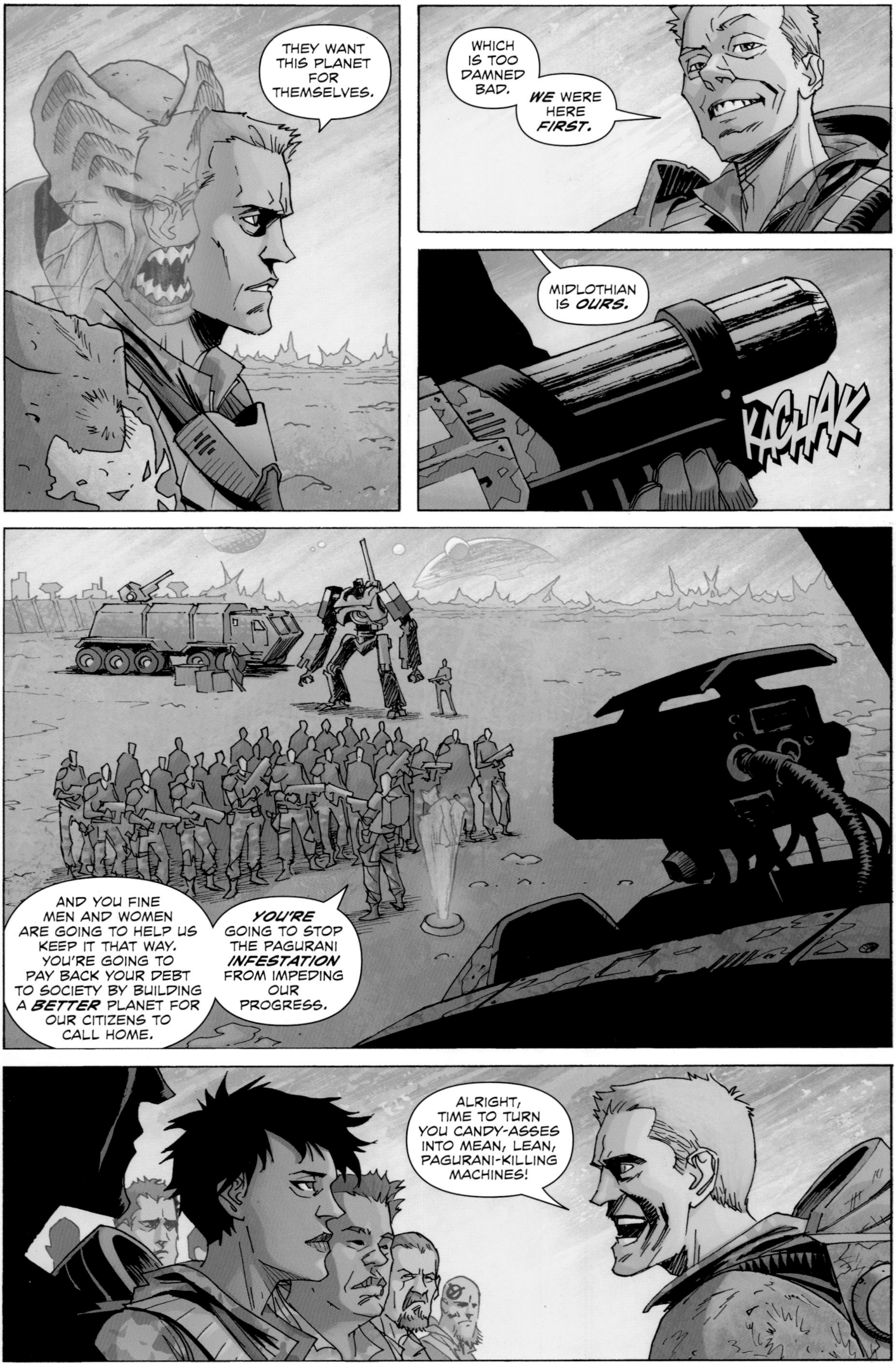
THEY WANT THIS PLANET FOR THEMSELVES.
WHICH IS TOO DAMNED BAD.
WE WERE HERE FIRST.
MIDLOTHIAN IS OURS.
KACHAK
AND YOU FINE MEN AND WOMEN ARE GOING TO HELP US KEEP IT THAT WAY. YOU'RE GOING TO PAY BACK YOUR DEBT TO SOCIETY BY BUILDING A BETTER PLANET FOR OUR CITIZENS TO CALL HOME.
YOU'RE GOING TO STOP THE PAGURANI INFESTATION FROM IMPEDING OUR PROGRESS.
ALRIGHT, TIME TO TURN YOU CANDY-ASSES INTO MEAN, LEAN, PAGURANI-KILLING MACHINES!

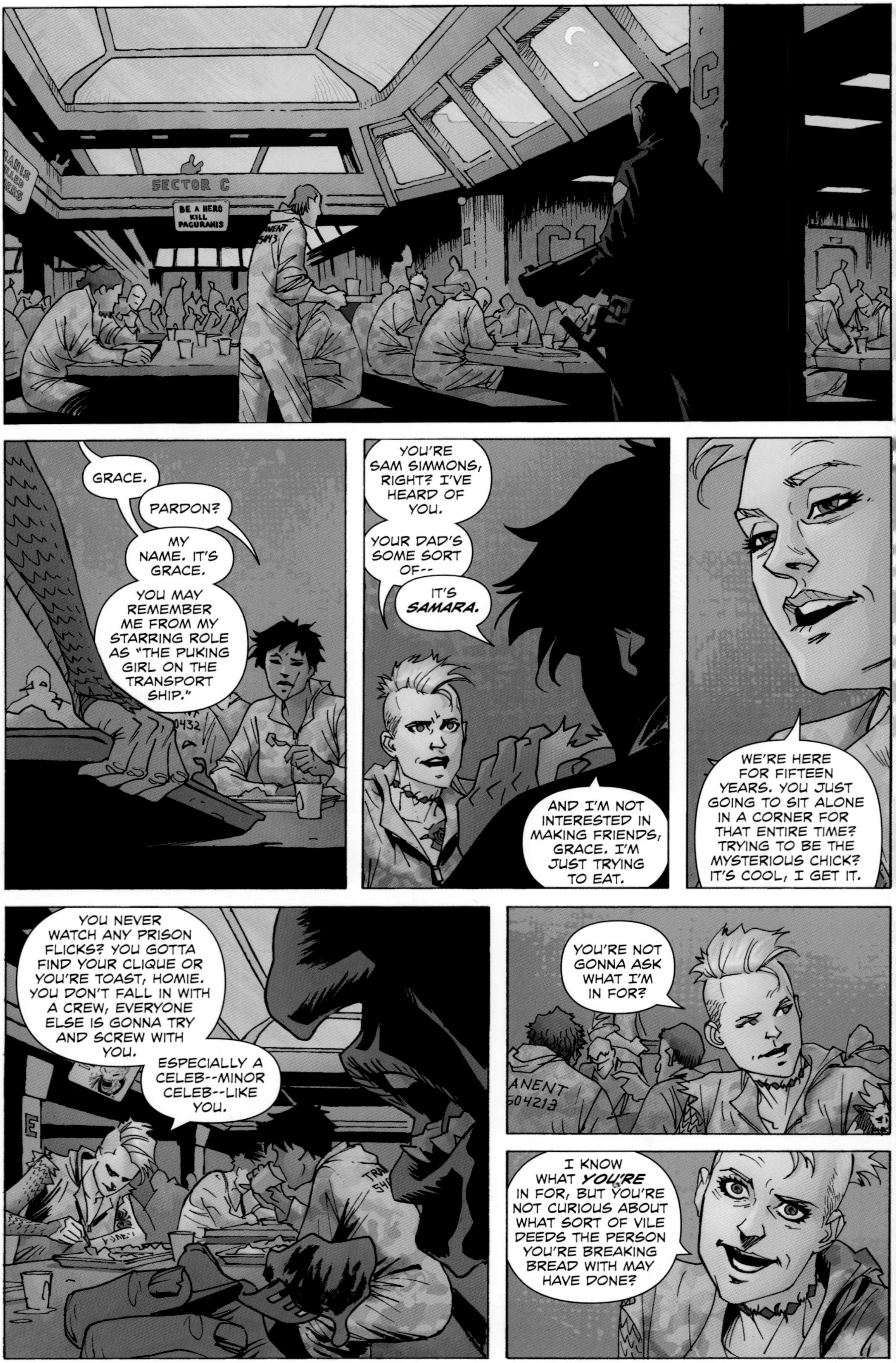
SECTOR C
BE A HERO KILL PAGURANIS
GRACE.
PARDON?
MY NAME. IT'S GRACE.
YOU MAY REMEMBER ME FROM MY STARRING ROLE AS "THE PUKING GIRL ON THE TRANSPORT SHIP."
YOU'RE SAM SIMMONS, RIGHT? I'VE HEARD OF YOU.
YOUR DAD'S SOME SORT OF--
IT'S *SAMARA.*
AND I'M NOT INTERESTED IN MAKING FRIENDS, GRACE. I'M JUST TRYING TO EAT.
WE'RE HERE FOR FIFTEEN YEARS. YOU JUST GOING TO SIT ALONE IN A CORNER FOR THAT ENTIRE TIME? TRYING TO BE THE MYSTERIOUS CHICK? IT'S COOL, I GET IT.
YOU NEVER WATCH ANY PRISON FLICKS? YOU GOTTA FIND YOUR CLIQUE OR YOU'RE TOAST, HOMIE. YOU DON'T FALL IN WITH A CREW, EVERYONE ELSE IS GONNA TRY AND SCREW WITH YOU.
ESPECIALLY A CELEB--MINOR CELEB--LIKE YOU.
YOU'RE NOT GONNA ASK WHAT I'M IN FOR?
I KNOW WHAT *YOU'RE* IN FOR, BUT YOU'RE NOT CURIOUS ABOUT WHAT SORT OF VILE DEEDS THE PERSON YOU'RE BREAKING BREAD WITH MAY HAVE DONE?

I'M IN FOR SHOPLIFTING. *SHOP. LIFTING.* CAN YOU BELIEVE IT? STEALING NAIL POLISH. *NAIL POLISH!* STORE SAID I ROBBED THEM AT GUNPOINT. WHO USES A GUN TO STEAL NAIL POLISH?

I'D NEVER EVEN TOUCHED A GUN BEFORE TODAY.

BUT, YOU KNOW...GUN *EQUALS* AUTOMATIC LIFE.

LIFE OR MIDLOTHIAN, LIKE THERE'S A REAL CHOICE.

IT'S A SHAM. I BET MOST OF THE PEOPLE HERE ARE INNOCENT AND DON'T--

WILL YOU *PLEASE* SHUT UP?

DON'T BE SO DAMNED NAÏVE.

LOOK AROUND YOU. YOU REALLY THINK ANYONE HERE'S INNOCENT? THAT NONE OF US BELONG HERE?

SECTOR E

GLOBAL OUTR ENTE WANTS YO

IT'S GOING TO BE A LONG FIFTEEN YEARS IF YOU DON'T ACCEPT WHY YOU'RE HERE.

SPOILED RICH--

AWWWWW... YOU AND YOUR WIDDLE GIRLFRIEND HAVING A SPAT?

HEH.

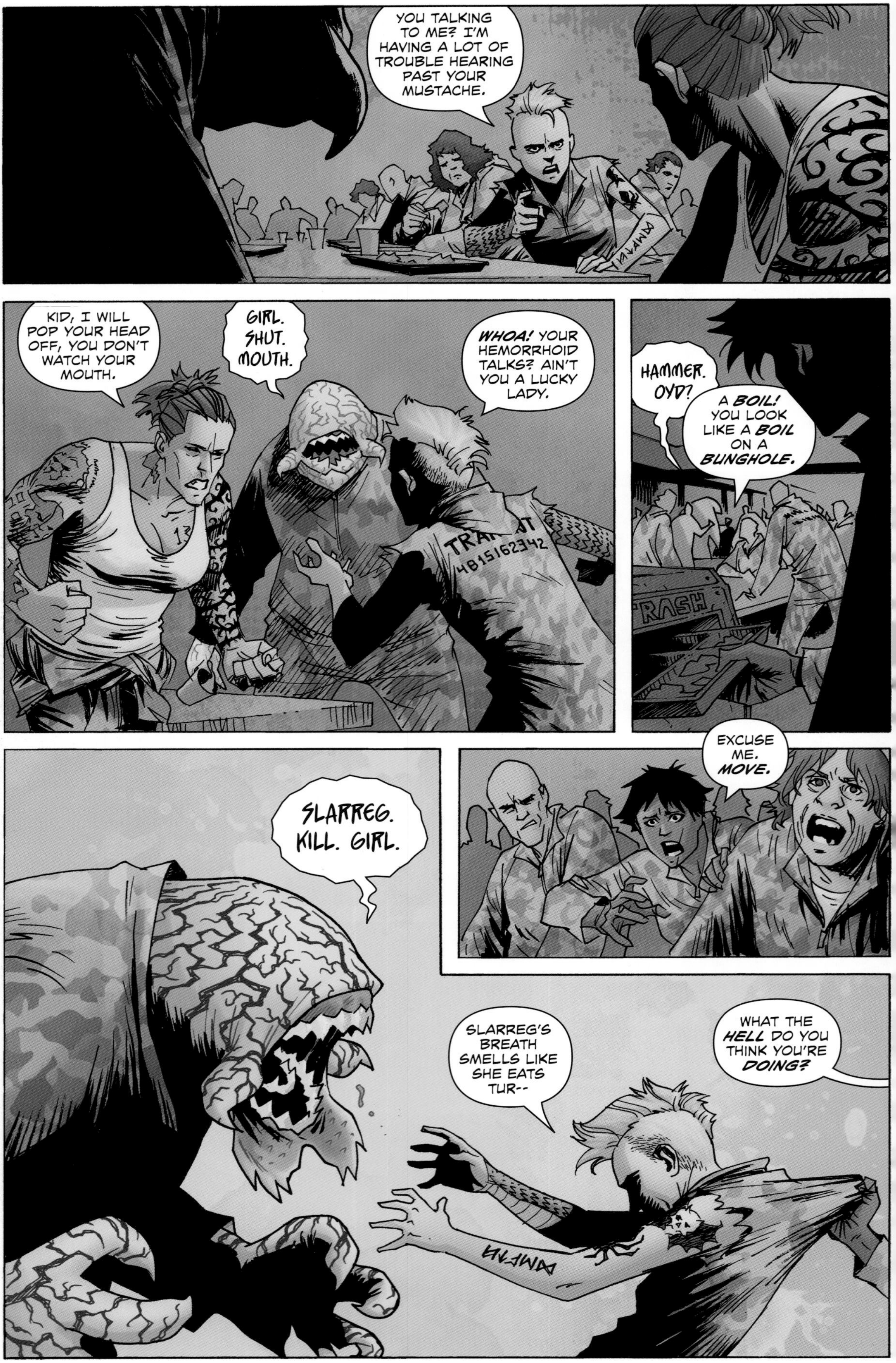
YOU TALKING TO ME? I'M HAVING A LOT OF TROUBLE HEARING PAST YOUR MUSTACHE.
KID, I WILL POP YOUR HEAD OFF, YOU DON'T WATCH YOUR MOUTH.
GIRL. SHUT. MOUTH.
WHOA! YOUR HEMORRHOID TALKS? AIN'T YOU A LUCKY LADY.
TRANSIT
4815162342
HAMMER. OYD?
A BOIL! YOU LOOK LIKE A BOIL ON A BUNGHOLE.
TRASH
SLARREG. KILL. GIRL.
EXCUSE ME. MOVE.
SLARREG'S BREATH SMELLS LIKE SHE EATS TUR--
WHAT THE HELL DO YOU THINK YOU'RE DOING?

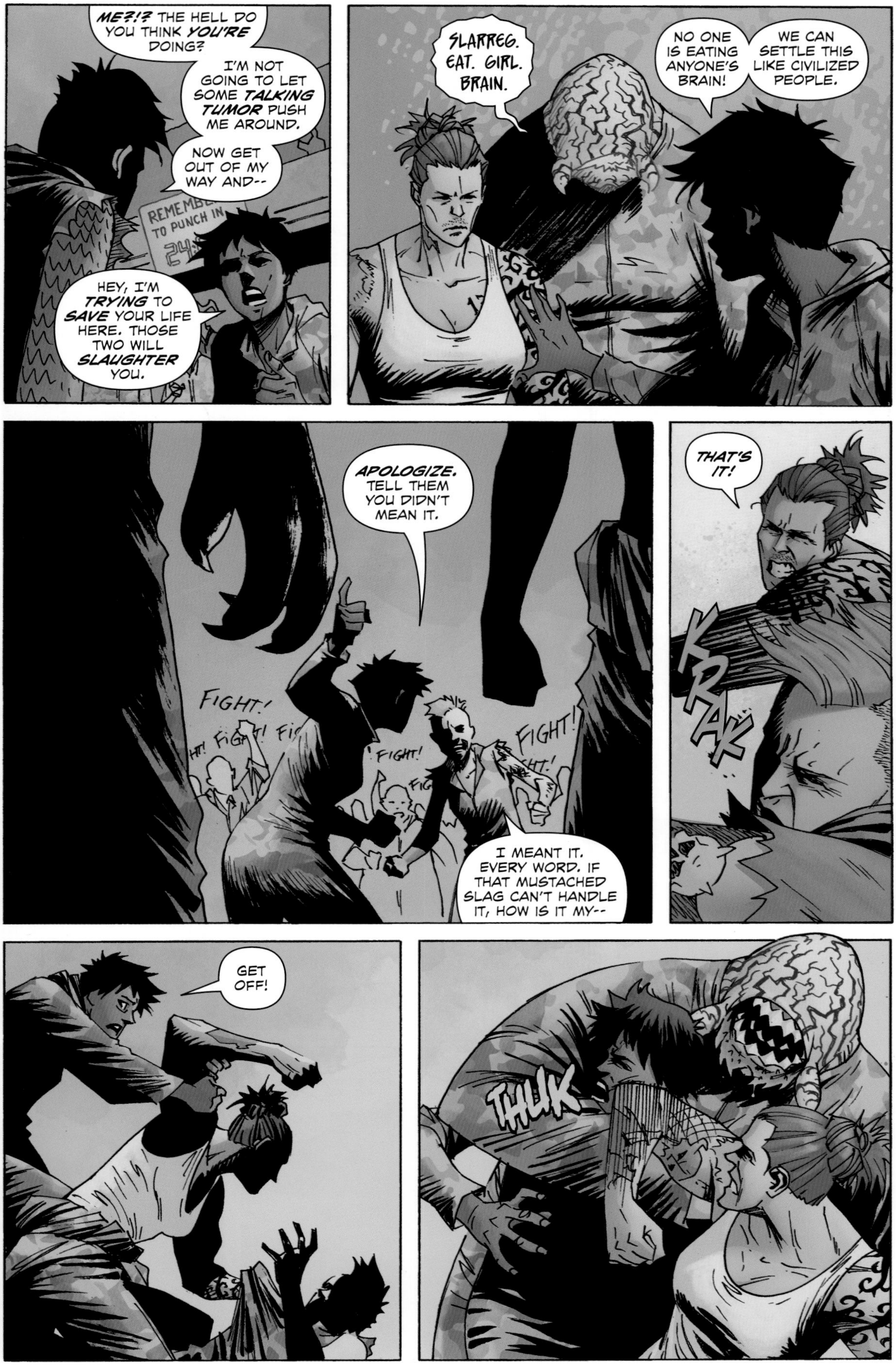
ME?!? THE HELL DO YOU THINK YOU'RE DOING?
I'M NOT GOING TO LET SOME TALKING TUMOR PUSH ME AROUND.
NOW GET OUT OF MY WAY AND--
REMEMBER TO PUNCH IN
HEY, I'M TRYING TO SAVE YOUR LIFE HERE. THOSE TWO WILL SLAUGHTER YOU.
SLARREG. EAT. GIRL. BRAIN.
NO ONE IS EATING ANYONE'S BRAIN!
WE CAN SETTLE THIS LIKE CIVILIZED PEOPLE.
APOLOGIZE. TELL THEM YOU DIDN'T MEAN IT.
FIGHT!
FIGHT!
FIGHT!
FIGHT!
I MEANT IT. EVERY WORD. IF THAT MUSTACHED SLAG CAN'T HANDLE IT, HOW IS IT MY--
THAT'S IT!
KRAK
GET OFF!
THUK

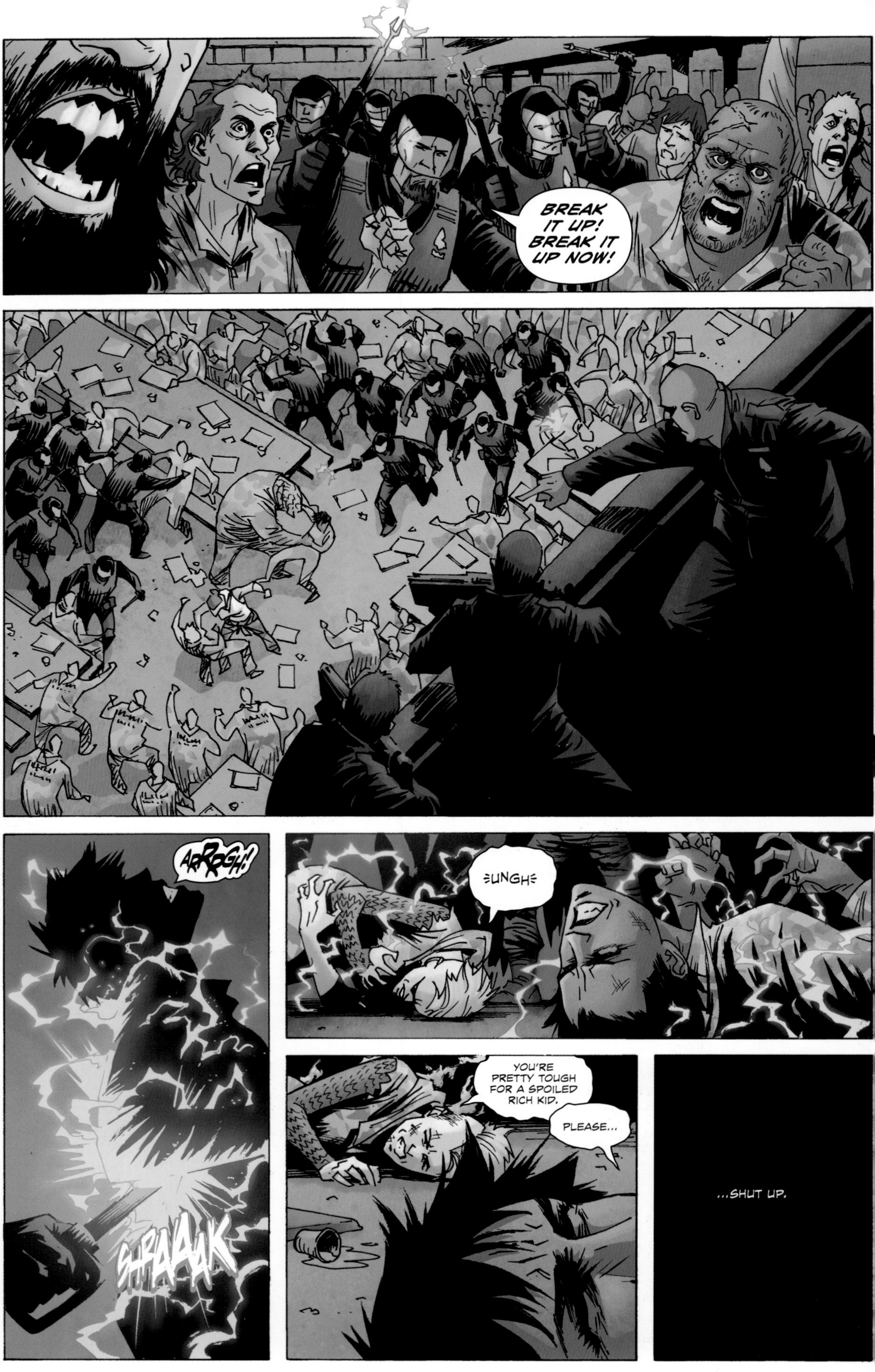
BREAK IT UP! BREAK IT UP NOW!
ARRGH!
SHRAAAK
UNGH
YOU'RE PRETTY TOUGH FOR A SPOILED RICH KID.
PLEASE...
...SHUT UP.

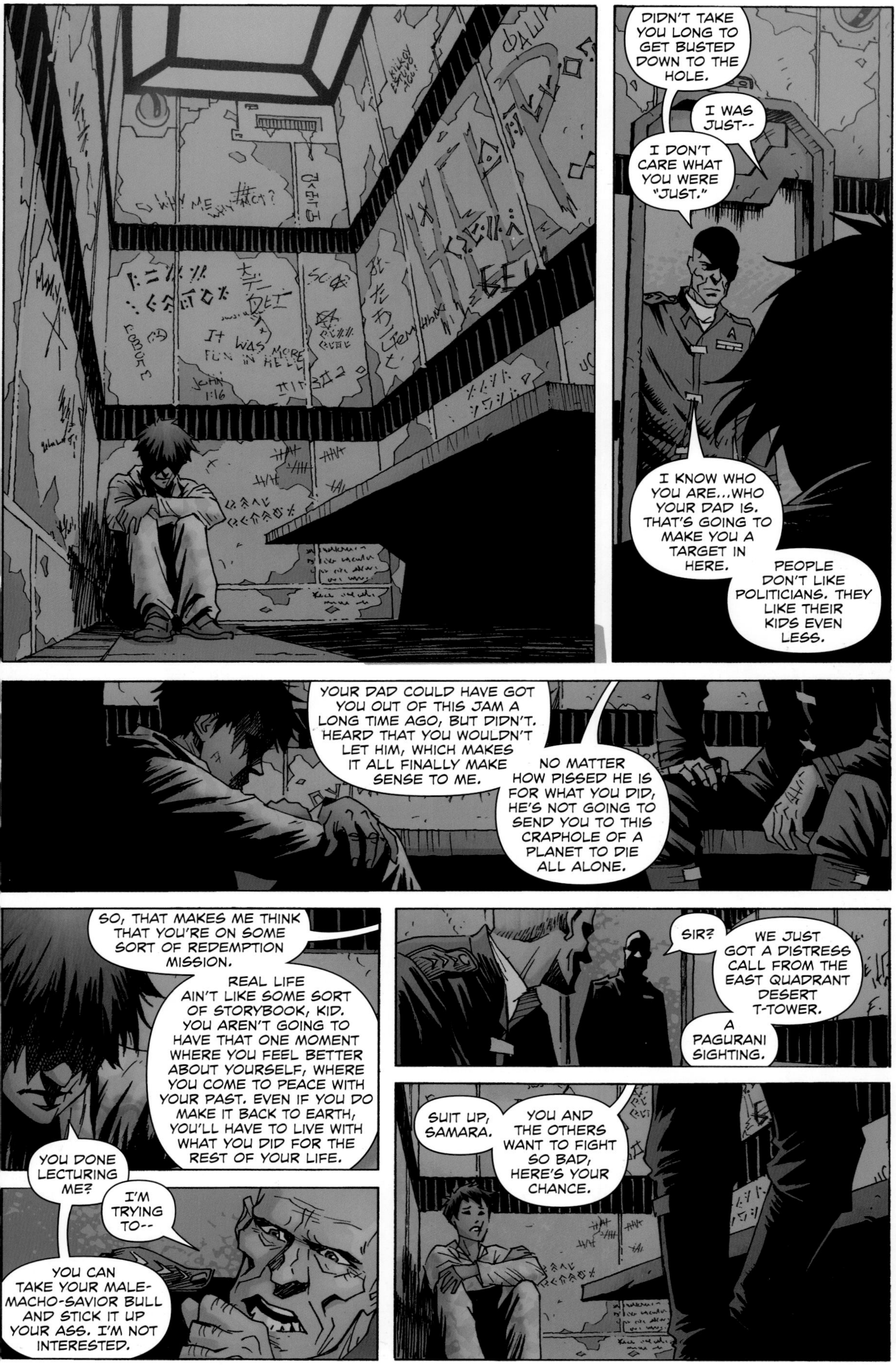
WHY ME
IT WAS MORE FUN IN HELL
JOHN 1:16
DIDN'T TAKE YOU LONG TO GET BUSTED DOWN TO THE HOLE.
I WAS JUST--
I DON'T CARE WHAT YOU WERE "JUST."
I KNOW WHO YOU ARE...WHO YOUR DAD IS. THAT'S GOING TO MAKE YOU A TARGET IN HERE.
PEOPLE DON'T LIKE POLITICIANS. THEY LIKE THEIR KIDS EVEN LESS.
YOUR DAD COULD HAVE GOT YOU OUT OF THIS JAM A LONG TIME AGO, BUT DIDN'T. HEARD THAT YOU WOULDN'T LET HIM, WHICH MAKES IT ALL FINALLY MAKE SENSE TO ME.
NO MATTER HOW PISSED HE IS FOR WHAT YOU DID, HE'S NOT GOING TO SEND YOU TO THIS CRAPHOLE OF A PLANET TO DIE ALL ALONE.
SO, THAT MAKES ME THINK THAT YOU'RE ON SOME SORT OF REDEMPTION MISSION.
REAL LIFE AIN'T LIKE SOME SORT OF STORYBOOK, KID. YOU AREN'T GOING TO HAVE THAT ONE MOMENT WHERE YOU FEEL BETTER ABOUT YOURSELF, WHERE YOU COME TO PEACE WITH YOUR PAST. EVEN IF YOU DO MAKE IT BACK TO EARTH, YOU'LL HAVE TO LIVE WITH WHAT YOU DID FOR THE REST OF YOUR LIFE.
YOU DONE LECTURING ME?
I'M TRYING TO--
YOU CAN TAKE YOUR MALE-MACHO-SAVIOR BULL AND STICK IT UP YOUR ASS. I'M NOT INTERESTED.
SIR?
WE JUST GOT A DISTRESS CALL FROM THE EAST QUADRANT DESERT T-TOWER.
A PAGURANI SIGHTING.
SUIT UP, SAMARA.
YOU AND THE OTHERS WANT TO FIGHT SO BAD, HERE'S YOUR CHANCE.

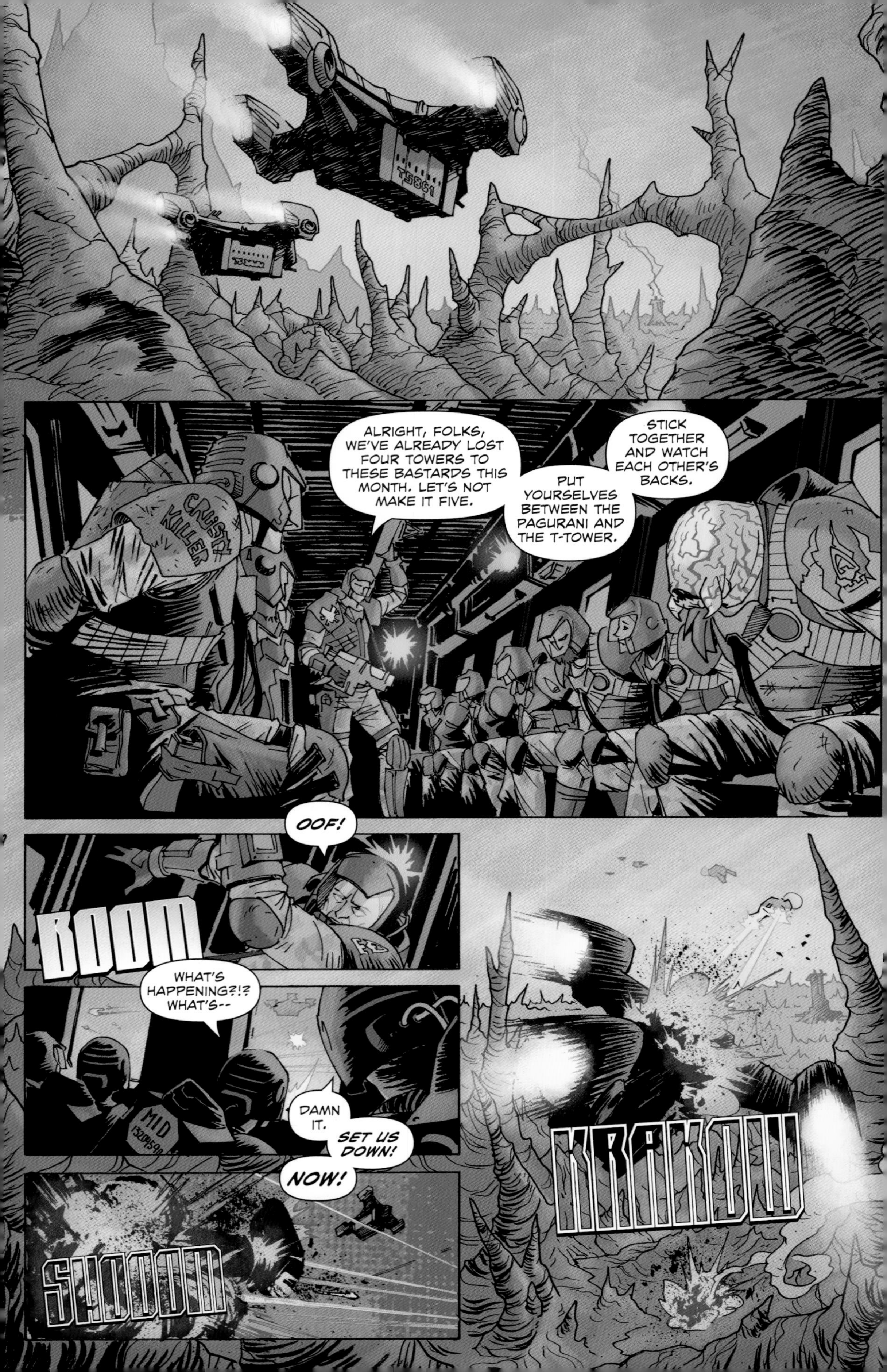
TS861
CRUSTY KILLER
ALRIGHT, FOLKS, WE'VE ALREADY LOST FOUR TOWERS TO THESE BASTARDS THIS MONTH. LET'S NOT MAKE IT FIVE.
PUT YOURSELVES BETWEEN THE PAGURANI AND THE T-TOWER.
STICK TOGETHER AND WATCH EACH OTHER'S BACKS.
OOF!
BOOM
WHAT'S HAPPENING?!? WHAT'S--
MID
DAMN IT.
SET US DOWN!
NOW!
SHOOOM
KRAKOW

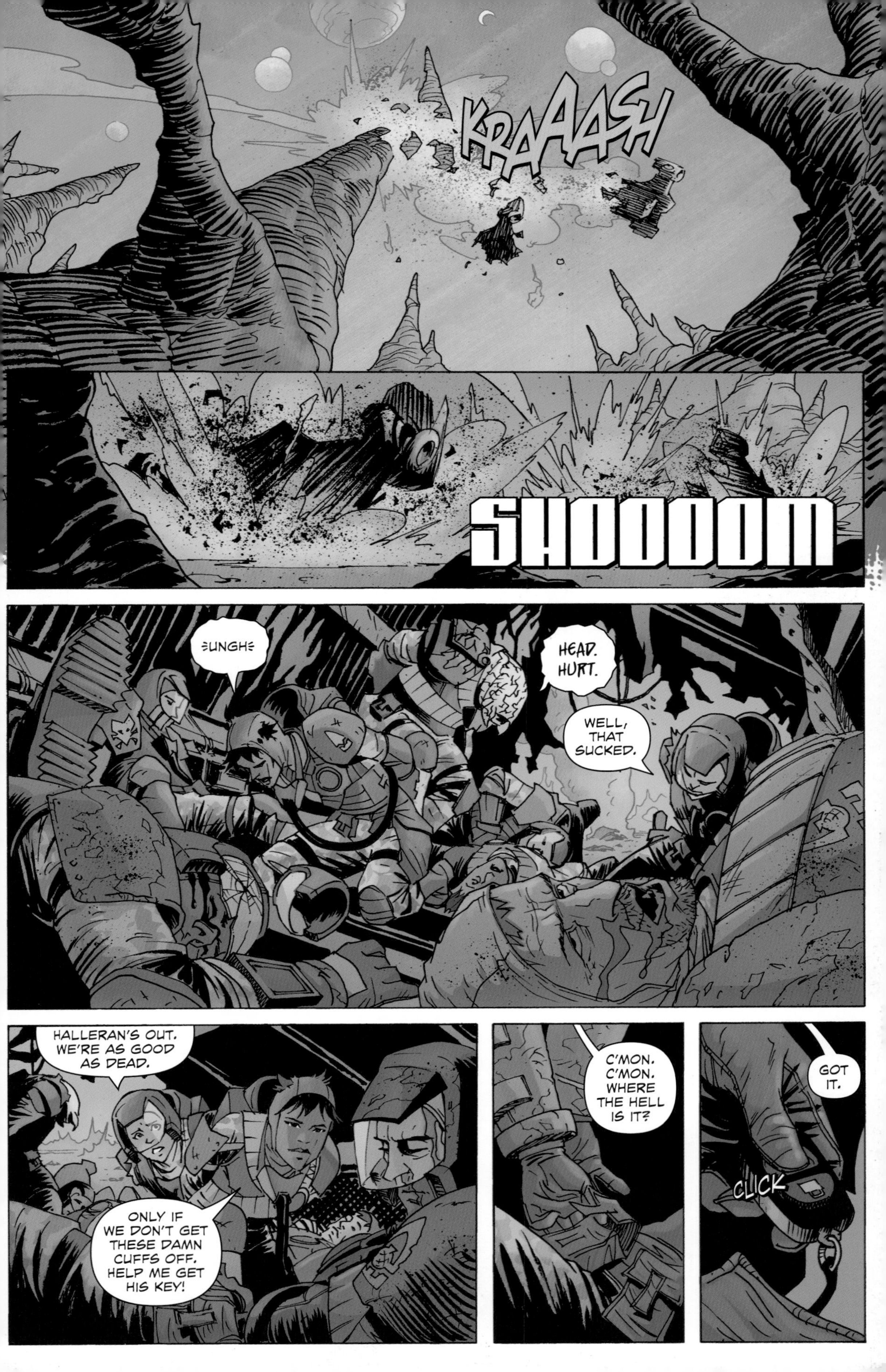
KRAAASH
SHOOOOM
UNGH
HEAD. HURT.
WELL, THAT SUCKED.
HALLERAN'S OUT. WE'RE AS GOOD AS DEAD.
ONLY IF WE DON'T GET THESE DAMN CUFFS OFF. HELP ME GET HIS KEY!
C'MON. C'MON. WHERE THE HELL IS IT?
GOT IT.
CLICK

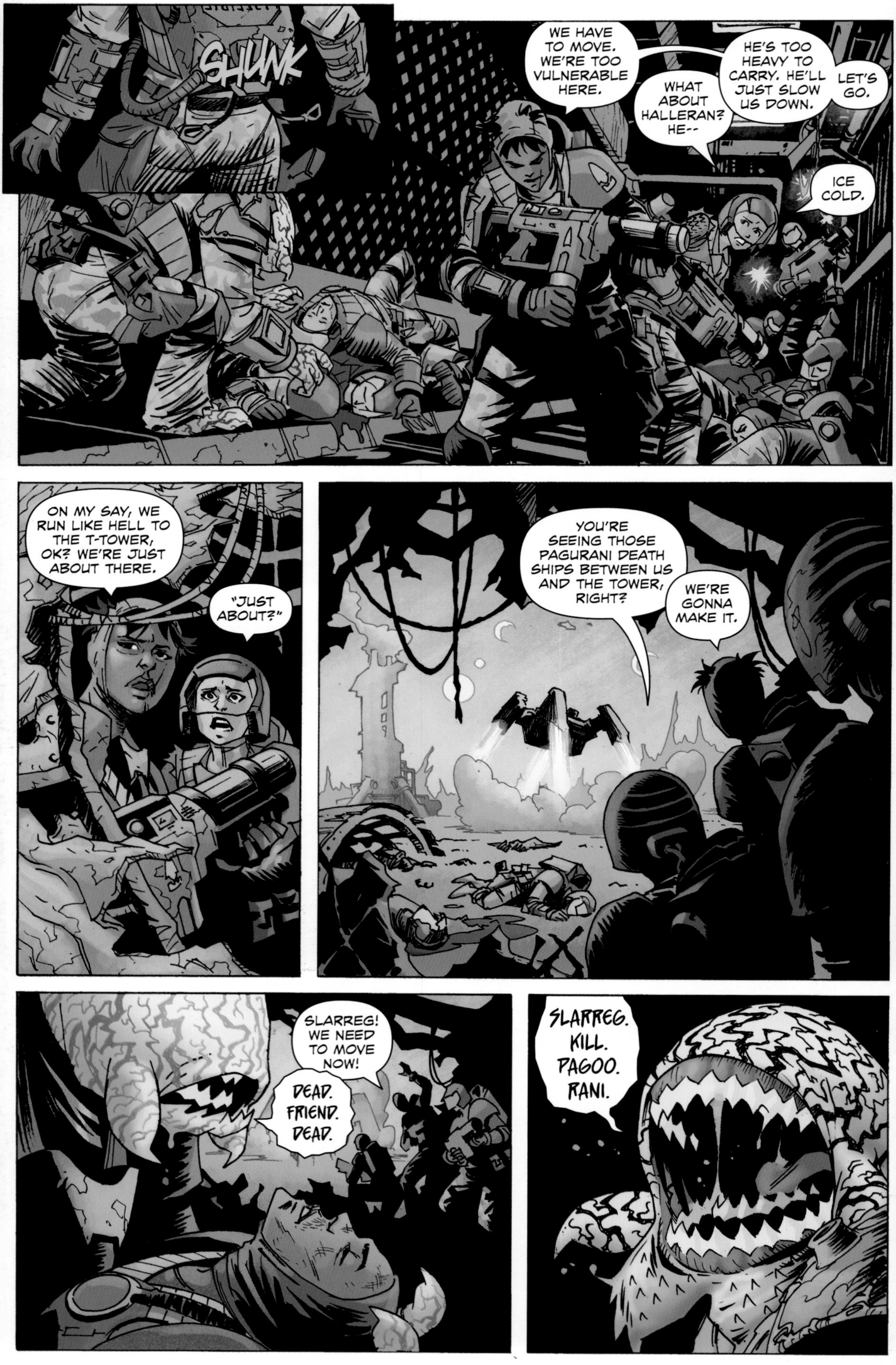
SHUNK
WE HAVE TO MOVE. WE'RE TOO VULNERABLE HERE.
WHAT ABOUT HALLERAN? HE--
HE'S TOO HEAVY TO CARRY. HE'LL JUST SLOW US DOWN.
LET'S GO.
ICE COLD.
ON MY SAY, WE RUN LIKE HELL TO THE T-TOWER, OK? WE'RE JUST ABOUT THERE.
"JUST ABOUT?"
YOU'RE SEEING THOSE PAGURANI DEATH SHIPS BETWEEN US AND THE TOWER, RIGHT?
WE'RE GONNA MAKE IT.
SLARREG! WE NEED TO MOVE NOW!
DEAD. FRIEND. DEAD.
SLARREG. KILL. PAGOO. RANI.

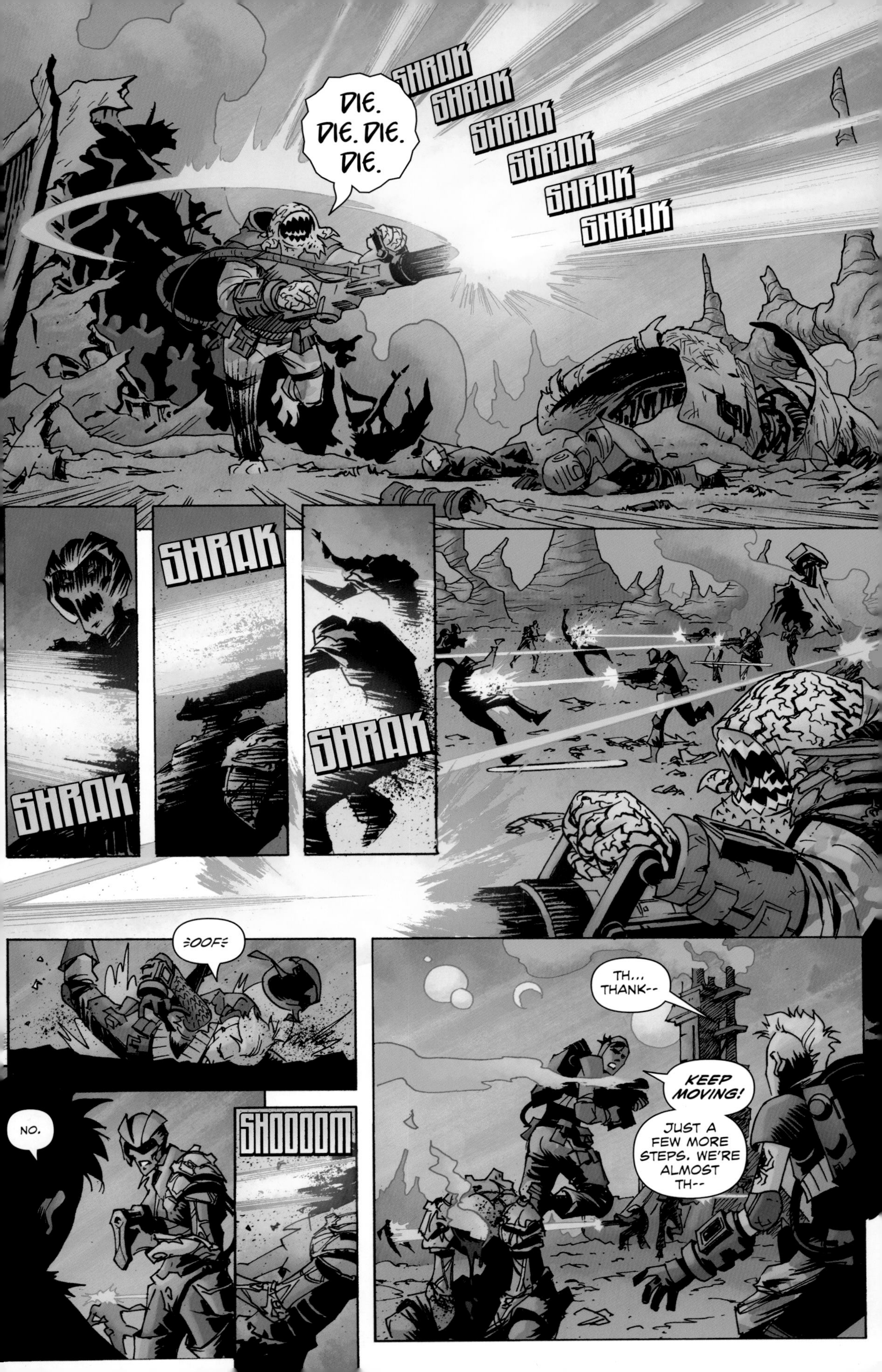
DIE.
DIE. DIE.
DIE.
SHRAK
SHRAK
SHRAK
SHRAK
SHRAK
SHRAK
SHRAK
SHRAK
SHRAK
=OOF=
NO.
SHOOOOM!
TH... THANK--
KEEP MOVING!
JUST A FEW MORE STEPS. WE'RE ALMOST TH--

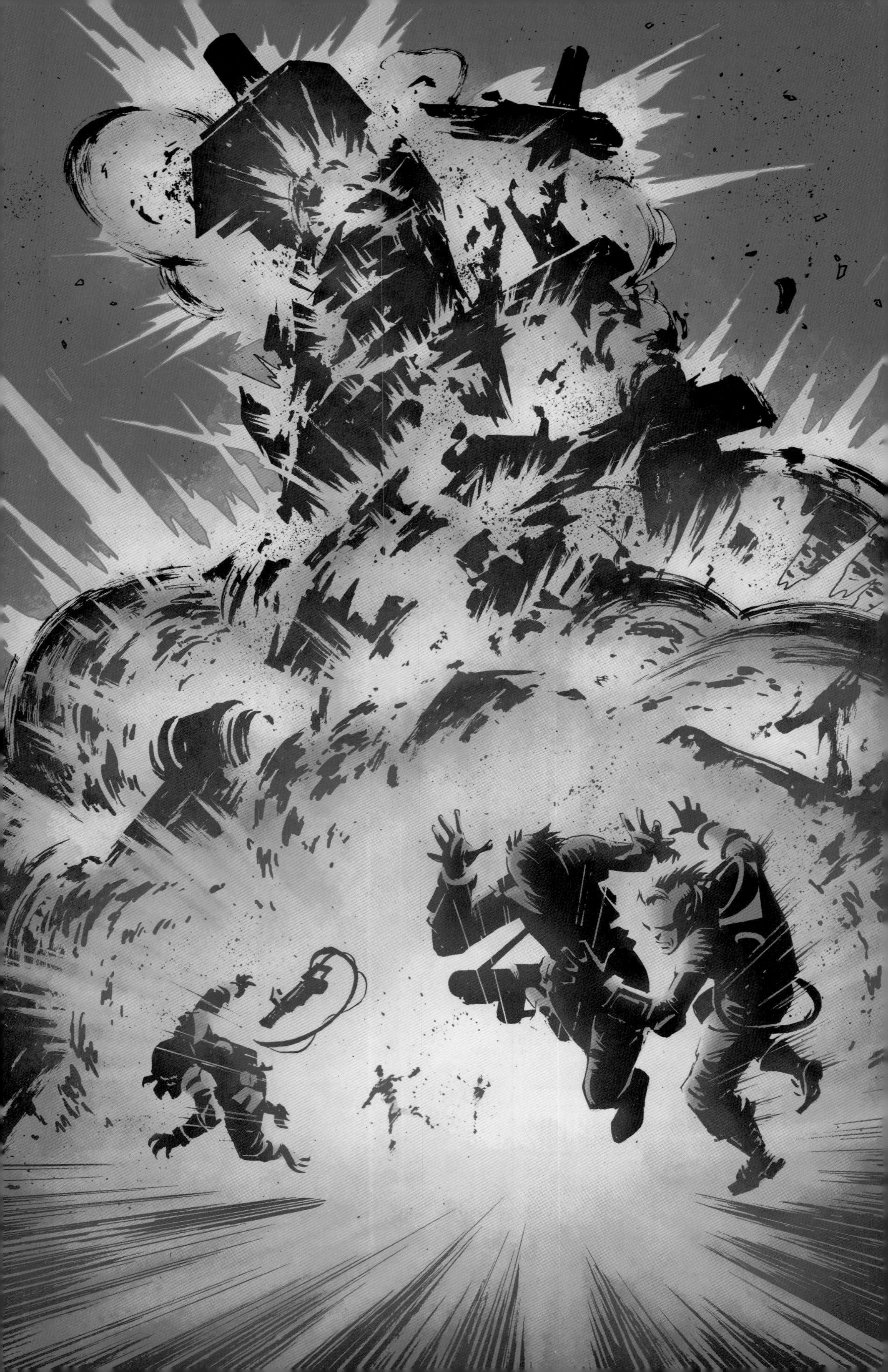

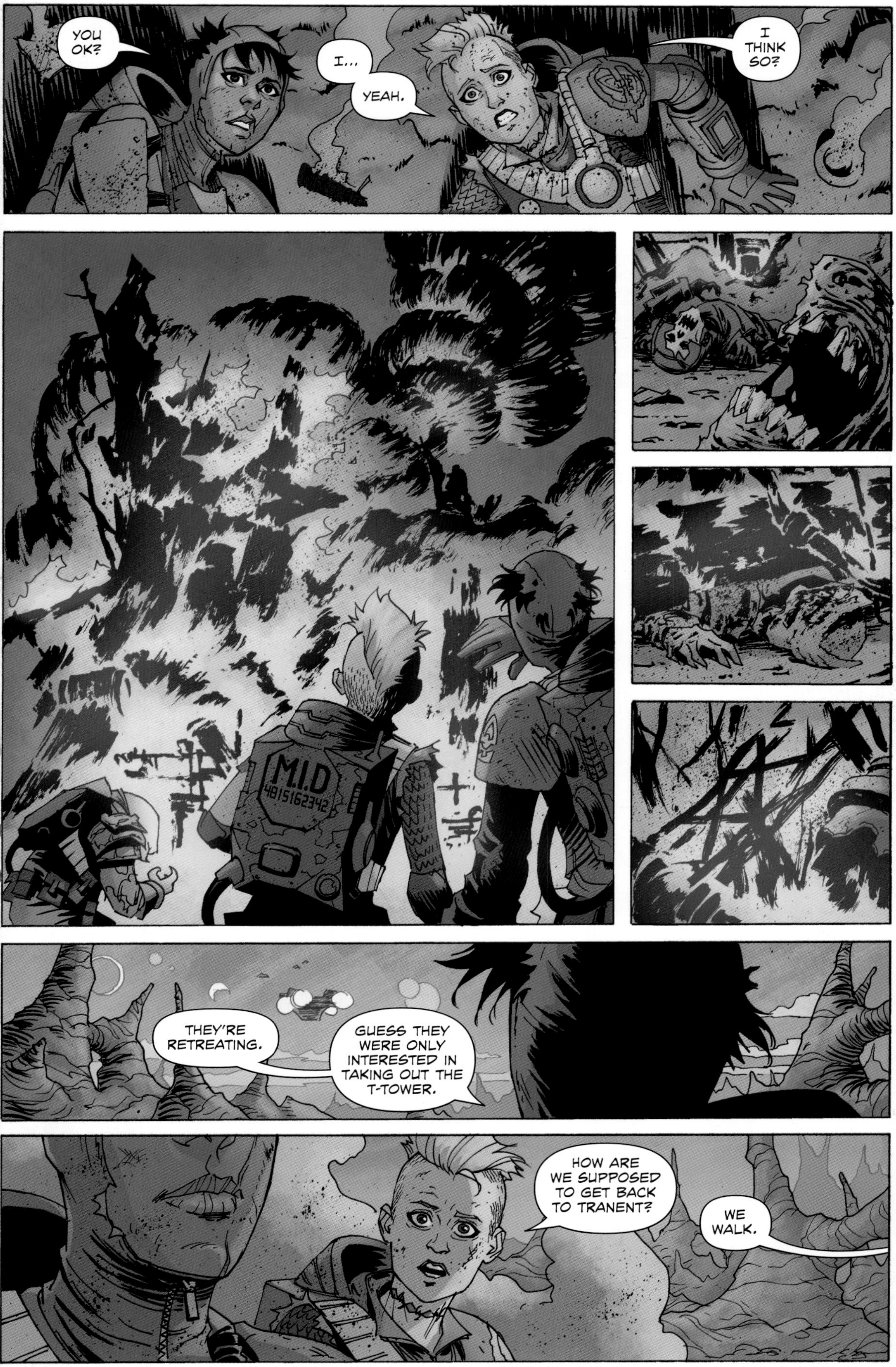
YOU OK?
I...
YEAH.
I THINK SO?
M.I.D
4815162342
THEY'RE RETREATING.
GUESS THEY WERE ONLY INTERESTED IN TAKING OUT THE T-TOWER.
HOW ARE WE SUPPOSED TO GET BACK TO TRANENT?
WE WALK.

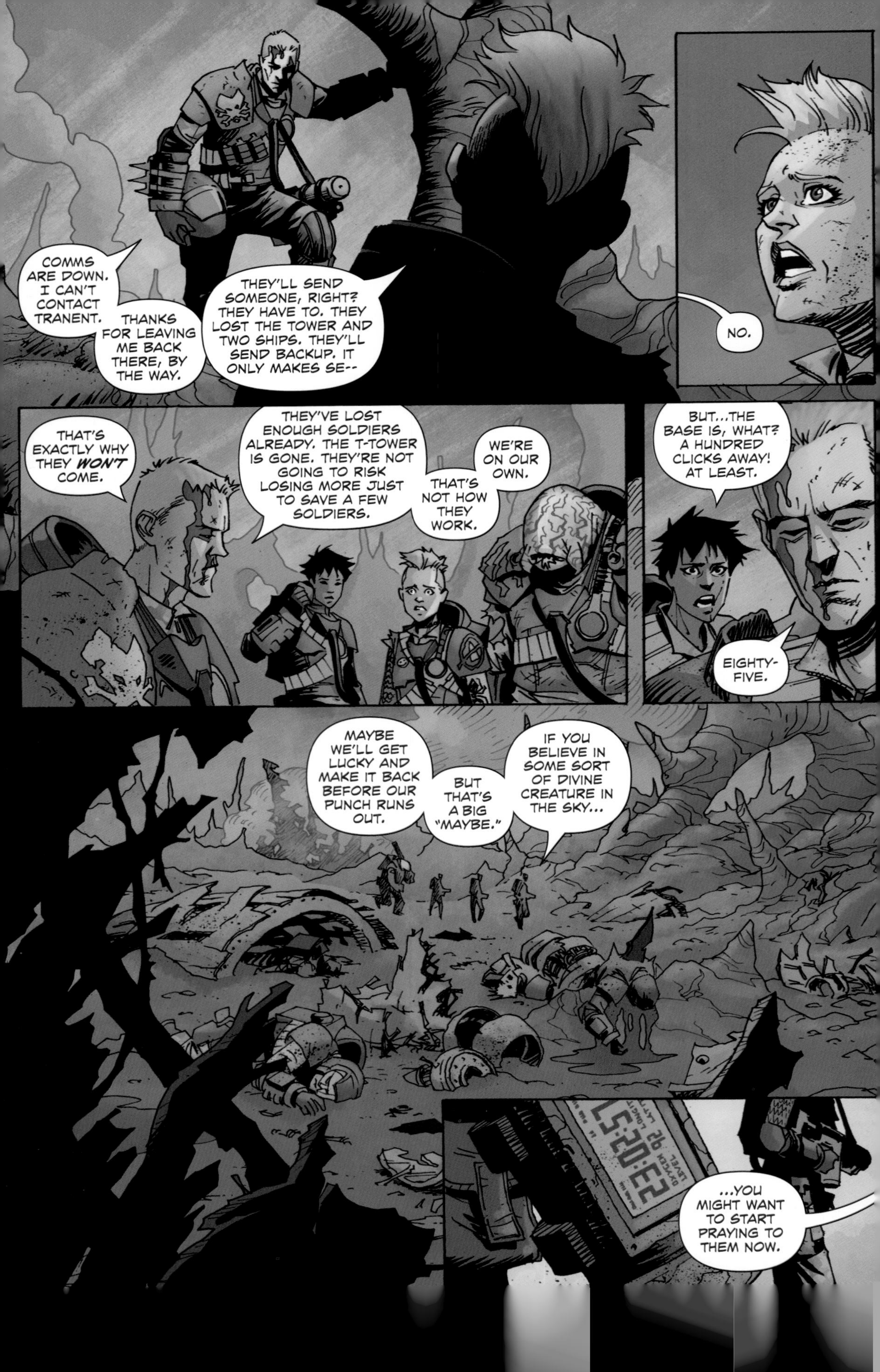
COMMS ARE DOWN. I CAN'T CONTACT TRANENT.
THANKS FOR LEAVING ME BACK THERE, BY THE WAY.
THEY'LL SEND SOMEONE, RIGHT? THEY HAVE TO. THEY LOST THE TOWER AND TWO SHIPS. THEY'LL SEND BACKUP. IT ONLY MAKES SE--
NO.
THAT'S EXACTLY WHY THEY *WON'T* COME.
THEY'VE LOST ENOUGH SOLDIERS ALREADY. THE T-TOWER IS GONE. THEY'RE NOT GOING TO RISK LOSING MORE JUST TO SAVE A FEW SOLDIERS.
THAT'S NOT HOW THEY WORK.
WE'RE ON OUR OWN.
BUT...THE BASE IS, WHAT? A HUNDRED CLICKS AWAY! AT LEAST.
EIGHTY-FIVE.
MAYBE WE'LL GET LUCKY AND MAKE IT BACK BEFORE OUR PUNCH RUNS OUT.
BUT THAT'S A BIG "MAYBE."
IF YOU BELIEVE IN SOME SORT OF DIVINE CREATURE IN THE SKY...
...YOU MIGHT WANT TO START PRAYING TO THEM NOW.

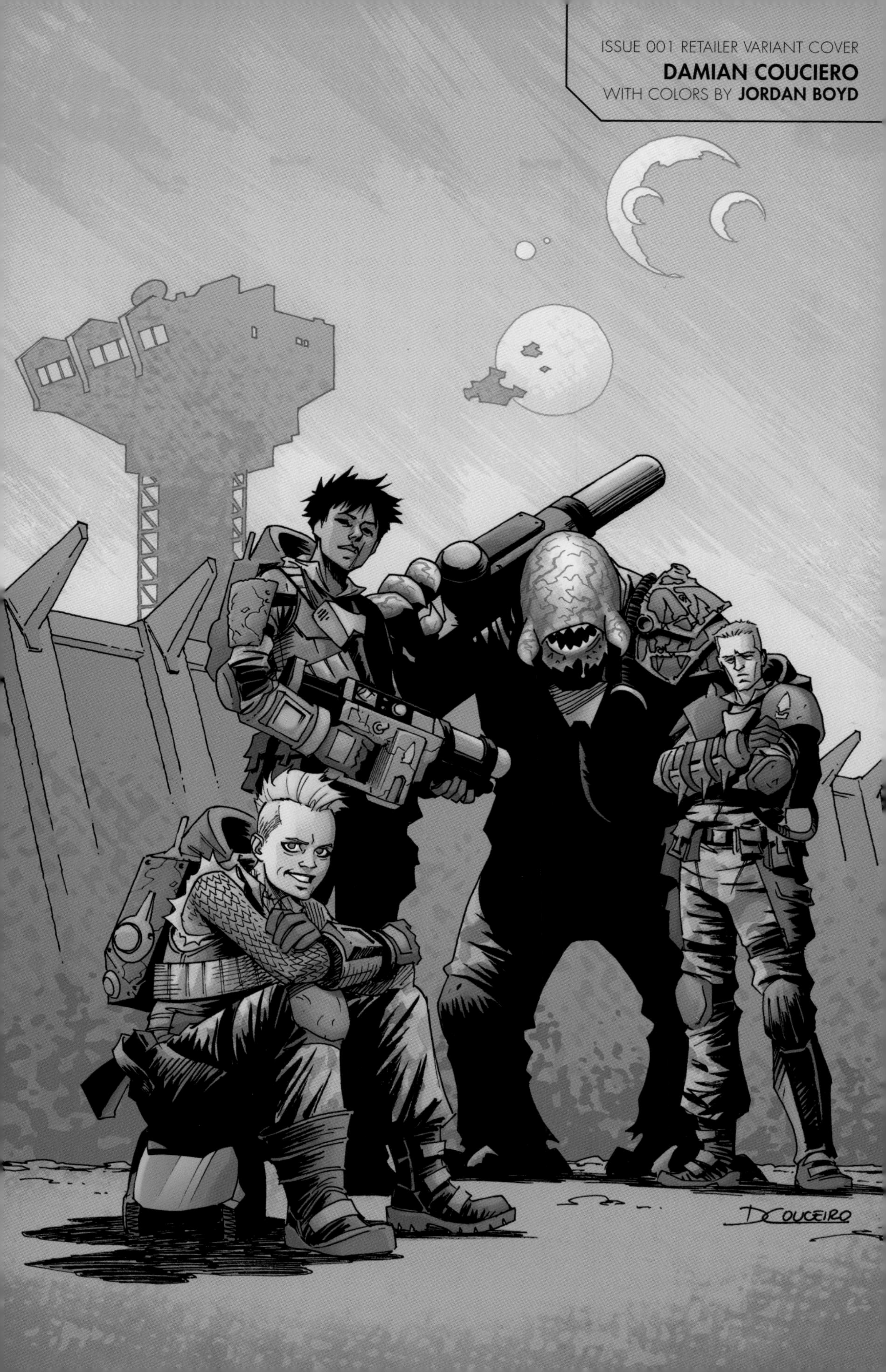
DCOUCEIRO

ISSUE 001 RETAILER VARIANT COVER
DAMIAN COUCIERO
WITH COLORS BY **JORDAN BOYD**

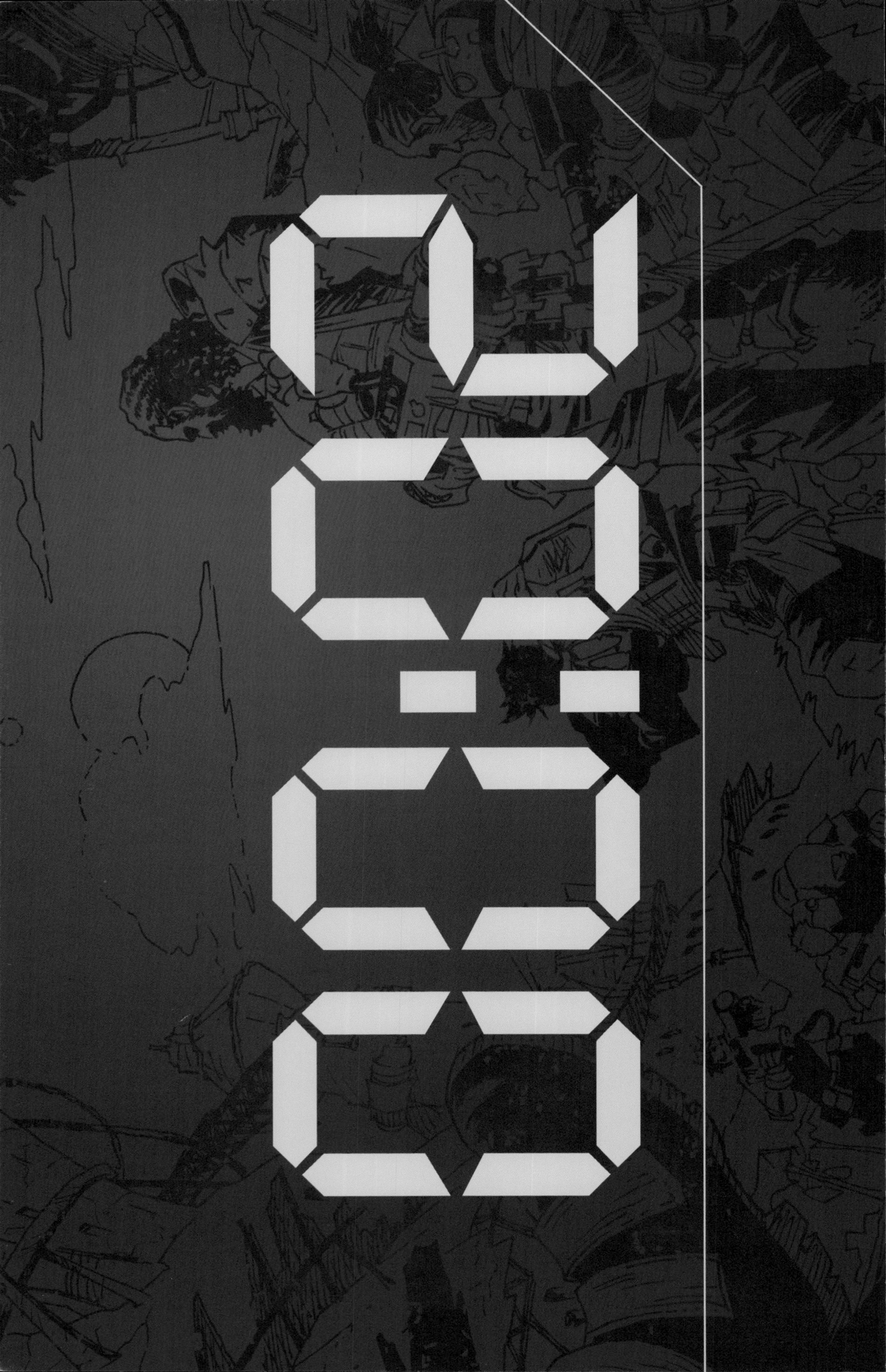
20:00

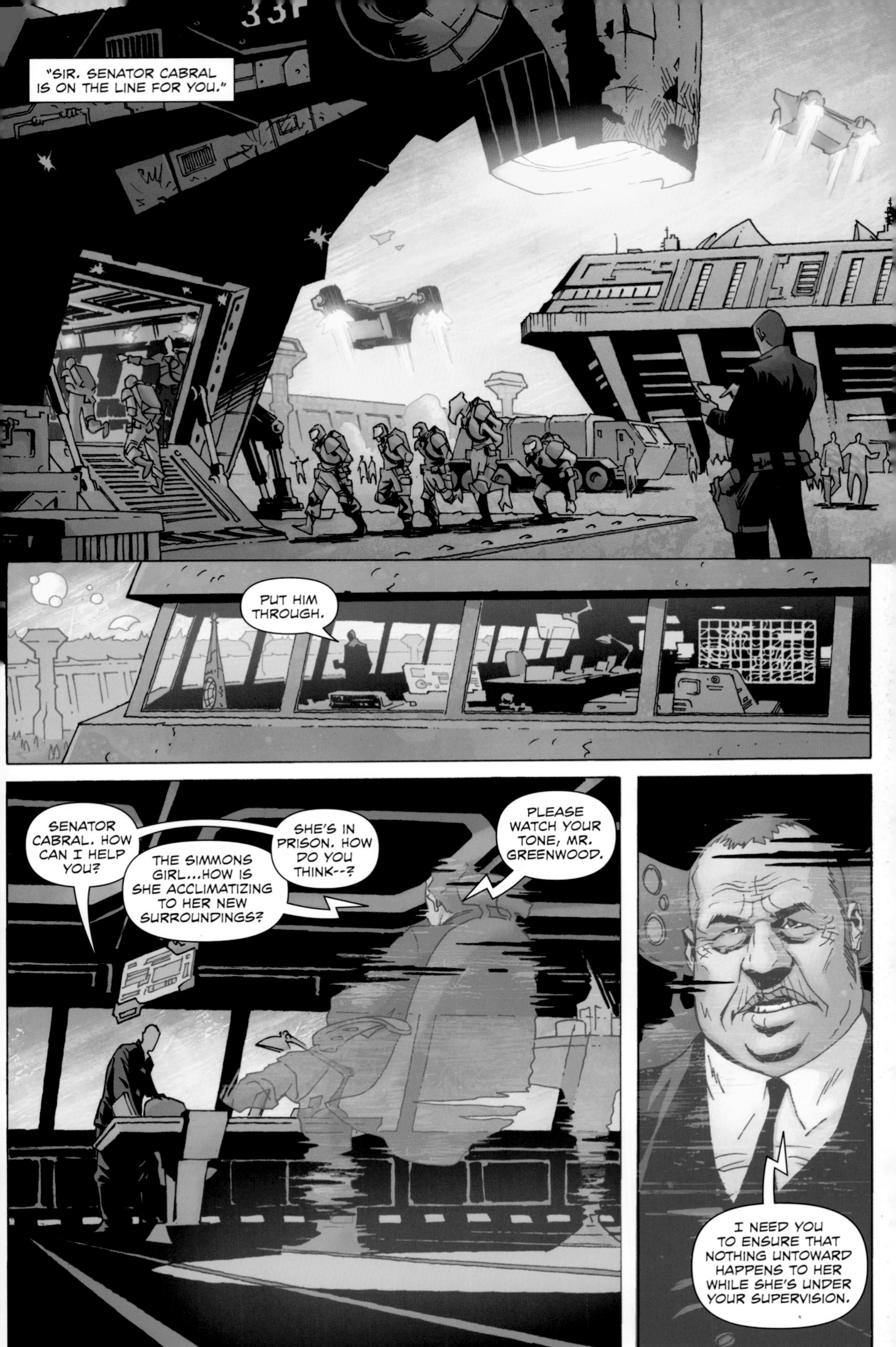

"SIR. SENATOR CABRAL IS ON THE LINE FOR YOU."
PUT HIM THROUGH.
SENATOR CABRAL. HOW CAN I HELP YOU?
THE SIMMONS GIRL...HOW IS SHE ACCLIMATIZING TO HER NEW SURROUNDINGS?
SHE'S IN PRISON. HOW DO YOU THINK--?
PLEASE WATCH YOUR TONE, MR. GREENWOOD.
I NEED YOU TO ENSURE THAT NOTHING UNTOWARD HAPPENS TO HER WHILE SHE'S UNDER YOUR SUPERVISION.

I'M COUNTING ON YOU FOR THAT. THAT SHE REMAINS SAFE... FOR THE TIME BEING.

WE NEED HER.

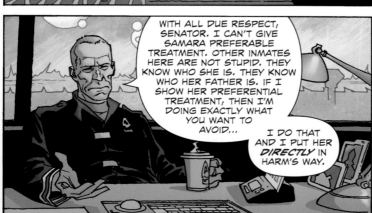

WITH ALL DUE RESPECT, SENATOR. I CAN'T GIVE SAMARA PREFERABLE TREATMENT. OTHER INMATES HERE ARE NOT STUPID. THEY KNOW WHO SHE IS. THEY KNOW WHO HER FATHER IS. IF I SHOW HER PREFERENTIAL TREATMENT, THEN I'M DOING EXACTLY WHAT YOU WANT TO AVOID...

I DO THAT AND I PUT HER *DIRECTLY* IN HARM'S WAY.

THIS ISN'T A DAY CARE, SENATOR. THIS IS A PRISON. THIS IS A WAR.

"I'M NOT GOING TO TELL YOU HOW TO RUN YOUR PRISON, GREENWOOD.

"BUT, SAMARA SIMMONS PRESENTS A...A STRATEGIC ADVANTAGE FOR US AND FOR G.O.E.

"SENATOR SIMMONS HAS NEVER BEEN A FAN OF THE M.I.D. PROGRAM--LESS SO, NOW THAT HIS DAUGHTER IS IN IT."

HOWEVER, IF WE CAN ENSURE THAT HIS DAUGHTER STAYS SAFE...

"...PULL SOME STRINGS" TO GET HER HOME TO HER FAMILY EARLY AND UNHARMED...

...THEN I SUSPECT THAT WE CAN EXPECT THAT SENATOR SIMMONS CAN... *RE-EXAMINE* SOME OF HIS POLICIES.

I'M SURE THAT I DON'T NEED TO TELL YOU WHY IT WOULD BE SO VALUABLE TO HAVE A MAN WHO'S ALWAYS BEEN A POLITICAL ADVERSARY IN OUR DEBT. THIS BENEFITS US ALL.

I WOULD LIKE TO SCHEDULE A CALL BETWEEN FATHER AND DAUGHTER FOR TOMORROW.

UNTIL THEN, CONSIDER WHAT WE'VE DISCUSSED. *CAREFULLY.*

YES, SIR.

SCREW ME.

MCHENRY!

WHAT'S THE WORD ON HALLERAN'S CREW?

DAMN.

WE LOST CONTACT WITH THEM SHORTLY AFTER THEY WERE ATTACKED.

THEY'RE DECEASED AS FAR AS WE CAN TELL.

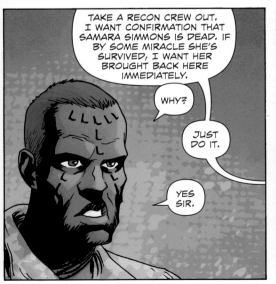

TAKE A RECON CREW OUT. I WANT CONFIRMATION THAT SAMARA SIMMONS IS DEAD. IF BY SOME MIRACLE SHE'S SURVIVED, I WANT HER BROUGHT BACK HERE IMMEDIATELY.

WHY?

JUST DO IT.

YES SIR.

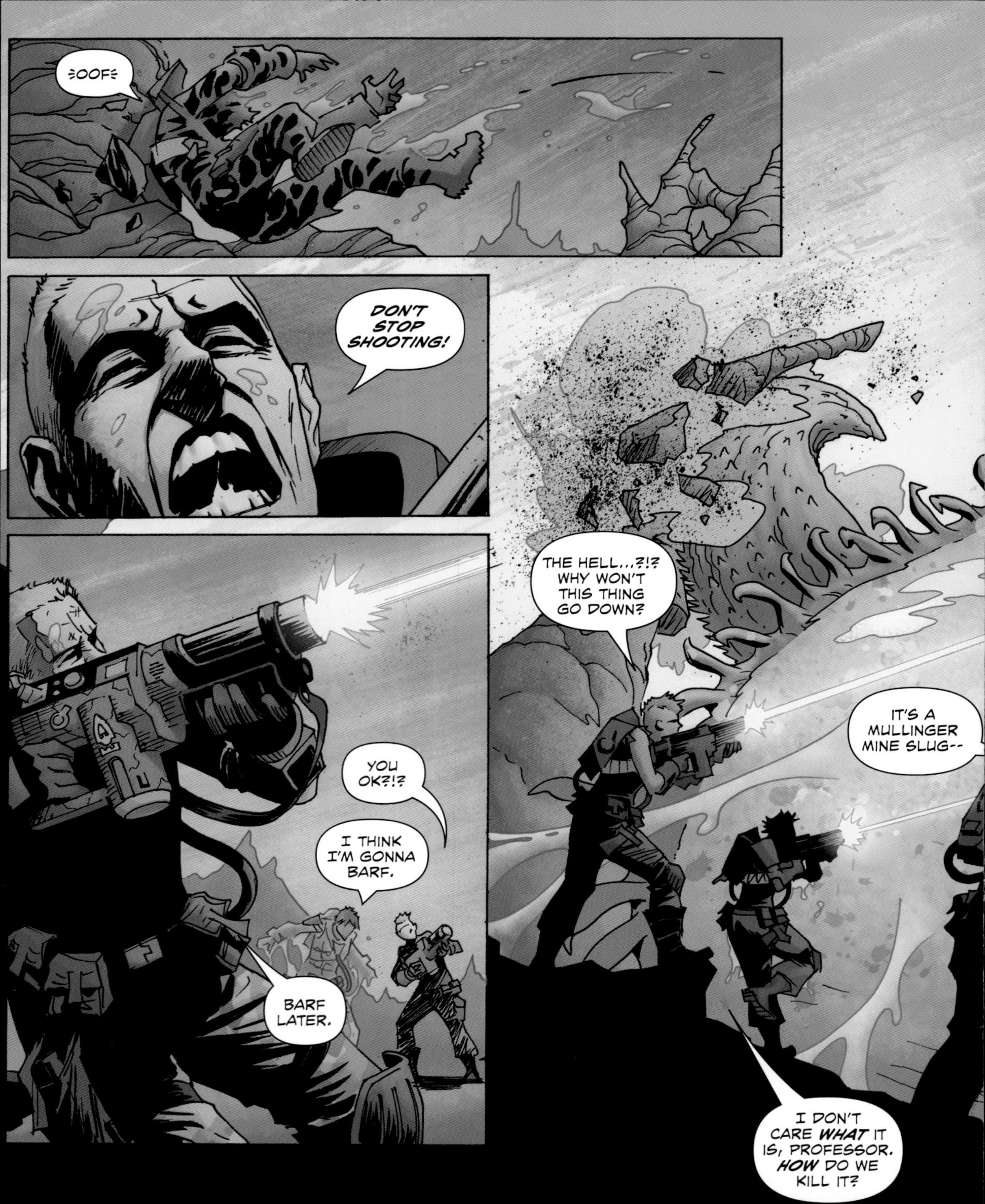

OOF
DON'T STOP SHOOTING!
THE HELL...?!? WHY WON'T THIS THING GO DOWN?
IT'S A MULLINGER MINE SLUG--
YOU OK?!?
I THINK I'M GONNA BARF.
BARF LATER.
I DON'T CARE *WHAT* IT IS, PROFESSOR. *HOW* DO WE KILL IT?

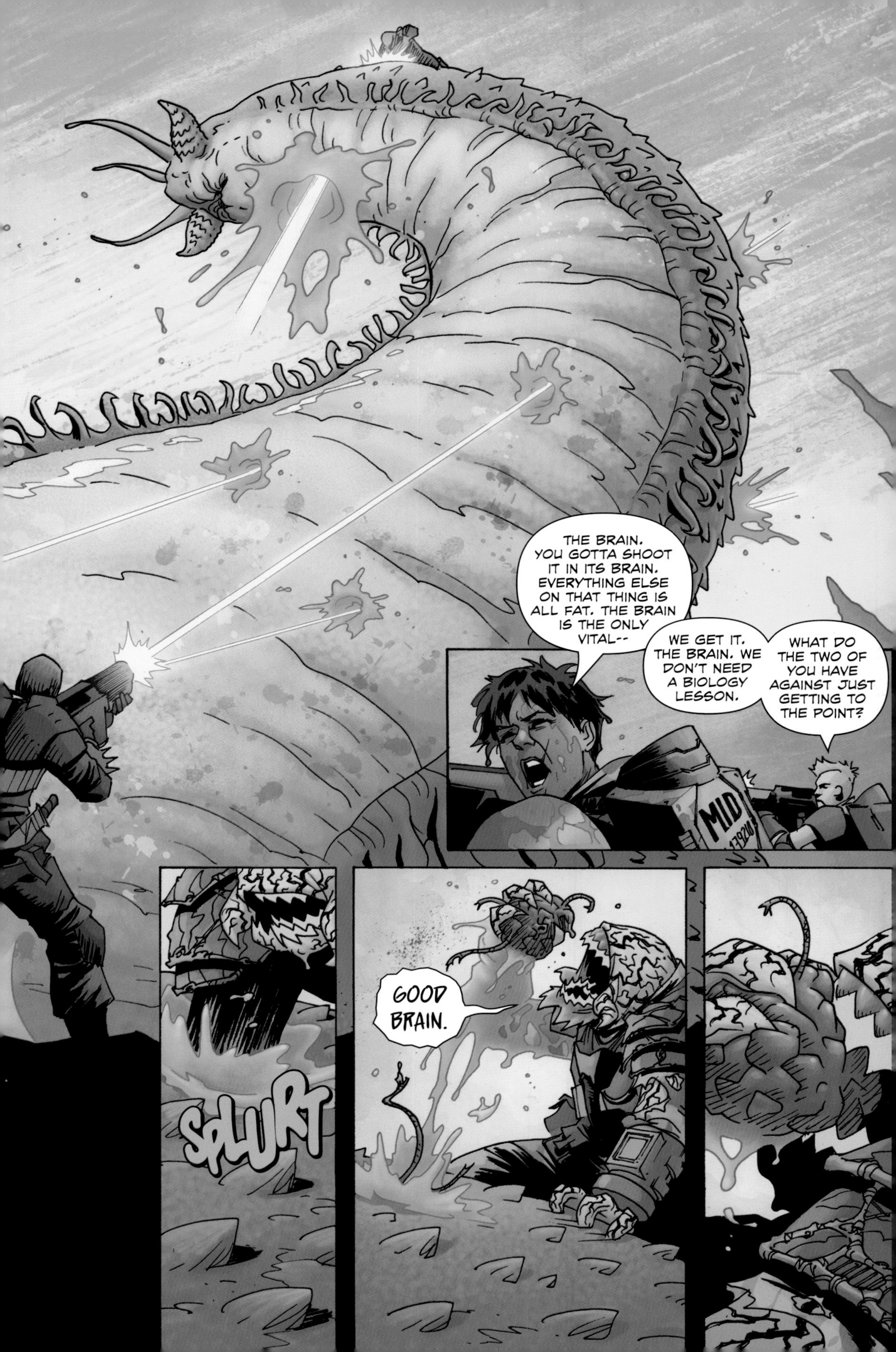
THE BRAIN. YOU GOTTA SHOOT IT IN ITS BRAIN. EVERYTHING ELSE ON THAT THING IS ALL FAT. THE BRAIN IS THE ONLY VITAL--
WE GET IT. THE BRAIN. WE DON'T NEED A BIOLOGY LESSON.
WHAT DO THE TWO OF YOU HAVE AGAINST JUST GETTING TO THE POINT?
MID
SPLURT
GOOD BRAIN.

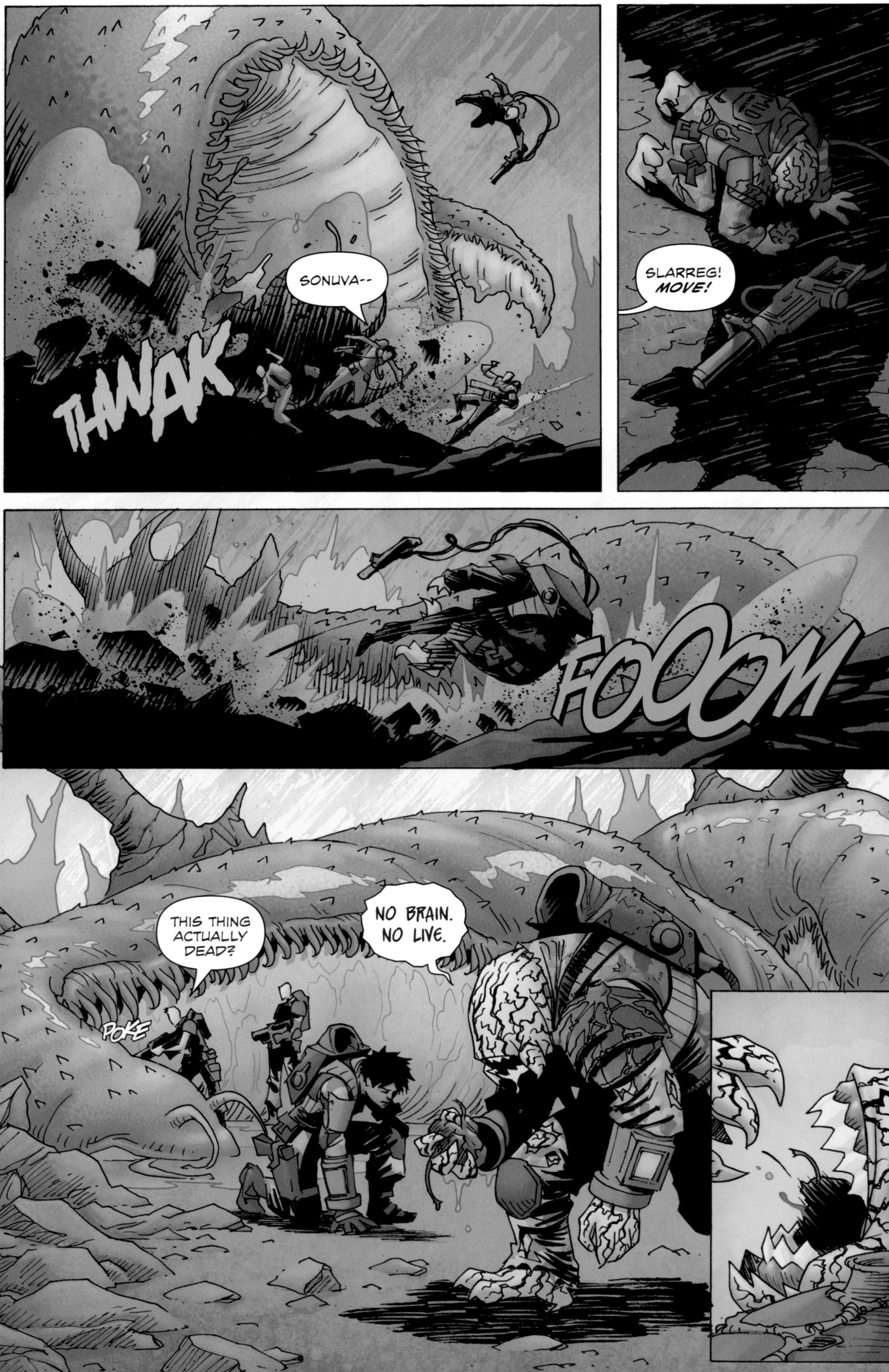
SONUVA--
THWAK
SLARREG! MOVE!
FOOOOM
THIS THING ACTUALLY DEAD?
NO BRAIN. NO LIVE.
POKE

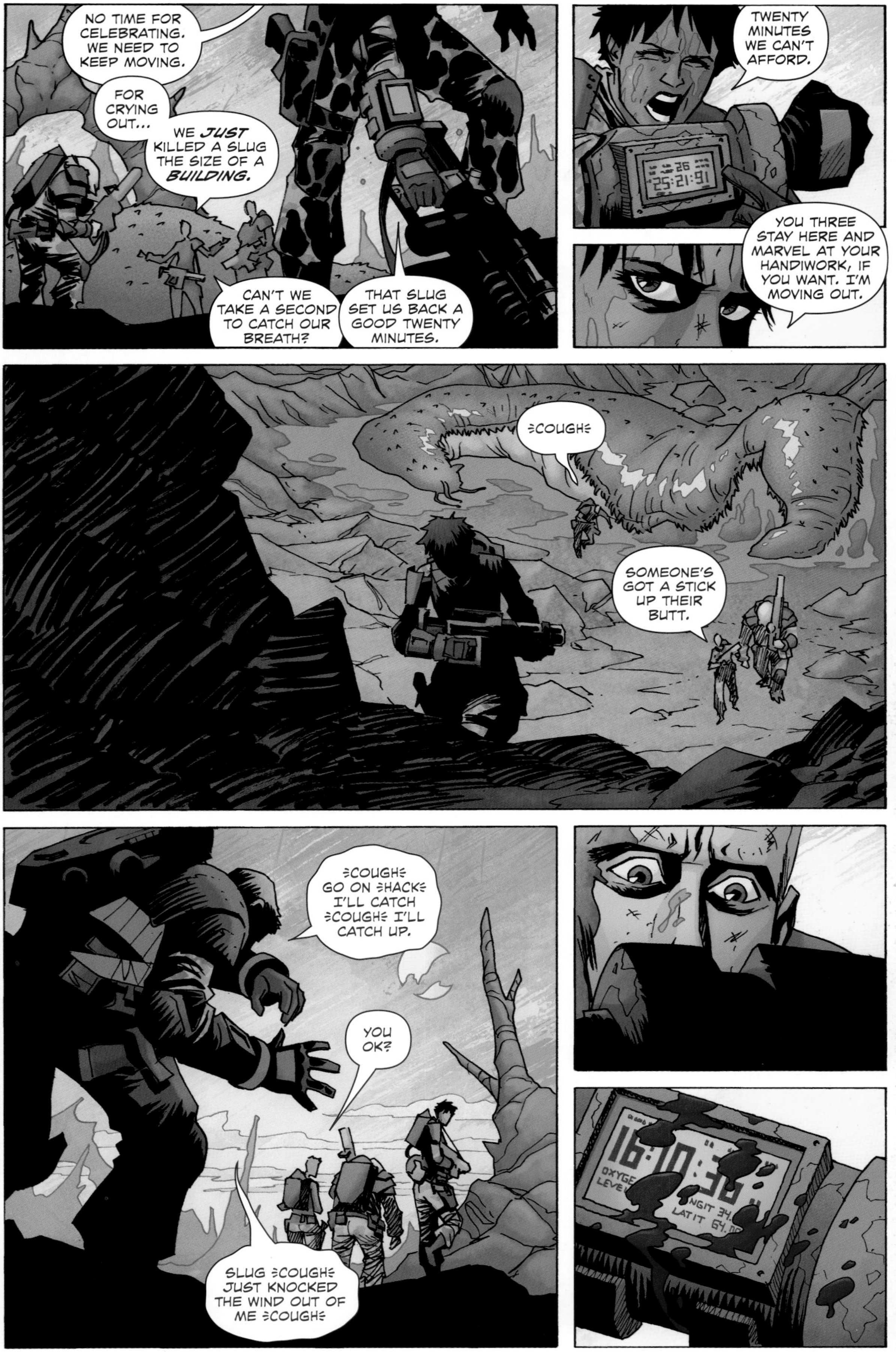
NO TIME FOR CELEBRATING. WE NEED TO KEEP MOVING.
FOR CRYING OUT...
WE *JUST* KILLED A SLUG THE SIZE OF A *BUILDING.*
CAN'T WE TAKE A SECOND TO CATCH OUR BREATH?
THAT SLUG SET US BACK A GOOD TWENTY MINUTES.
TWENTY MINUTES WE CAN'T AFFORD.
YOU THREE STAY HERE AND MARVEL AT YOUR HANDIWORK, IF YOU WANT. I'M MOVING OUT.
=COUGH=
SOMEONE'S GOT A STICK UP THEIR BUTT.
=COUGH= GO ON =HACK= I'LL CATCH =COUGH= I'LL CATCH UP.
YOU OK?
SLUG =COUGH= JUST KNOCKED THE WIND OUT OF ME =COUGH=

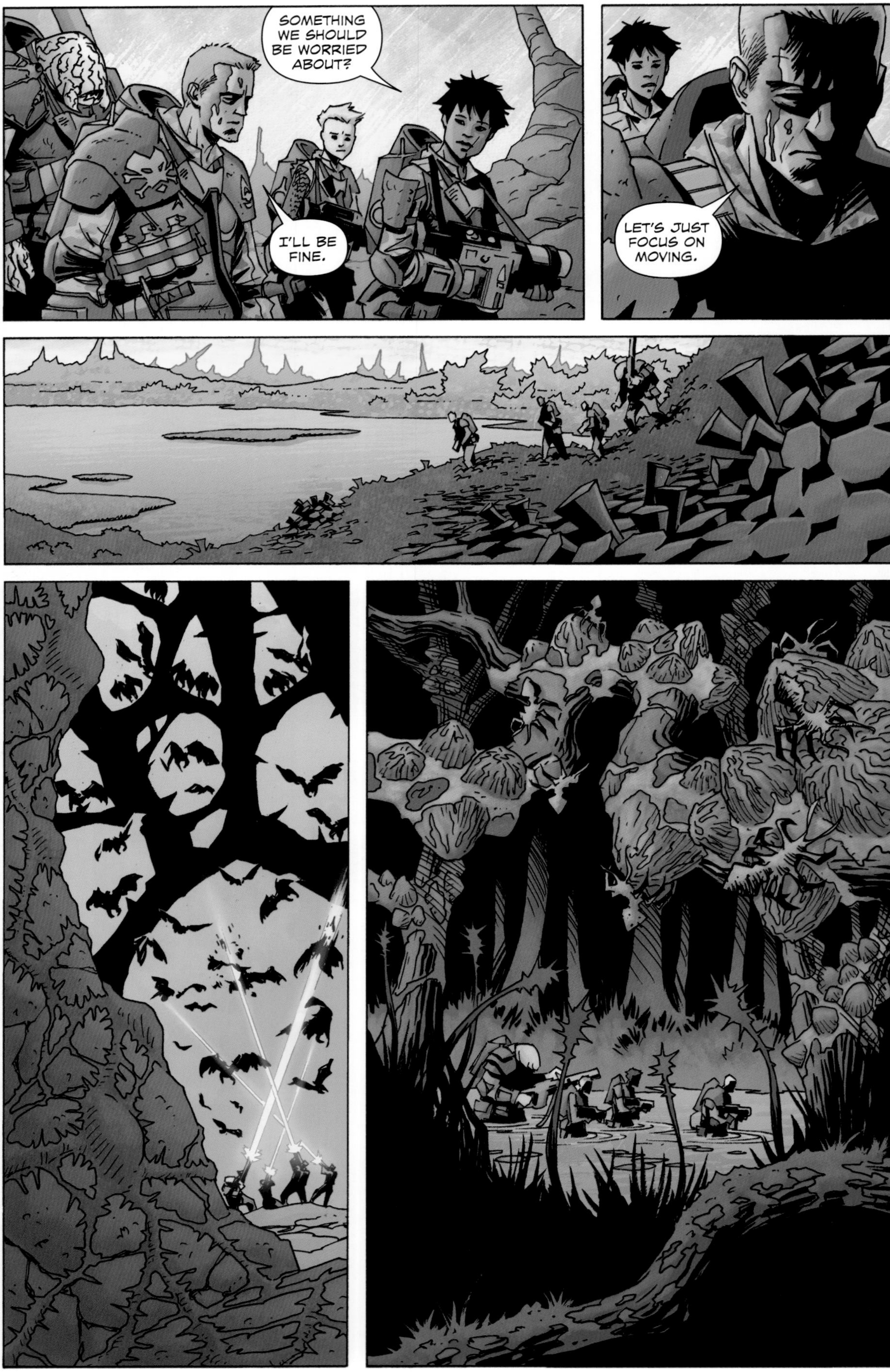
SOMETHING WE SHOULD BE WORRIED ABOUT?
I'LL BE FINE.
LET'S JUST FOCUS ON MOVING.

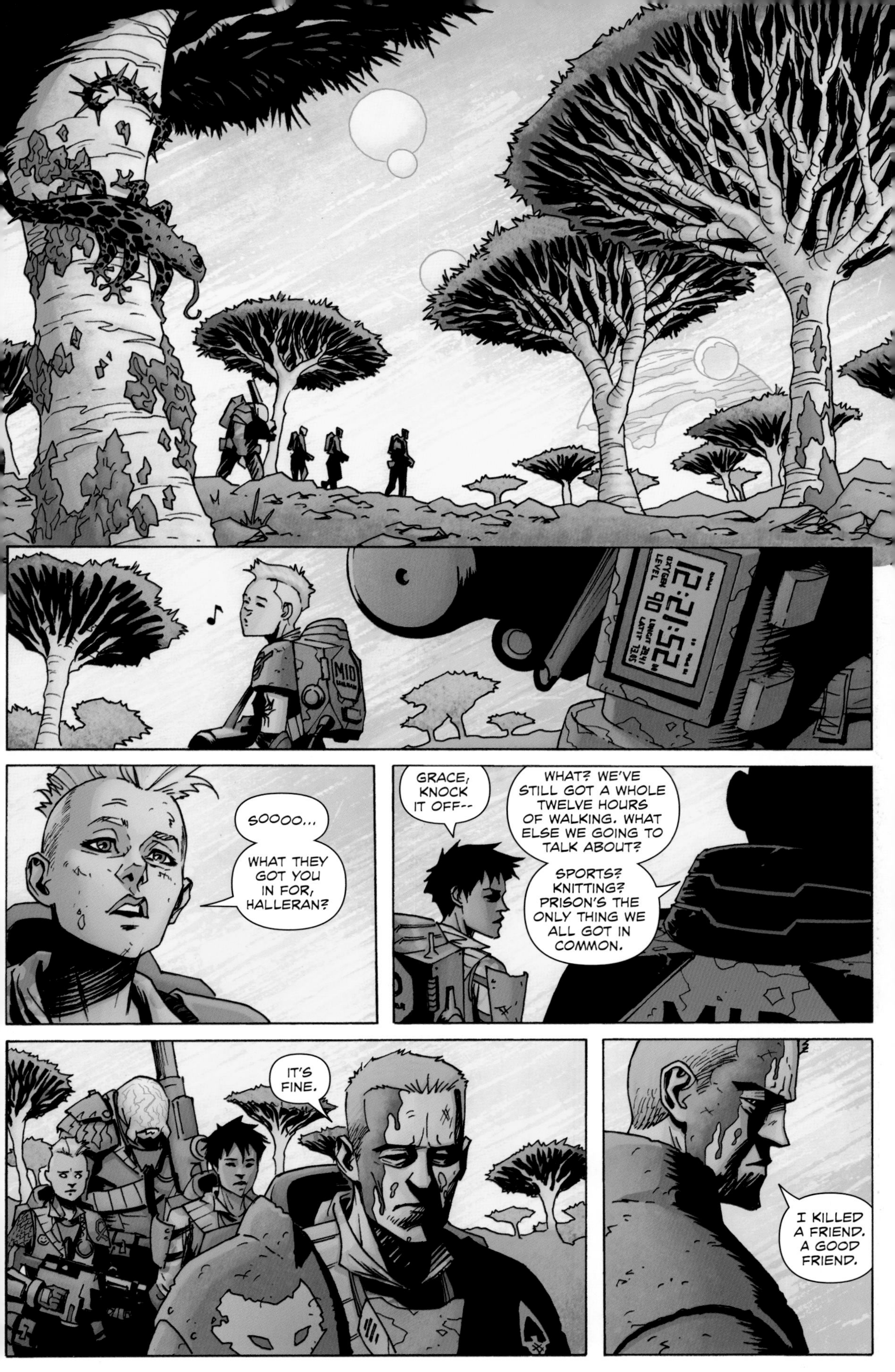
12:21:52
OXYGEN LEVEL 90
SOOOO...
WHAT THEY GOT YOU IN FOR, HALLERAN?
GRACE, KNOCK IT OFF--
WHAT? WE'VE STILL GOT A WHOLE TWELVE HOURS OF WALKING. WHAT ELSE WE GOING TO TALK ABOUT?
SPORTS? KNITTING? PRISON'S THE ONLY THING WE ALL GOT IN COMMON.
IT'S FINE.
I KILLED A FRIEND. A GOOD FRIEND.

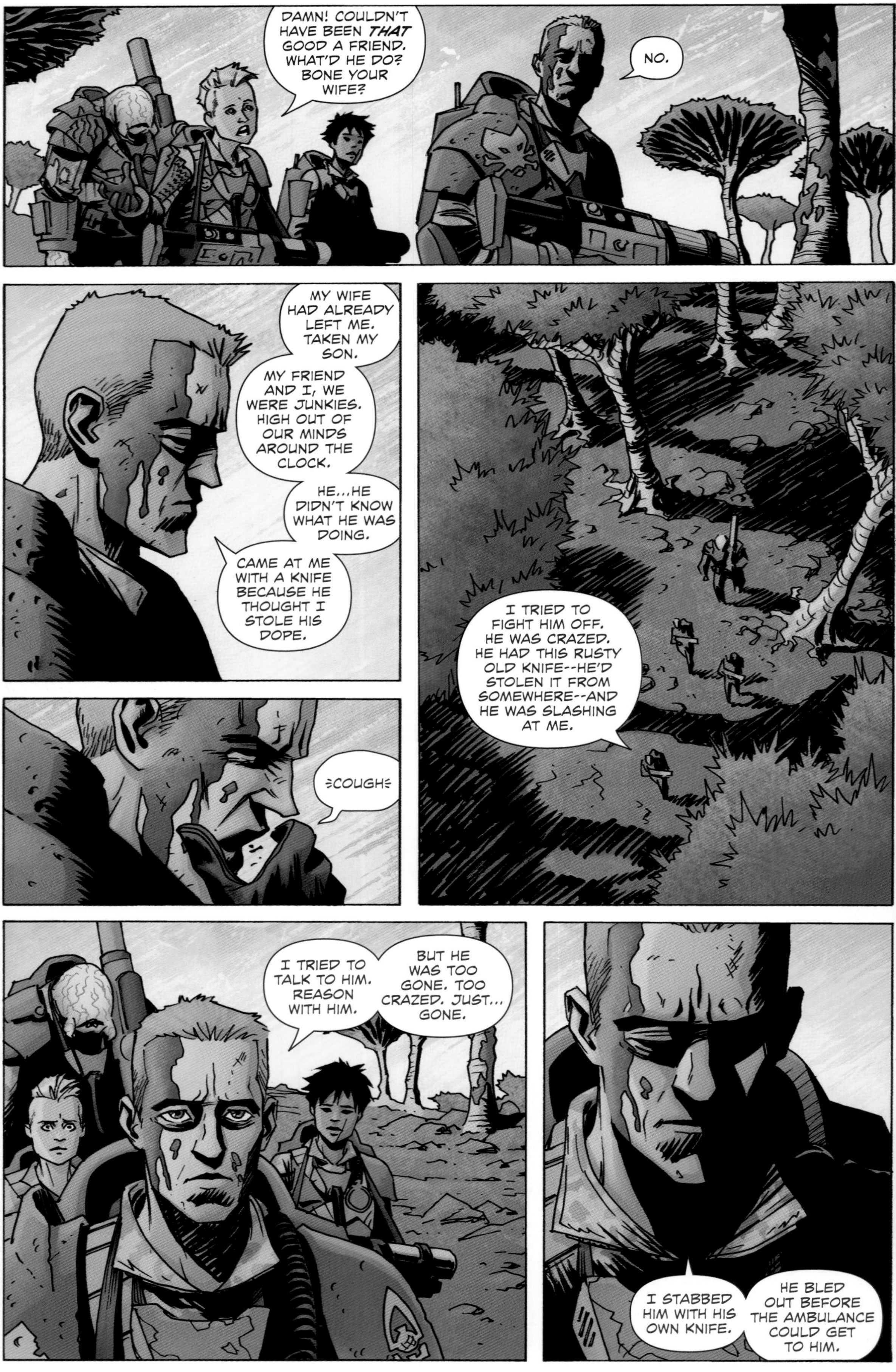
DAMN! COULDN'T HAVE BEEN *THAT* GOOD A FRIEND. WHAT'D HE DO? BONE YOUR WIFE?
NO.
MY WIFE HAD ALREADY LEFT ME. TAKEN MY SON.
MY FRIEND AND I, WE WERE JUNKIES. HIGH OUT OF OUR MINDS AROUND THE CLOCK.
HE...HE DIDN'T KNOW WHAT HE WAS DOING.
CAME AT ME WITH A KNIFE BECAUSE HE THOUGHT I STOLE HIS DOPE.
I TRIED TO FIGHT HIM OFF. HE WAS CRAZED. HE HAD THIS RUSTY OLD KNIFE--HE'D STOLEN IT FROM SOMEWHERE--AND HE WAS SLASHING AT ME.
COUGH
I TRIED TO TALK TO HIM. REASON WITH HIM.
BUT HE WAS TOO GONE. TOO CRAZED. JUST... GONE.
I STABBED HIM WITH HIS OWN KNIFE.
HE BLED OUT BEFORE THE AMBULANCE COULD GET TO HIM.

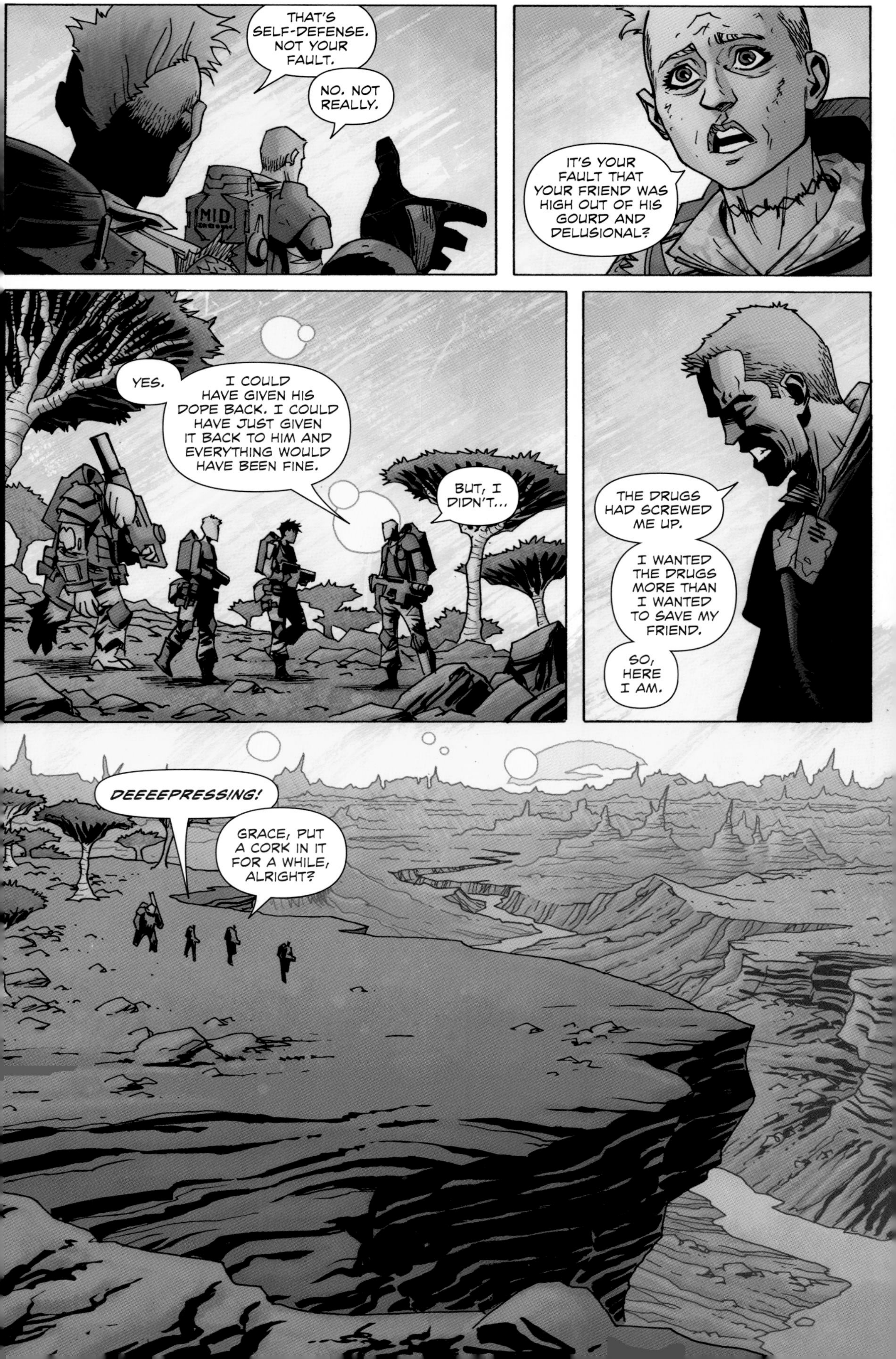

THAT'S SELF-DEFENSE. NOT YOUR FAULT.
NO. NOT REALLY.
IT'S YOUR FAULT THAT YOUR FRIEND WAS HIGH OUT OF HIS GOURD AND DELUSIONAL?
YES.
I COULD HAVE GIVEN HIS DOPE BACK. I COULD HAVE JUST GIVEN IT BACK TO HIM AND EVERYTHING WOULD HAVE BEEN FINE.
BUT, I DIDN'T...
THE DRUGS HAD SCREWED ME UP.
I WANTED THE DRUGS MORE THAN I WANTED TO SAVE MY FRIEND.
SO, HERE I AM.
DEEEEPRESSING!
GRACE, PUT A CORK IN IT FOR A WHILE, ALRIGHT?

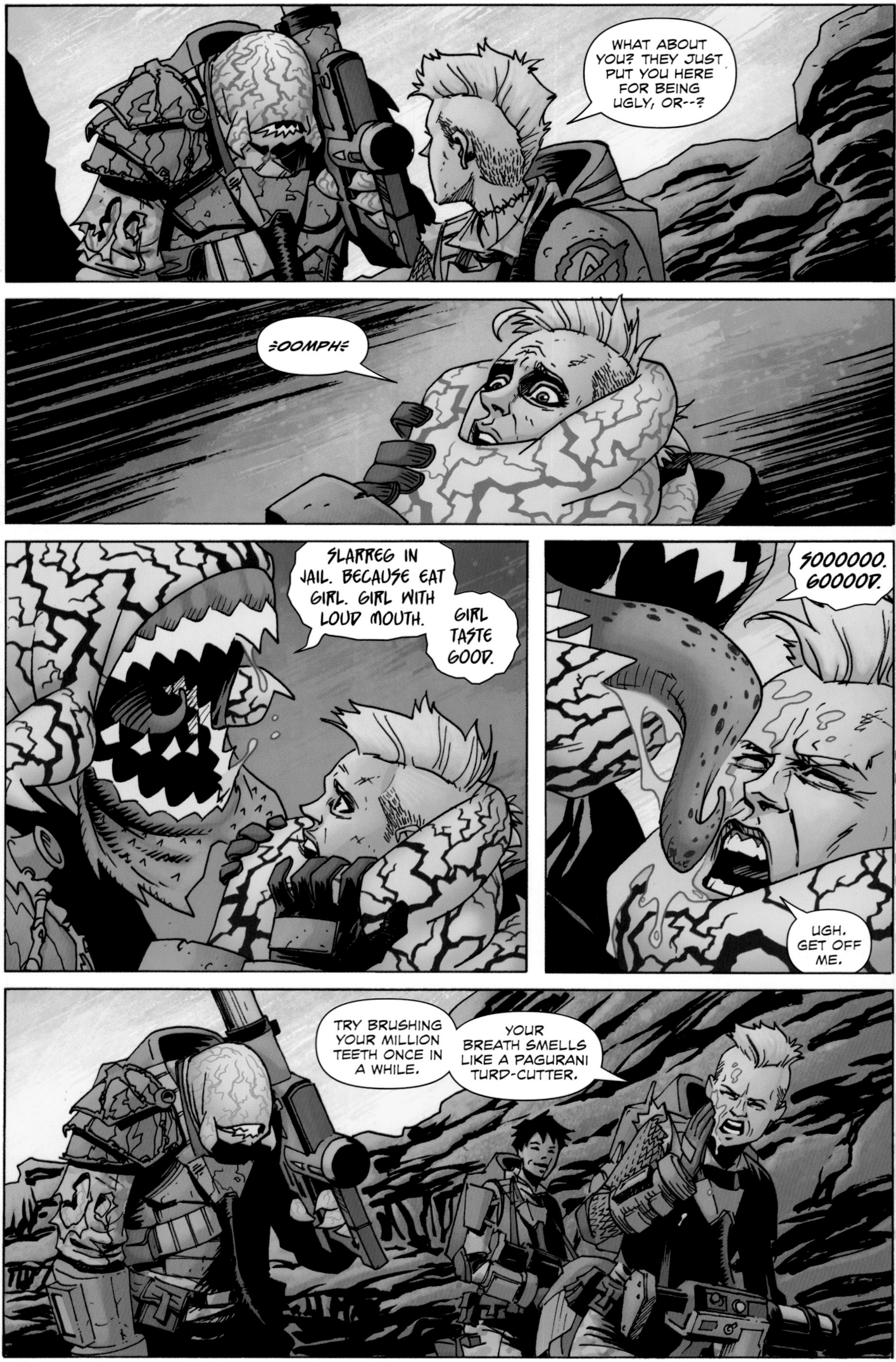
WHAT ABOUT YOU? THEY JUST PUT YOU HERE FOR BEING UGLY, OR--?
=OOMPH=
SLARREG IN JAIL. BECAUSE EAT GIRL. GIRL WITH LOUD MOUTH.
GIRL TASTE GOOD.
SOOOOOO. GOOOOD.
UGH. GET OFF ME.
YOUR BREATH SMELLS LIKE A PAGURANI TURD-CUTTER.
TRY BRUSHING YOUR MILLION TEETH ONCE IN A WHILE.

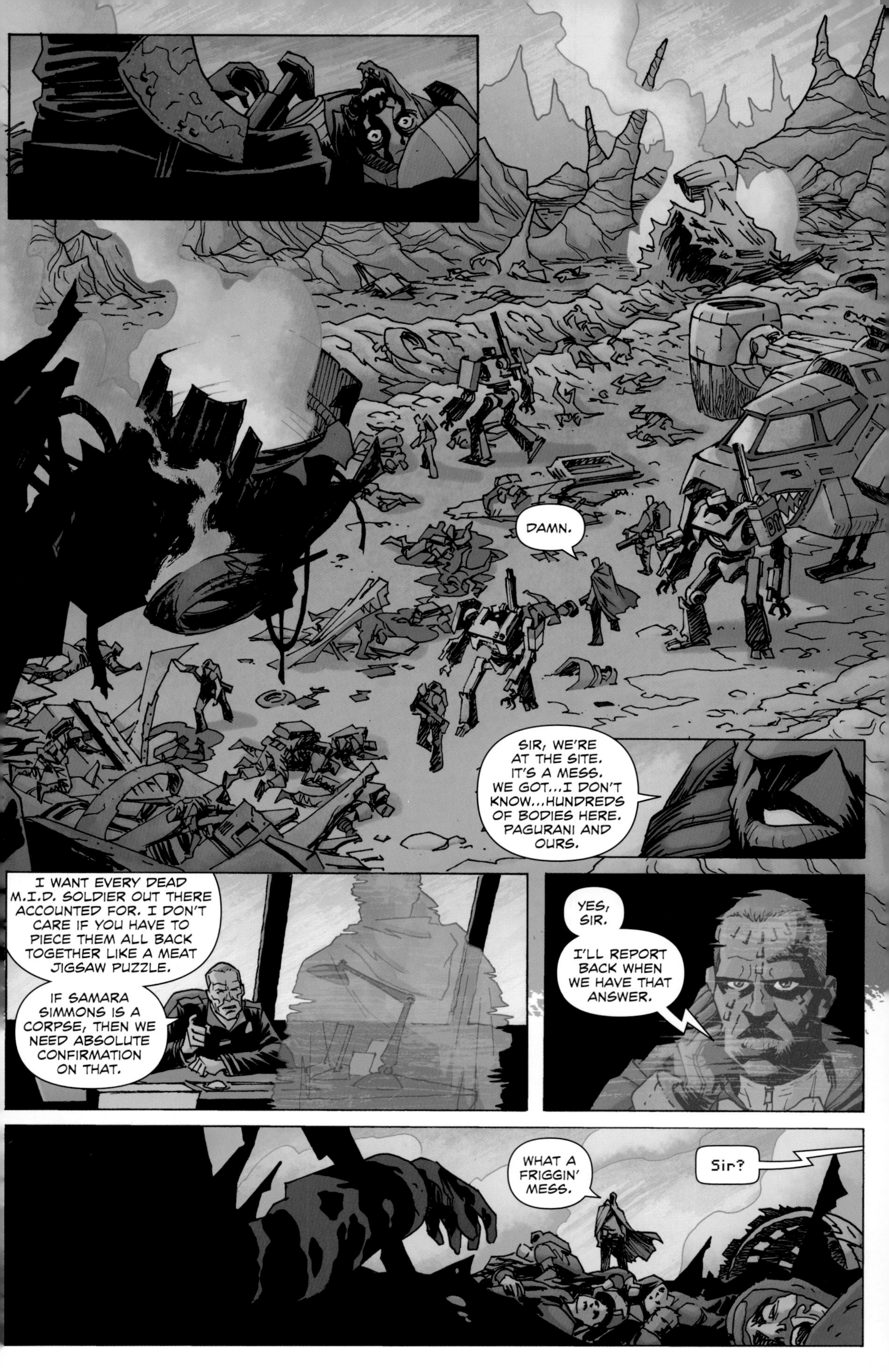
DAMN.
SIR, WE'RE AT THE SITE. IT'S A MESS. WE GOT...I DON'T KNOW...HUNDREDS OF BODIES HERE. PAGURANI AND OURS.
I WANT EVERY DEAD M.I.D. SOLDIER OUT THERE ACCOUNTED FOR. I DON'T CARE IF YOU HAVE TO PIECE THEM ALL BACK TOGETHER LIKE A MEAT JIGSAW PUZZLE.
IF SAMARA SIMMONS IS A CORPSE, THEN WE NEED ABSOLUTE CONFIRMATION ON THAT.
YES, SIR.
I'LL REPORT BACK WHEN WE HAVE THAT ANSWER.
WHAT A FRIGGIN' MESS.
Sir?

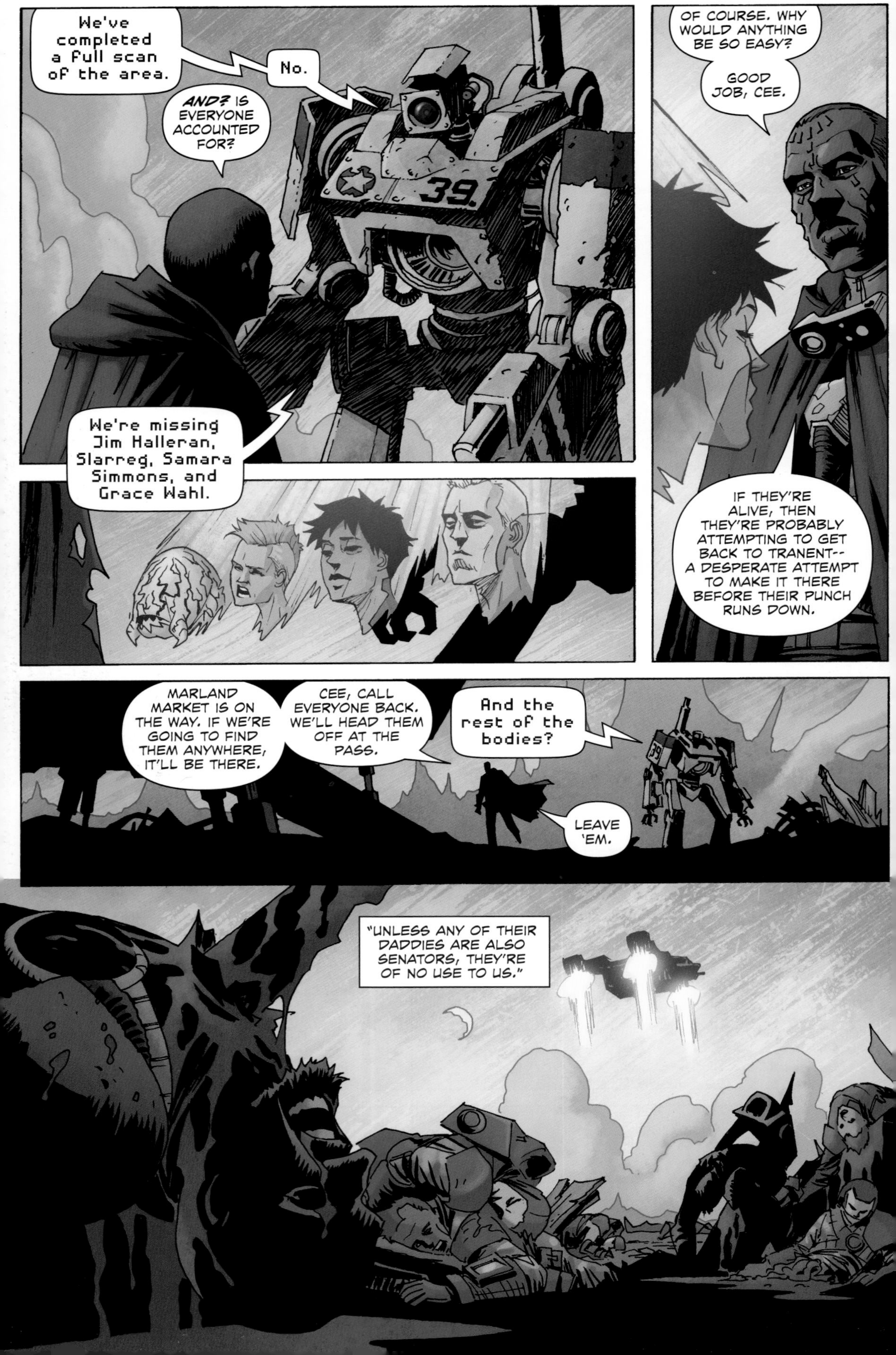
We've completed a full scan of the area.
AND? IS EVERYONE ACCOUNTED FOR?
No.
We're missing Jim Halleran, Slarreg, Samara Simmons, and Grace Wahl.
OF COURSE. WHY WOULD ANYTHING BE SO EASY?
GOOD JOB, CEE.
IF THEY'RE ALIVE, THEN THEY'RE PROBABLY ATTEMPTING TO GET BACK TO TRANENT-- A DESPERATE ATTEMPT TO MAKE IT THERE BEFORE THEIR PUNCH RUNS DOWN.
39
MARLAND MARKET IS ON THE WAY. IF WE'RE GOING TO FIND THEM ANYWHERE, IT'LL BE THERE.
CEE, CALL EVERYONE BACK. WE'LL HEAD THEM OFF AT THE PASS.
And the rest of the bodies?
LEAVE 'EM.
"UNLESS ANY OF THEIR DADDIES ARE ALSO SENATORS, THEY'RE OF NO USE TO US."

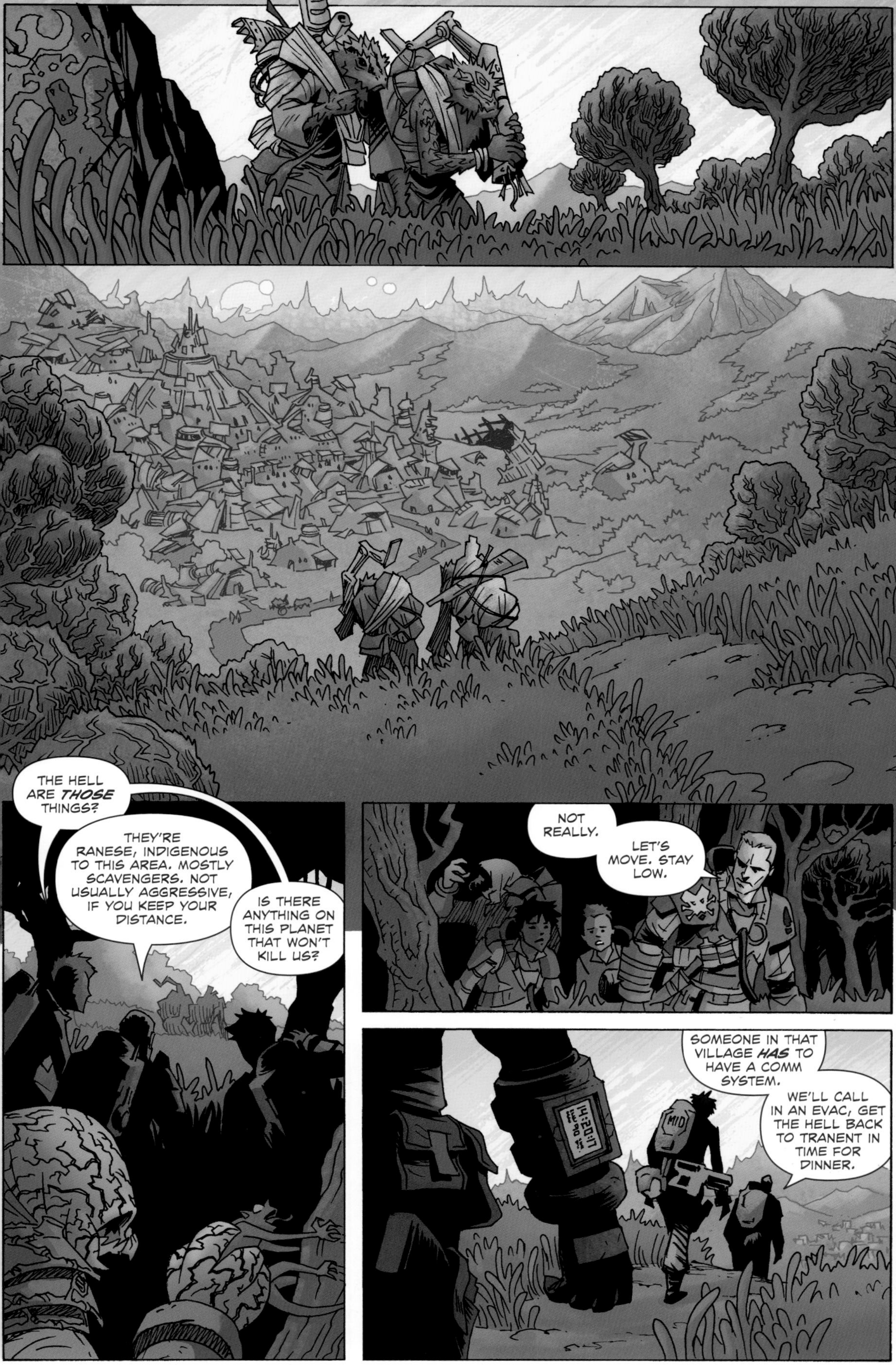
THE HELL ARE *THOSE* THINGS?
THEY'RE RANESE, INDIGENOUS TO THIS AREA. MOSTLY SCAVENGERS. NOT USUALLY AGGRESSIVE, IF YOU KEEP YOUR DISTANCE.
IS THERE ANYTHING ON THIS PLANET THAT WON'T KILL US?
NOT REALLY.
LET'S MOVE. STAY LOW.
SOMEONE IN THAT VILLAGE *HAS* TO HAVE A COMM SYSTEM.
WE'LL CALL IN AN EVAC, GET THE HELL BACK TO TRANENT IN TIME FOR DINNER.
MID

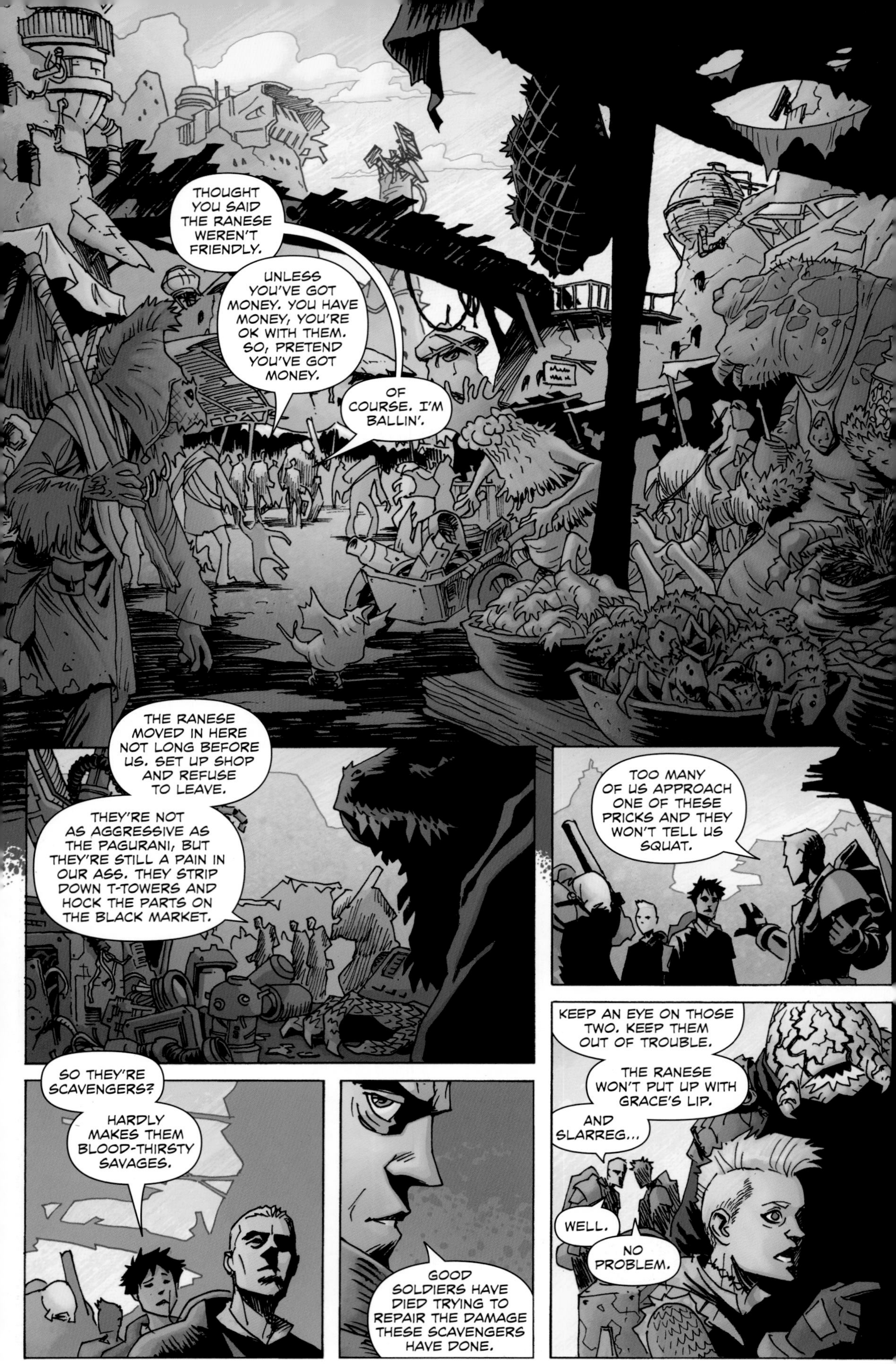

THOUGHT YOU SAID THE RANESE WEREN'T FRIENDLY.
UNLESS YOU'VE GOT MONEY. YOU HAVE MONEY, YOU'RE OK WITH THEM. SO, PRETEND YOU'VE GOT MONEY.
OF COURSE. I'M BALLIN'.
THE RANESE MOVED IN HERE NOT LONG BEFORE US. SET UP SHOP AND REFUSE TO LEAVE.
THEY'RE NOT AS AGGRESSIVE AS THE PAGURANI, BUT THEY'RE STILL A PAIN IN OUR ASS. THEY STRIP DOWN T-TOWERS AND HOCK THE PARTS ON THE BLACK MARKET.
TOO MANY OF US APPROACH ONE OF THESE PRICKS AND THEY WON'T TELL US SQUAT.
SO THEY'RE SCAVENGERS?
HARDLY MAKES THEM BLOOD-THIRSTY SAVAGES.
GOOD SOLDIERS HAVE DIED TRYING TO REPAIR THE DAMAGE THESE SCAVENGERS HAVE DONE.
KEEP AN EYE ON THOSE TWO. KEEP THEM OUT OF TROUBLE.
THE RANESE WON'T PUT UP WITH GRACE'S LIP.
AND SLARREG...
WELL.
NO PROBLEM.

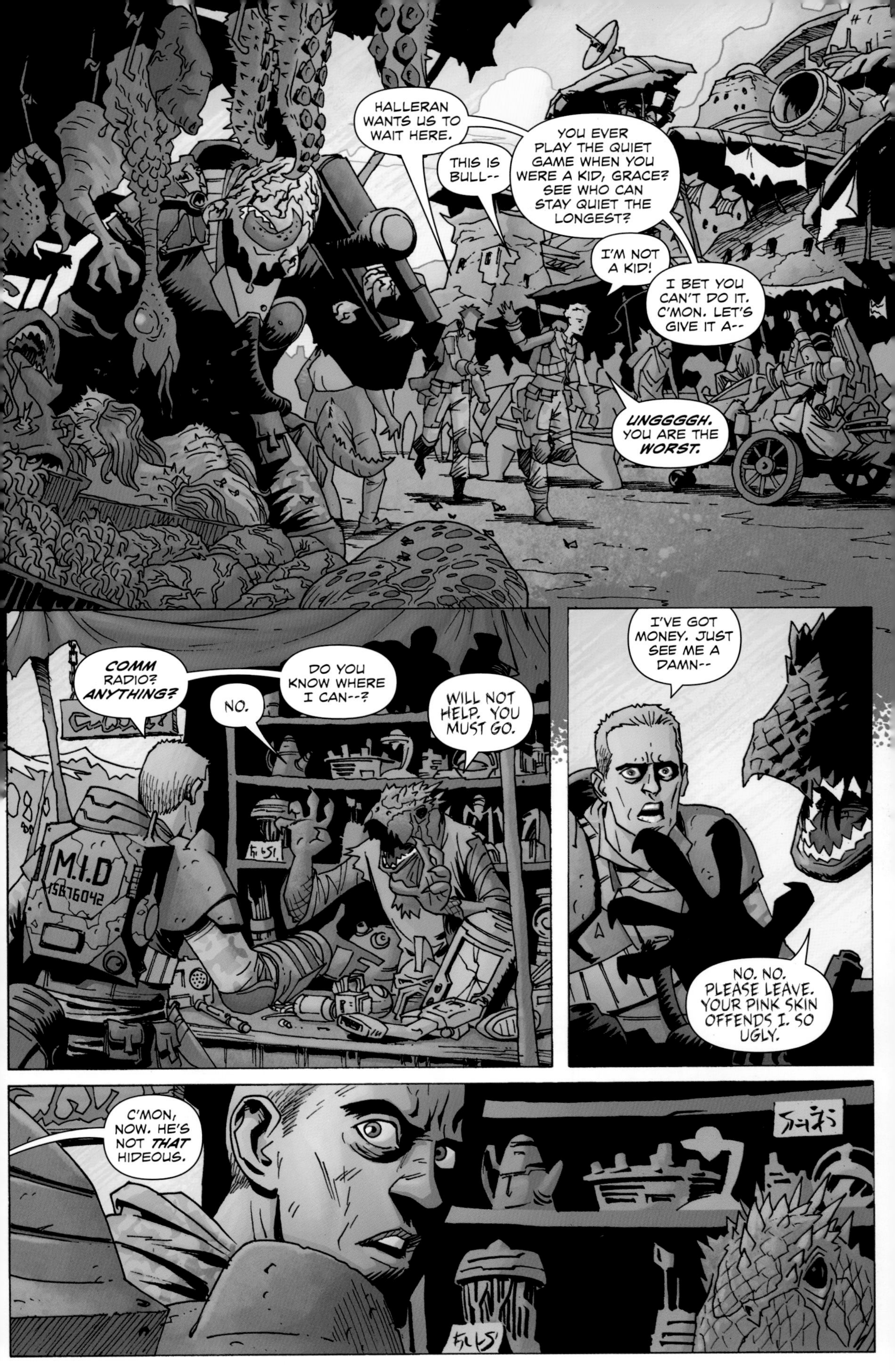
HALLERAN WANTS US TO WAIT HERE.
THIS IS BULL--
YOU EVER PLAY THE QUIET GAME WHEN YOU WERE A KID, GRACE? SEE WHO CAN STAY QUIET THE LONGEST?
I'M NOT A KID!
I BET YOU CAN'T DO IT. C'MON. LET'S GIVE IT A--
UNGGGGH. YOU ARE THE WORST.
DO YOU KNOW WHERE I CAN--?
COMM RADIO? ANYTHING?
NO.
WILL NOT HELP. YOU MUST GO.
M.I.D
I'VE GOT MONEY. JUST SEE ME A DAMN--
NO. NO. PLEASE LEAVE. YOUR PINK SKIN OFFENDS I. SO UGLY.
C'MON, NOW. HE'S NOT THAT HIDEOUS.

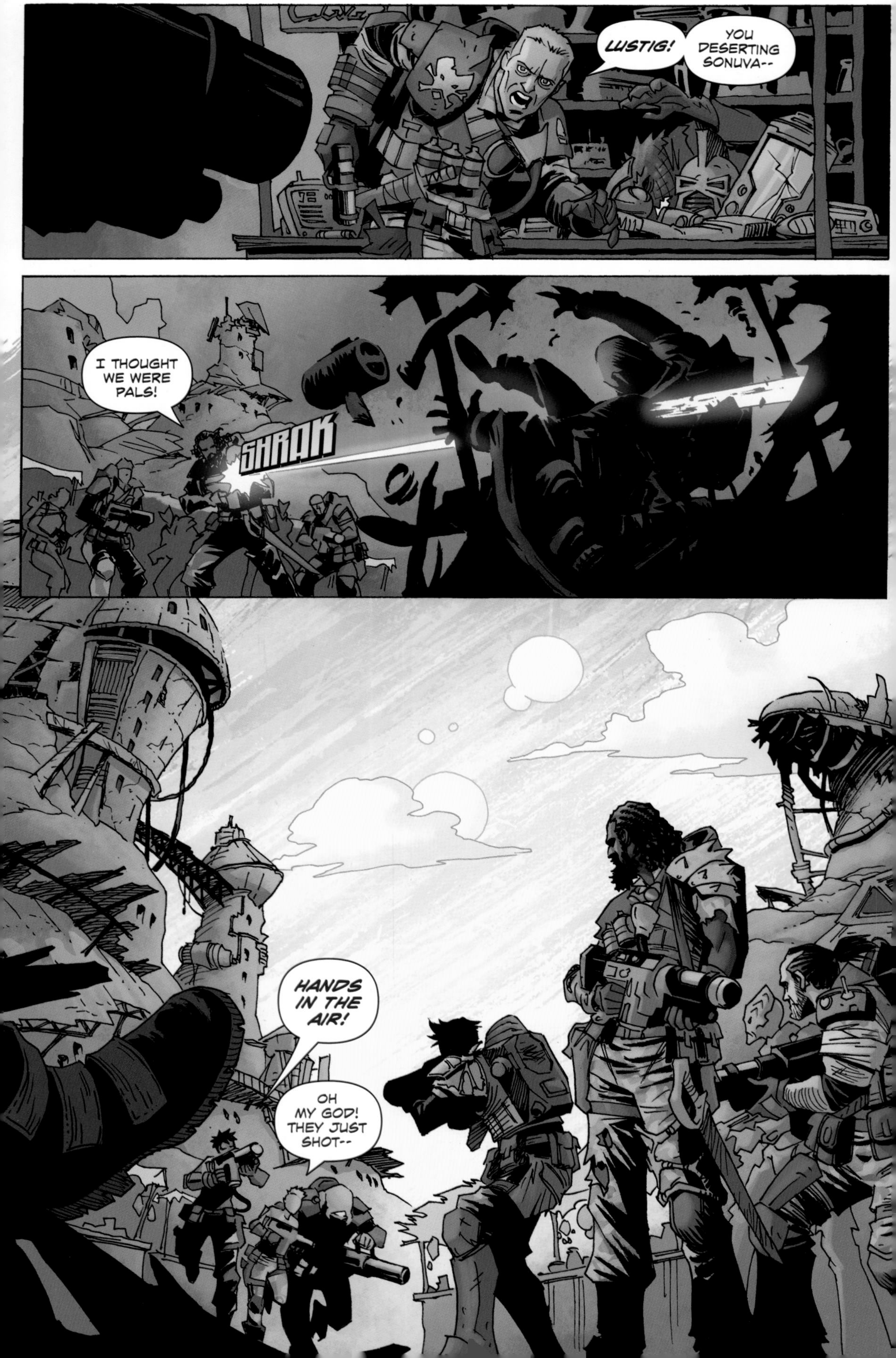
LUSTIG!
YOU DESERTING SONUVA--
I THOUGHT WE WERE PALS!
SHRAK
HANDS IN THE AIR!
OH MY GOD! THEY JUST SHOT--

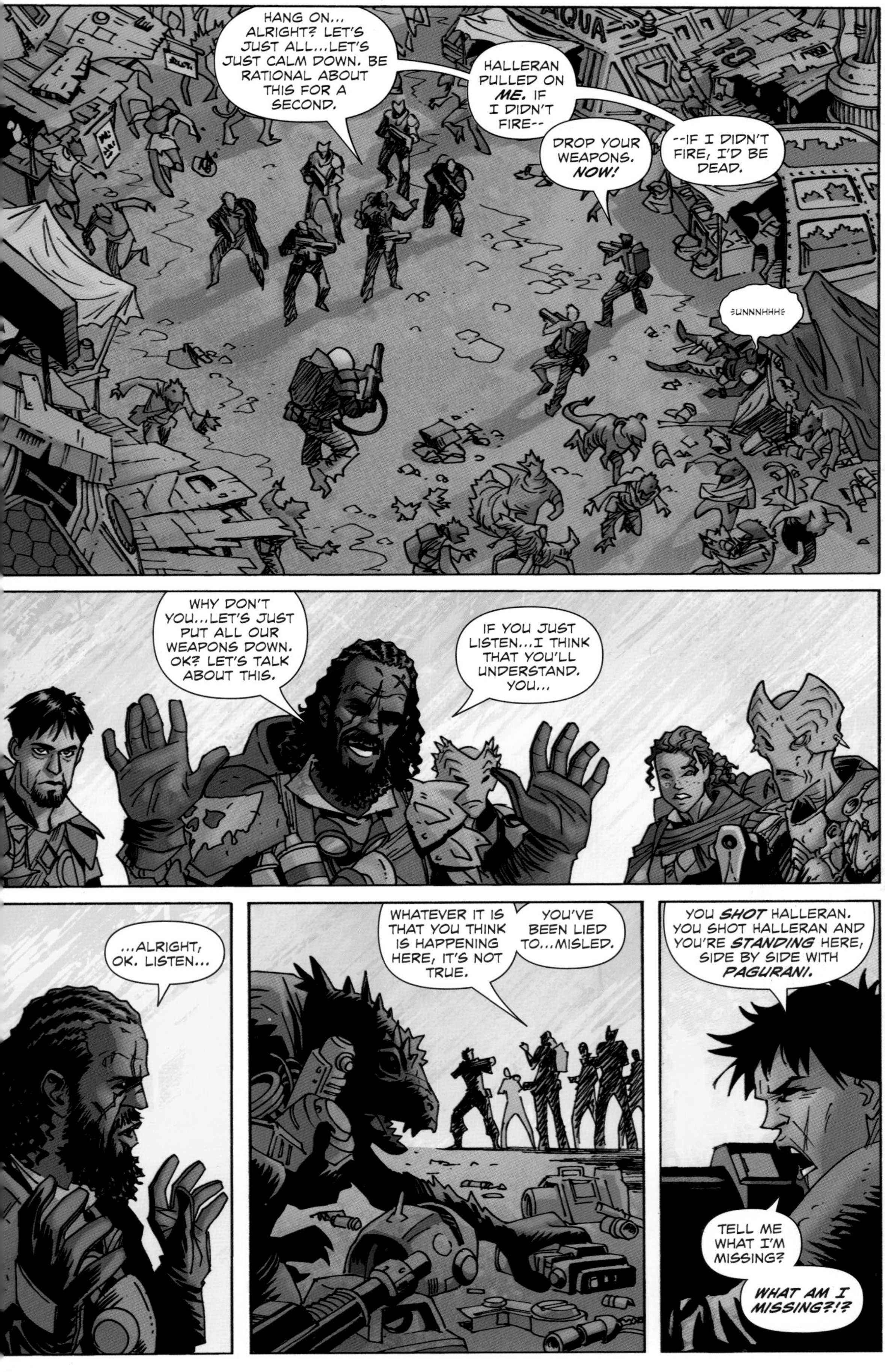
HANG ON... ALRIGHT? LET'S JUST ALL...LET'S JUST CALM DOWN. BE RATIONAL ABOUT THIS FOR A SECOND.
HALLERAN PULLED ON *ME.* IF I DIDN'T FIRE--
DROP YOUR WEAPONS. *NOW!*
--IF I DIDN'T FIRE, I'D BE DEAD.
UNNNHHH
WHY DON'T YOU...LET'S JUST PUT ALL OUR WEAPONS DOWN. OK? LET'S TALK ABOUT THIS.
IF YOU JUST LISTEN...I THINK THAT YOU'LL UNDERSTAND. YOU...
...ALRIGHT, OK. LISTEN...
WHATEVER IT IS THAT YOU THINK IS HAPPENING HERE, IT'S NOT TRUE.
YOU'VE BEEN LIED TO...MISLED.
YOU *SHOT* HALLERAN. YOU SHOT HALLERAN AND YOU'RE *STANDING* HERE, SIDE BY SIDE WITH *PAGURANI.*
TELL ME WHAT I'M MISSING?
WHAT AM I MISSING?!?

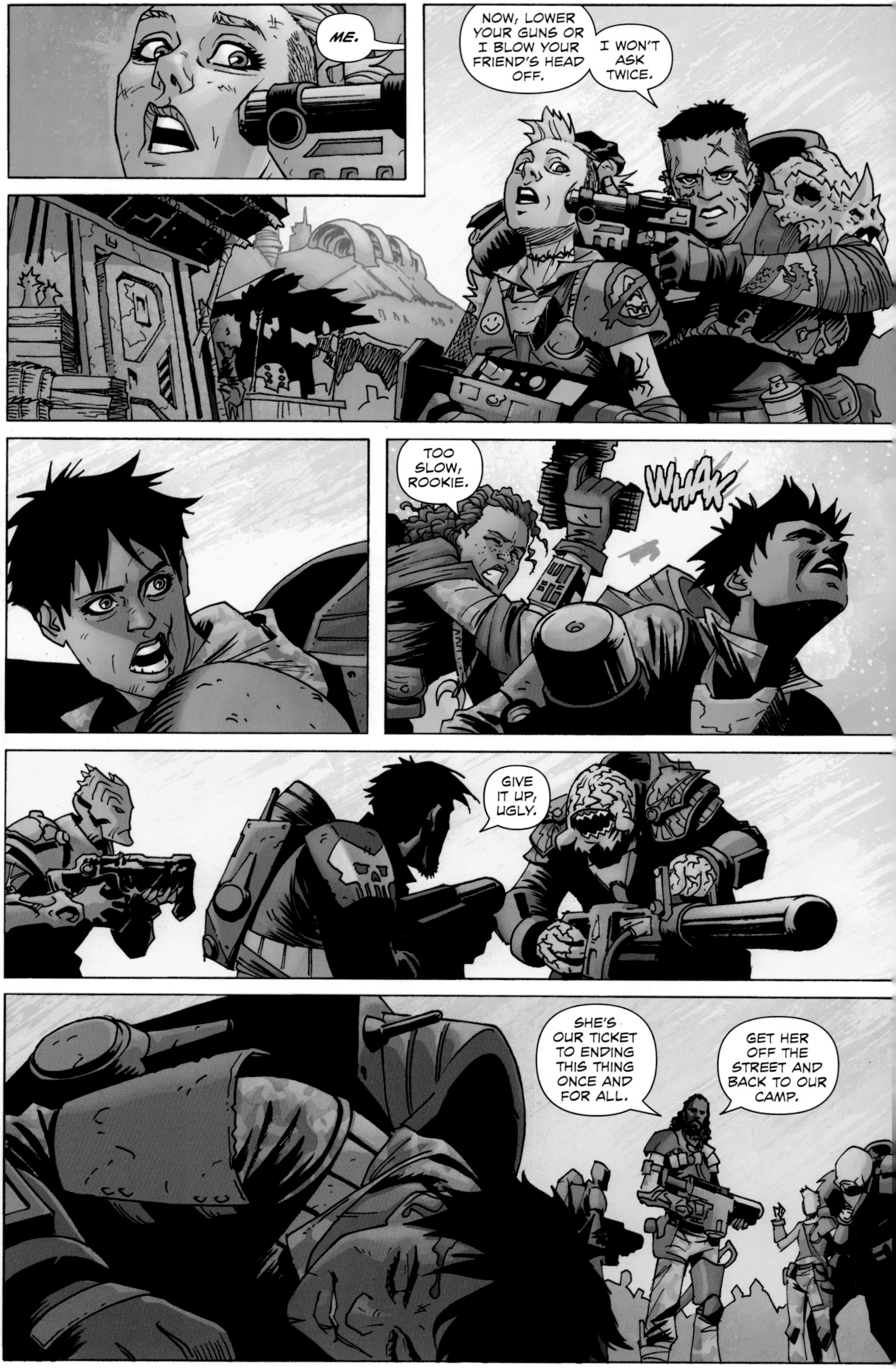

ME.
NOW, LOWER YOUR GUNS OR I BLOW YOUR FRIEND'S HEAD OFF.
I WON'T ASK TWICE.
TOO SLOW, ROOKIE.
WHAK
GIVE IT UP, UGLY.
SHE'S OUR TICKET TO ENDING THIS THING ONCE AND FOR ALL.
GET HER OFF THE STREET AND BACK TO OUR CAMP.

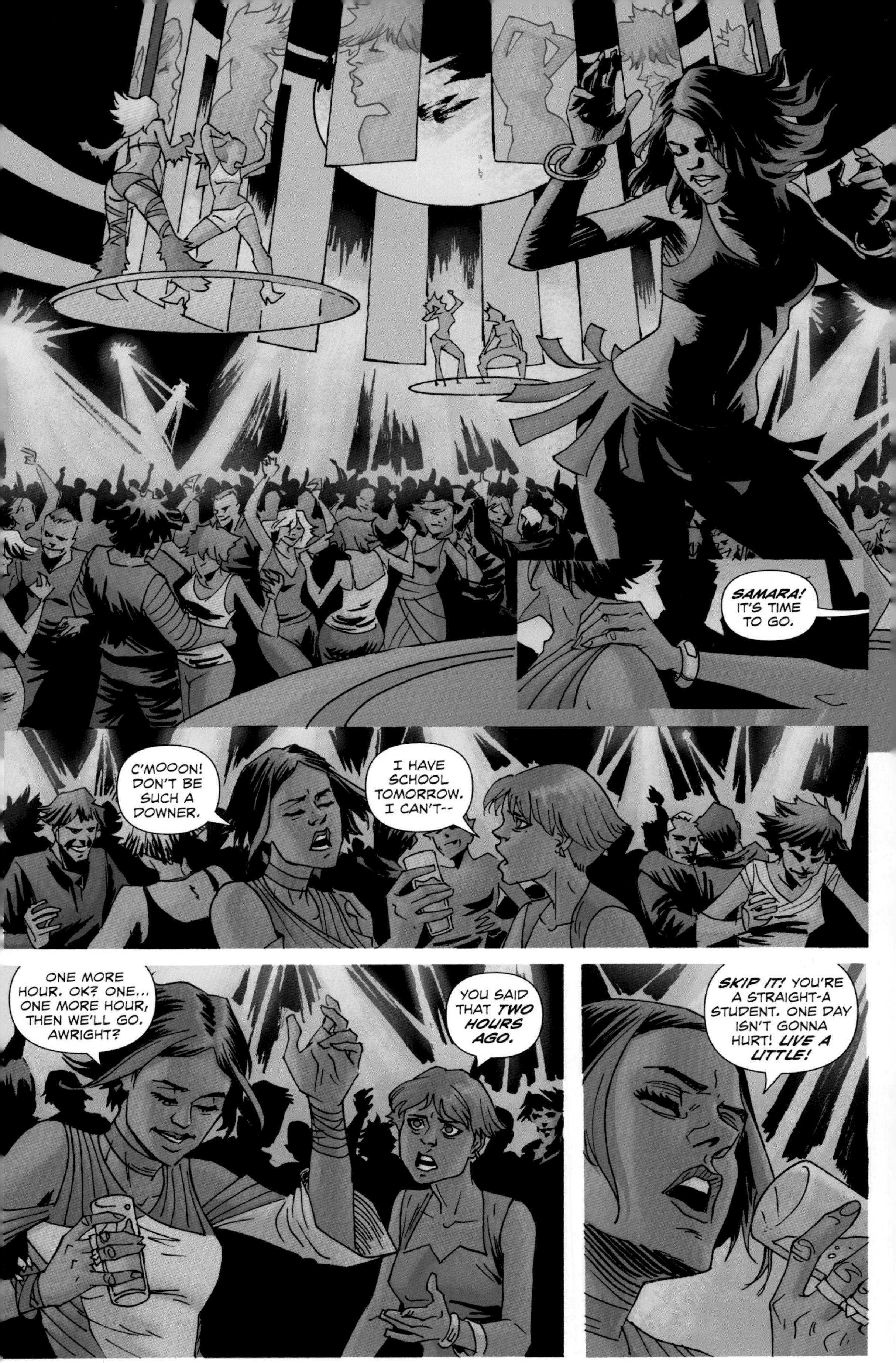

SAMARA! IT'S TIME TO GO.
C'MOOON! DON'T BE SUCH A DOWNER.
I HAVE SCHOOL TOMORROW. I CAN'T--
ONE MORE HOUR. OK? ONE... ONE MORE HOUR, THEN WE'LL GO. AWRIGHT?
YOU SAID THAT *TWO HOURS AGO.*
SKIP IT! YOU'RE A STRAIGHT-A STUDENT. ONE DAY ISN'T GONNA HURT! *LIVE A LITTLE!*

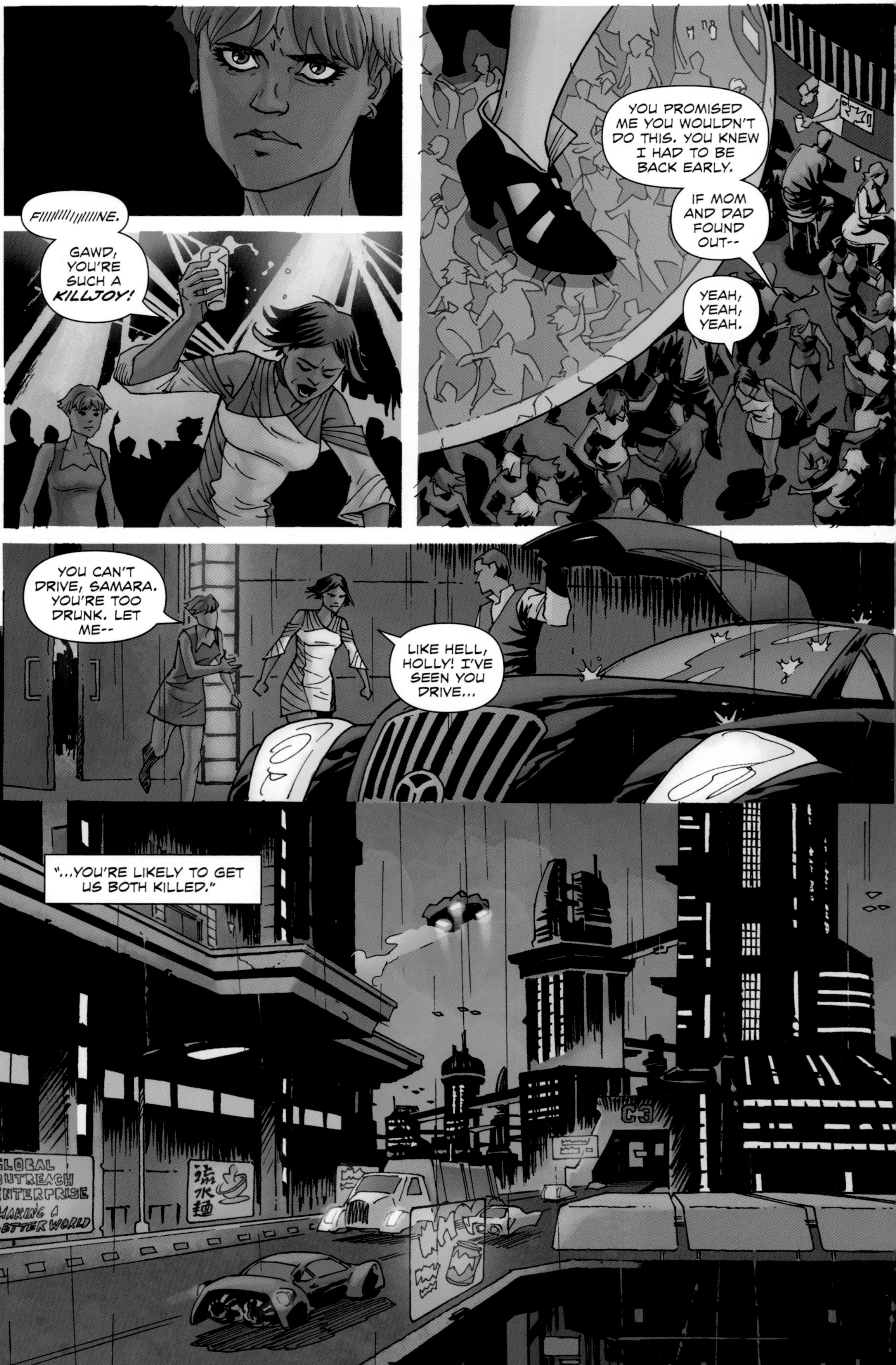
FIIIIIIIIIIIIIINE.
GAWD, YOU'RE SUCH A KILLJOY!
YOU PROMISED ME YOU WOULDN'T DO THIS. YOU KNEW I HAD TO BE BACK EARLY.
IF MOM AND DAD FOUND OUT--
YEAH, YEAH, YEAH.
YOU CAN'T DRIVE, SAMARA. YOU'RE TOO DRUNK. LET ME--
LIKE HELL, HOLLY! I'VE SEEN YOU DRIVE...
"...YOU'RE LIKELY TO GET US BOTH KILLED."
GLOBAL OUTREACH ENTERPRISE
MAKING A BETTER WORLD
C3

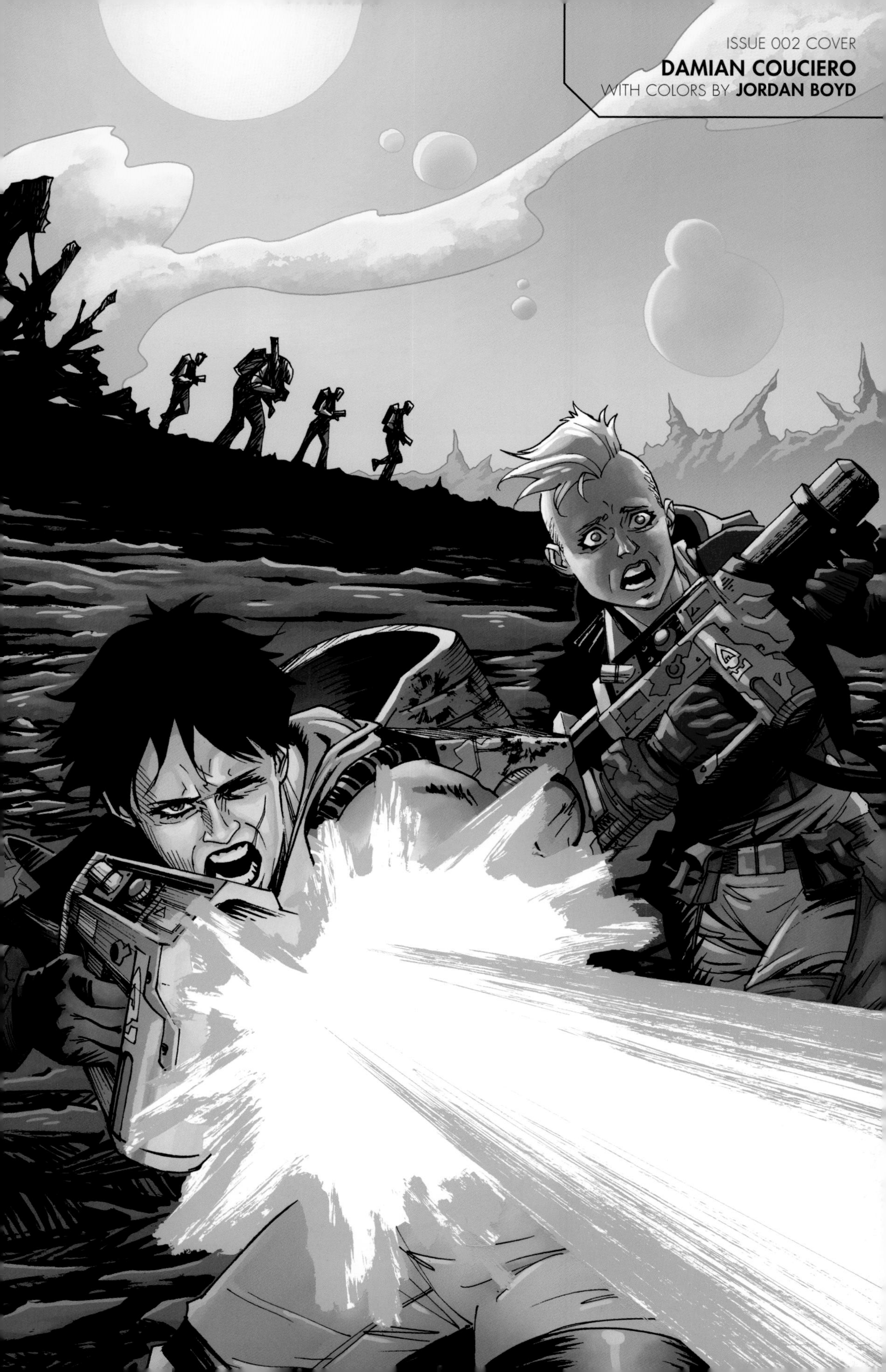

ISSUE 002 COVER
DAMIAN COUCIERO
WITH COLORS BY **JORDAN BOYD**

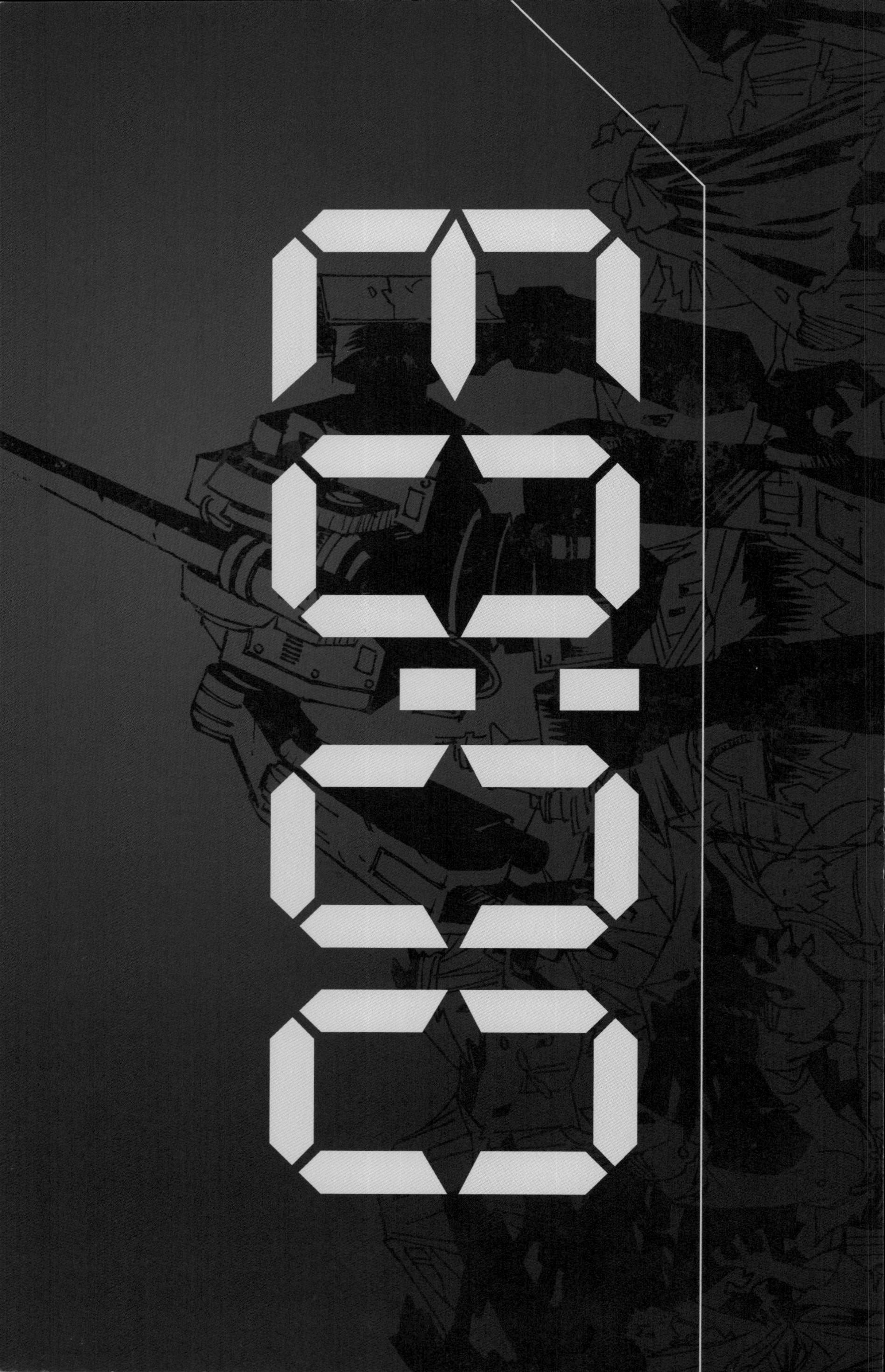

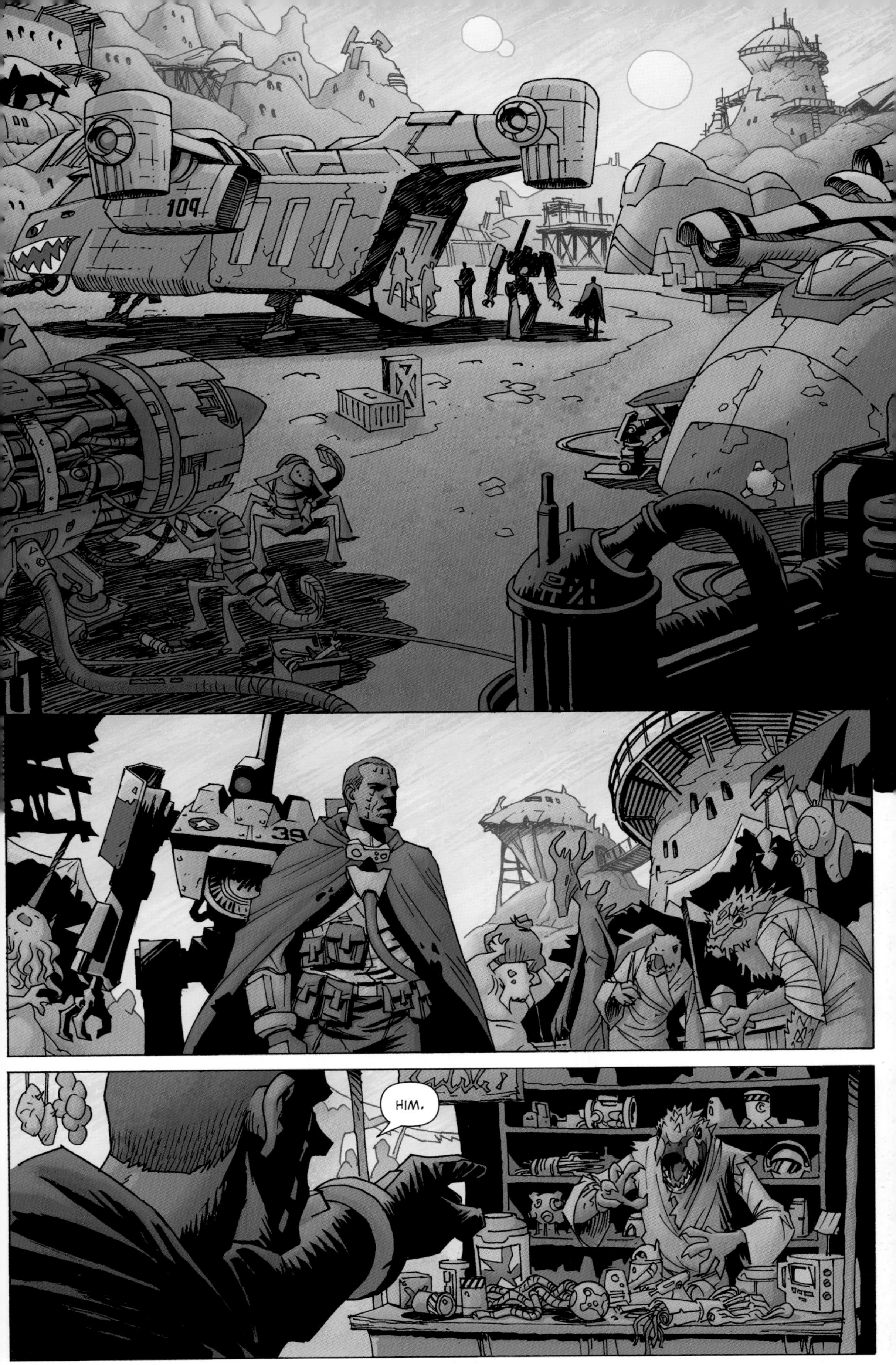
HIM.

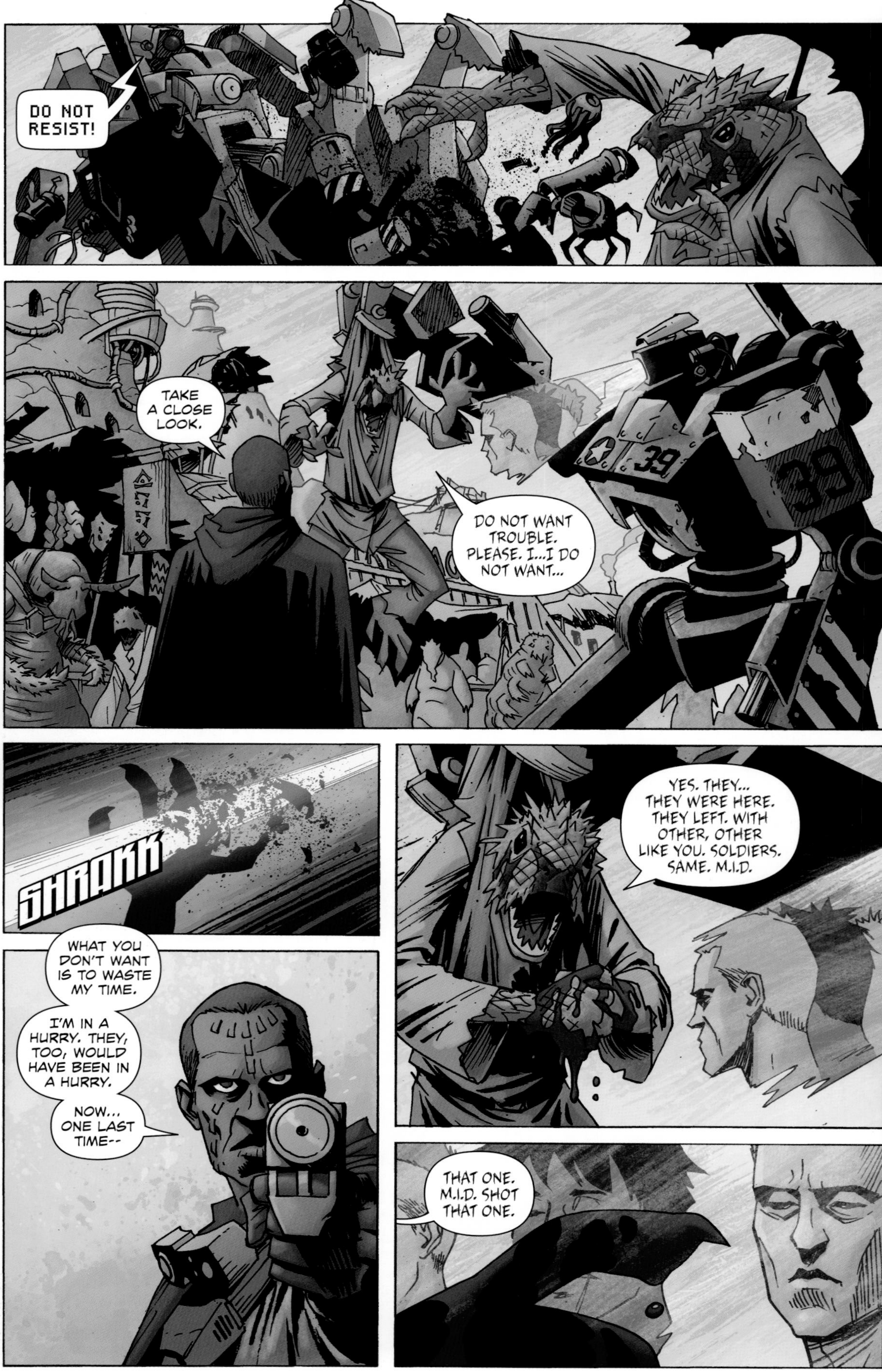
DO NOT RESIST!
TAKE A CLOSE LOOK.
DO NOT WANT TROUBLE. PLEASE. I...I DO NOT WANT...
SHRAKK
WHAT YOU DON'T WANT IS TO WASTE MY TIME.
I'M IN A HURRY. THEY, TOO, WOULD HAVE BEEN IN A HURRY.
NOW... ONE LAST TIME--
YES. THEY... THEY WERE HERE. THEY LEFT. WITH OTHER, OTHER LIKE YOU. SOLDIERS. SAME. M.I.D.
THAT ONE. M.I.D. SHOT THAT ONE.

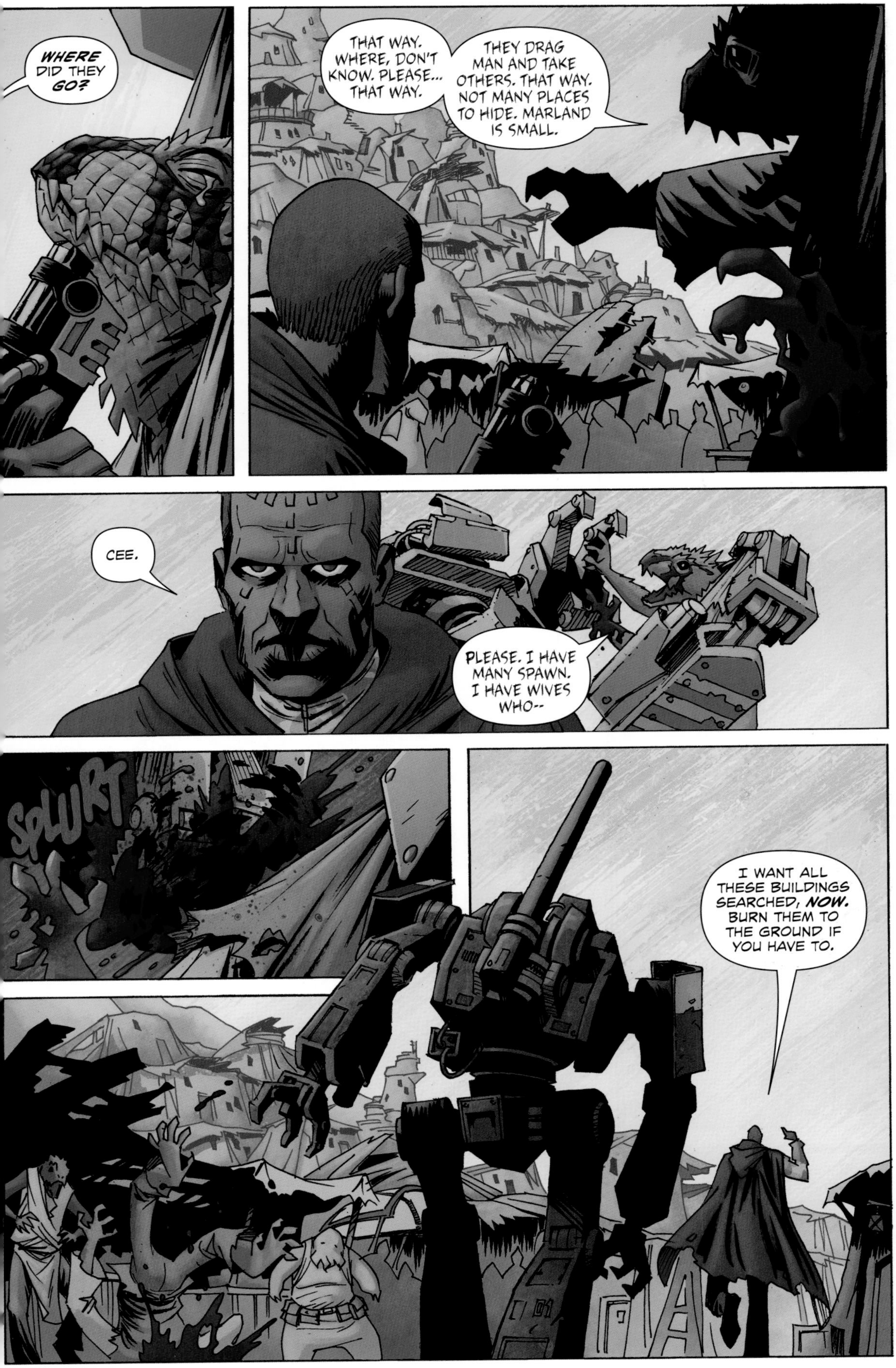
WHERE DID THEY GO?
THAT WAY. WHERE, DON'T KNOW. PLEASE... THAT WAY.
THEY DRAG MAN AND TAKE OTHERS. THAT WAY. NOT MANY PLACES TO HIDE. MARLAND IS SMALL.
CEE.
PLEASE. I HAVE MANY SPAWN. I HAVE WIVES WHO--
SPLURT
I WANT ALL THESE BUILDINGS SEARCHED, NOW. BURN THEM TO THE GROUND IF YOU HAVE TO.

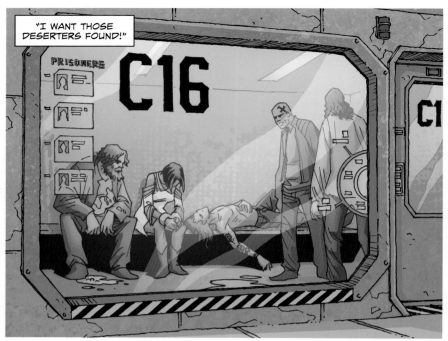

"I WANT THOSE DESERTERS FOUND!"

PRISONERS
C16
C1

SAMARA SIMMONS?

YOUR PARENTS ARE HERE. THEY'VE POSTED YOUR BAIL.

MOM... DAD... I...

IS HOLLY OK? THEY WON'T TALK TO ME ABOUT...

I'M SO SORRY. I--

ARE YOU OK? DID YOU--

MOM. PLEASE, TELL ME THAT HOLLY'S OK. PLEASE...

HOW COULD YOU?

DRIVING DRUNK? ARE YOU INSANE?

PHIL, PLEASE... NOT NOW...

SHE'S DEAD BECAUSE OF YOU.

"YOU KILLED YOUR OWN SISTER."

UNGH...

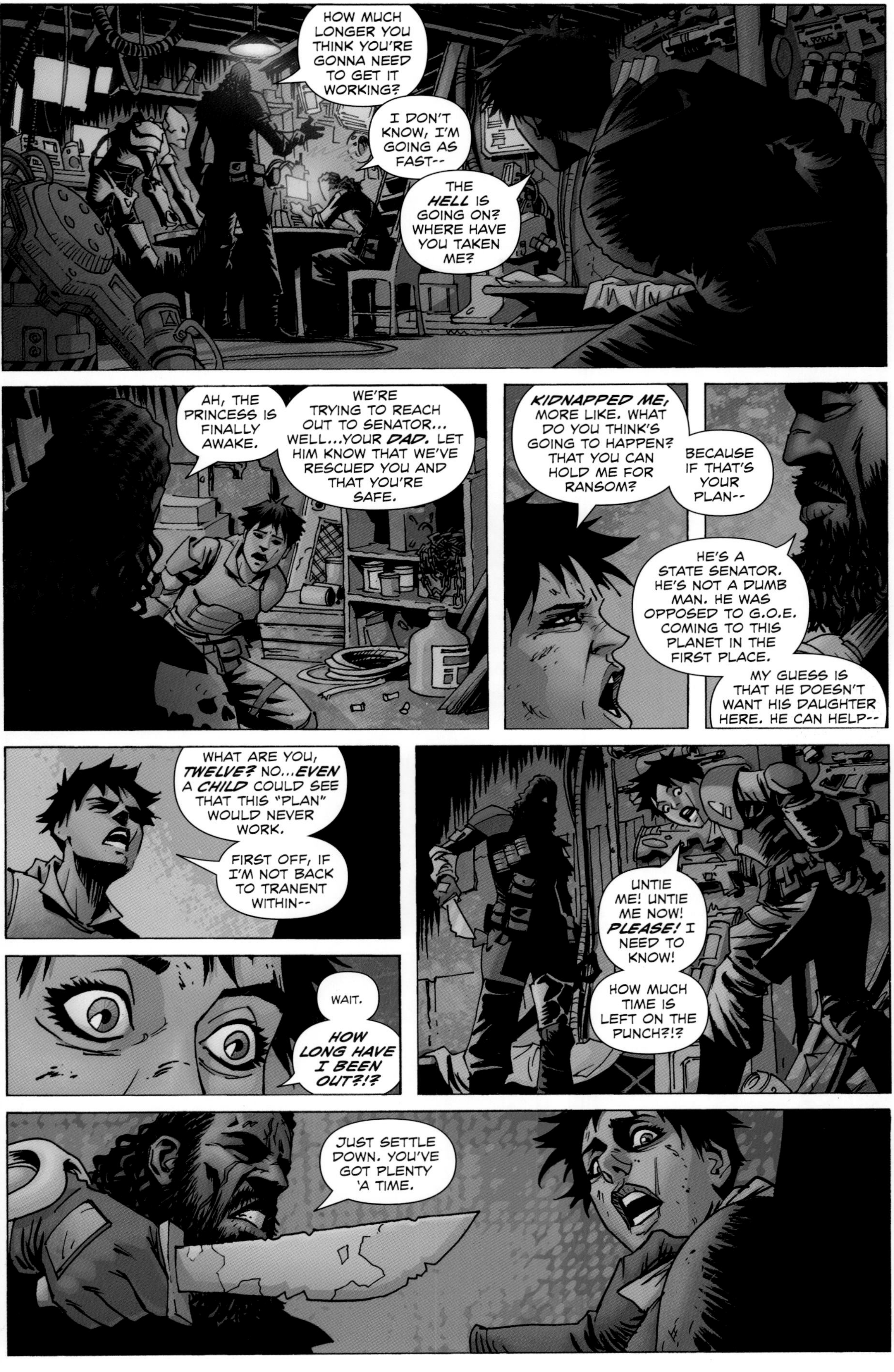
HOW MUCH LONGER YOU THINK YOU'RE GONNA NEED TO GET IT WORKING?
I DON'T KNOW, I'M GOING AS FAST--
THE *HELL* IS GOING ON? WHERE HAVE YOU TAKEN ME?
AH, THE PRINCESS IS FINALLY AWAKE.
WE'RE TRYING TO REACH OUT TO SENATOR... WELL...YOUR *DAD.* LET HIM KNOW THAT WE'VE RESCUED YOU AND THAT YOU'RE SAFE.
KIDNAPPED ME, MORE LIKE. WHAT DO YOU THINK'S GOING TO HAPPEN? THAT YOU CAN HOLD ME FOR RANSOM?
BECAUSE IF THAT'S YOUR PLAN--
HE'S A STATE SENATOR. HE'S NOT A DUMB MAN. HE WAS OPPOSED TO G.O.E. COMING TO THIS PLANET IN THE FIRST PLACE.
MY GUESS IS THAT HE DOESN'T WANT HIS DAUGHTER HERE. HE CAN HELP--
WHAT ARE YOU, *TWELVE?* NO...*EVEN* A *CHILD* COULD SEE THAT THIS "PLAN" WOULD NEVER WORK.
FIRST OFF, IF I'M NOT BACK TO TRANENT WITHIN--
WAIT.
HOW LONG HAVE I BEEN OUT?!?
UNTIE ME! UNTIE ME NOW! *PLEASE!* I NEED TO KNOW!
HOW MUCH TIME IS LEFT ON THE PUNCH?!?
JUST SETTLE DOWN. YOU'VE GOT PLENTY 'A TIME.

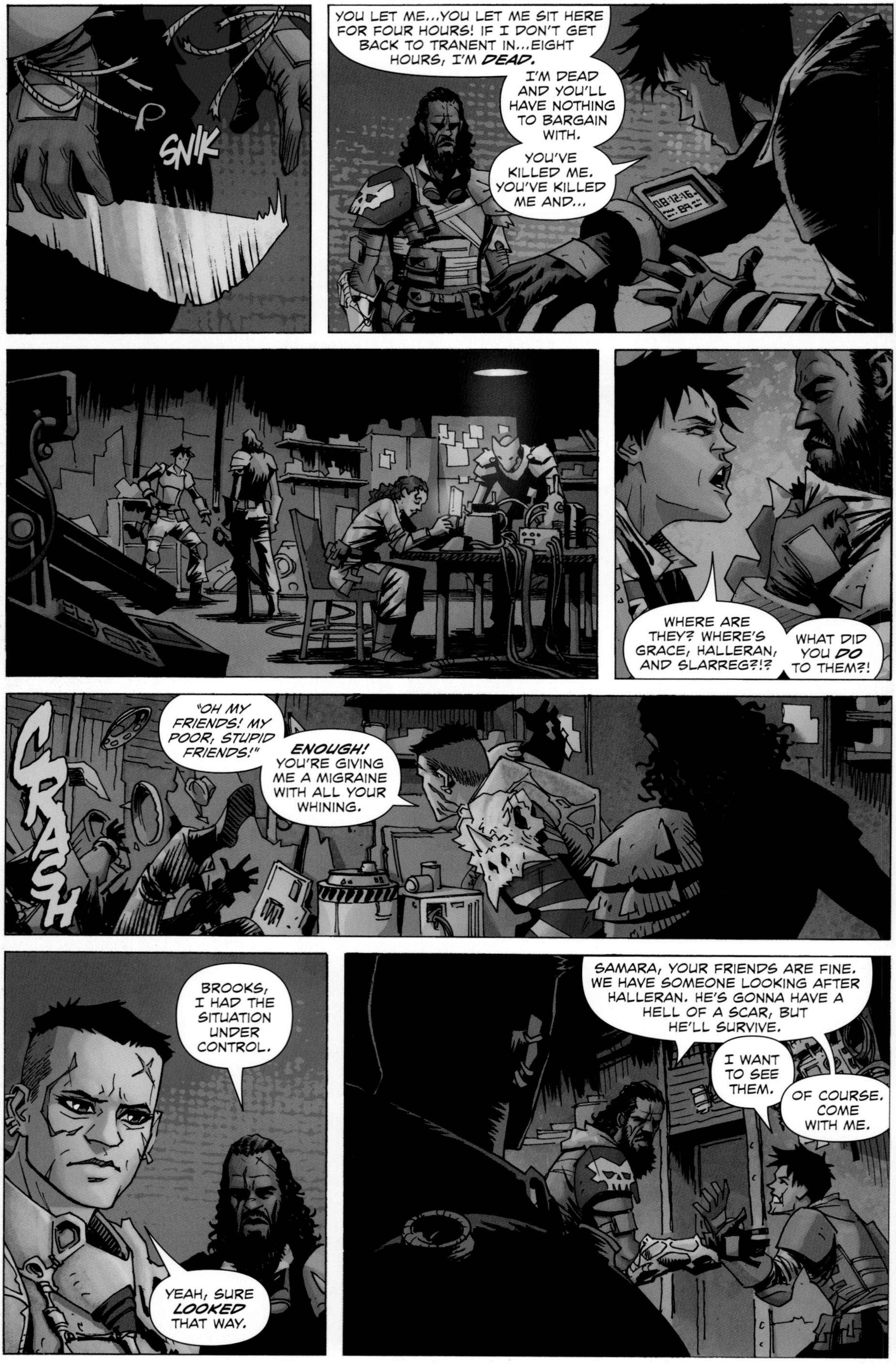
SNIK
YOU LET ME...YOU LET ME SIT HERE FOR FOUR HOURS! IF I DON'T GET BACK TO TRANENT IN...EIGHT HOURS, I'M DEAD.
I'M DEAD AND YOU'LL HAVE NOTHING TO BARGAIN WITH.
YOU'VE KILLED ME. YOU'VE KILLED ME AND...
08:12:16
WHERE ARE THEY? WHERE'S GRACE, HALLERAN, AND SLARREG?!?
WHAT DID YOU DO TO THEM?!
CRASH
"OH MY FRIENDS! MY POOR, STUPID FRIENDS!"
ENOUGH! YOU'RE GIVING ME A MIGRAINE WITH ALL YOUR WHINING.
BROOKS, I HAD THE SITUATION UNDER CONTROL.
YEAH, SURE LOOKED THAT WAY.
SAMARA, YOUR FRIENDS ARE FINE. WE HAVE SOMEONE LOOKING AFTER HALLERAN. HE'S GONNA HAVE A HELL OF A SCAR, BUT HE'LL SURVIVE.
I WANT TO SEE THEM.
OF COURSE. COME WITH ME.

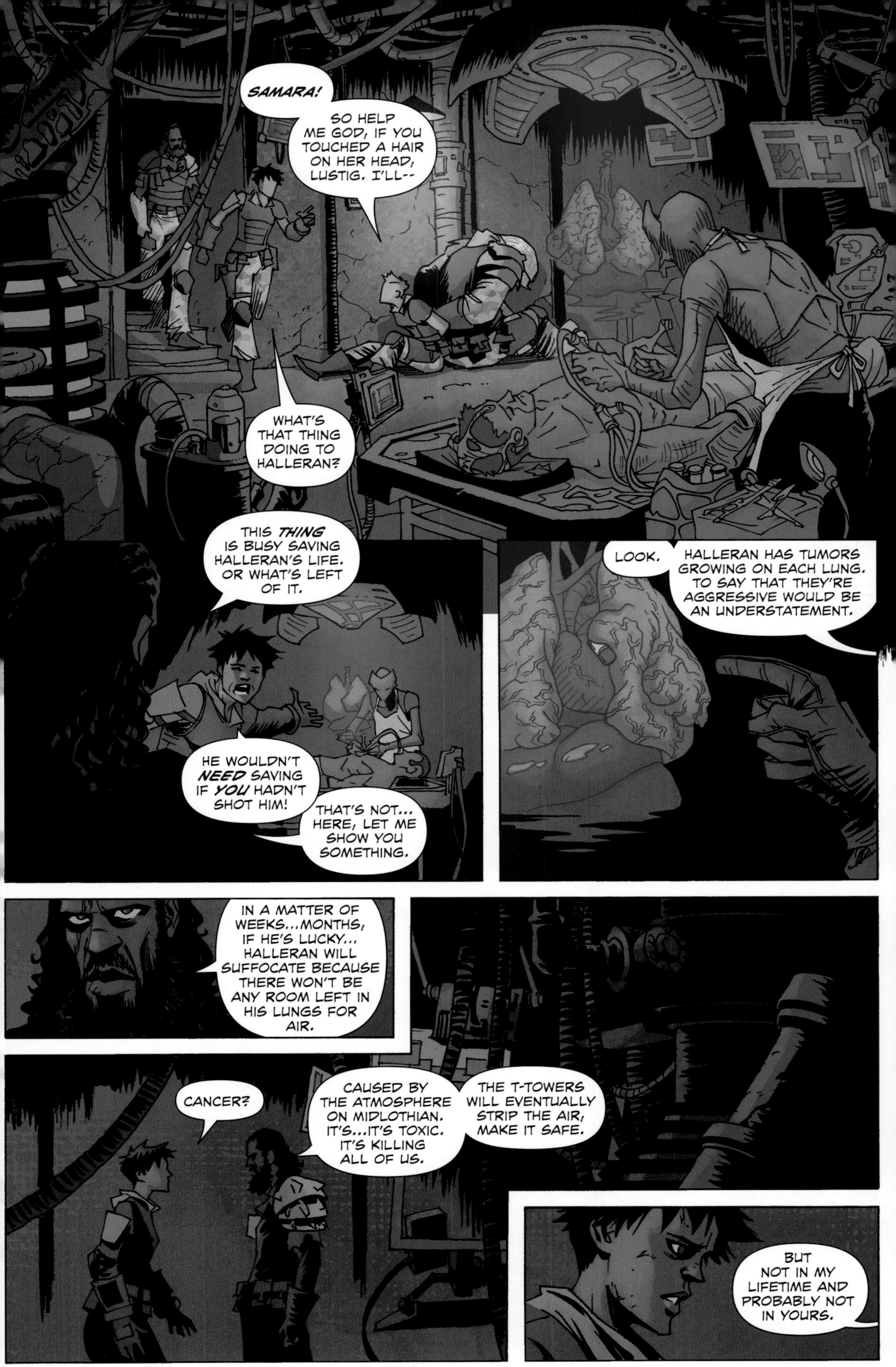
SAMARA!
SO HELP ME GOD, IF YOU TOUCHED A HAIR ON HER HEAD, LUSTIG. I'LL--
WHAT'S THAT THING DOING TO HALLERAN?
THIS THING IS BUSY SAVING HALLERAN'S LIFE. OR WHAT'S LEFT OF IT.
HE WOULDN'T NEED SAVING IF YOU HADN'T SHOT HIM!
THAT'S NOT... HERE, LET ME SHOW YOU SOMETHING.
LOOK.
HALLERAN HAS TUMORS GROWING ON EACH LUNG. TO SAY THAT THEY'RE AGGRESSIVE WOULD BE AN UNDERSTATEMENT.
IN A MATTER OF WEEKS...MONTHS, IF HE'S LUCKY... HALLERAN WILL SUFFOCATE BECAUSE THERE WON'T BE ANY ROOM LEFT IN HIS LUNGS FOR AIR.
CANCER?
CAUSED BY THE ATMOSPHERE ON MIDLOTHIAN. IT'S...IT'S TOXIC. IT'S KILLING ALL OF US.
THE T-TOWERS WILL EVENTUALLY STRIP THE AIR, MAKE IT SAFE.
BUT NOT IN MY LIFETIME AND PROBABLY NOT IN YOURS.

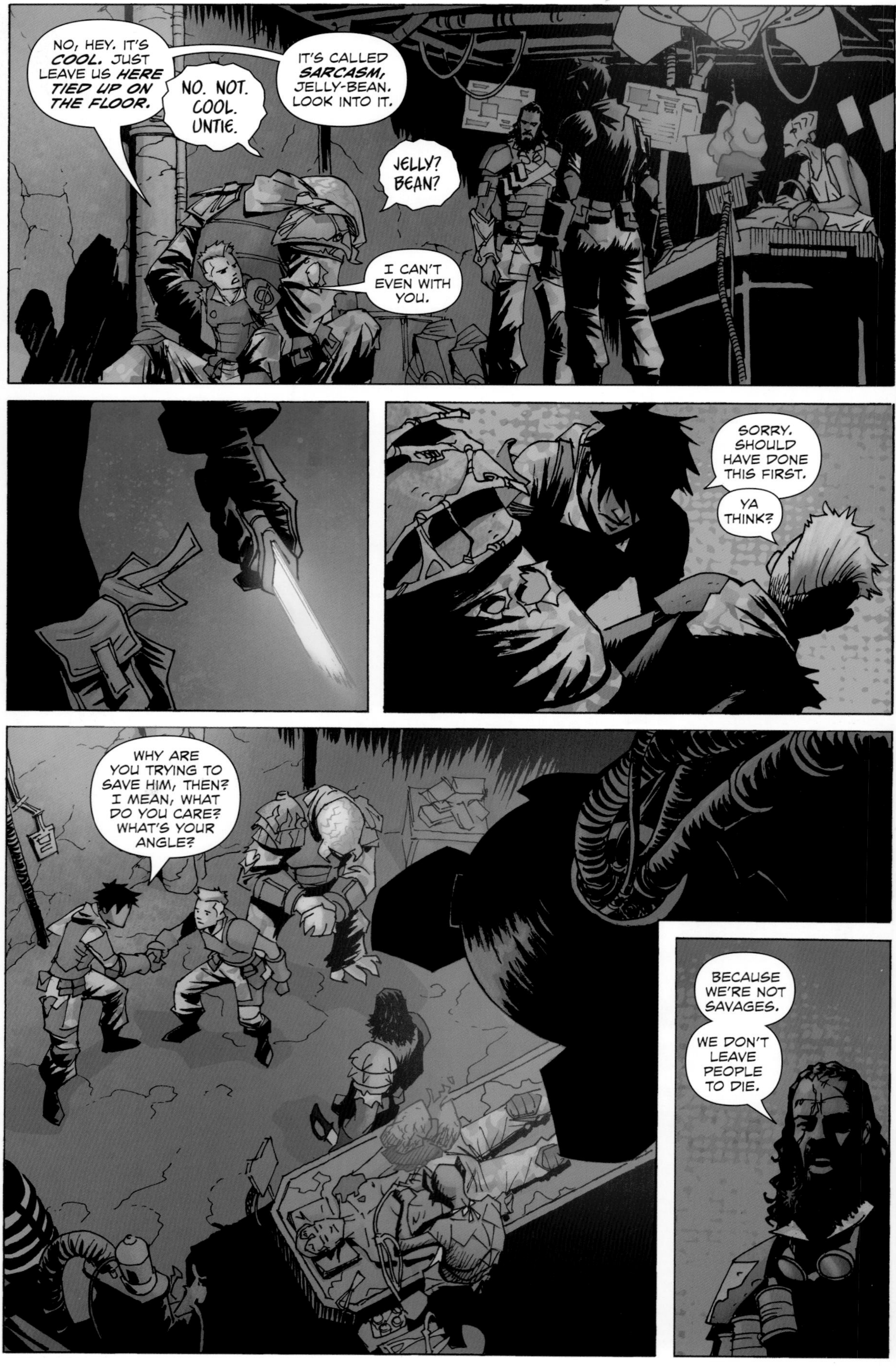
NO, HEY. IT'S *COOL.* JUST LEAVE US ***HERE TIED UP ON THE FLOOR.***
NO. NOT. COOL. UNTIE.
IT'S CALLED ***SARCASM,*** JELLY-BEAN. LOOK INTO IT.
JELLY? BEAN?
I CAN'T EVEN WITH YOU.
SORRY. SHOULD HAVE DONE THIS FIRST.
YA THINK?
WHY ARE YOU TRYING TO SAVE HIM, THEN? I MEAN, WHAT DO YOU CARE? WHAT'S YOUR ANGLE?
BECAUSE WE'RE NOT SAVAGES.
WE DON'T LEAVE PEOPLE TO DIE.

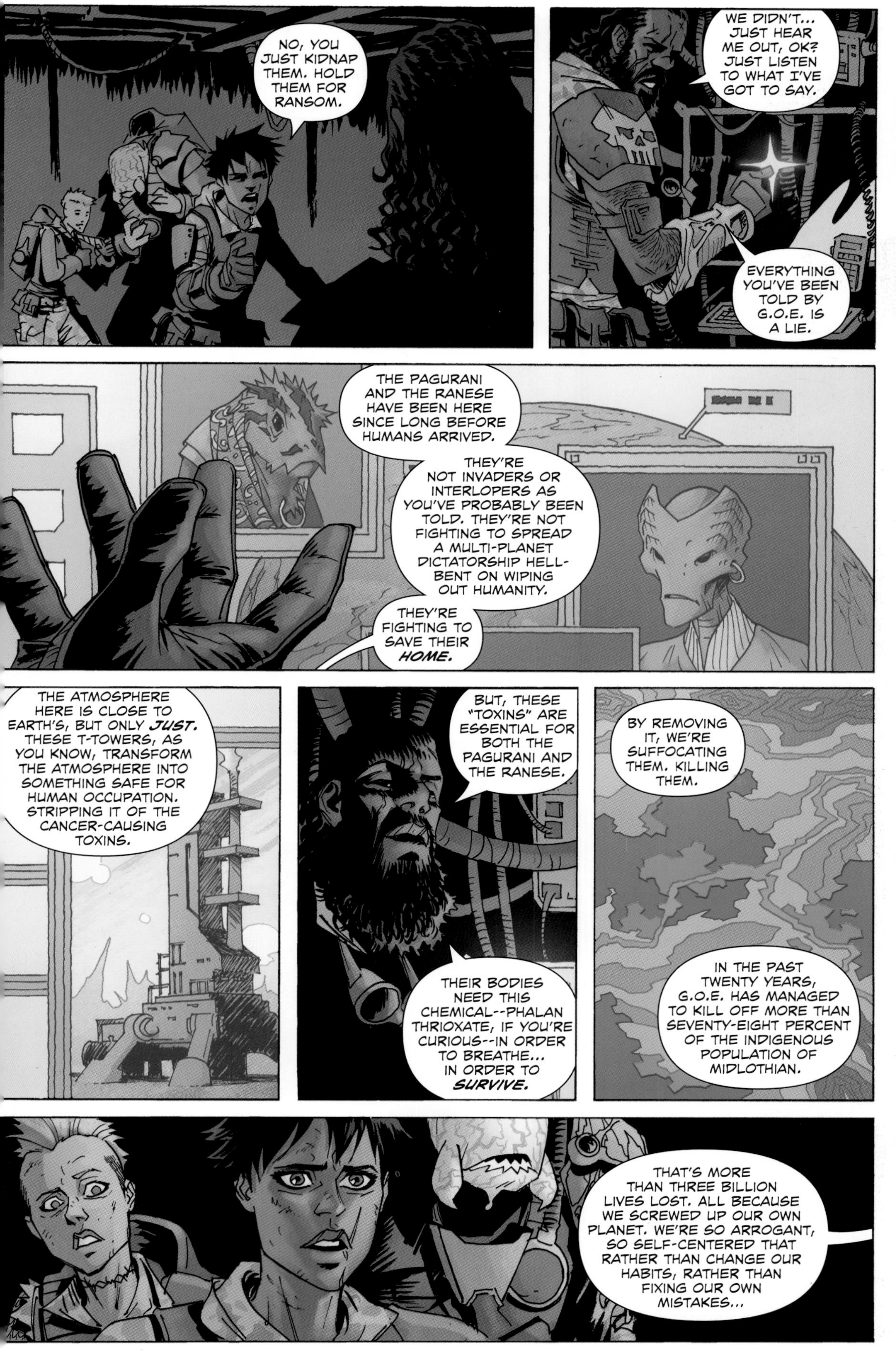
NO, YOU JUST KIDNAP THEM. HOLD THEM FOR RANSOM.
WE DIDN'T... JUST HEAR ME OUT, OK? JUST LISTEN TO WHAT I'VE GOT TO SAY.
EVERYTHING YOU'VE BEEN TOLD BY G.O.E. IS A LIE.
THE PAGURANI AND THE RANESE HAVE BEEN HERE SINCE LONG BEFORE HUMANS ARRIVED.
THEY'RE NOT INVADERS OR INTERLOPERS AS YOU'VE PROBABLY BEEN TOLD. THEY'RE NOT FIGHTING TO SPREAD A MULTI-PLANET DICTATORSHIP HELL-BENT ON WIPING OUT HUMANITY.
THEY'RE FIGHTING TO SAVE THEIR *HOME.*
THE ATMOSPHERE HERE IS CLOSE TO EARTH'S, BUT ONLY *JUST.* THESE T-TOWERS, AS YOU KNOW, TRANSFORM THE ATMOSPHERE INTO SOMETHING SAFE FOR HUMAN OCCUPATION. STRIPPING IT OF THE CANCER-CAUSING TOXINS.
BUT, THESE "TOXINS" ARE ESSENTIAL FOR BOTH THE PAGURANI AND THE RANESE.
THEIR BODIES NEED THIS CHEMICAL--PHALAN THRIOXATE--IF YOU'RE CURIOUS--IN ORDER TO BREATHE... IN ORDER TO *SURVIVE.*
BY REMOVING IT, WE'RE SUFFOCATING THEM. KILLING THEM.
IN THE PAST TWENTY YEARS, G.O.E. HAS MANAGED TO KILL OFF MORE THAN SEVENTY-EIGHT PERCENT OF THE INDIGENOUS POPULATION OF MIDLOTHIAN.
THAT'S MORE THAN THREE BILLION LIVES LOST. ALL BECAUSE WE SCREWED UP OUR OWN PLANET. WE'RE SO ARROGANT, SO SELF-CENTERED THAT RATHER THAN CHANGE OUR HABITS, RATHER THAN FIXING OUR OWN MISTAKES...

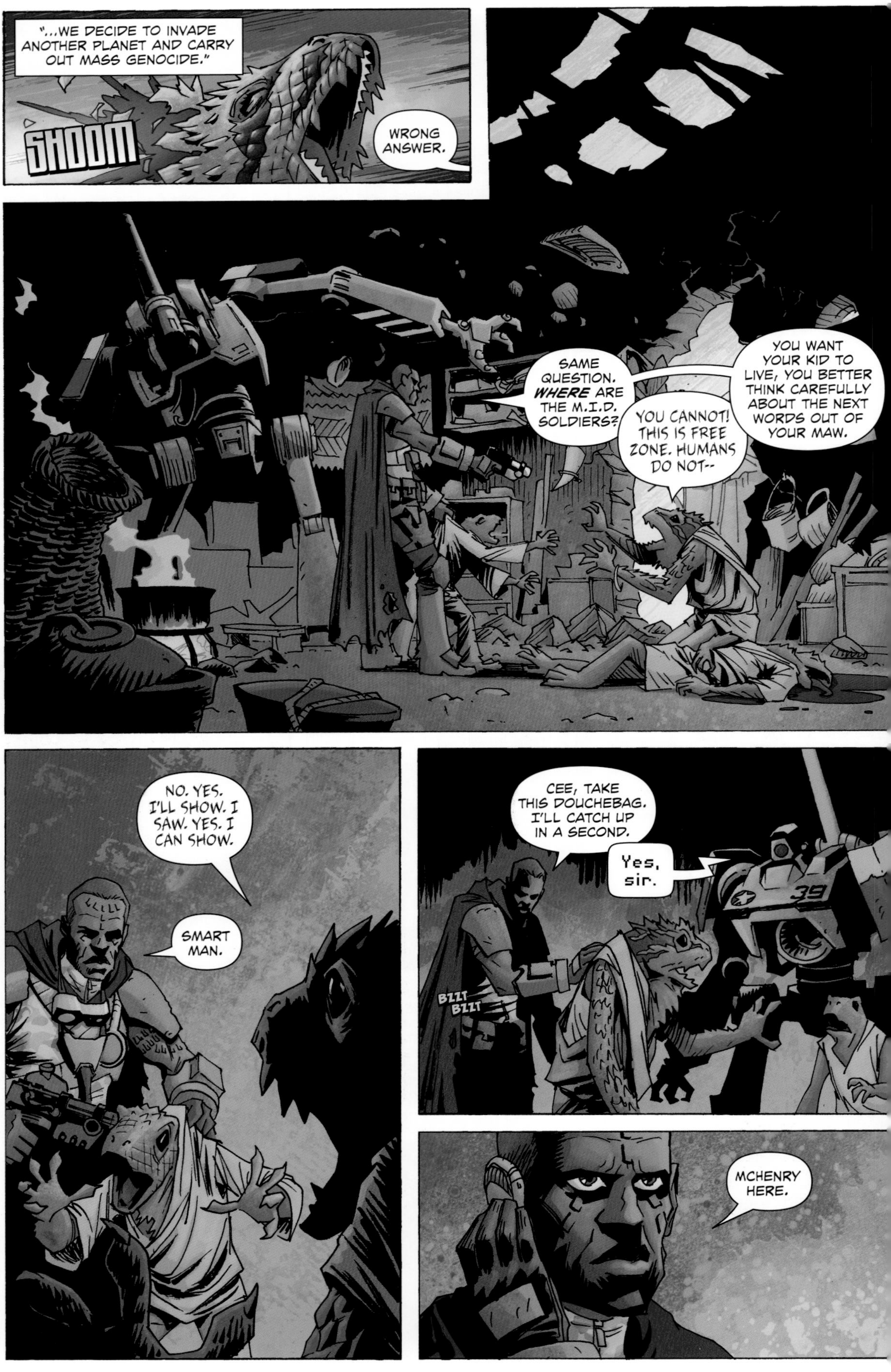
"...WE DECIDE TO INVADE ANOTHER PLANET AND CARRY OUT MASS GENOCIDE."
SHOOM
WRONG ANSWER.
SAME QUESTION. WHERE ARE THE M.I.D. SOLDIERS?
YOU WANT YOUR KID TO LIVE, YOU BETTER THINK CAREFULLY ABOUT THE NEXT WORDS OUT OF YOUR MAW.
YOU CANNOT! THIS IS FREE ZONE. HUMANS DO NOT--
NO. YES. I'LL SHOW. I SAW. YES. I CAN SHOW.
SMART MAN.
CEE, TAKE THIS DOUCHEBAG. I'LL CATCH UP IN A SECOND.
Yes, sir.
39
BZZT BZZT
MCHENRY HERE.

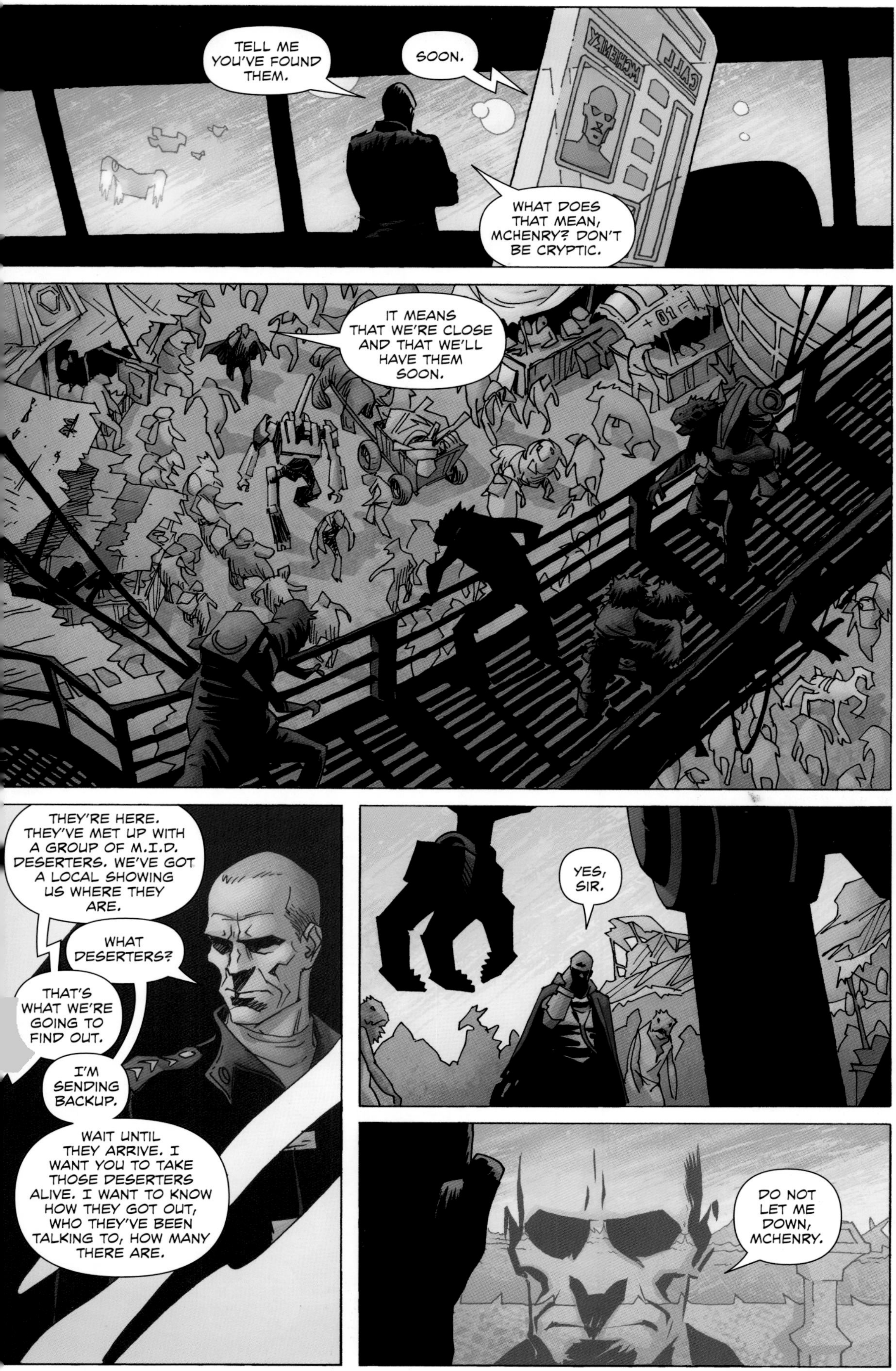

TELL ME YOU'VE FOUND THEM.
SOON.
WHAT DOES THAT MEAN, MCHENRY? DON'T BE CRYPTIC.
CALL MCHENRY
IT MEANS THAT WE'RE CLOSE AND THAT WE'LL HAVE THEM SOON.
THEY'RE HERE. THEY'VE MET UP WITH A GROUP OF M.I.D. DESERTERS. WE'VE GOT A LOCAL SHOWING US WHERE THEY ARE.
WHAT DESERTERS?
THAT'S WHAT WE'RE GOING TO FIND OUT.
I'M SENDING BACKUP.
WAIT UNTIL THEY ARRIVE. I WANT YOU TO TAKE THOSE DESERTERS ALIVE. I WANT TO KNOW HOW THEY GOT OUT, WHO THEY'VE BEEN TALKING TO, HOW MANY THERE ARE.
YES, SIR.
DO NOT LET ME DOWN, MCHENRY.

NO?

NO.

I DON'T KNOW YOU. YOU KNOCK ME OUT, DRAG US TO YOUR SKETCHY SECRET HIDEOUT, AND THEN TRY TO FEED ME SOME CONSPIRACY THEORY ABOUT THE BIG BAD GOVERNMENT...AND YOU WANT *WHAT?*

THAT I JUST SHRUG MY SHOULDERS AND AGREE TO CALL UP MY DAD FOR AID... THAT YOU AND I FIGHT BACK-TO-BACK AGAINST THE *LARGEST MILITARY FORCE* IN THE *GALAXY?*

I'M ASKING YOU TO HELP US STOP THIS. THE G.O.E. AND THEIR M.I.D. PROGRAM IS *SLAUGHTERING* PAGURANI AND RANESE BY *THE MILLIONS.* THEY'RE DRIVING THEM TO *EXTINCTION.*

THE PAGURANI ARE KILLING *US!* THEY KILLED OVER A DOZEN PEOPLE EARLIER TODAY! *OUR PEOPLE!* AND NOW YOU WANT US TO SAVE THEM?

JUST LOOKING AT THEM MAKES ME WANT TO PUKE.

BUT, YOU'RE NOT GIVING US A CHOICE, ARE YOU?

YOU HAVE A CHOICE. YOU CAN BE A WILLING PARTICIPANT OR YOU CAN BE A CAPTIVE. WE CAN'T LET YOU GO, NOW THAT YOU'VE SEEN US.

I'D PREFER THAT YOU WORKED WITH US, THOUGH.

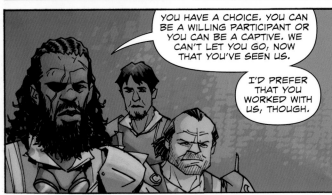

HEY DILDO, IN CASE YOU FORGOT WE GOT EXPLOSIVES ALL UP IN OUR GUTS.

WE'RE NOT BACK TO TRANENT AND SOON--

WE CAN DISABLE THE PUNCH SYSTEM.

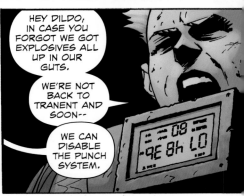

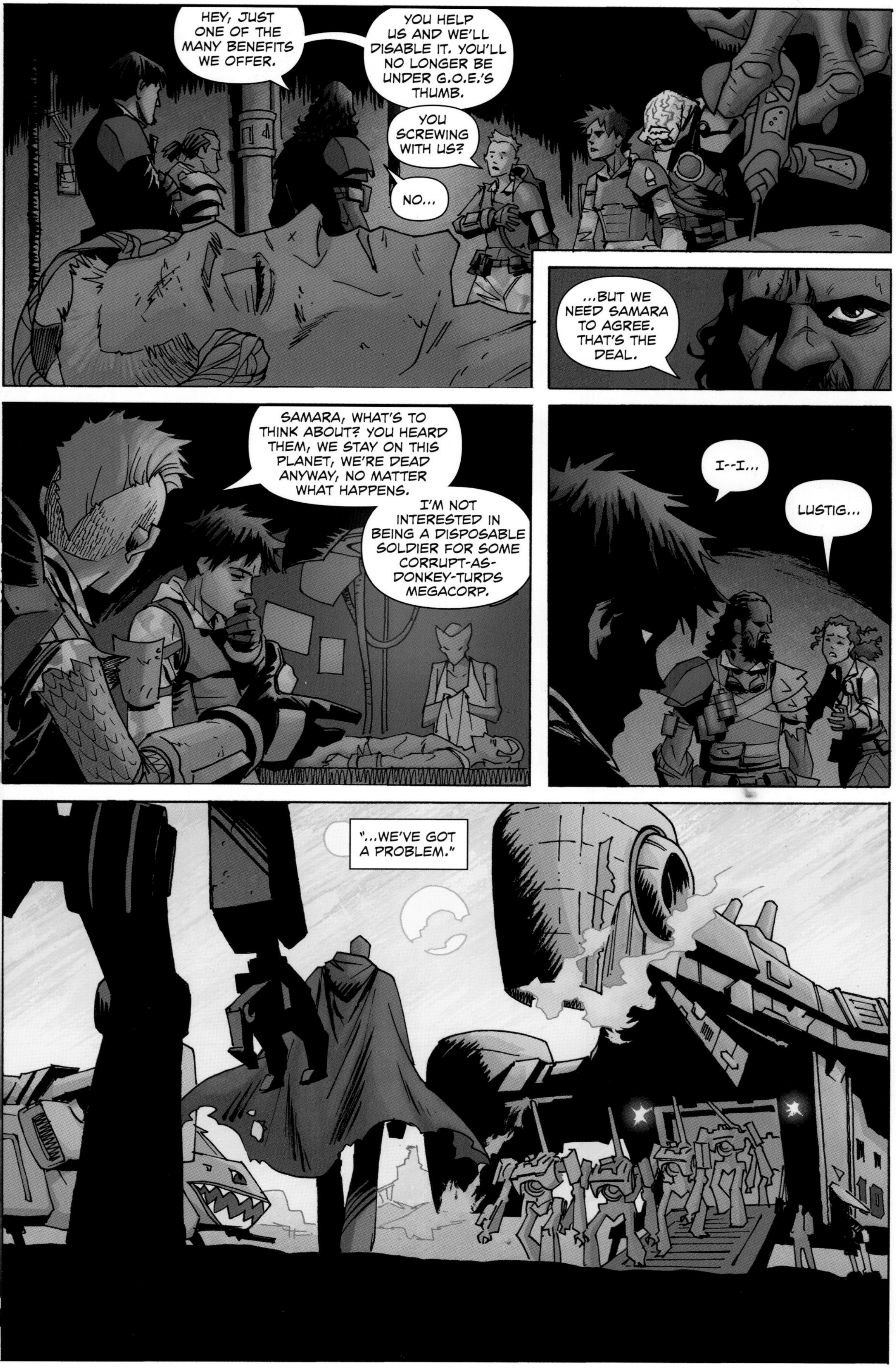
HEY, JUST ONE OF THE MANY BENEFITS WE OFFER.
YOU HELP US AND WE'LL DISABLE IT. YOU'LL NO LONGER BE UNDER G.O.E.'S THUMB.
YOU SCREWING WITH US?
NO...
...BUT WE NEED SAMARA TO AGREE. THAT'S THE DEAL.
SAMARA, WHAT'S TO THINK ABOUT? YOU HEARD THEM, WE STAY ON THIS PLANET, WE'RE DEAD ANYWAY, NO MATTER WHAT HAPPENS.
I'M NOT INTERESTED IN BEING A DISPOSABLE SOLDIER FOR SOME CORRUPT-AS-DONKEY-TURDS MEGACORP.
I--I...
LUSTIG...
"...WE'VE GOT A PROBLEM."

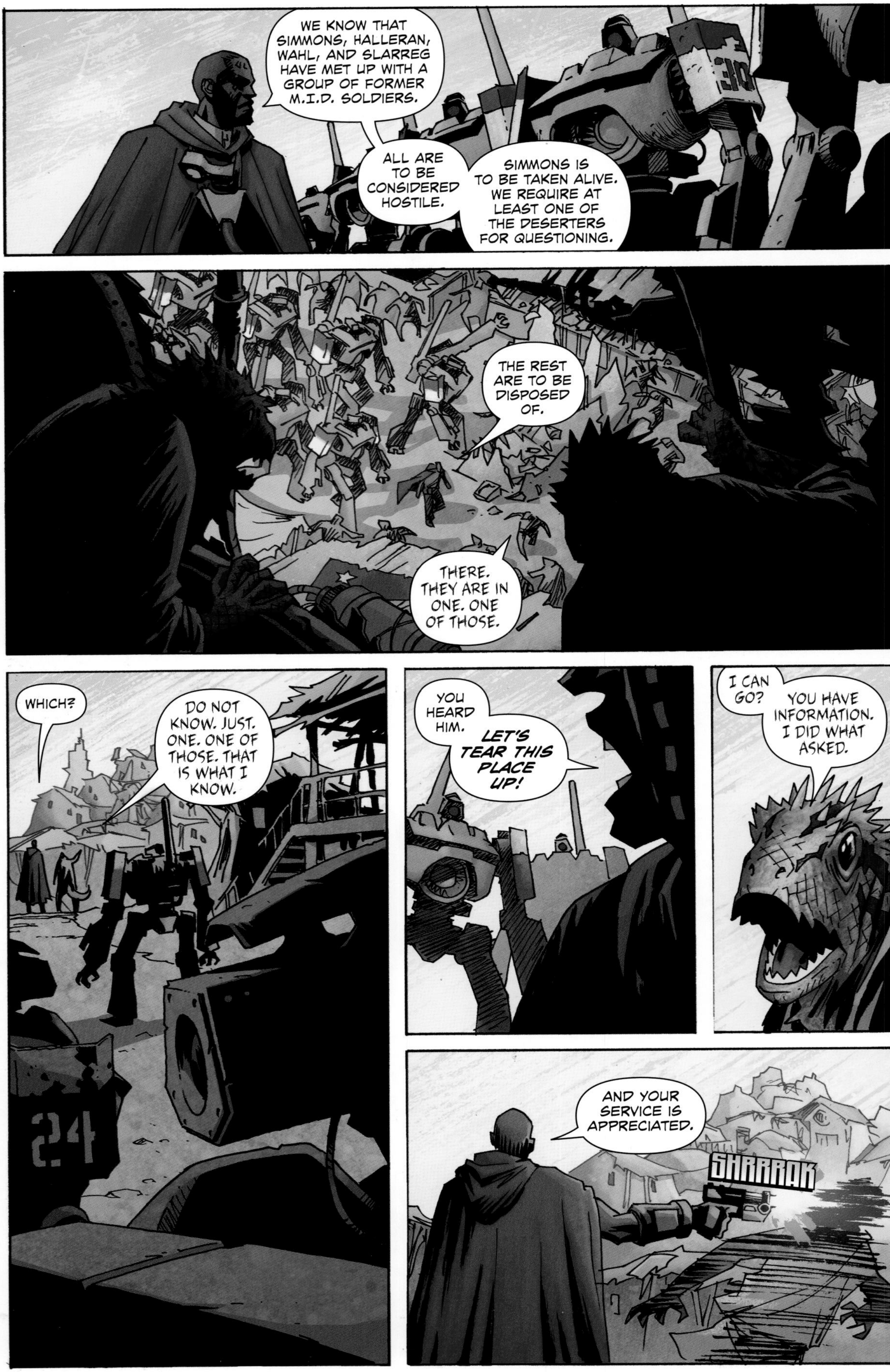
WE KNOW THAT SIMMONS, HALLERAN, WAHL, AND SLARREG HAVE MET UP WITH A GROUP OF FORMER M.I.D. SOLDIERS.
ALL ARE TO BE CONSIDERED HOSTILE.
SIMMONS IS TO BE TAKEN ALIVE. WE REQUIRE AT LEAST ONE OF THE DESERTERS FOR QUESTIONING.
THE REST ARE TO BE DISPOSED OF.
THERE. THEY ARE IN ONE. ONE OF THOSE.
WHICH?
DO NOT KNOW. JUST. ONE. ONE OF THOSE. THAT IS WHAT I KNOW.
YOU HEARD HIM.
LET'S TEAR THIS PLACE UP!
I CAN GO?
YOU HAVE INFORMATION. I DID WHAT ASKED.
AND YOUR SERVICE IS APPRECIATED.
SHRRRAK

LET'S GO! WE DON'T HAVE MUCH TIME.

JAS, LEAVE THE COMMS, WE'VE GOT ENOUGH BACK AT THE BASE.

NO WAY. IT TOOK ME MONTHS TO GET THIS TOGETH--

LEAVE IT!

IT'S TIME TO CLEAR OUT.

I'M NOT LEAVING HALLERAN.

WE DON'T HAVE A CHOICE.

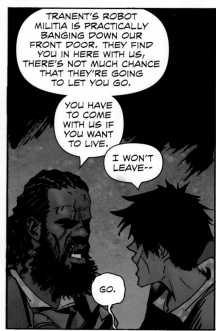

TRANENT'S ROBOT MILITIA IS PRACTICALLY BANGING DOWN OUR FRONT DOOR. THEY FIND YOU IN HERE WITH US, THERE'S NOT MUCH CHANCE THAT THEY'RE GOING TO LET YOU GO.

YOU HAVE TO COME WITH US IF YOU WANT TO LIVE.

I WON'T LEAVE--

GO.

LUSTIG'S RIGHT.

NO ONE SURVIVES. NO ONE MAKES IT BACK TO EARTH.

I KEPT HOPING... HOPING THAT THEY'D FIX IT. THAT THE AIR WOULD BE SAFE. THAT SOMEHOW I WAS THE EXCEPTION.

BUT...

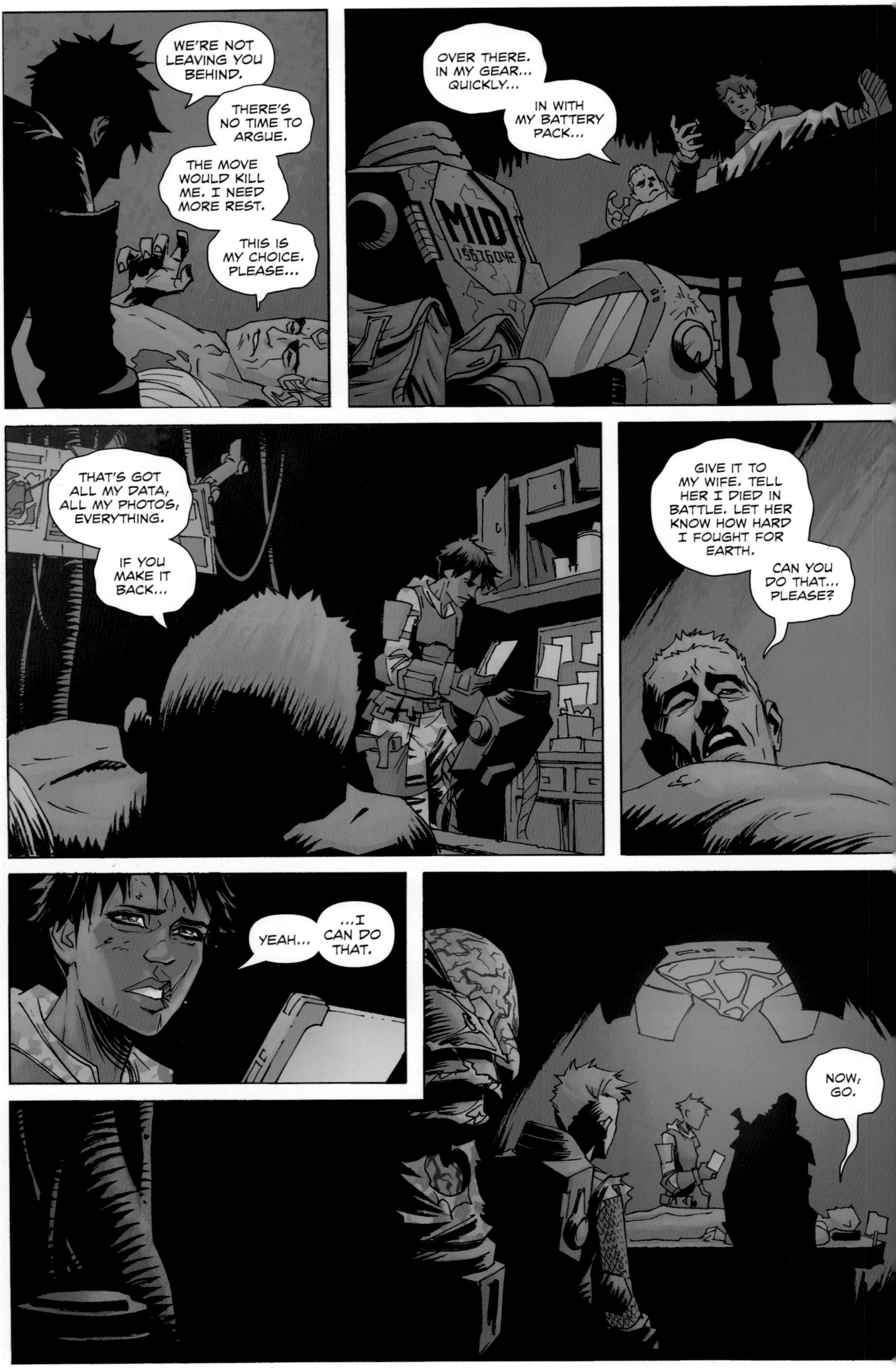
WE'RE NOT LEAVING YOU BEHIND.
THERE'S NO TIME TO ARGUE.
THE MOVE WOULD KILL ME. I NEED MORE REST.
THIS IS MY CHOICE. PLEASE...
OVER THERE. IN MY GEAR... QUICKLY...
IN WITH MY BATTERY PACK...
MID
THAT'S GOT ALL MY DATA, ALL MY PHOTOS, EVERYTHING.
IF YOU MAKE IT BACK...
GIVE IT TO MY WIFE. TELL HER I DIED IN BATTLE. LET HER KNOW HOW HARD I FOUGHT FOR EARTH.
CAN YOU DO THAT... PLEASE?
YEAH...
...I CAN DO THAT.
NOW, GO.

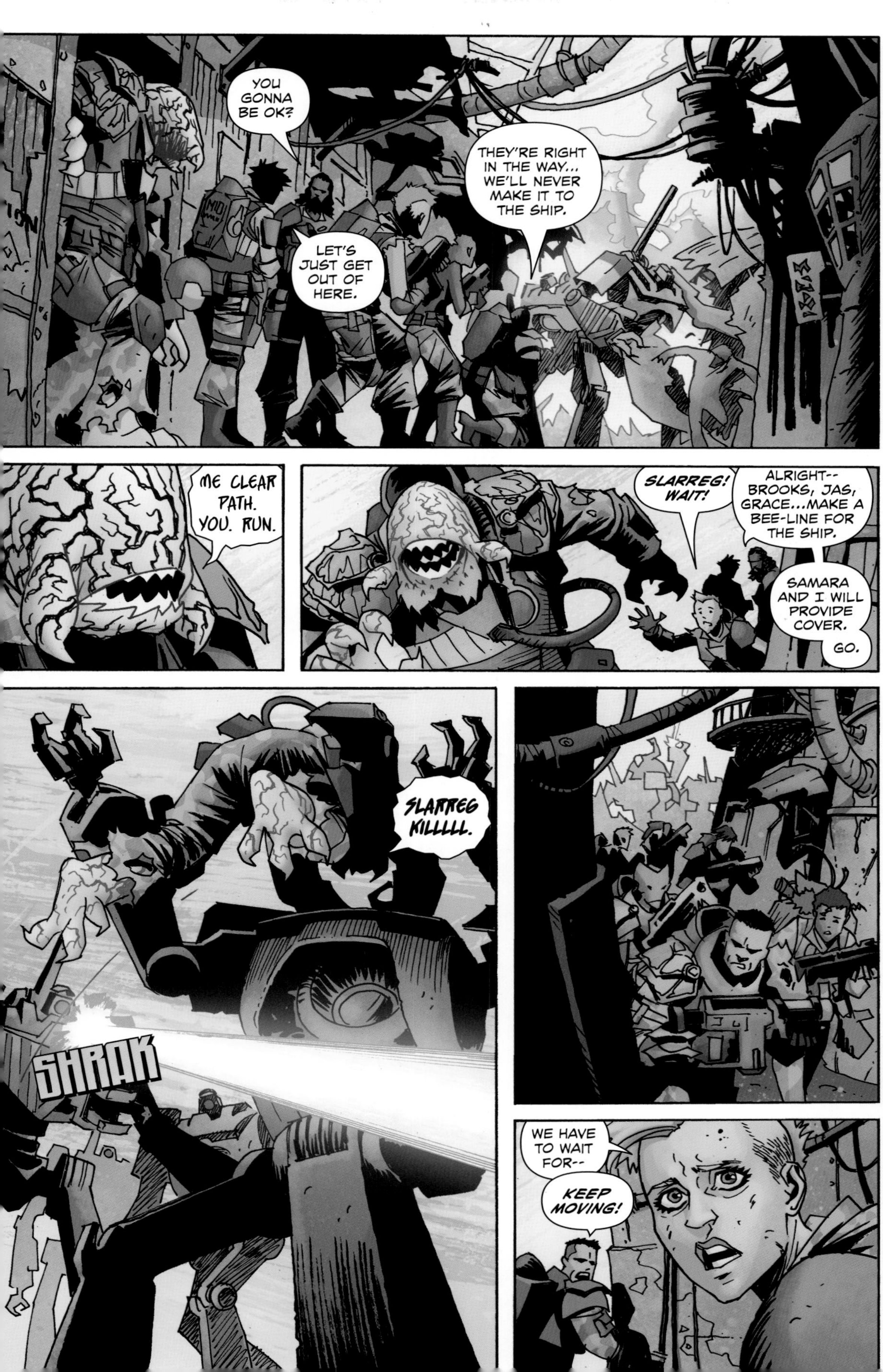
YOU GONNA BE OK?
LET'S JUST GET OUT OF HERE.
THEY'RE RIGHT IN THE WAY... WE'LL NEVER MAKE IT TO THE SHIP.
ME CLEAR PATH. YOU. RUN.
SLARREG! WAIT!
ALRIGHT-- BROOKS, JAS, GRACE...MAKE A BEE-LINE FOR THE SHIP.
SAMARA AND I WILL PROVIDE COVER.
GO.
SLARREG KILLLLL.
SHRAK
WE HAVE TO WAIT FOR--
KEEP MOVING!

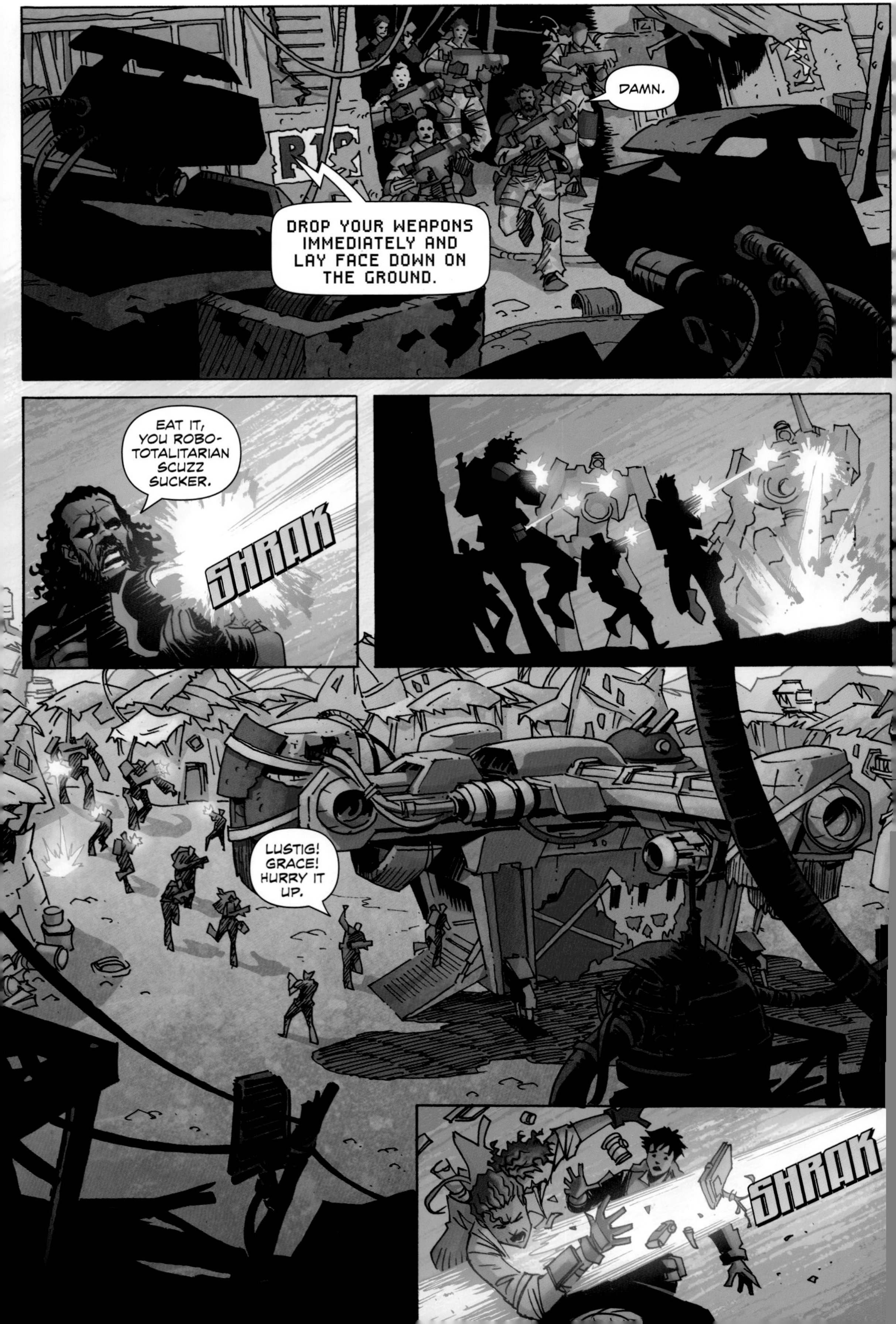
DROP YOUR WEAPONS IMMEDIATELY AND LAY FACE DOWN ON THE GROUND.
DAMN.
EAT IT, YOU ROBO-TOTALITARIAN SCUZZ SUCKER.
SHRAK
LUSTIG! GRACE! HURRY IT UP.
SHRAK

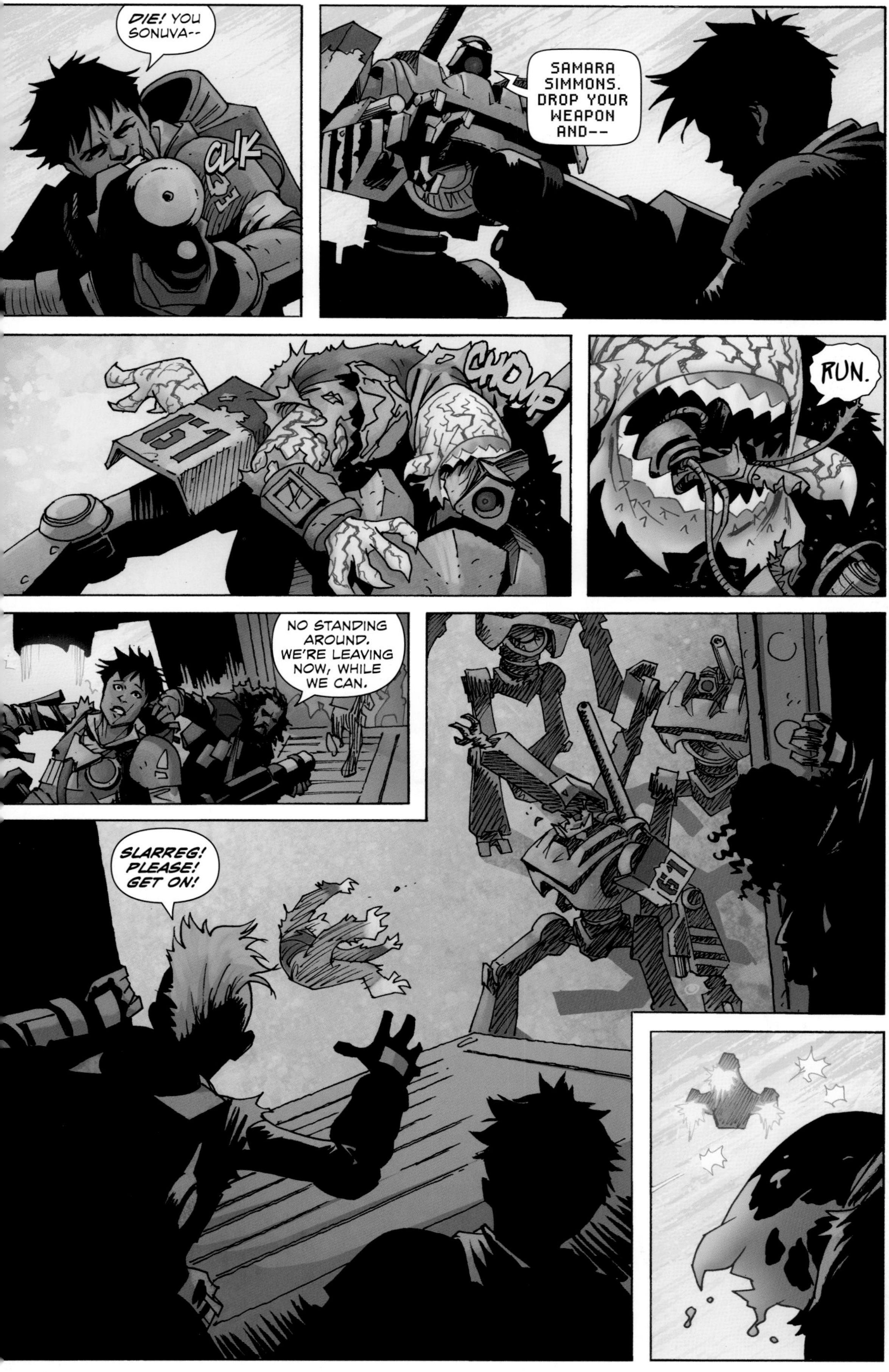
DIE! YOU SONUVA--
CLIK
SAMARA SIMMONS. DROP YOUR WEAPON AND--
CHOMP
RUN.
NO STANDING AROUND. WE'RE LEAVING NOW, WHILE WE CAN.
SLARREG! PLEASE! GET ON!

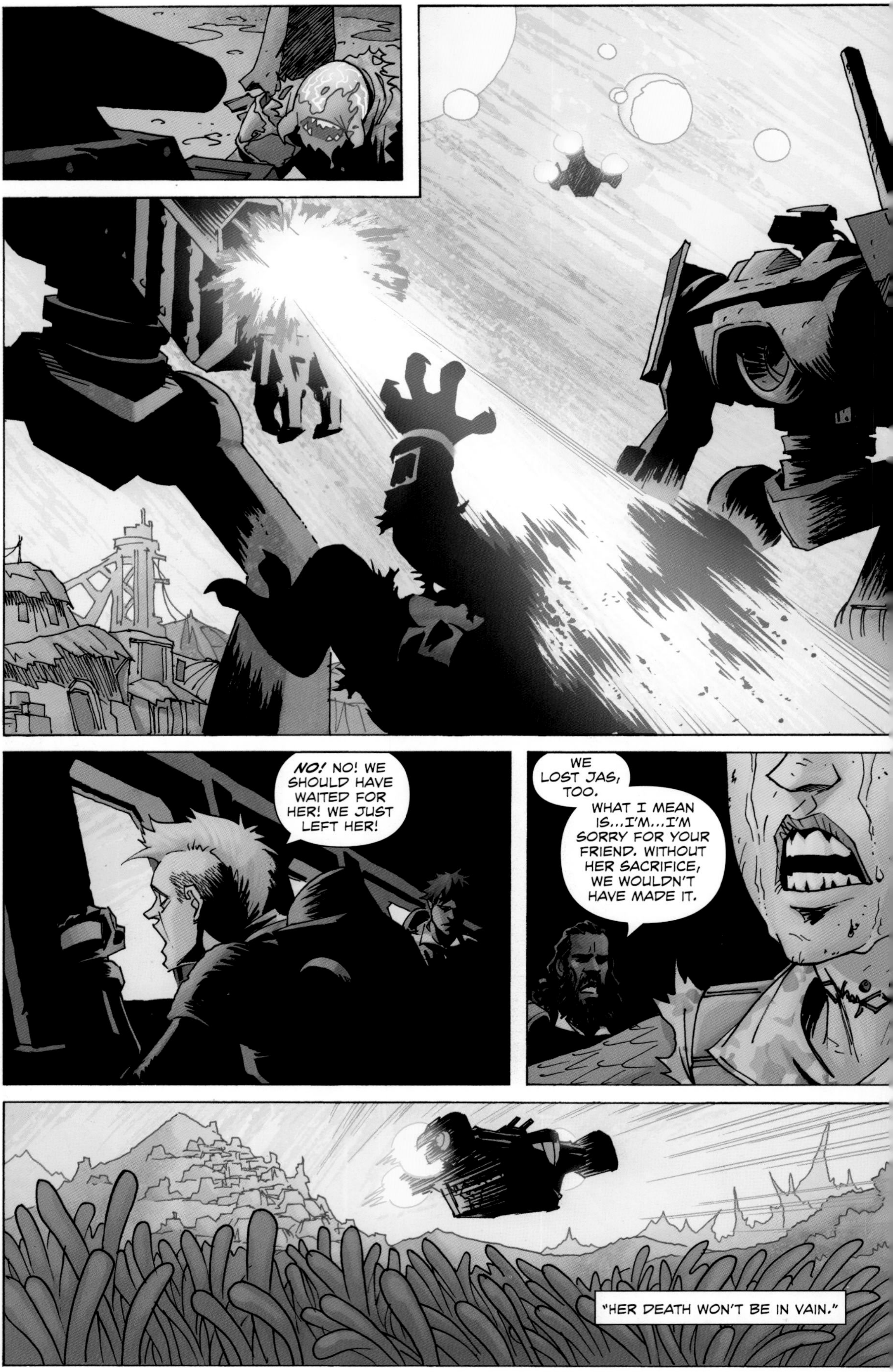
NO! NO! WE SHOULD HAVE WAITED FOR HER! WE JUST LEFT HER!
WE LOST JAS, TOO.
WHAT I MEAN IS...I'M...I'M SORRY FOR YOUR FRIEND. WITHOUT HER SACRIFICE, WE WOULDN'T HAVE MADE IT.
"HER DEATH WON'T BE IN VAIN."

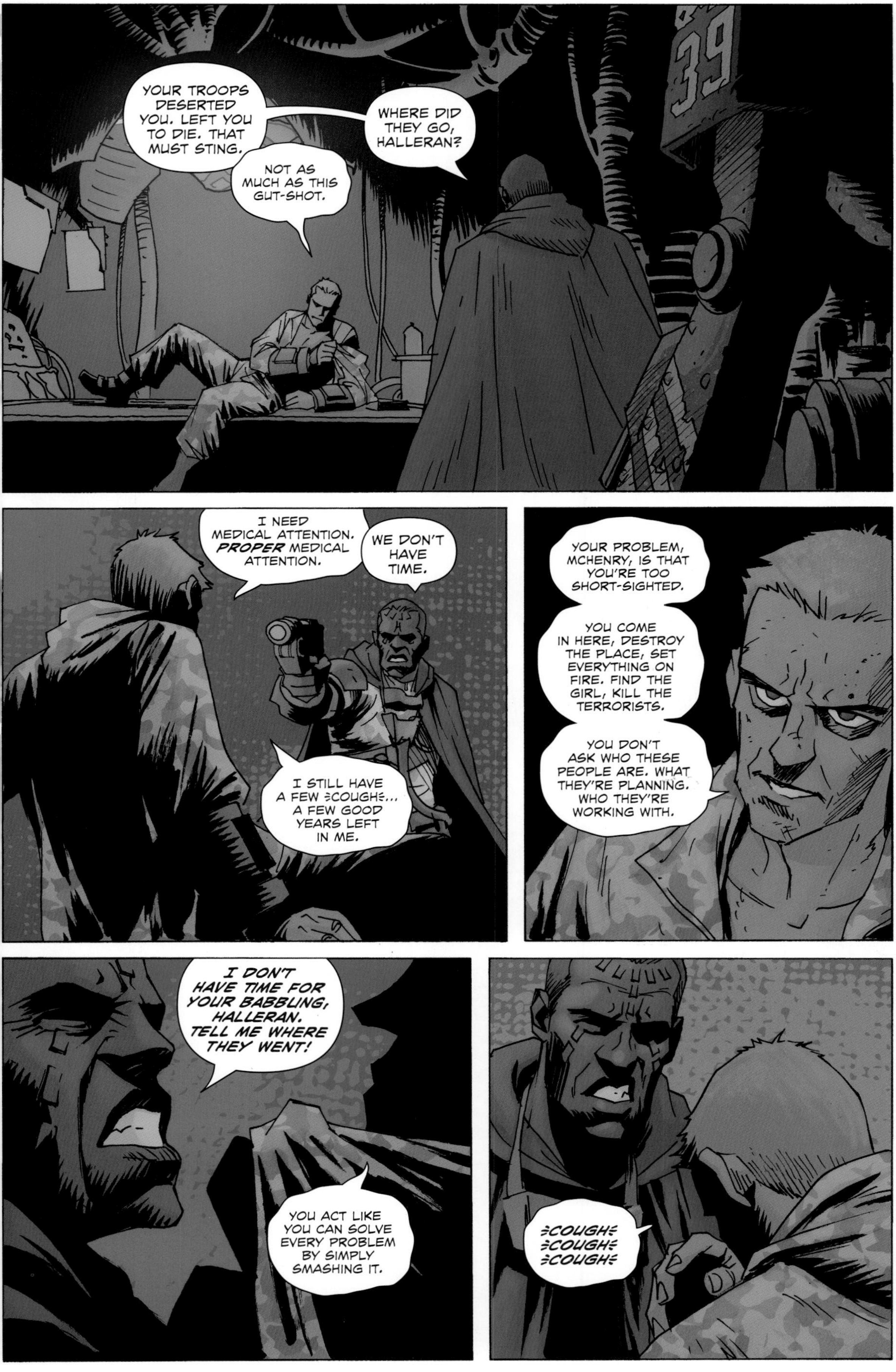
39
YOUR TROOPS DESERTED YOU. LEFT YOU TO DIE. THAT MUST STING.
WHERE DID THEY GO, HALLERAN?
NOT AS MUCH AS THIS GUT-SHOT.
I NEED MEDICAL ATTENTION. *PROPER* MEDICAL ATTENTION.
WE DON'T HAVE TIME.
I STILL HAVE A FEW ≈COUGH≈... A FEW GOOD YEARS LEFT IN ME.
YOUR PROBLEM, MCHENRY, IS THAT YOU'RE TOO SHORT-SIGHTED.
YOU COME IN HERE, DESTROY THE PLACE, SET EVERYTHING ON FIRE. FIND THE GIRL, KILL THE TERRORISTS.
YOU DON'T ASK WHO THESE PEOPLE ARE. WHAT THEY'RE PLANNING. WHO THEY'RE WORKING WITH.
I DON'T HAVE TIME FOR YOUR BABBLING, HALLERAN. TELL ME WHERE THEY WENT!
YOU ACT LIKE YOU CAN SOLVE EVERY PROBLEM BY SIMPLY SMASHING IT.
≈COUGH≈ ≈COUGH≈ ≈COUGH≈

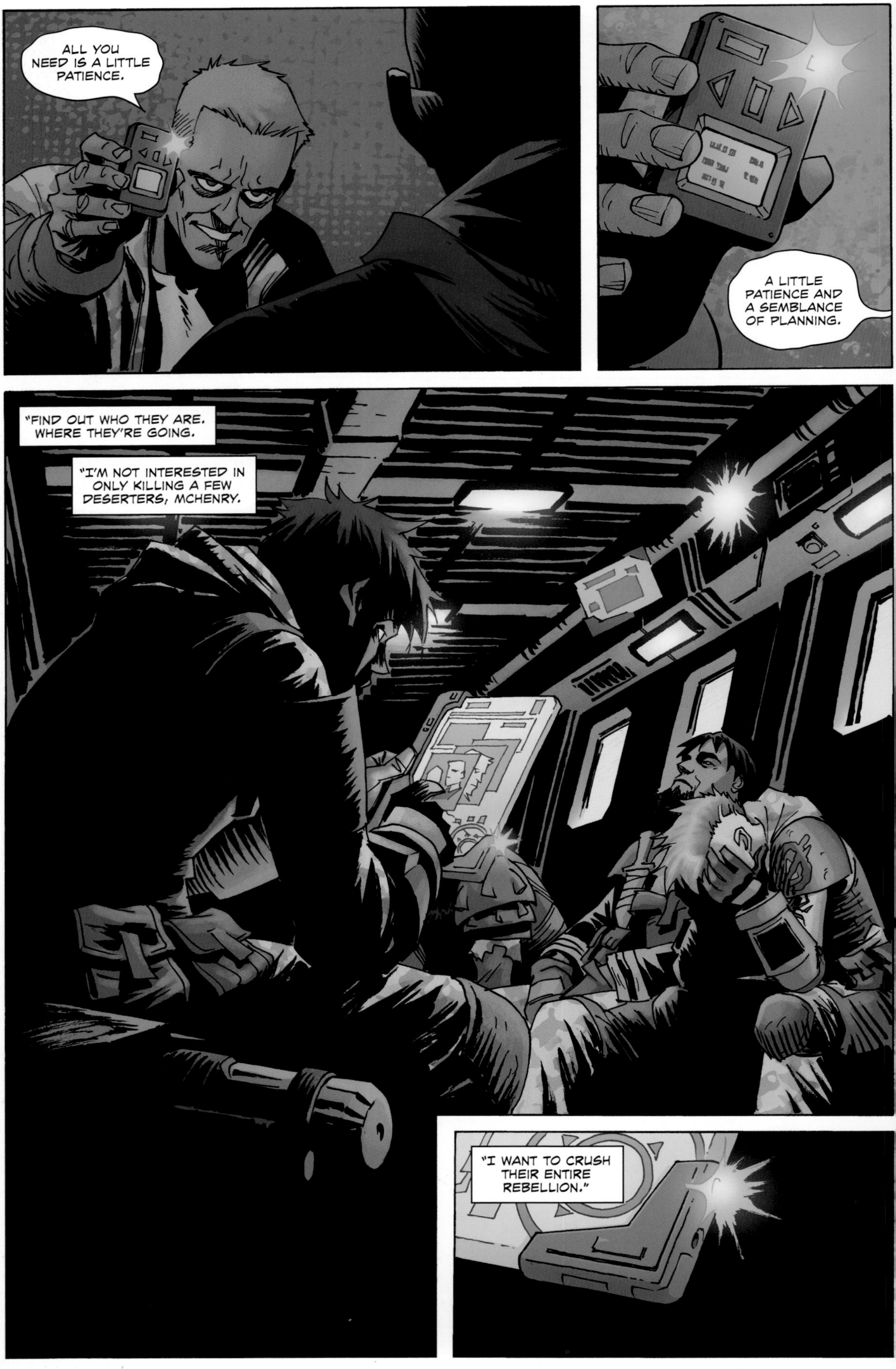
ALL YOU NEED IS A LITTLE PATIENCE.
A LITTLE PATIENCE AND A SEMBLANCE OF PLANNING.
"FIND OUT WHO THEY ARE. WHERE THEY'RE GOING.
"I'M NOT INTERESTED IN ONLY KILLING A FEW DESERTERS, MCHENRY.
"I WANT TO CRUSH THEIR ENTIRE REBELLION."

ISSUE 003 COVER
DAMIAN COUCIERO
WITH COLORS BY **JORDAN BOYD**

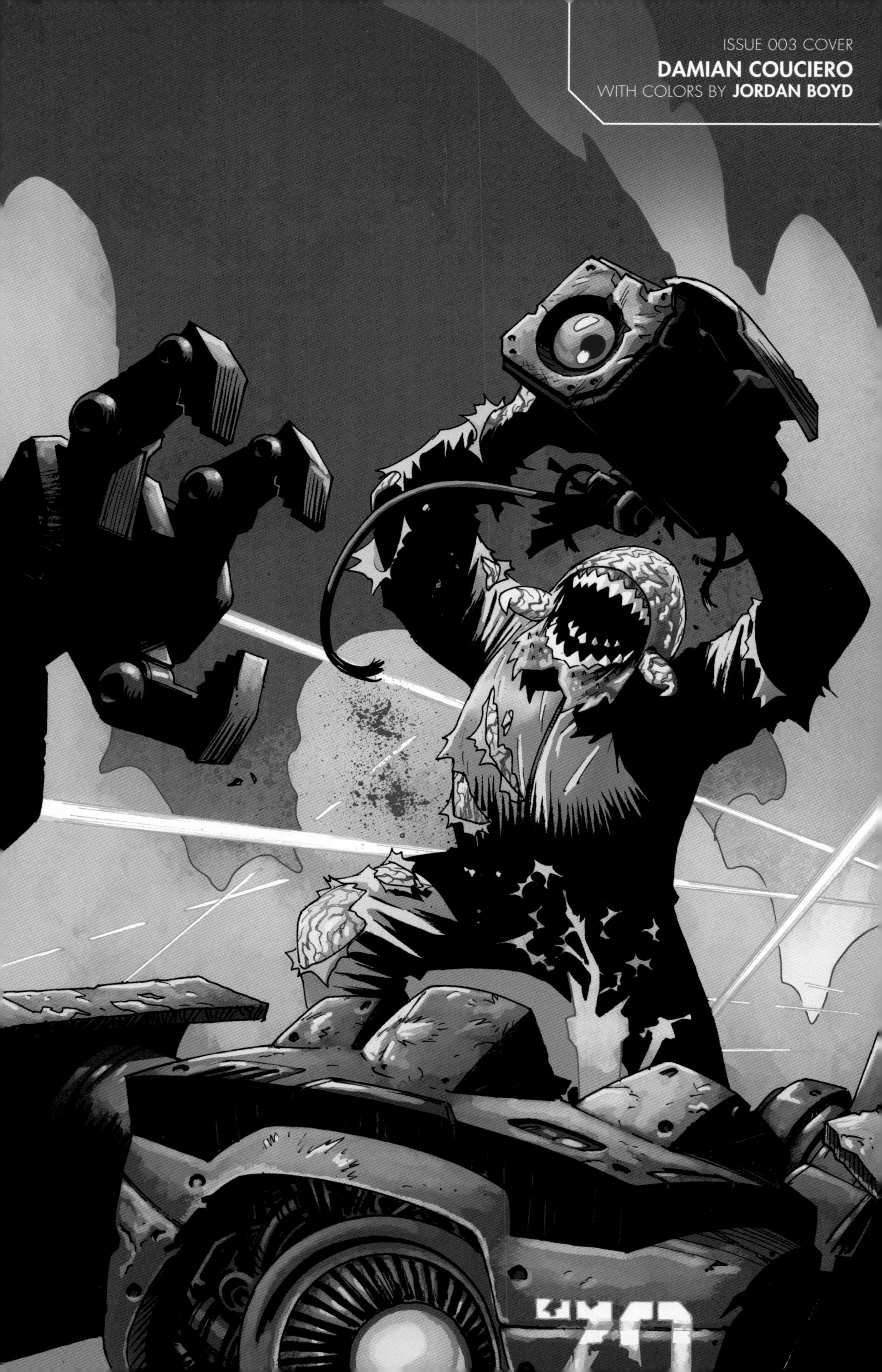

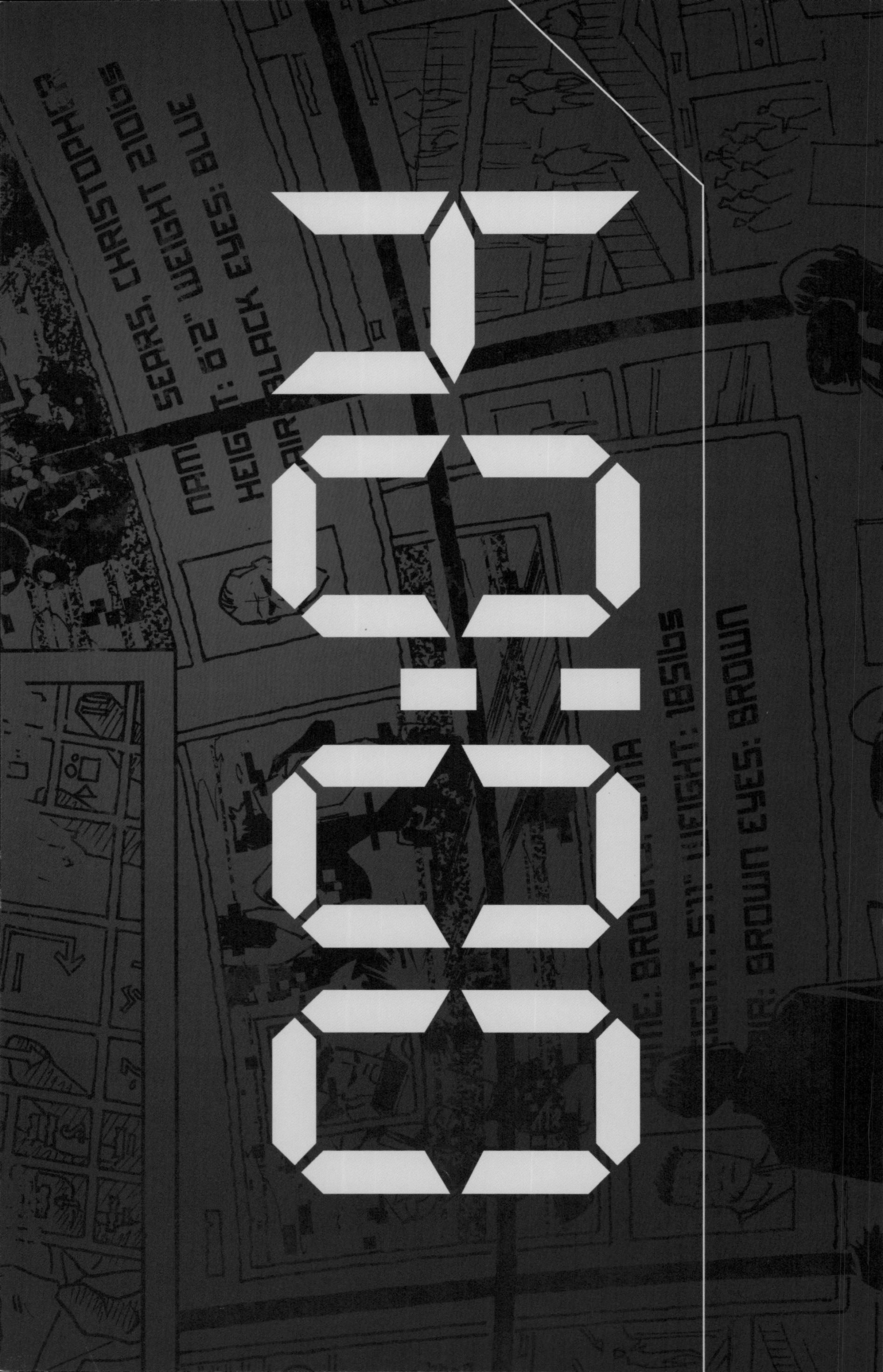
1:00:00
SEARS, CHRISTOPHER
6'2" WEIGHT 210lbs
BLACK EYES: BLUE
WEIGHT: 185lbs
BROWN EYES: BROWN

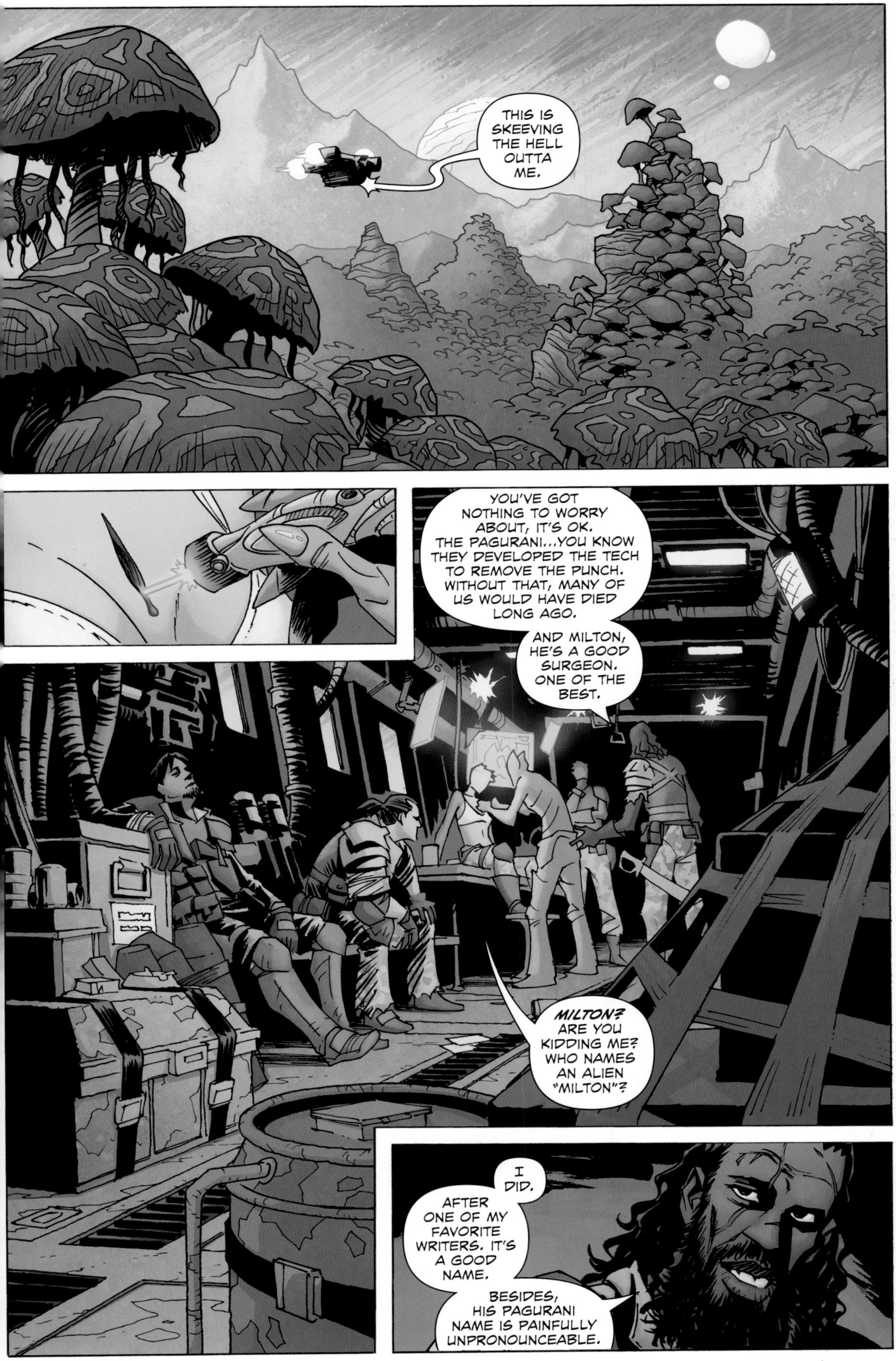
THIS IS SKEEVING THE HELL OUTTA ME.
YOU'VE GOT NOTHING TO WORRY ABOUT, IT'S OK. THE PAGURANI...YOU KNOW THEY DEVELOPED THE TECH TO REMOVE THE PUNCH. WITHOUT THAT, MANY OF US WOULD HAVE DIED LONG AGO.
AND MILTON, HE'S A GOOD SURGEON. ONE OF THE BEST.
MILTON? ARE YOU KIDDING ME? WHO NAMES AN ALIEN "MILTON"?
I DID.
AFTER ONE OF MY FAVORITE WRITERS. IT'S A GOOD NAME.
BESIDES, HIS PAGURANI NAME IS PAINFULLY UNPRONOUNCEABLE.

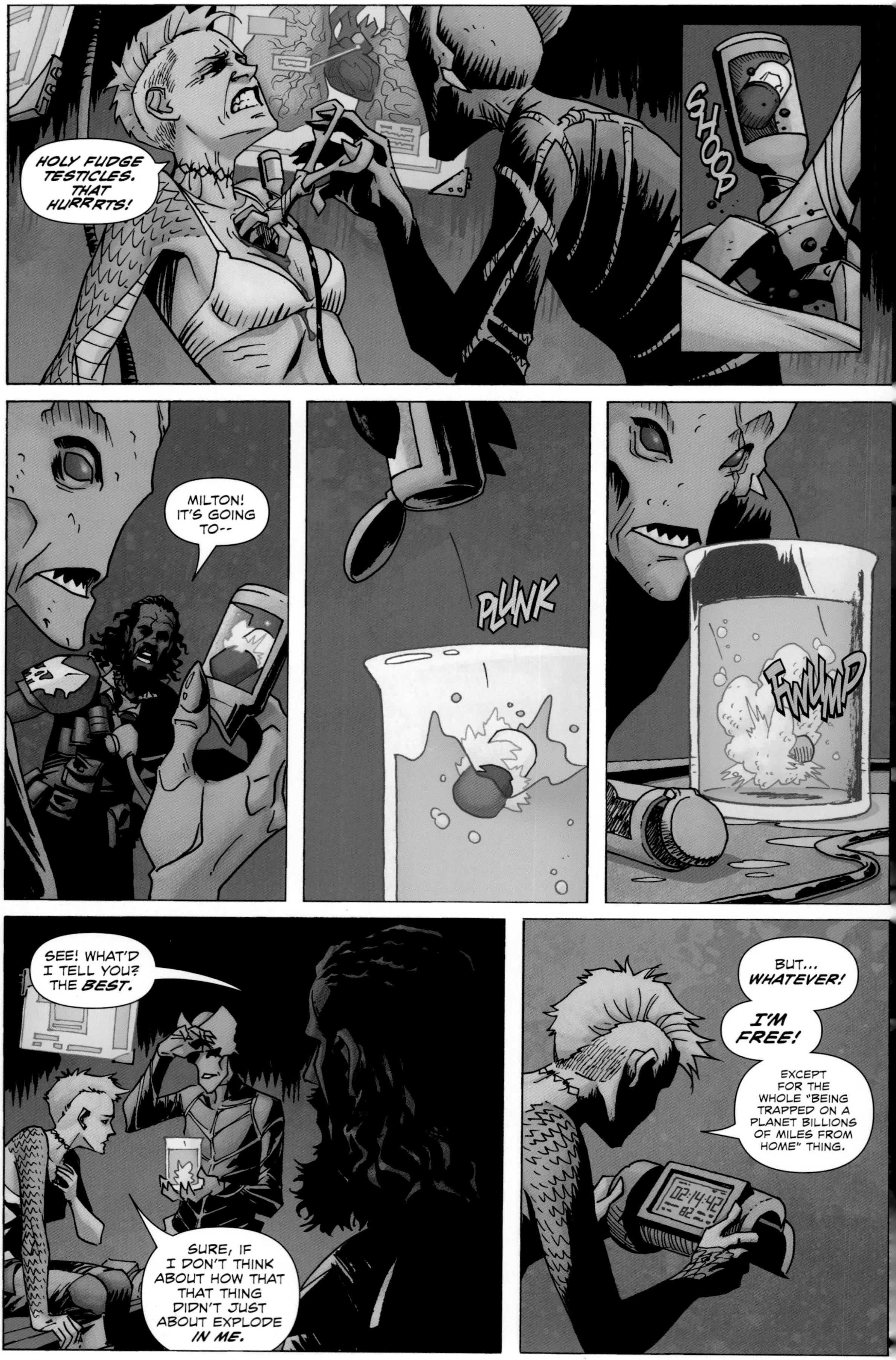
HOLY FUDGE TESTICLES. THAT HURRRTS!
SHOOP
MILTON! IT'S GOING TO--
PLUNK
FWUMP
SEE! WHAT'D I TELL YOU? THE *BEST.*
SURE, IF I DON'T THINK ABOUT HOW THAT THAT THING DIDN'T JUST ABOUT EXPLODE *IN ME.*
BUT... *WHATEVER!*
I'M FREE!
EXCEPT FOR THE WHOLE "BEING TRAPPED ON A PLANET BILLIONS OF MILES FROM HOME" THING.
02:14:42
82

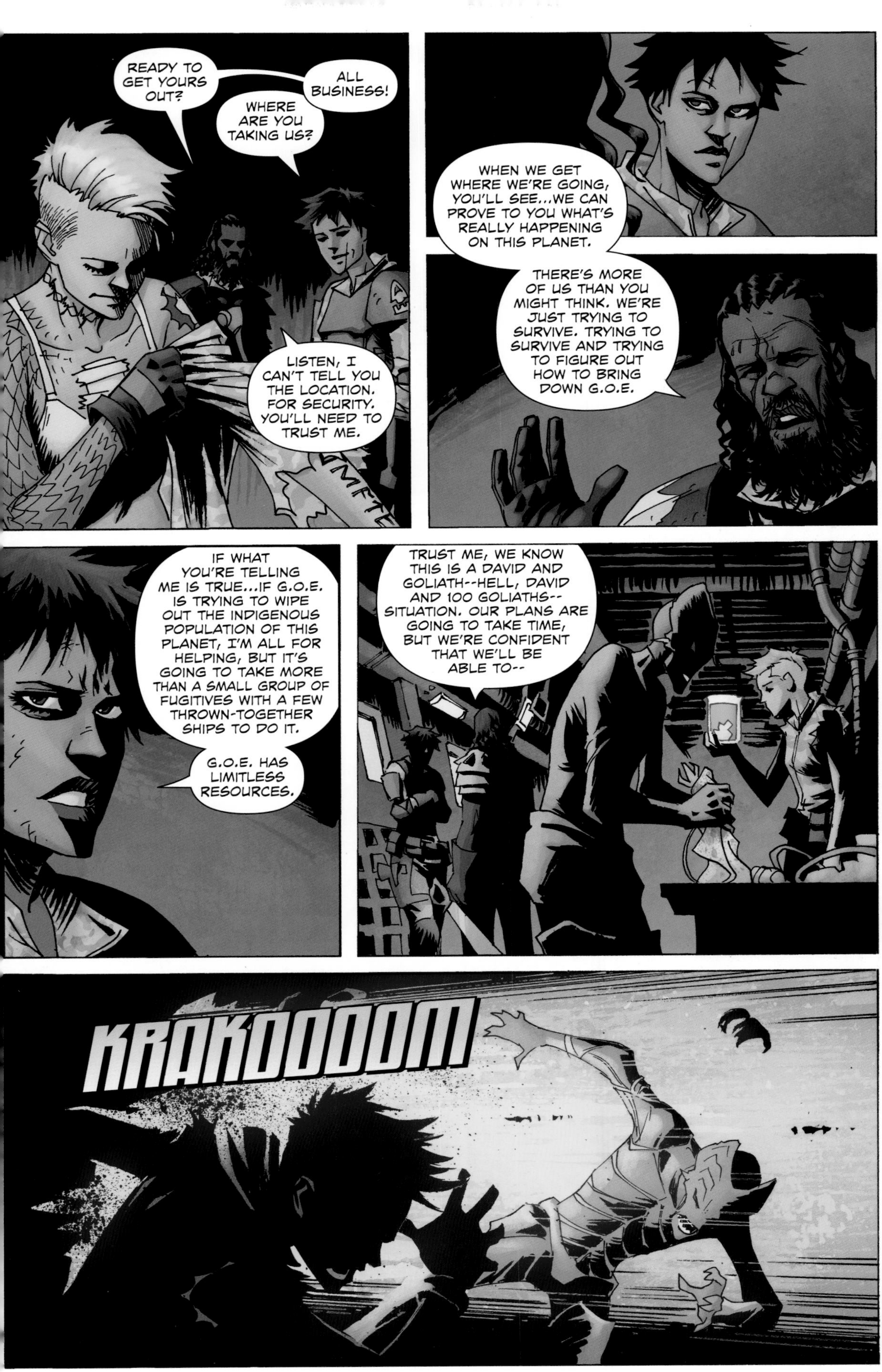
READY TO GET YOURS OUT?
ALL BUSINESS!
WHERE ARE YOU TAKING US?
LISTEN, I CAN'T TELL YOU THE LOCATION. FOR SECURITY. YOU'LL NEED TO TRUST ME.
WHEN WE GET WHERE WE'RE GOING, YOU'LL SEE...WE CAN PROVE TO YOU WHAT'S REALLY HAPPENING ON THIS PLANET.
THERE'S MORE OF US THAN YOU MIGHT THINK. WE'RE JUST TRYING TO SURVIVE. TRYING TO SURVIVE AND TRYING TO FIGURE OUT HOW TO BRING DOWN G.O.E.
IF WHAT YOU'RE TELLING ME IS TRUE...IF G.O.E. IS TRYING TO WIPE OUT THE INDIGENOUS POPULATION OF THIS PLANET, I'M ALL FOR HELPING, BUT IT'S GOING TO TAKE MORE THAN A SMALL GROUP OF FUGITIVES WITH A FEW THROWN-TOGETHER SHIPS TO DO IT.
G.O.E. HAS LIMITLESS RESOURCES.
TRUST ME, WE KNOW THIS IS A DAVID AND GOLIATH--HELL, DAVID AND 100 GOLIATHS--SITUATION. OUR PLANS ARE GOING TO TAKE TIME, BUT WE'RE CONFIDENT THAT WE'LL BE ABLE TO--
KRAKOOOOM

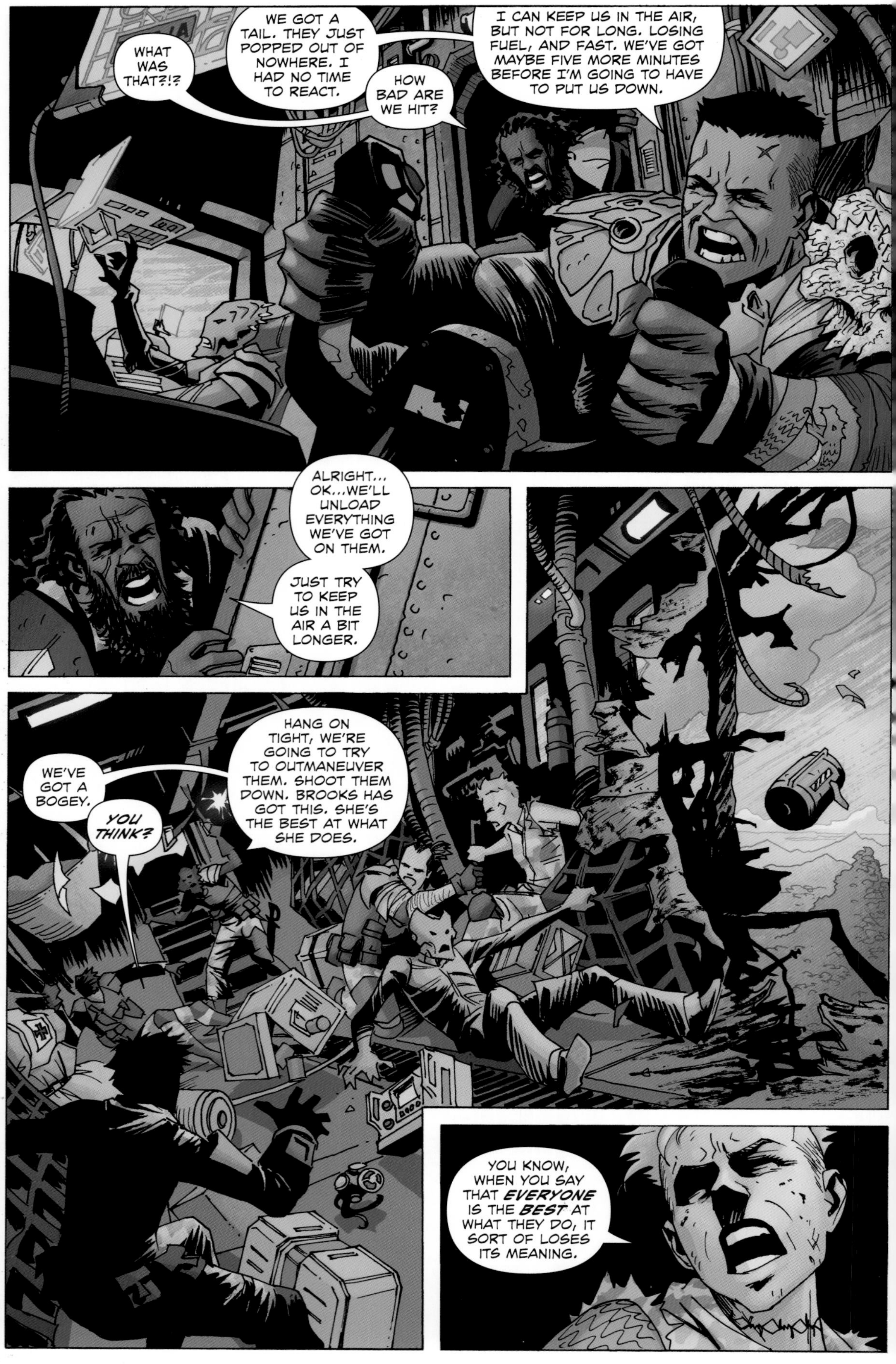
WHAT WAS THAT?!?
WE GOT A TAIL. THEY JUST POPPED OUT OF NOWHERE. I HAD NO TIME TO REACT.
HOW BAD ARE WE HIT?
I CAN KEEP US IN THE AIR, BUT NOT FOR LONG. LOSING FUEL, AND FAST. WE'VE GOT MAYBE FIVE MORE MINUTES BEFORE I'M GOING TO HAVE TO PUT US DOWN.
ALRIGHT... OK...WE'LL UNLOAD EVERYTHING WE'VE GOT ON THEM.
JUST TRY TO KEEP US IN THE AIR A BIT LONGER.
WE'VE GOT A BOGEY.
YOU THINK?
HANG ON TIGHT, WE'RE GOING TO TRY TO OUTMANEUVER THEM. SHOOT THEM DOWN. BROOKS HAS GOT THIS. SHE'S THE BEST AT WHAT SHE DOES.
YOU KNOW, WHEN YOU SAY THAT EVERYONE IS THE BEST AT WHAT THEY DO, IT SORT OF LOSES ITS MEANING.

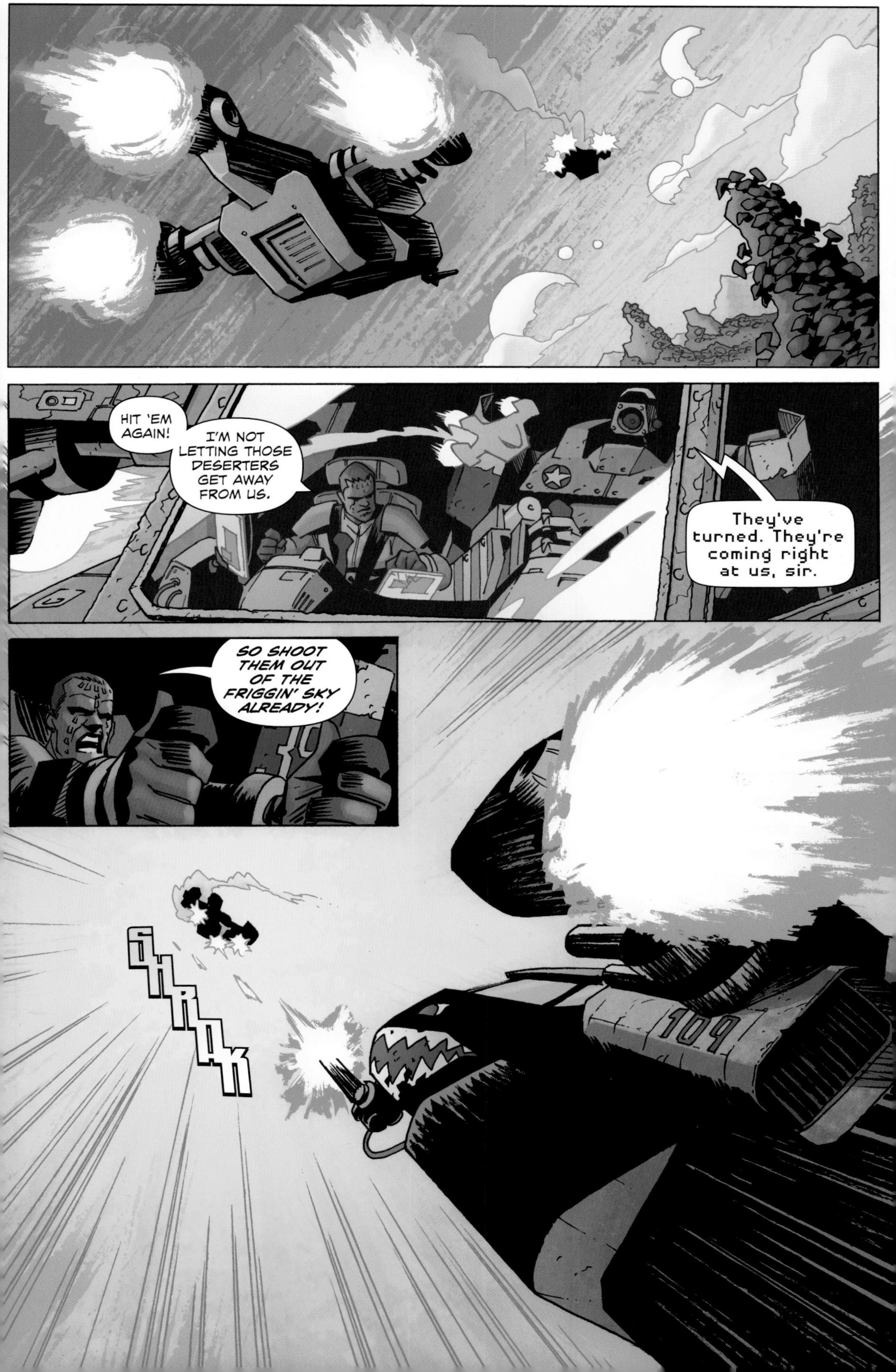
HIT 'EM AGAIN!
I'M NOT LETTING THOSE DESERTERS GET AWAY FROM US.
They've turned. They're coming right at us, sir.
SO SHOOT THEM OUT OF THE FRIGGIN' SKY ALREADY!
SHRAK

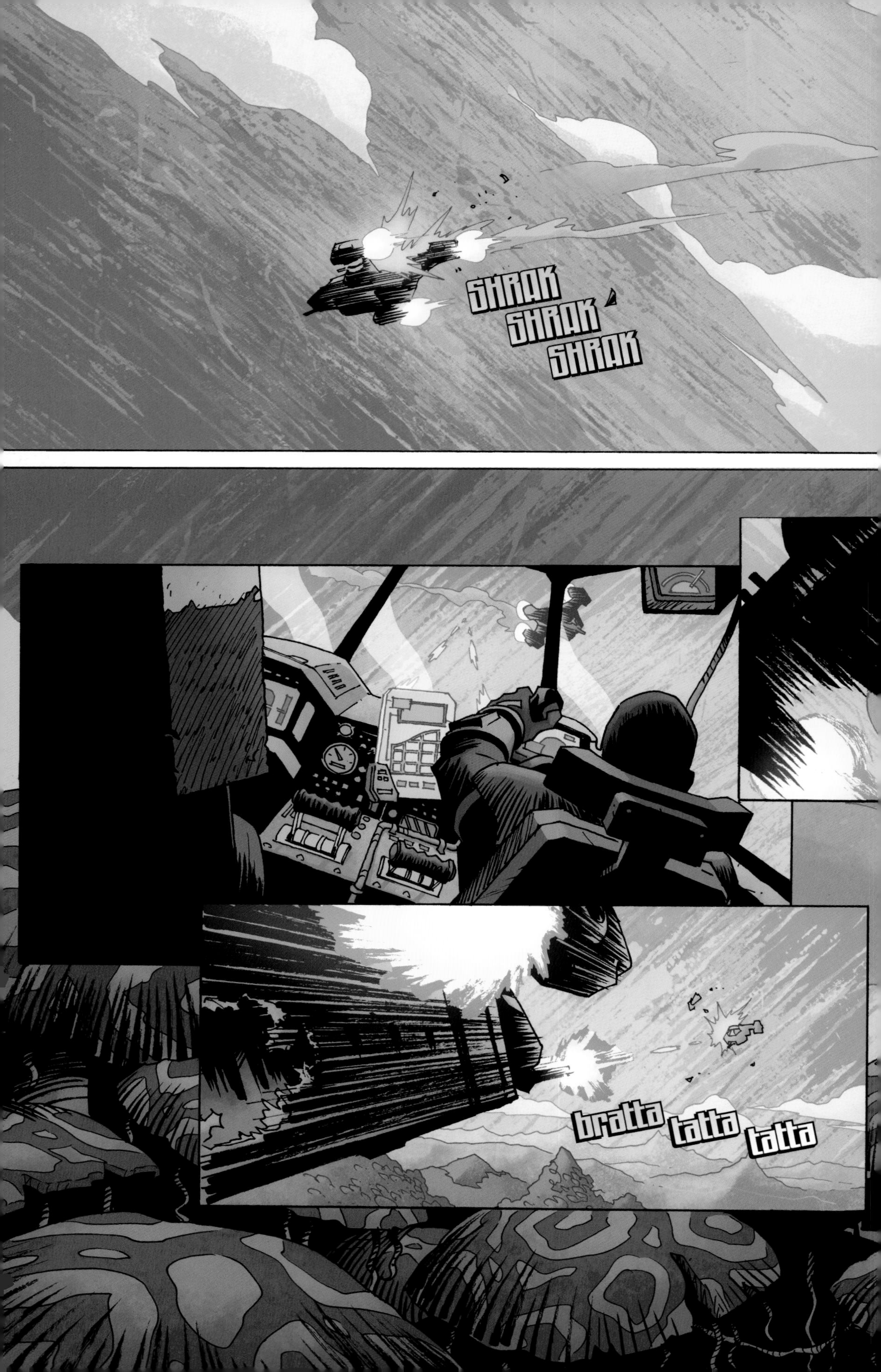
SHRAK
SHRAK
SHRAK
bratta tatta tatta

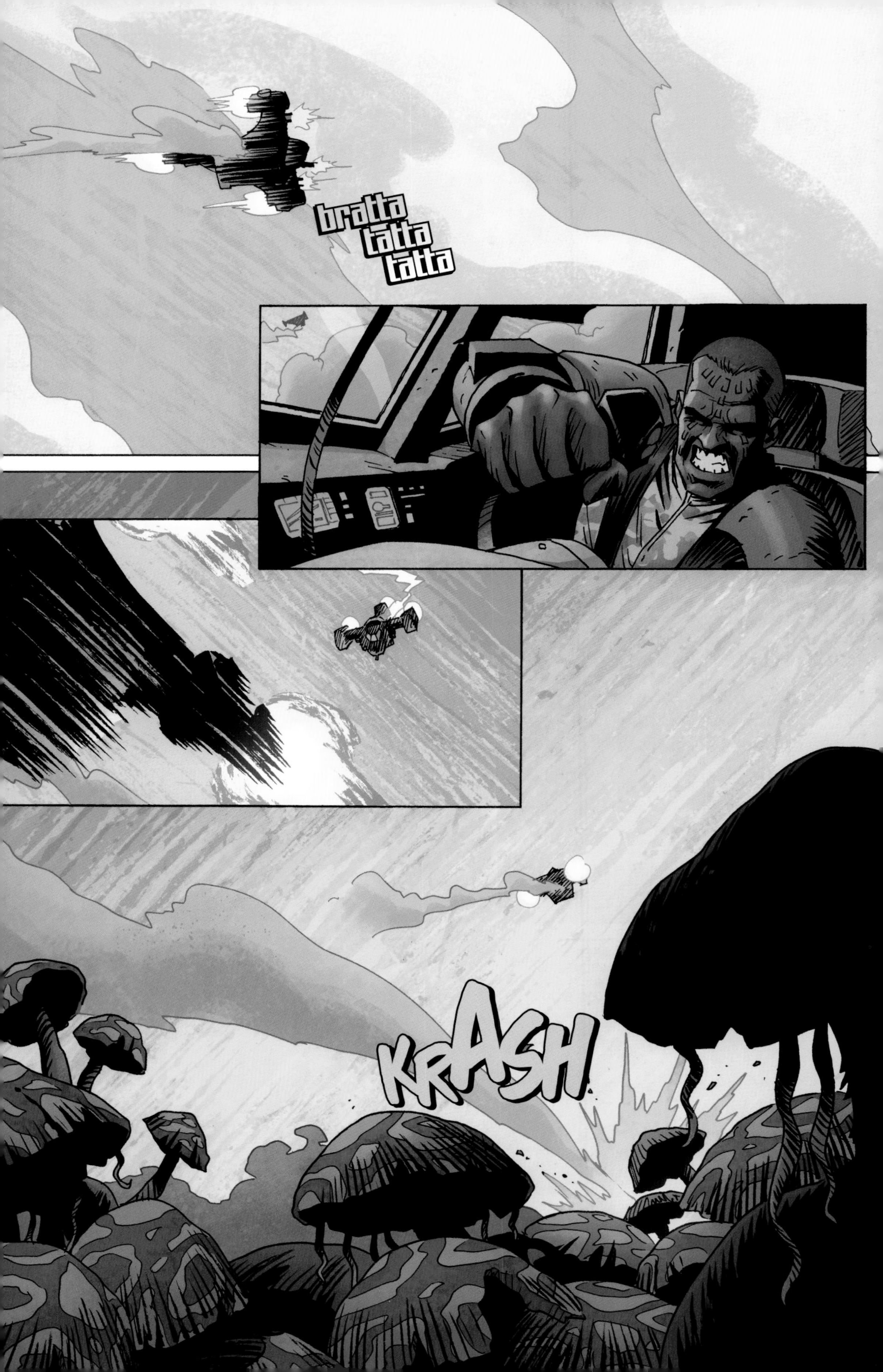
bratta tatta tatta
KRASH

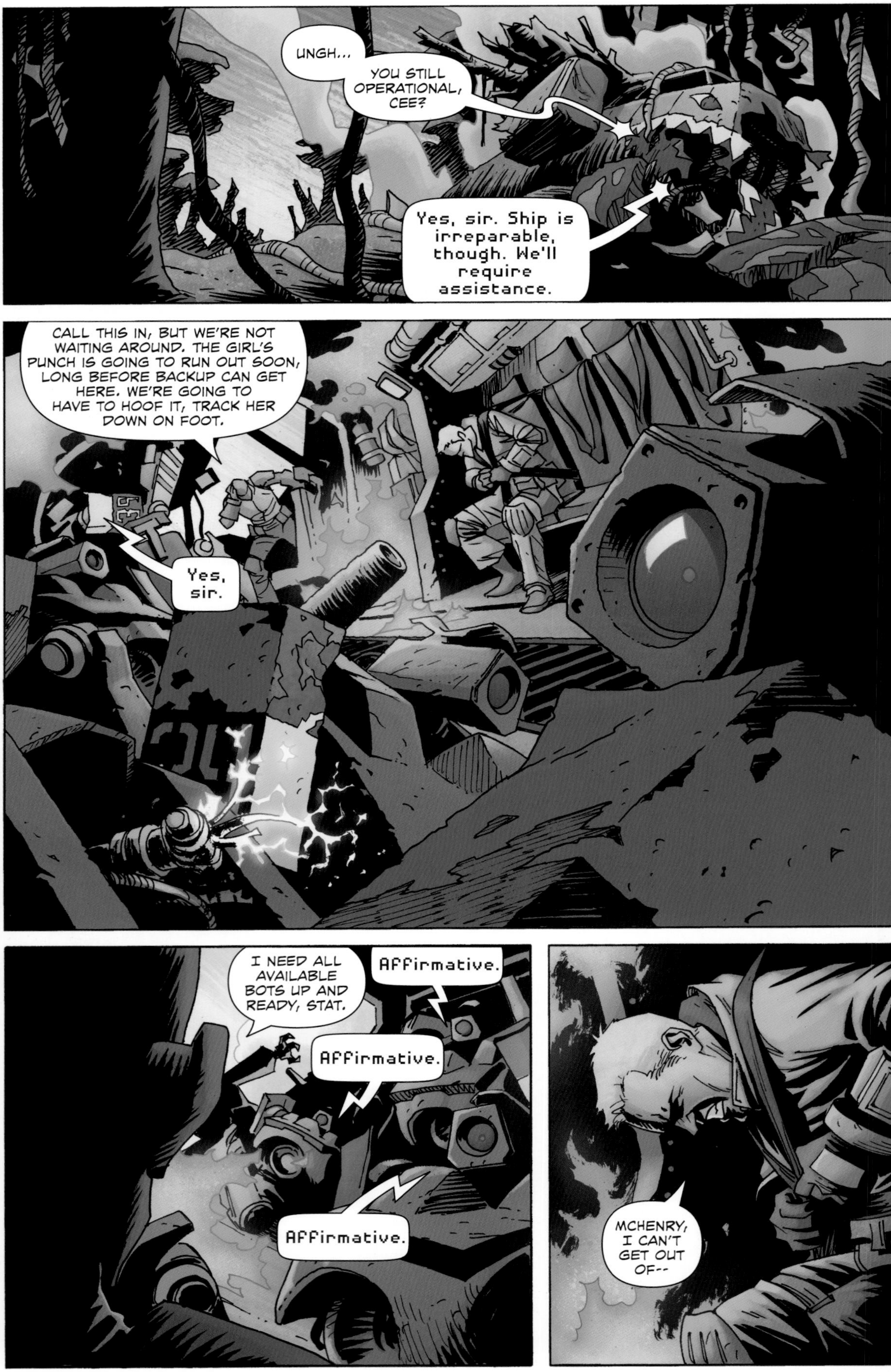
UNGH...
YOU STILL OPERATIONAL, CEE?
Yes, sir. Ship is irreparable, though. We'll require assistance.
CALL THIS IN, BUT WE'RE NOT WAITING AROUND. THE GIRL'S PUNCH IS GOING TO RUN OUT SOON, LONG BEFORE BACKUP CAN GET HERE. WE'RE GOING TO HAVE TO HOOF IT, TRACK HER DOWN ON FOOT.
Yes, sir.
I NEED ALL AVAILABLE BOTS UP AND READY, STAT.
Affirmative.
Affirmative.
Affirmative.
MCHENRY, I CAN'T GET OUT OF--

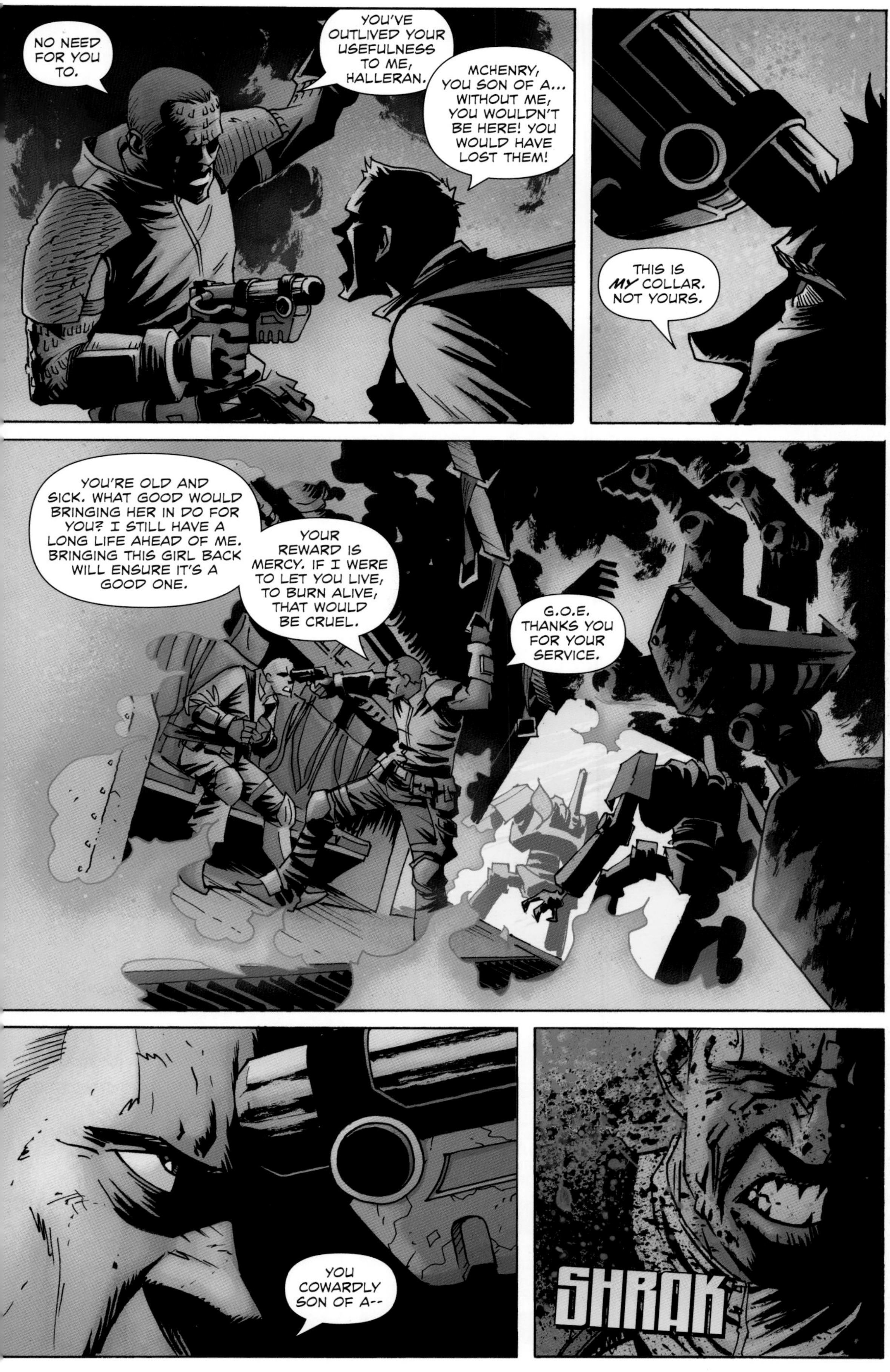
NO NEED FOR YOU TO.
YOU'VE OUTLIVED YOUR USEFULNESS TO ME, HALLERAN.
MCHENRY, YOU SON OF A... WITHOUT ME, YOU WOULDN'T BE HERE! YOU WOULD HAVE LOST THEM!
THIS IS MY COLLAR. NOT YOURS.
YOU'RE OLD AND SICK. WHAT GOOD WOULD BRINGING HER IN DO FOR YOU? I STILL HAVE A LONG LIFE AHEAD OF ME. BRINGING THIS GIRL BACK WILL ENSURE IT'S A GOOD ONE.
YOUR REWARD IS MERCY. IF I WERE TO LET YOU LIVE, TO BURN ALIVE, THAT WOULD BE CRUEL.
G.O.E. THANKS YOU FOR YOUR SERVICE.
YOU COWARDLY SON OF A--
SHRAK

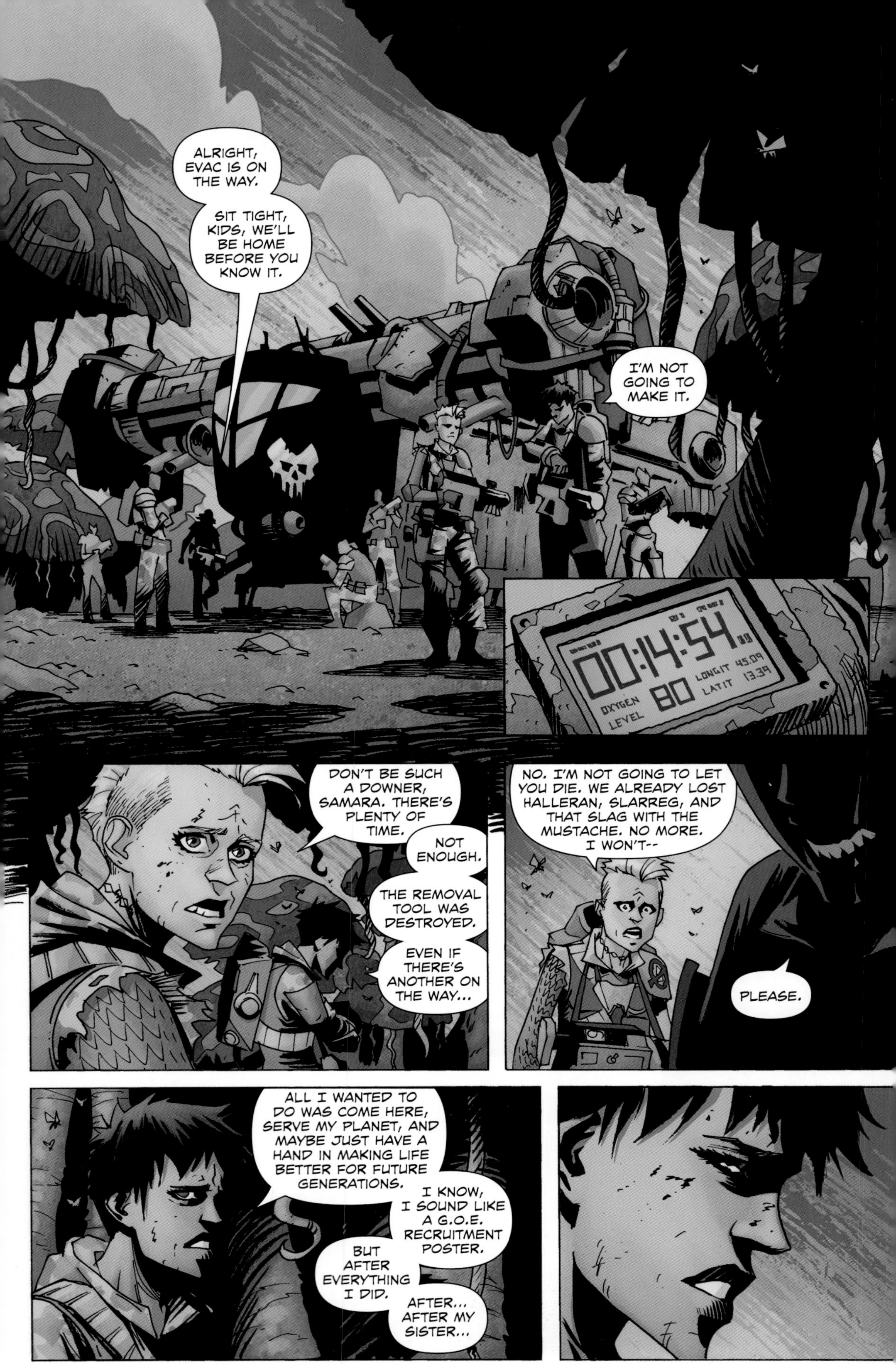
ALRIGHT, EVAC IS ON THE WAY.
SIT TIGHT, KIDS, WE'LL BE HOME BEFORE YOU KNOW IT.
I'M NOT GOING TO MAKE IT.
00:14:54
LONGIT 45.09
LATIT 13.39
OXYGEN LEVEL 80
DON'T BE SUCH A DOWNER, SAMARA. THERE'S PLENTY OF TIME.
NOT ENOUGH.
THE REMOVAL TOOL WAS DESTROYED.
EVEN IF THERE'S ANOTHER ON THE WAY...
NO. I'M NOT GOING TO LET YOU DIE. WE ALREADY LOST HALLERAN, SLARREG, AND THAT SLAG WITH THE MUSTACHE. NO MORE. I WON'T--
PLEASE.
ALL I WANTED TO DO WAS COME HERE, SERVE MY PLANET, AND MAYBE JUST HAVE A HAND IN MAKING LIFE BETTER FOR FUTURE GENERATIONS.
I KNOW, I SOUND LIKE A G.O.E. RECRUITMENT POSTER.
BUT AFTER EVERYTHING I DID.
AFTER... AFTER MY SISTER...

GOD. MY PARENTS COULDN'T EVEN LOOK ME IN THE FACE.

THEY TRIED AND I DON'T BLAME THEM. I KILLED MY SISTER. I KILLED THEIR DAUGHTER. I COULDN'T LOOK AT MYSELF IN THE MIRROR, EITHER.

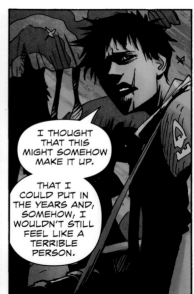

I THOUGHT THAT THIS MIGHT SOMEHOW MAKE IT UP.

THAT I COULD PUT IN THE YEARS AND, SOMEHOW, I WOULDN'T STILL FEEL LIKE A TERRIBLE PERSON.

BUT I SCREWED THIS UP TOO.

SAMARA, DON'T... IT'S NOT YOUR--

I NEED SOMEONE TO KNOW. THAT EVEN THOUGH I TOLD MYSELF I WAS COMING HERE AS SOME SORT OF PENANCE...

...I WAS REALLY JUST RUNNING AWAY FROM THE PROBLEM.

I'M A COWARD.

SAMARA SIMMONS!

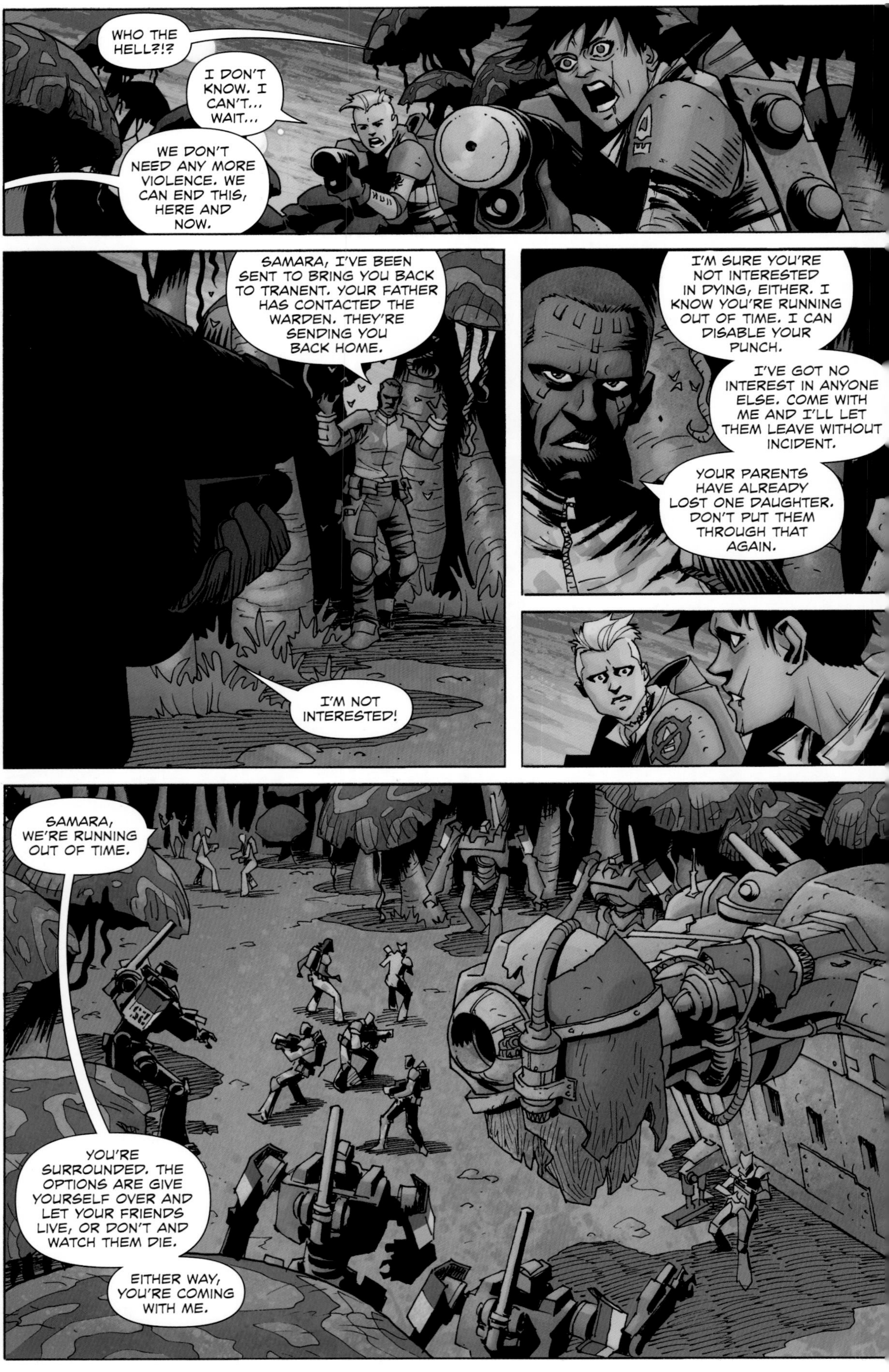
WHO THE HELL?!?
I DON'T KNOW. I CAN'T... WAIT...
WE DON'T NEED ANY MORE VIOLENCE. WE CAN END THIS, HERE AND NOW.
SAMARA, I'VE BEEN SENT TO BRING YOU BACK TO TRANENT. YOUR FATHER HAS CONTACTED THE WARDEN. THEY'RE SENDING YOU BACK HOME.
I'M NOT INTERESTED!
I'M SURE YOU'RE NOT INTERESTED IN DYING, EITHER. I KNOW YOU'RE RUNNING OUT OF TIME. I CAN DISABLE YOUR PUNCH.
I'VE GOT NO INTEREST IN ANYONE ELSE. COME WITH ME AND I'LL LET THEM LEAVE WITHOUT INCIDENT.
YOUR PARENTS HAVE ALREADY LOST ONE DAUGHTER. DON'T PUT THEM THROUGH THAT AGAIN.
SAMARA, WE'RE RUNNING OUT OF TIME.
YOU'RE SURROUNDED. THE OPTIONS ARE GIVE YOURSELF OVER AND LET YOUR FRIENDS LIVE, OR DON'T AND WATCH THEM DIE.
EITHER WAY, YOU'RE COMING WITH ME.

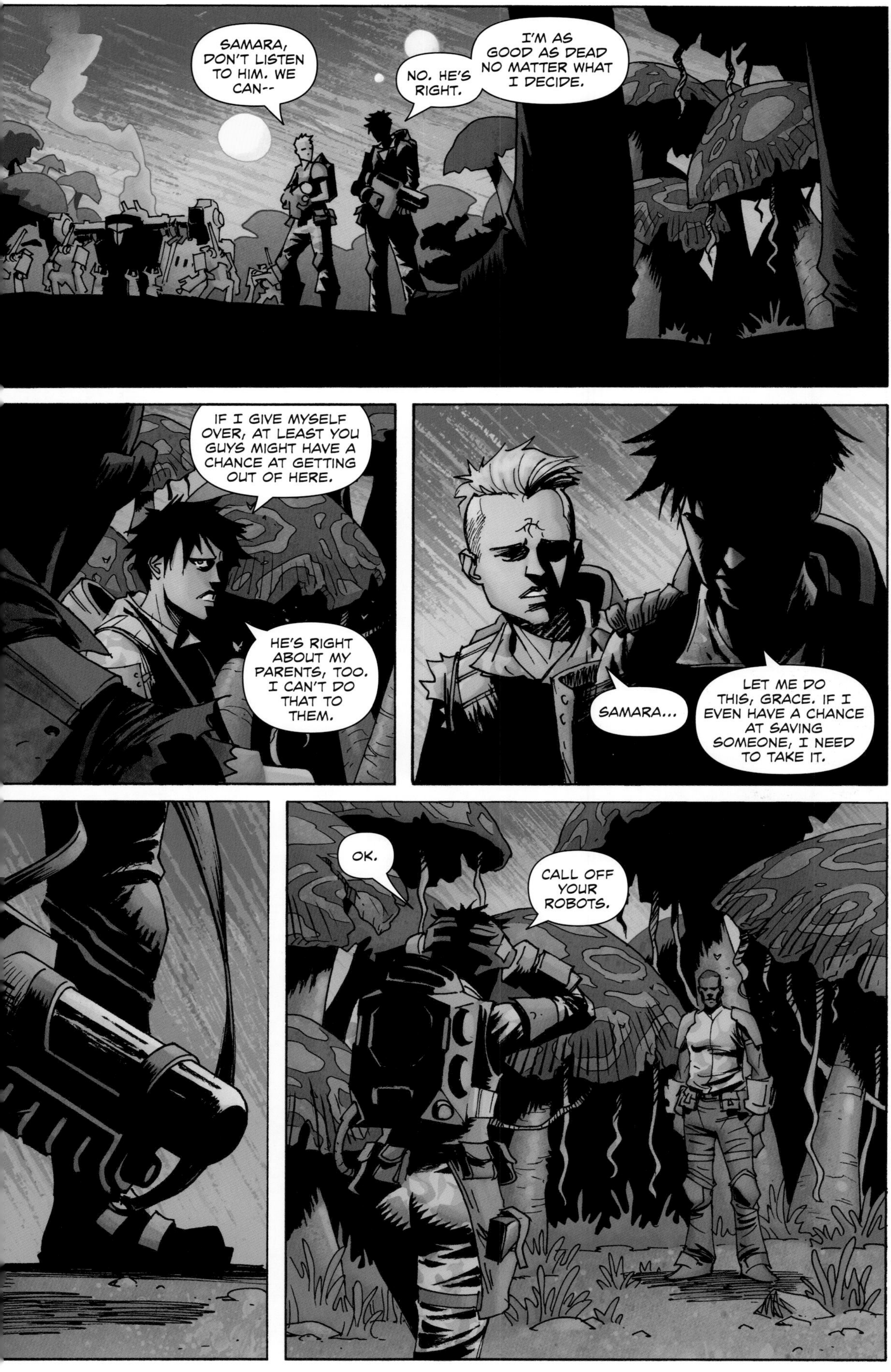
SAMARA, DON'T LISTEN TO HIM. WE CAN--
NO. HE'S RIGHT.
I'M AS GOOD AS DEAD NO MATTER WHAT I DECIDE.
IF I GIVE MYSELF OVER, AT LEAST YOU GUYS MIGHT HAVE A CHANCE AT GETTING OUT OF HERE.
HE'S RIGHT ABOUT MY PARENTS, TOO. I CAN'T DO THAT TO THEM.
SAMARA...
LET ME DO THIS, GRACE. IF I EVEN HAVE A CHANCE AT SAVING SOMEONE, I NEED TO TAKE IT.
OK.
CALL OFF YOUR ROBOTS.

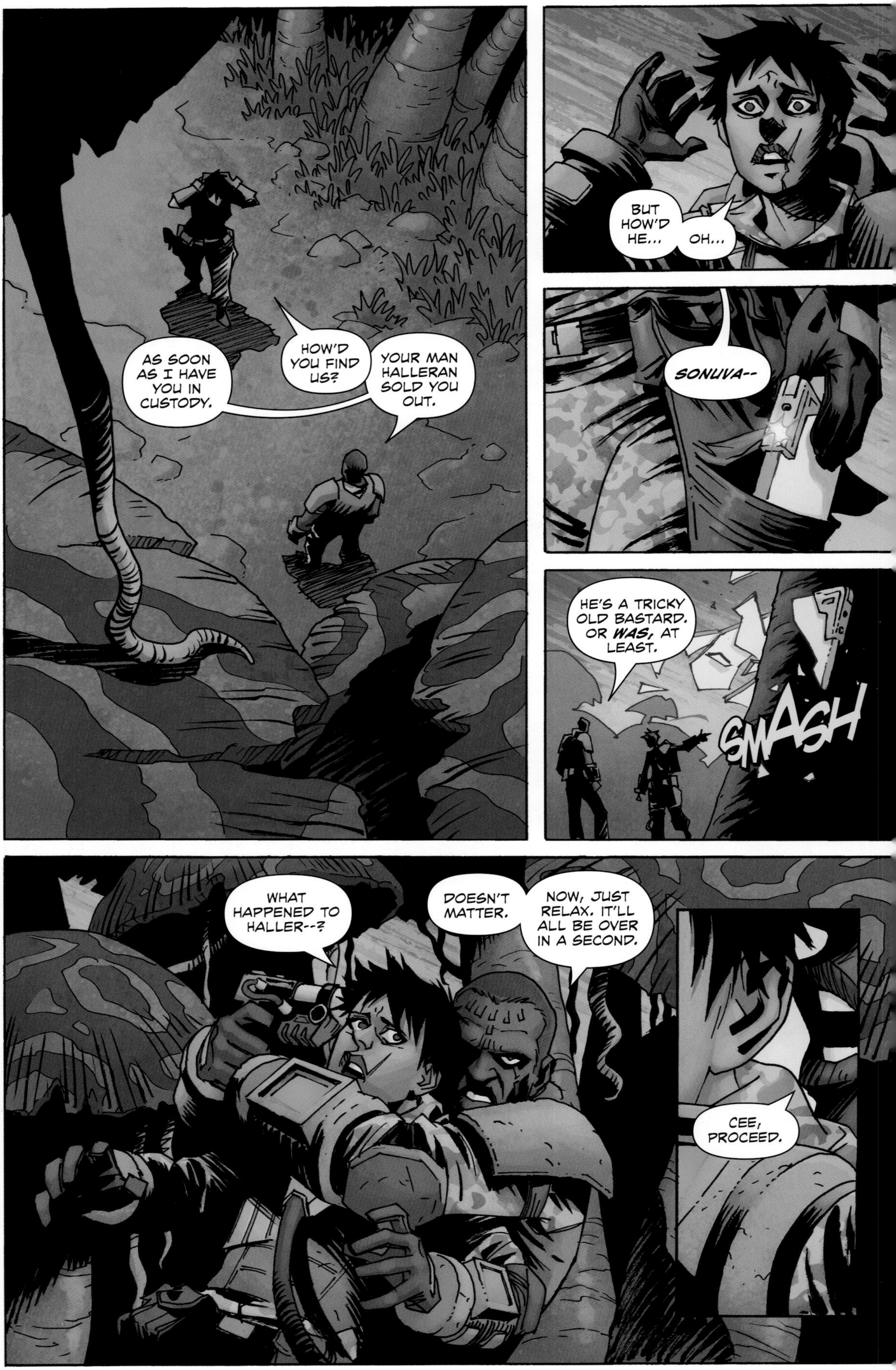
HOW'D YOU FIND US?
YOUR MAN HALLERAN SOLD YOU OUT.
AS SOON AS I HAVE YOU IN CUSTODY.
BUT HOW'D HE...
OH...
SONUVA--
HE'S A TRICKY OLD BASTARD. OR WAS, AT LEAST.
SMASH
WHAT HAPPENED TO HALLER--?
DOESN'T MATTER.
NOW, JUST RELAX. IT'LL ALL BE OVER IN A SECOND.
CEE, PROCEED.

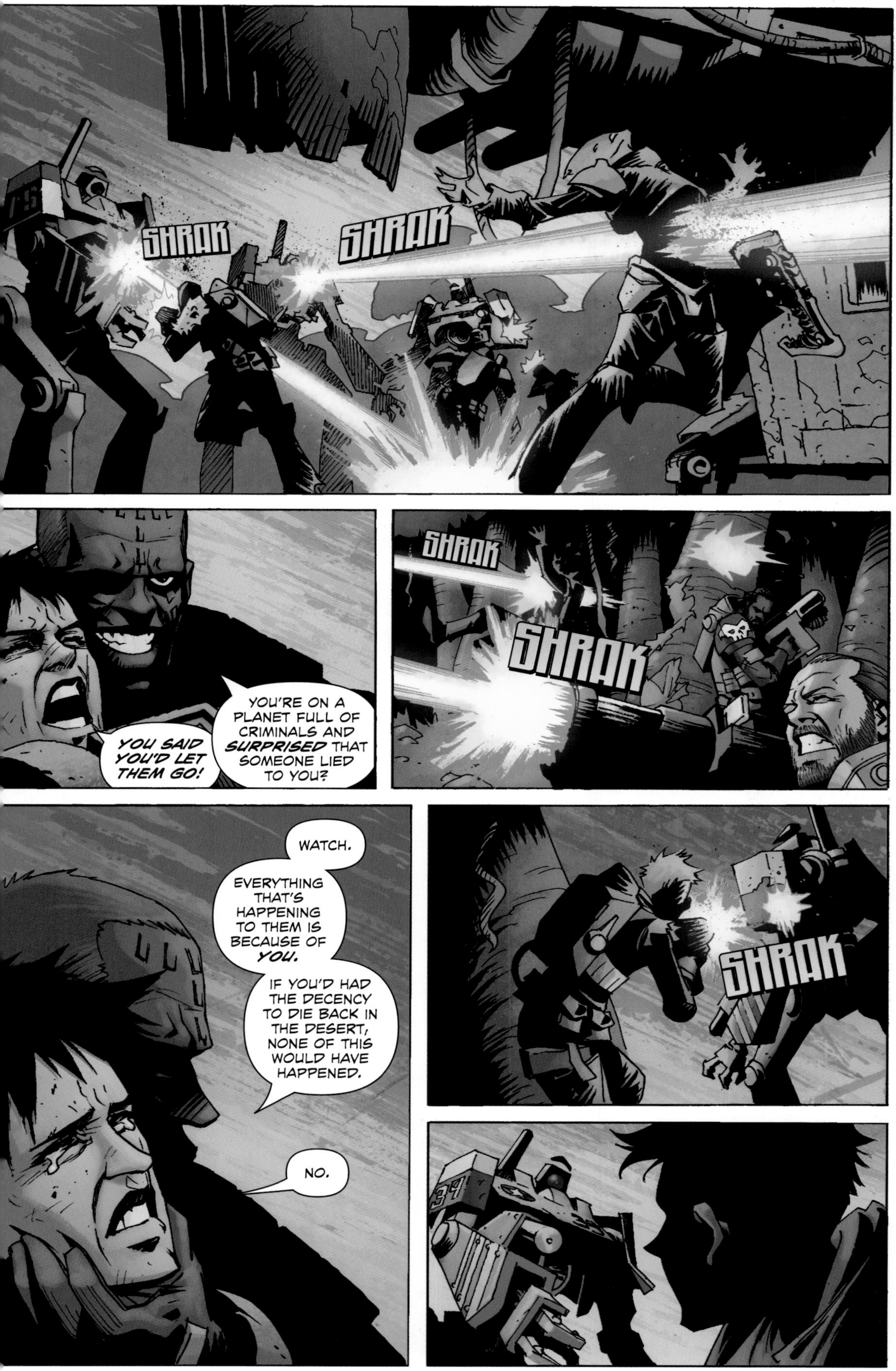
SHRAK
SHRAK
YOU SAID YOU'D LET THEM GO!
YOU'RE ON A PLANET FULL OF CRIMINALS AND SURPRISED THAT SOMEONE LIED TO YOU?
SHRAK
SHRAK
WATCH.
EVERYTHING THAT'S HAPPENING TO THEM IS BECAUSE OF YOU.
IF YOU'D HAD THE DECENCY TO DIE BACK IN THE DESERT, NONE OF THIS WOULD HAVE HAPPENED.
NO.
SHRAK

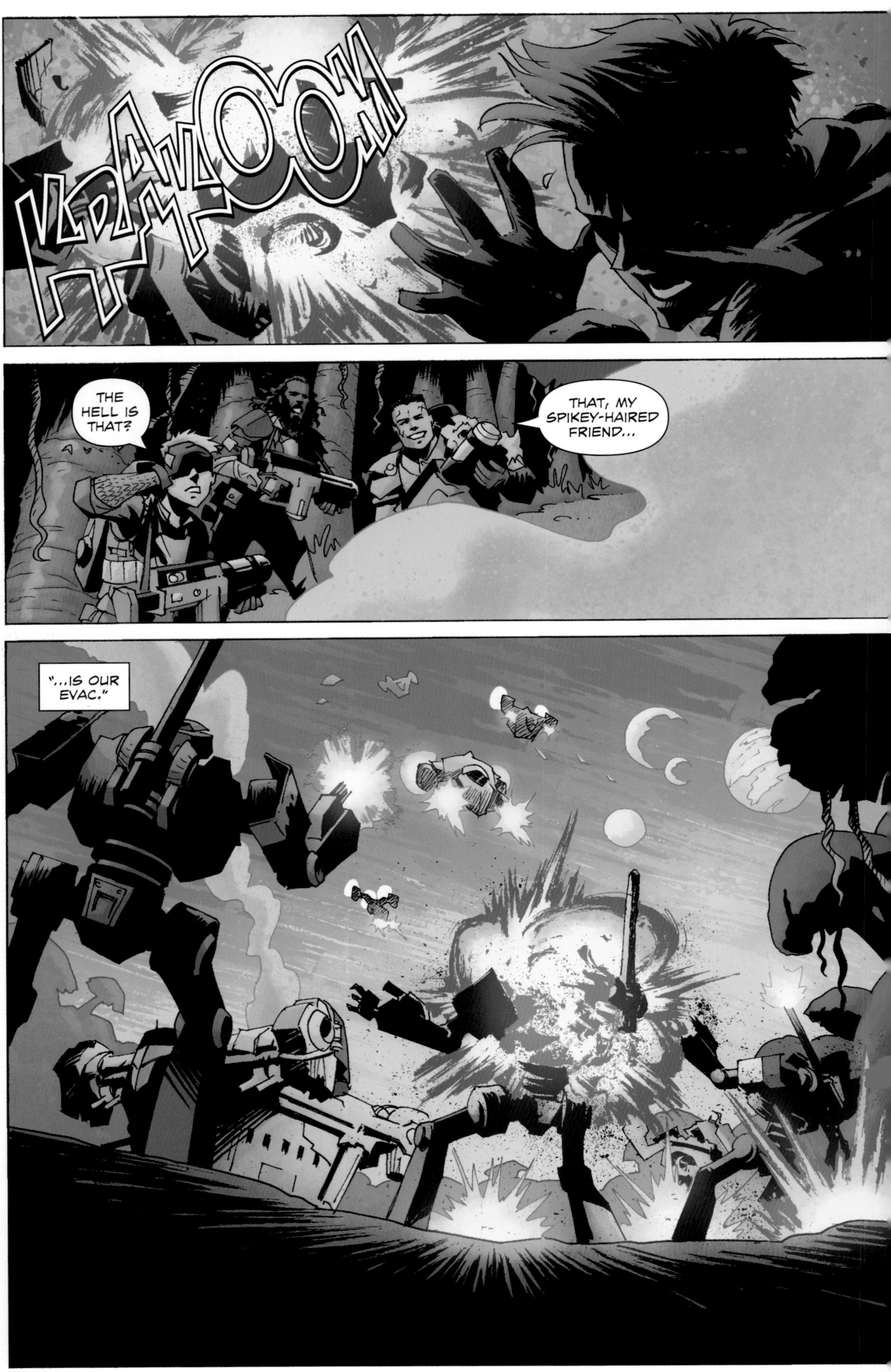
KRAWOOOM
THE HELL IS THAT?
THAT, MY SPIKEY-HAIRED FRIEND...
"...IS OUR EVAC."

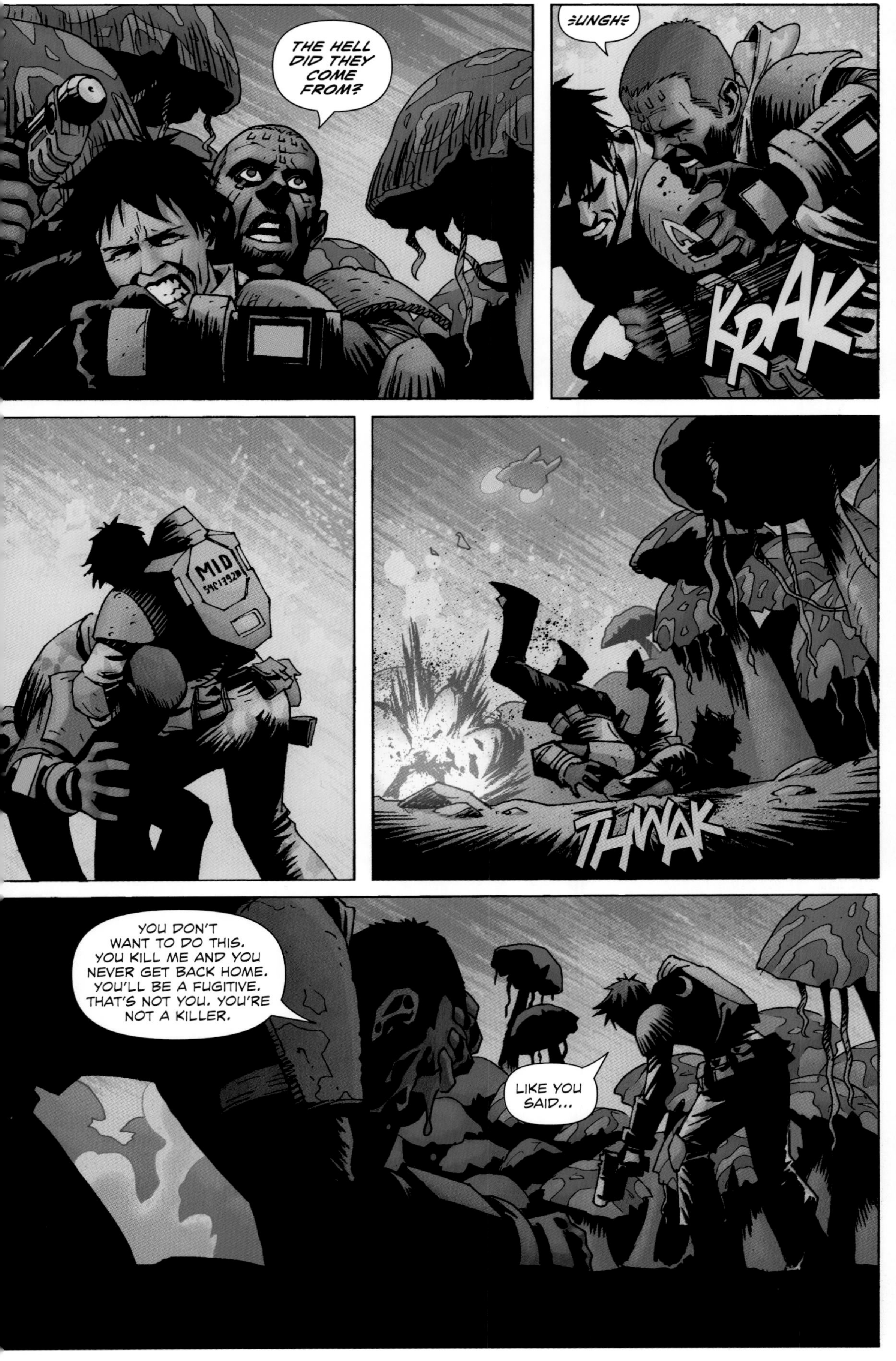
THE HELL DID THEY COME FROM?
UNGH
KRAK
MID
THWAK
YOU DON'T WANT TO DO THIS. YOU KILL ME AND YOU NEVER GET BACK HOME. YOU'LL BE A FUGITIVE. THAT'S NOT YOU. YOU'RE NOT A KILLER.
LIKE YOU SAID...

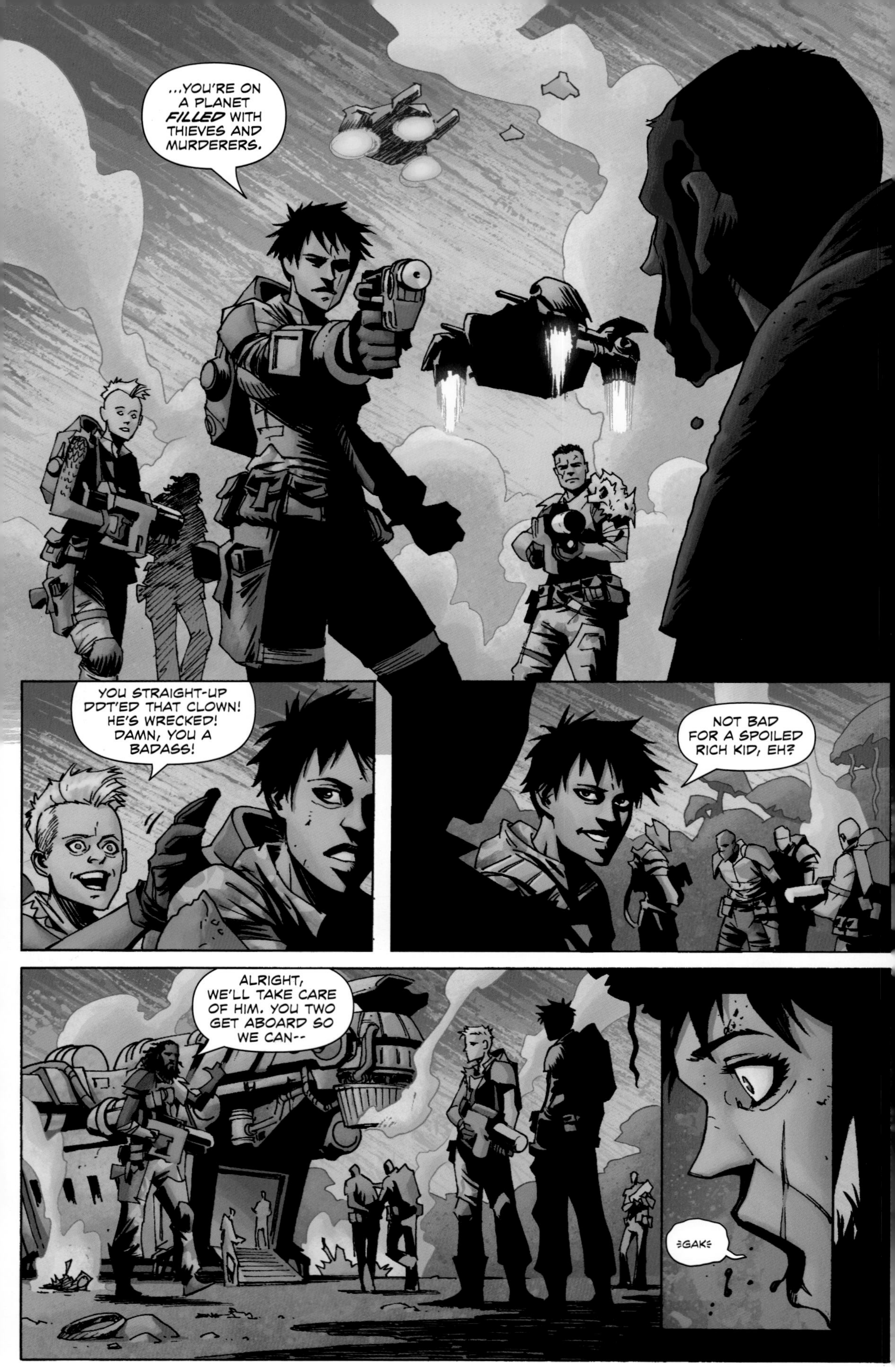
...YOU'RE ON A PLANET *FILLED* WITH THIEVES AND MURDERERS.
YOU STRAIGHT-UP DDT'ED THAT CLOWN! HE'S WRECKED! DAMN, YOU A BADASS!
NOT BAD FOR A SPOILED RICH KID, EH?
ALRIGHT, WE'LL TAKE CARE OF HIM. YOU TWO GET ABOARD SO WE CAN--
GAK

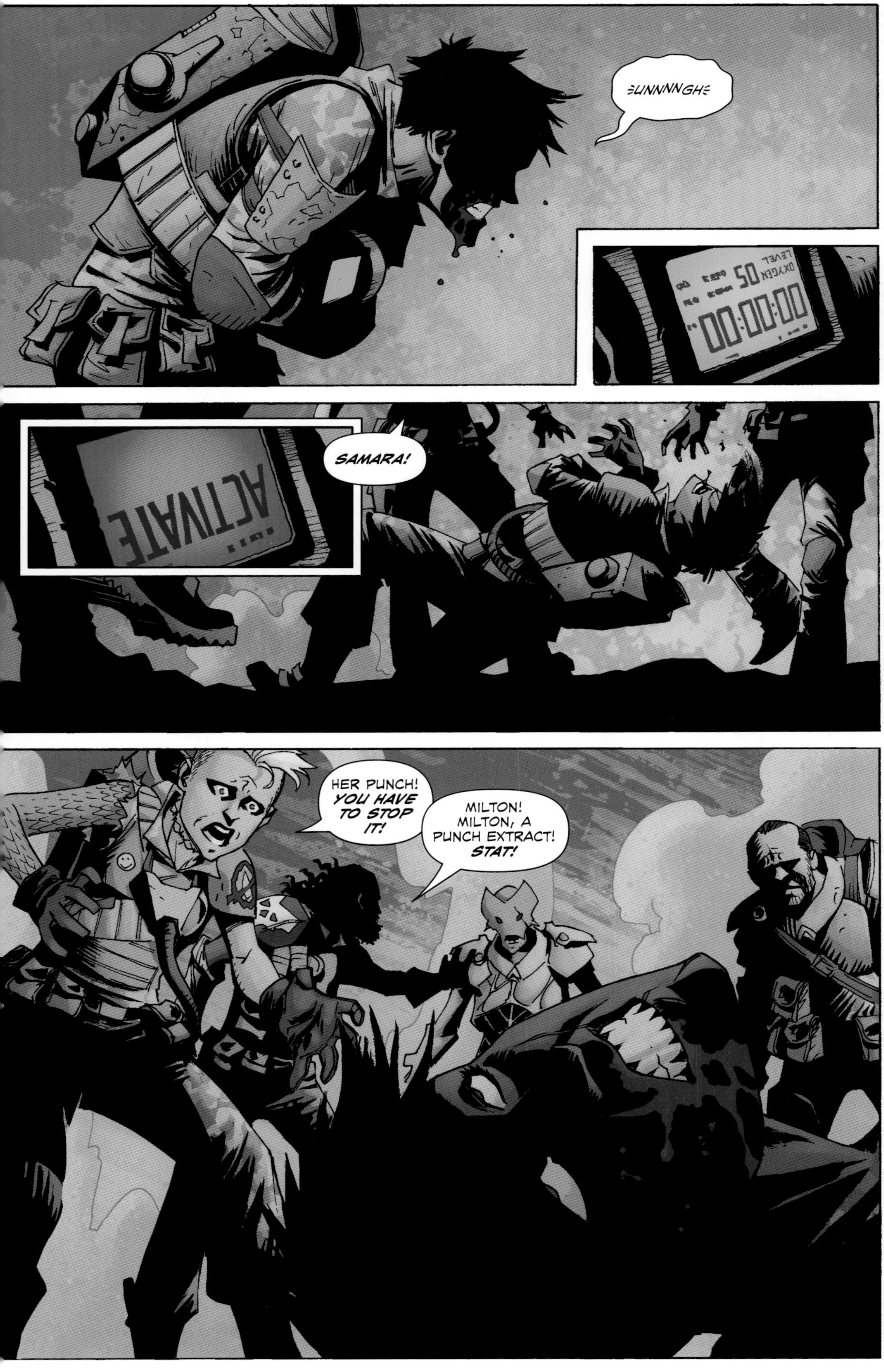
UNNNNGH
OXYGEN LEVEL 05
00:00:00
ACTIVATE
SAMARA!
HER PUNCH! YOU HAVE TO STOP IT!
MILTON! MILTON, A PUNCH EXTRACT! STAT!

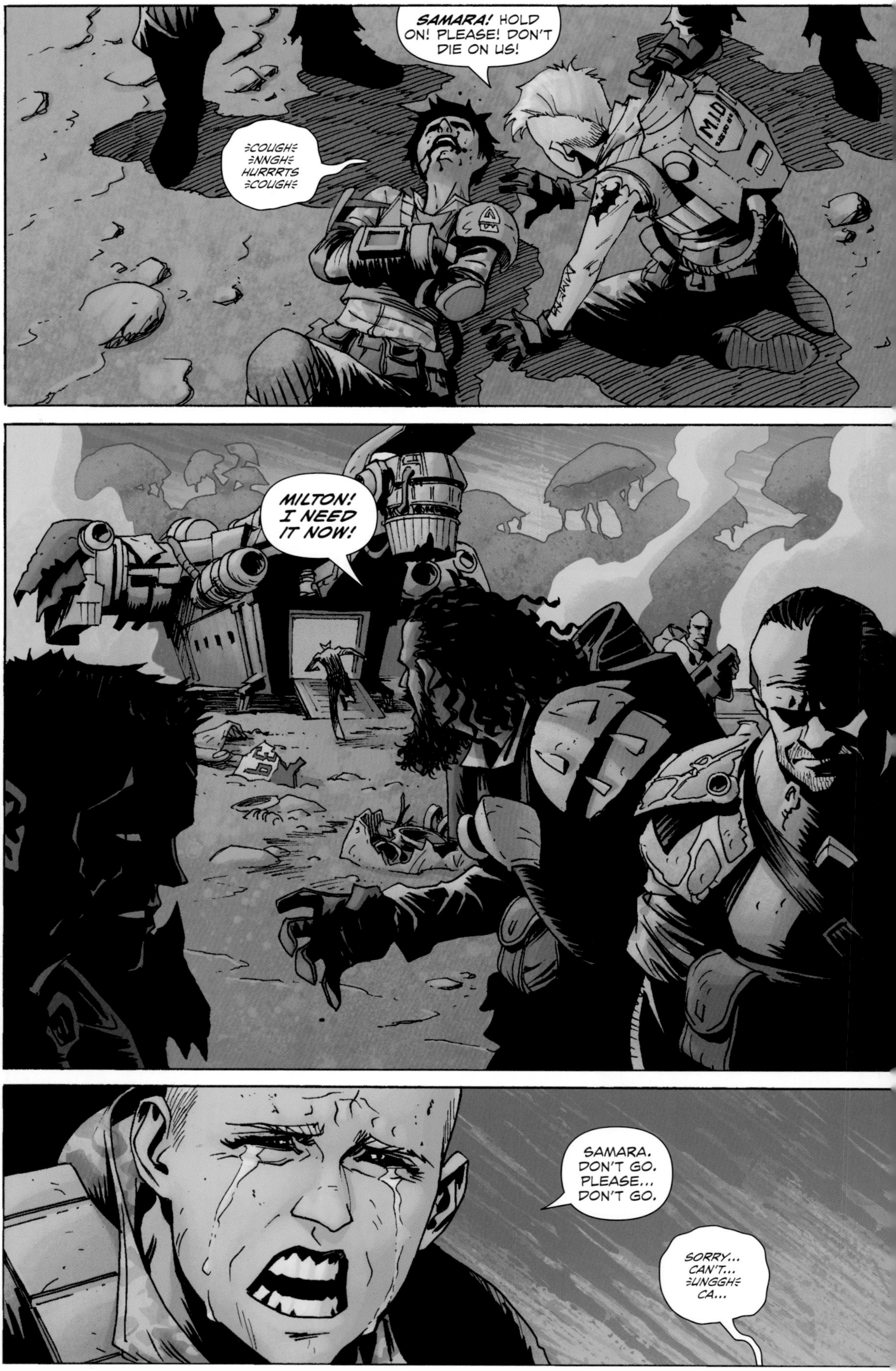
SAMARA! HOLD ON! PLEASE! DON'T DIE ON US!
COUGH NNGH HURRRTS COUGH
M.I.D.
MILTON! I NEED IT NOW!
SAMARA. DON'T GO. PLEASE... DON'T GO.
SORRY... CAN'T... UNGGH CA...

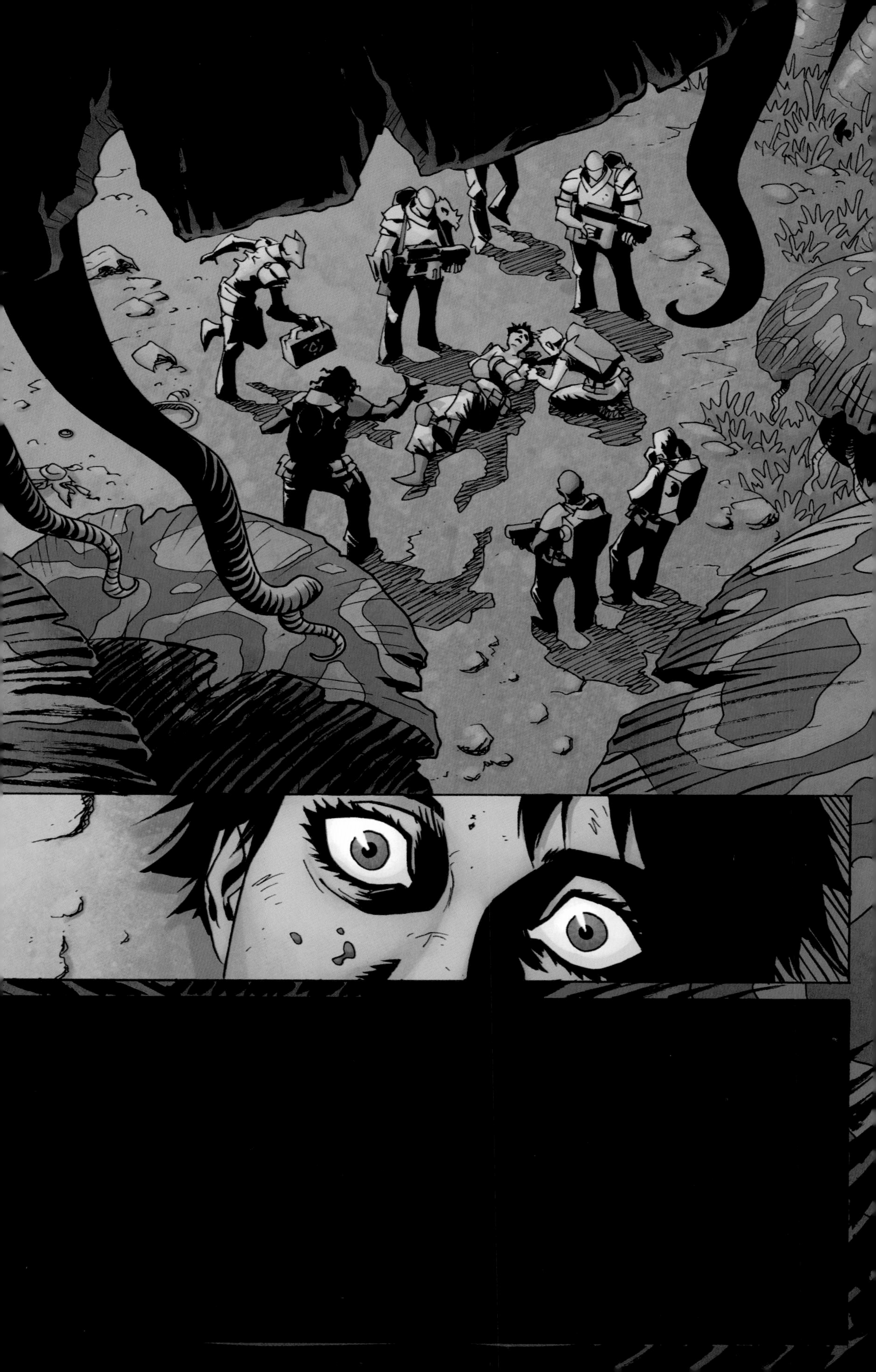

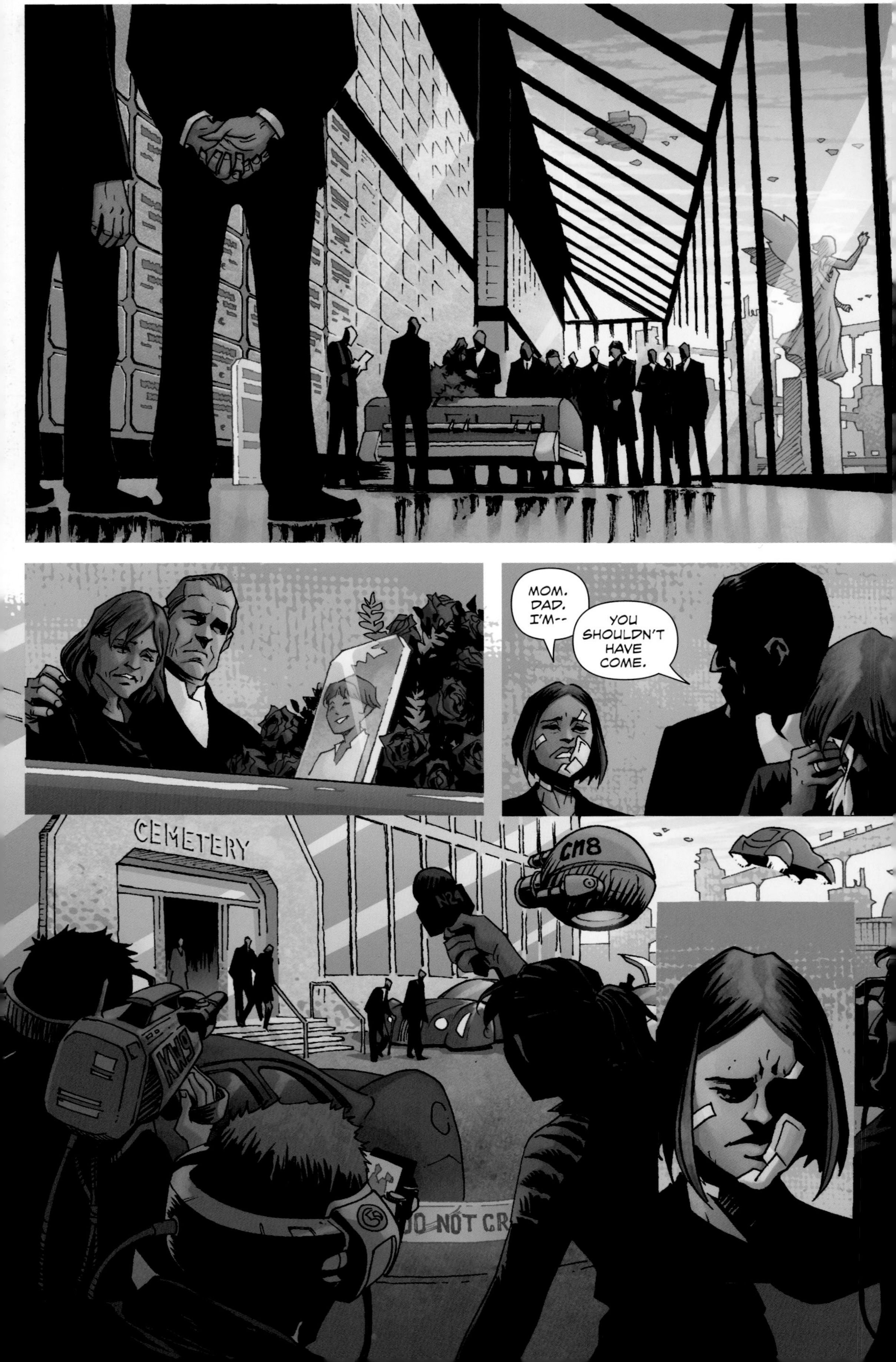

MOM. DAD. I'M--
YOU SHOULDN'T HAVE COME.
CEMETERY
CM8
N24
KW9
DO NOT CR

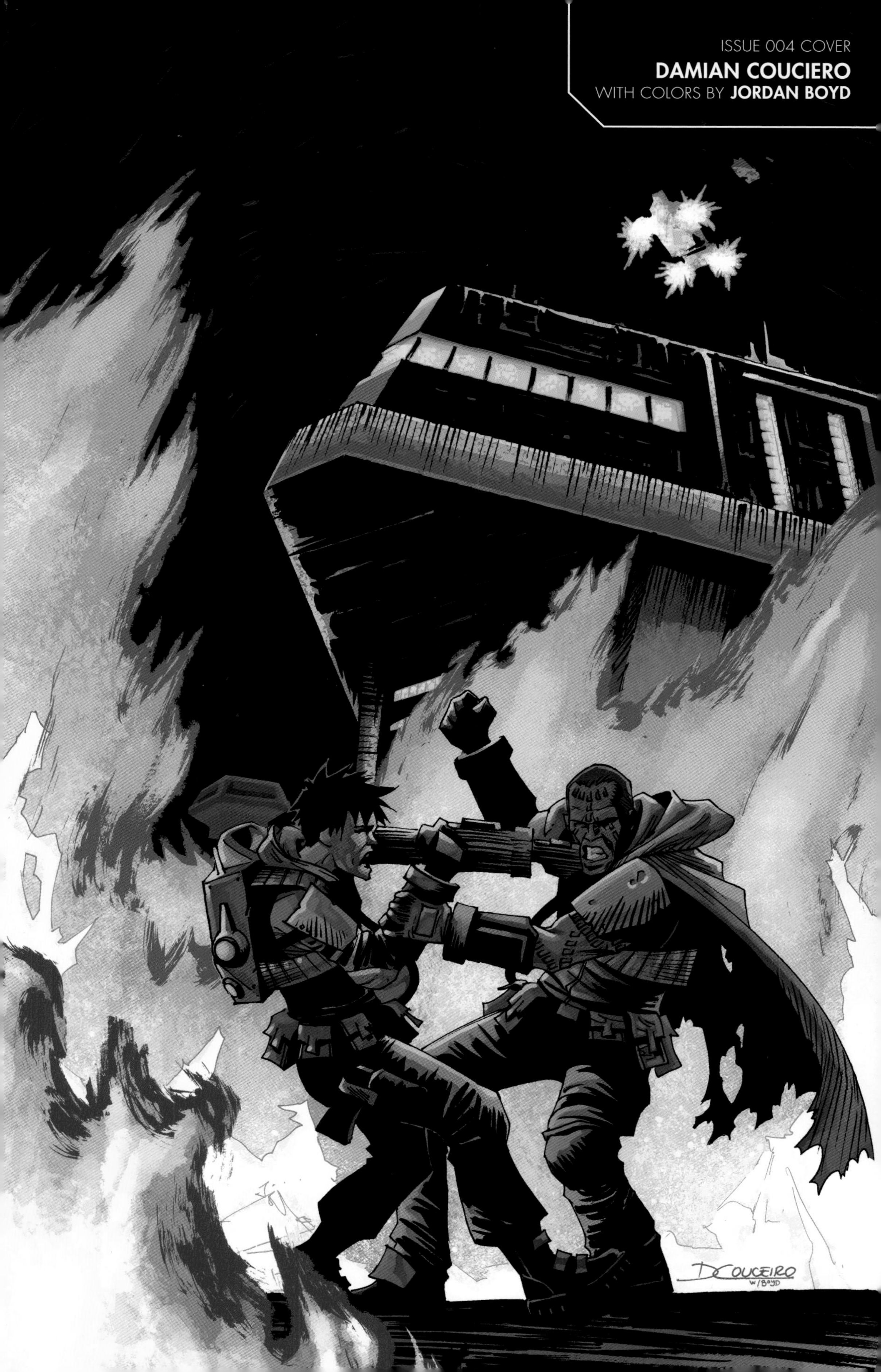
DCOUCEIRO
W/BOYD

ISSUE 004 COVER
DAMIAN COUCIERO
WITH COLORS BY **JORDAN BOYD**

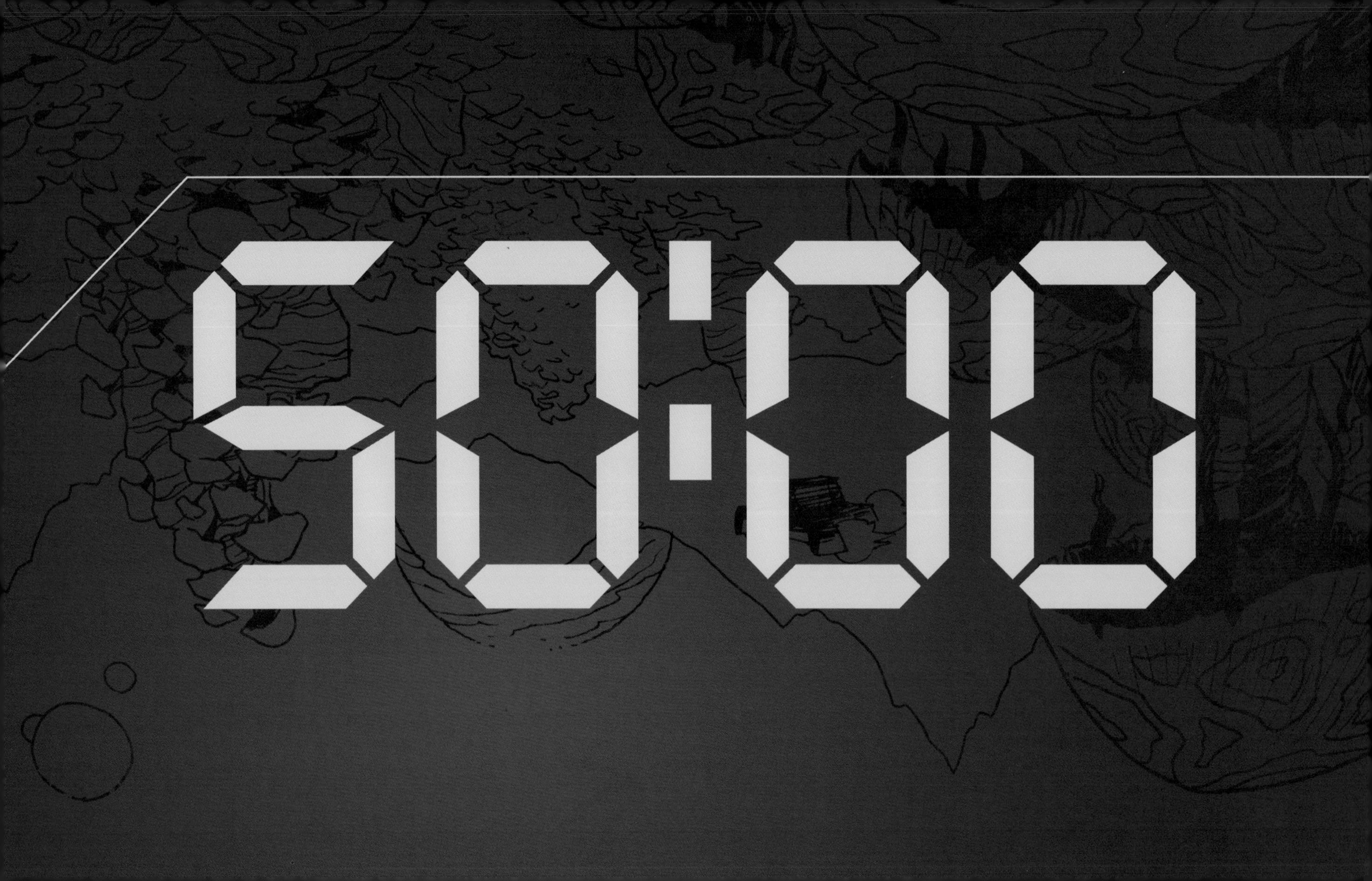
50:00

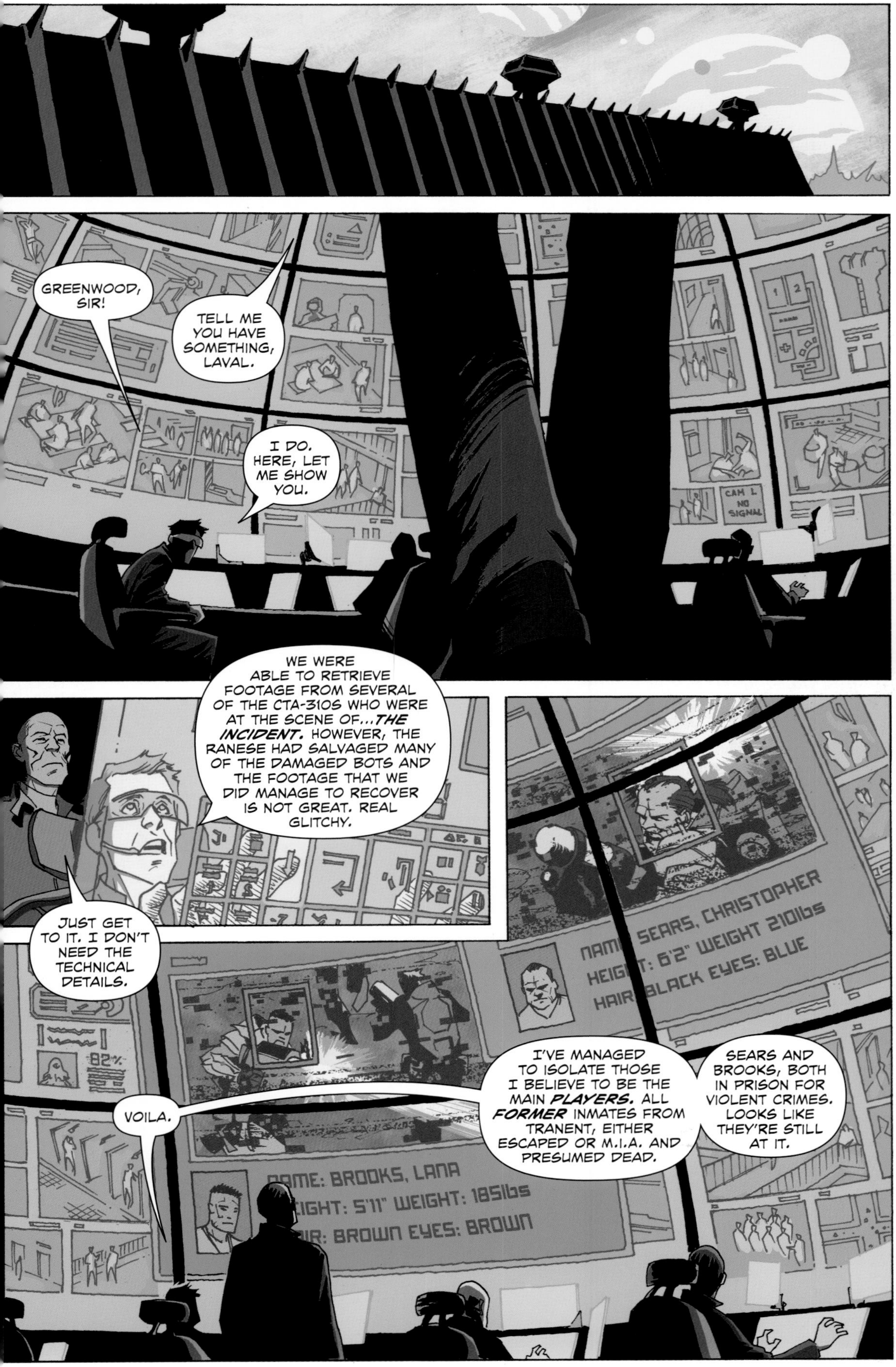
GREENWOOD, SIR!
TELL ME YOU HAVE SOMETHING, LAVAL.
I DO. HERE, LET ME SHOW YOU.
CAM L NO SIGNAL
WE WERE ABLE TO RETRIEVE FOOTAGE FROM SEVERAL OF THE CTA-310S WHO WERE AT THE SCENE OF... *THE INCIDENT.* HOWEVER, THE RANESE HAD SALVAGED MANY OF THE DAMAGED BOTS AND THE FOOTAGE THAT WE DID MANAGE TO RECOVER IS NOT GREAT. REAL GLITCHY.
JUST GET TO IT. I DON'T NEED THE TECHNICAL DETAILS.
VOILA.
I'VE MANAGED TO ISOLATE THOSE I BELIEVE TO BE THE MAIN *PLAYERS.* ALL *FORMER* INMATES FROM TRANENT, EITHER ESCAPED OR M.I.A. AND PRESUMED DEAD.
SEARS AND BROOKS, BOTH IN PRISON FOR VIOLENT CRIMES. LOOKS LIKE THEY'RE STILL AT IT.
SEARS, CHRISTOPHER
: 6'2" WEIGHT 210lbs
BLACK EYES: BLUE
82%
AME: BROOKS, LANA
EIGHT: 5'11" WEIGHT: 185lbs
IR: BROWN EYES: BROWN

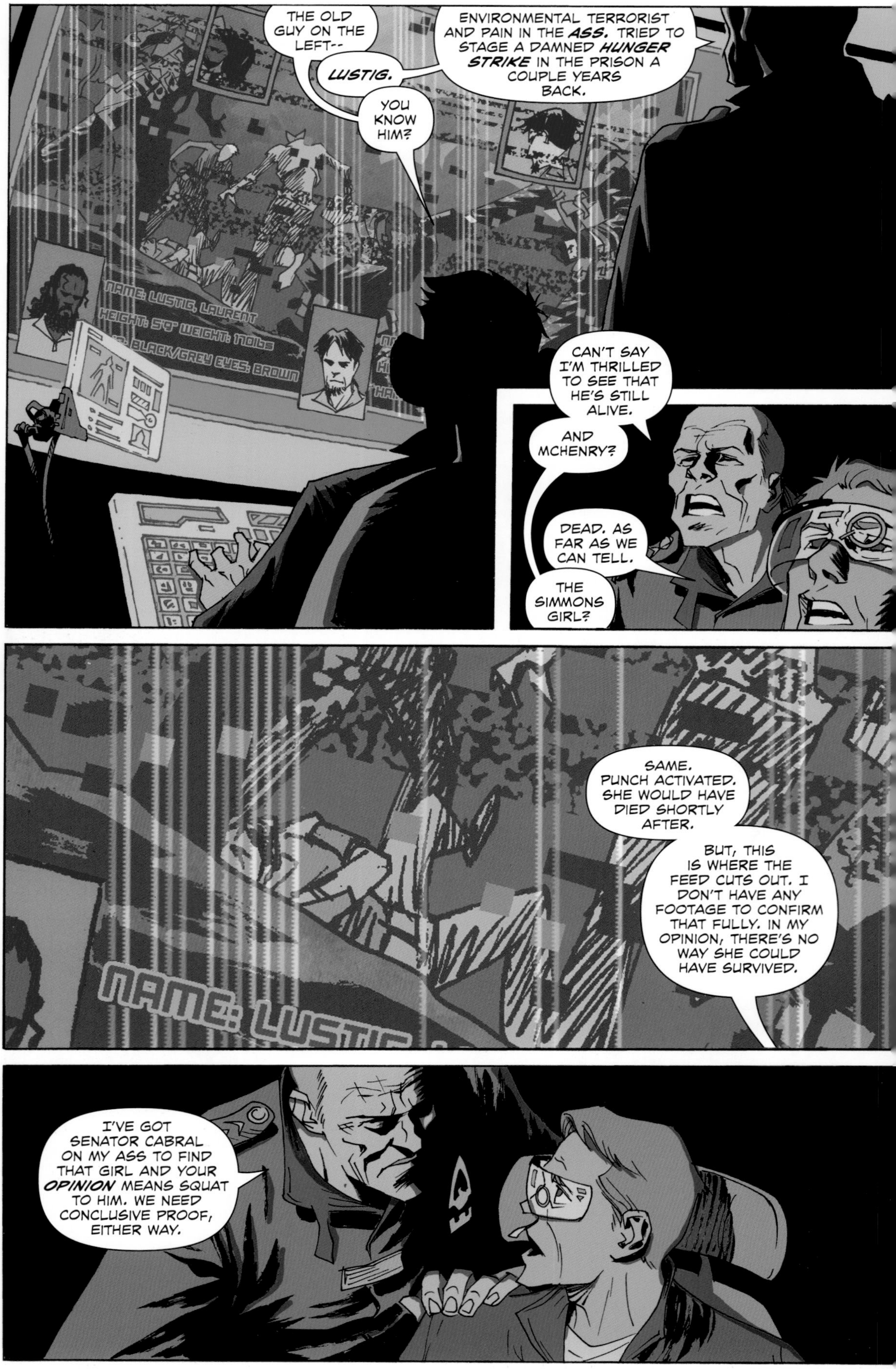

THE OLD GUY ON THE LEFT--
LUSTIG.
YOU KNOW HIM?
ENVIRONMENTAL TERRORIST AND PAIN IN THE ASS. TRIED TO STAGE A DAMNED HUNGER STRIKE IN THE PRISON A COUPLE YEARS BACK.
NAME: LUSTIG, LAURENT
HEIGHT: 5'9" WEIGHT: 110lbs
BLACK/GREY EYES: BROWN
CAN'T SAY I'M THRILLED TO SEE THAT HE'S STILL ALIVE.
AND MCHENRY?
DEAD. AS FAR AS WE CAN TELL.
THE SIMMONS GIRL?
SAME. PUNCH ACTIVATED. SHE WOULD HAVE DIED SHORTLY AFTER.
BUT, THIS IS WHERE THE FEED CUTS OUT. I DON'T HAVE ANY FOOTAGE TO CONFIRM THAT FULLY. IN MY OPINION, THERE'S NO WAY SHE COULD HAVE SURVIVED.
NAME: LUSTIG
I'VE GOT SENATOR CABRAL ON MY ASS TO FIND THAT GIRL AND YOUR OPINION MEANS SQUAT TO HIM. WE NEED CONCLUSIVE PROOF, EITHER WAY.

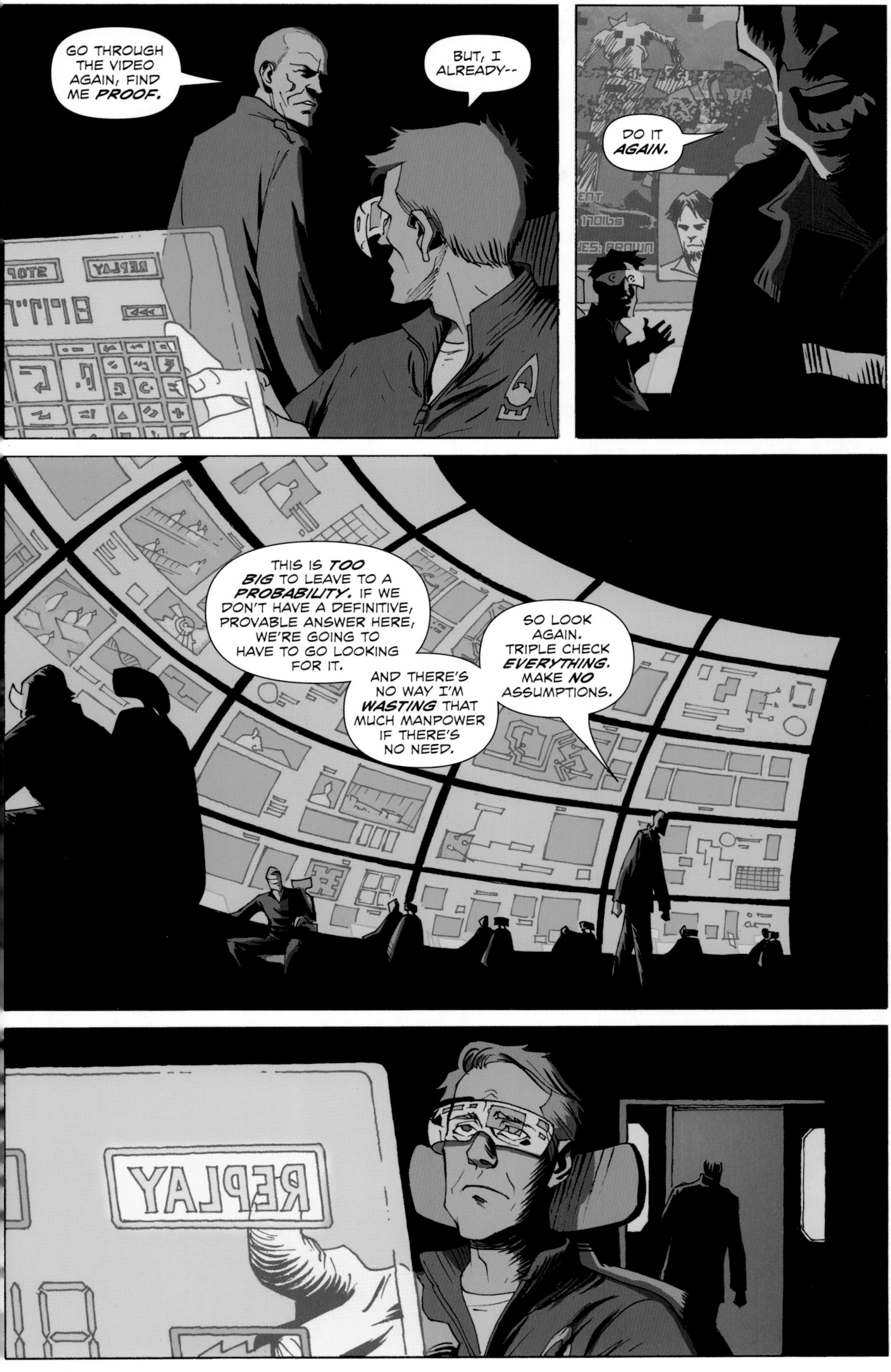
GO THROUGH THE VIDEO AGAIN, FIND ME *PROOF.*
BUT, I ALREADY--
DO IT *AGAIN.*
THIS IS *TOO BIG* TO LEAVE TO A *PROBABILITY.* IF WE DON'T HAVE A DEFINITIVE, PROVABLE ANSWER HERE, WE'RE GOING TO HAVE TO GO LOOKING FOR IT.
AND THERE'S NO WAY I'M *WASTING* THAT MUCH MANPOWER IF THERE'S NO NEED.
SO LOOK AGAIN. TRIPLE CHECK *EVERYTHING.* MAKE *NO* ASSUMPTIONS.

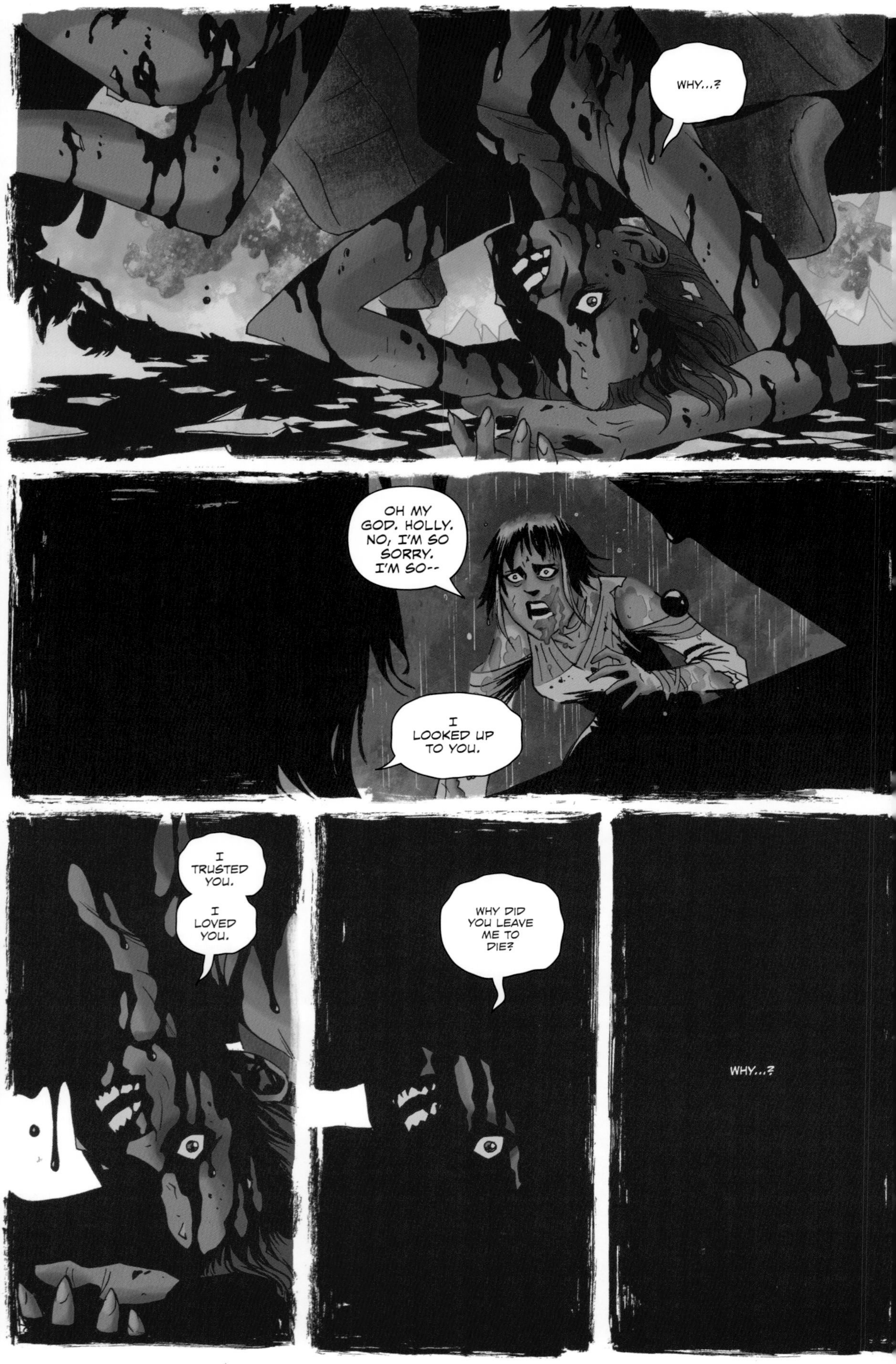
WHY...?
OH MY GOD. HOLLY. NO, I'M SO SORRY. I'M SO--
I LOOKED UP TO YOU.
I TRUSTED YOU.
I LOVED YOU.
WHY DID YOU LEAVE ME TO DIE?
WHY...?

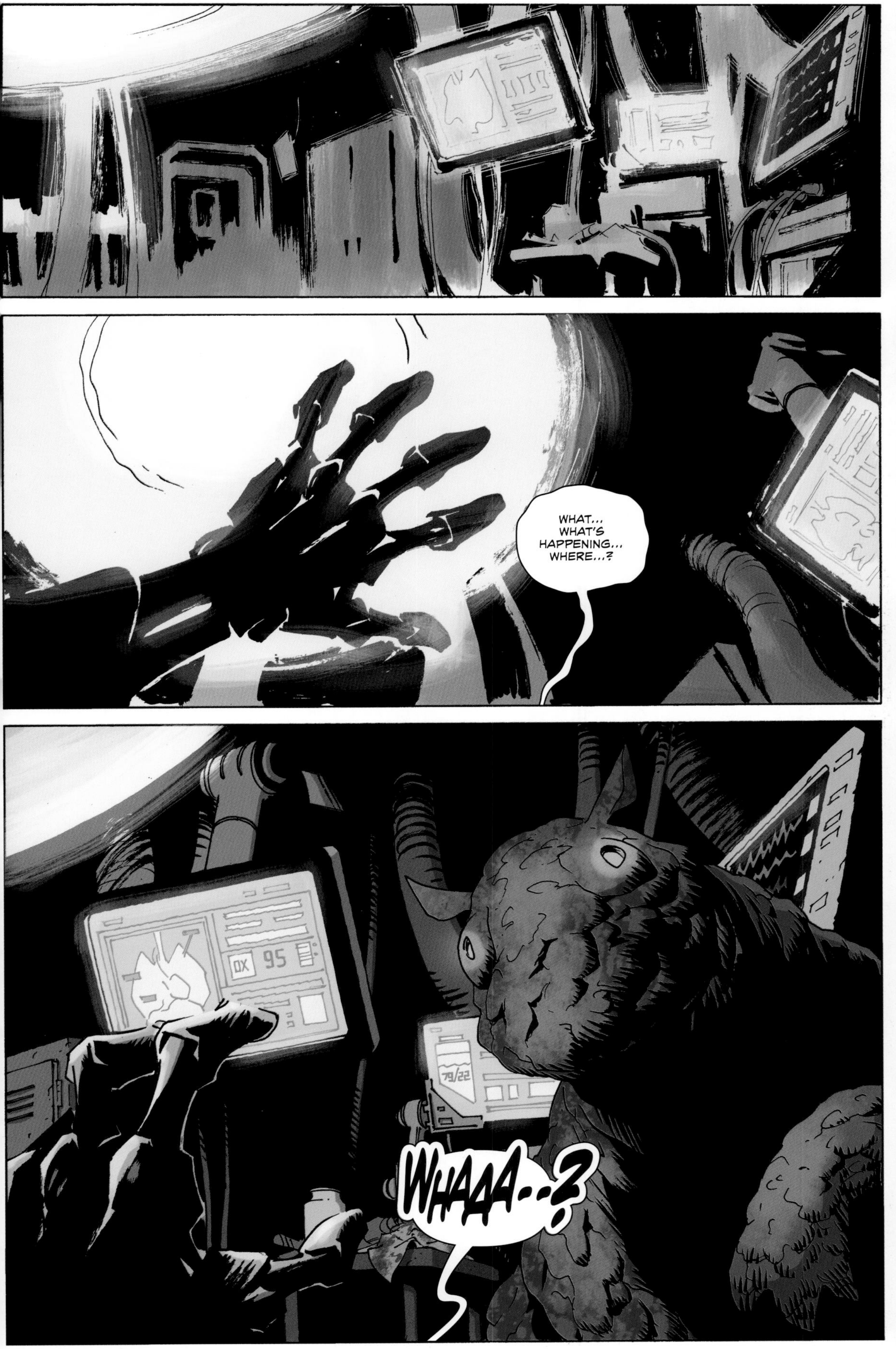
WHAT... WHAT'S HAPPENING... WHERE...?
OX 95
79/22
WHAAA--?

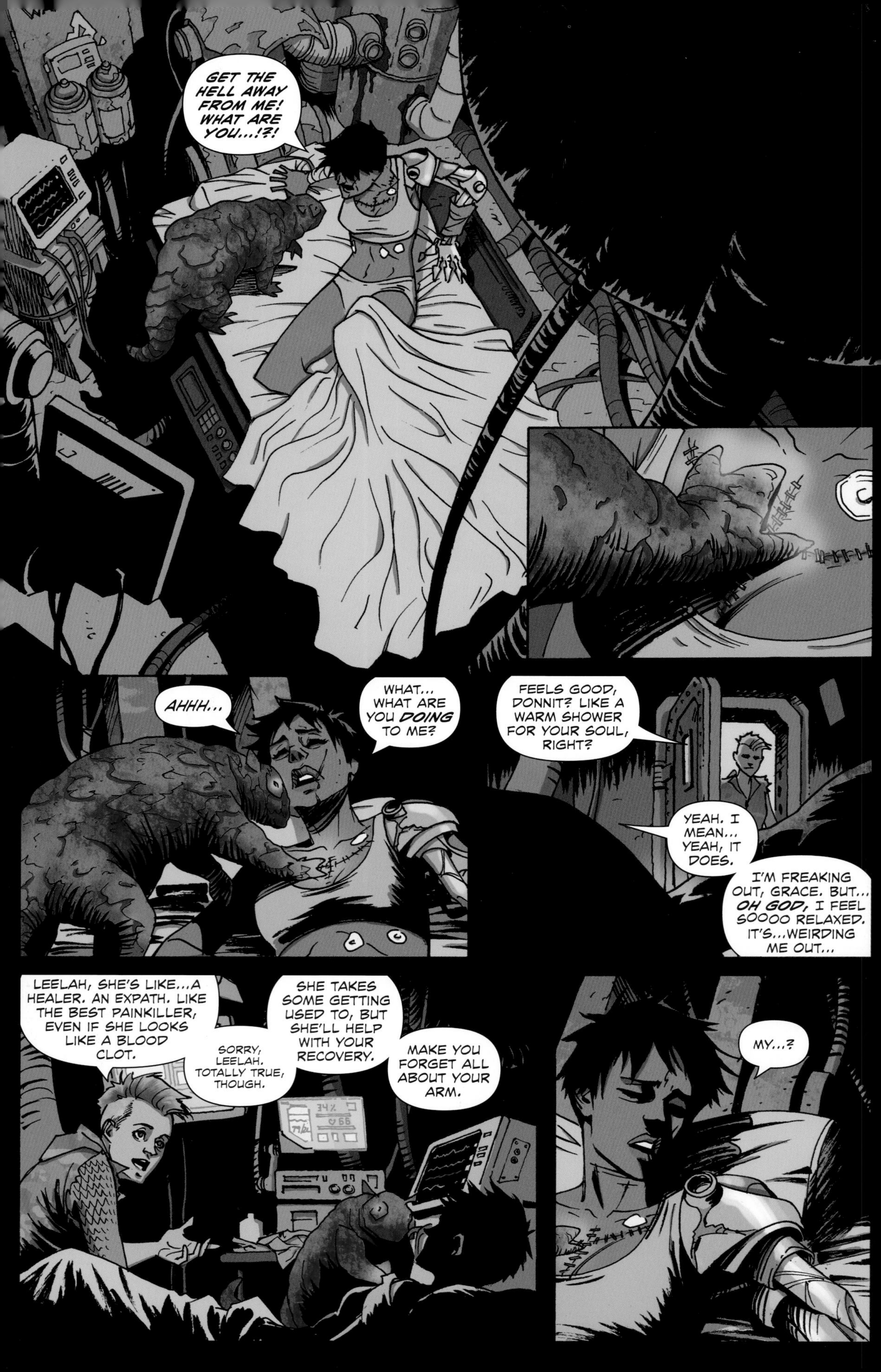

GET THE HELL AWAY FROM ME! WHAT ARE YOU...!?!
AHHH...
WHAT... WHAT ARE YOU DOING TO ME?
FEELS GOOD, DONNIT? LIKE A WARM SHOWER FOR YOUR SOUL, RIGHT?
YEAH. I MEAN... YEAH, IT DOES.
I'M FREAKING OUT, GRACE. BUT... OH GOD, I FEEL SOOOO RELAXED. IT'S...WEIRDING ME OUT...
LEELAH, SHE'S LIKE...A HEALER. AN EXPATH. LIKE THE BEST PAINKILLER, EVEN IF SHE LOOKS LIKE A BLOOD CLOT.
SORRY, LEELAH. TOTALLY TRUE, THOUGH.
SHE TAKES SOME GETTING USED TO, BUT SHE'LL HELP WITH YOUR RECOVERY.
MAKE YOU FORGET ALL ABOUT YOUR ARM.
MY...?

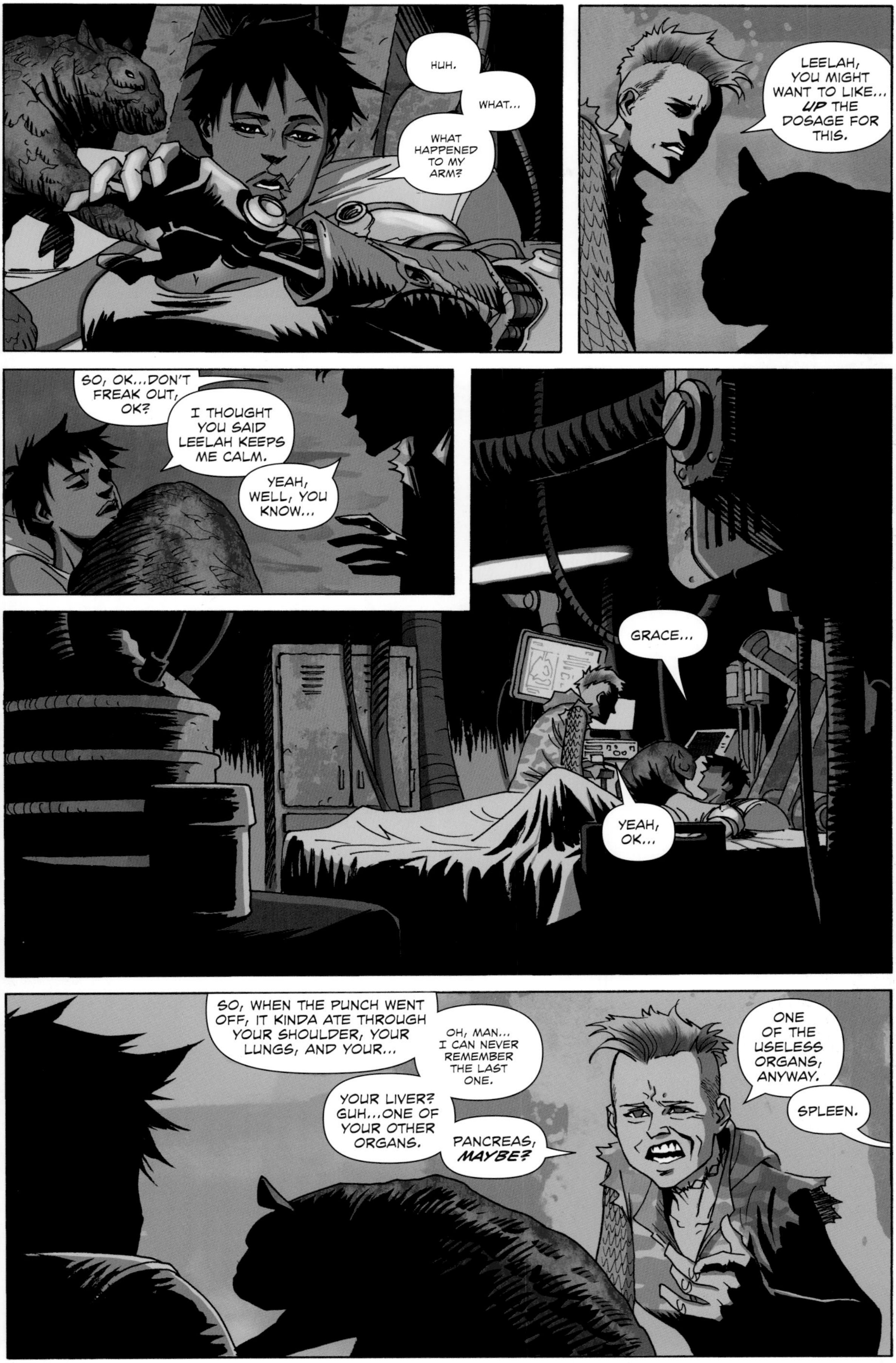
HUH.
WHAT...
WHAT HAPPENED TO MY ARM?
LEELAH, YOU MIGHT WANT TO LIKE... *UP* THE DOSAGE FOR THIS.
SO, OK...DON'T FREAK OUT, OK?
I THOUGHT YOU SAID LEELAH KEEPS ME CALM.
YEAH, WELL, YOU KNOW...
GRACE...
YEAH, OK...
SO, WHEN THE PUNCH WENT OFF, IT KINDA ATE THROUGH YOUR SHOULDER, YOUR LUNGS, AND YOUR...
OH, MAN... I CAN NEVER REMEMBER THE LAST ONE.
YOUR LIVER? GUH...ONE OF YOUR OTHER ORGANS.
PANCREAS, *MAYBE?*
ONE OF THE USELESS ORGANS, ANYWAY.
SPLEEN.

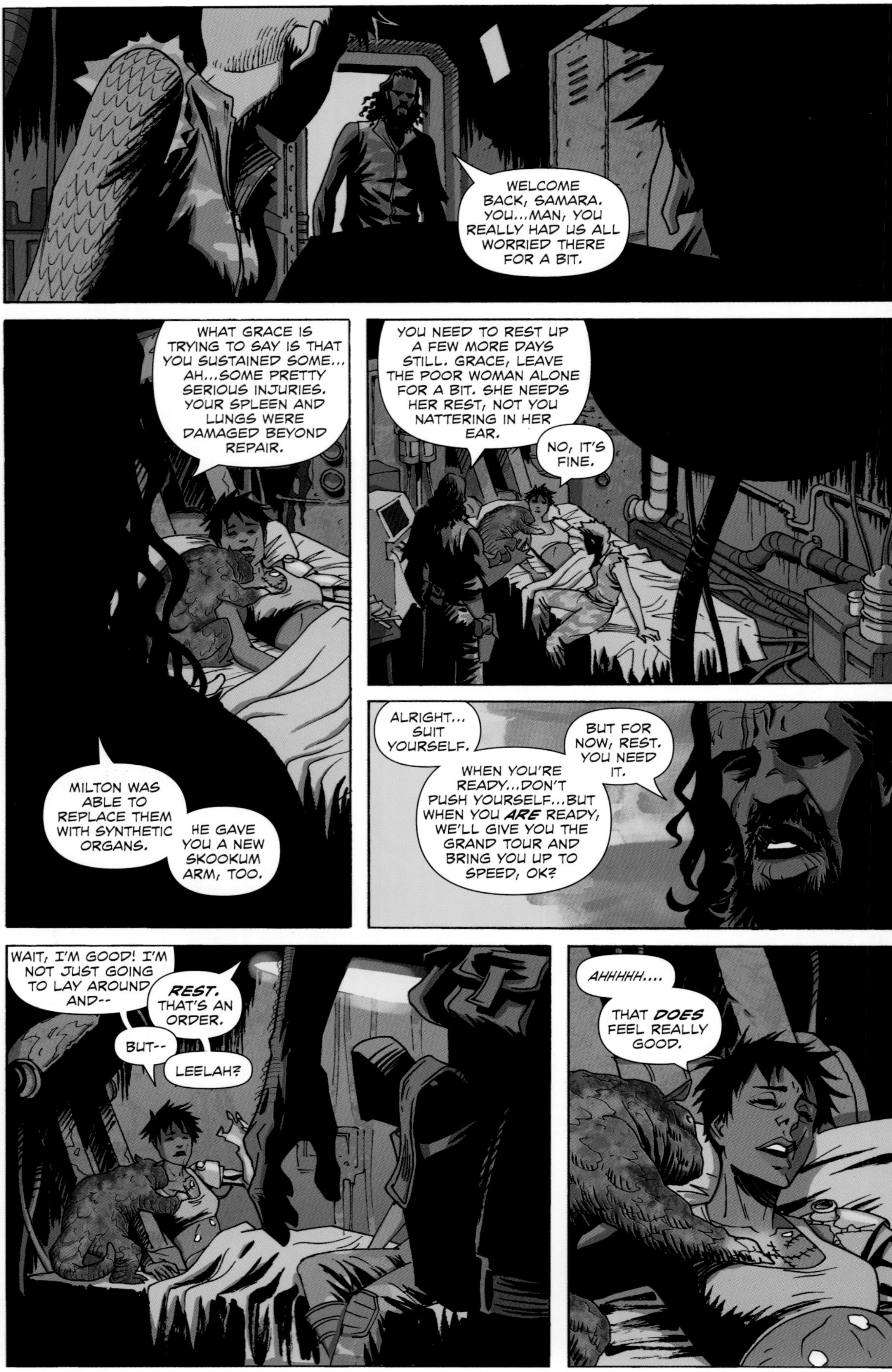
WELCOME BACK, SAMARA. YOU...MAN, YOU REALLY HAD US ALL WORRIED THERE FOR A BIT.
WHAT GRACE IS TRYING TO SAY IS THAT YOU SUSTAINED SOME... AH...SOME PRETTY SERIOUS INJURIES. YOUR SPLEEN AND LUNGS WERE DAMAGED BEYOND REPAIR.
MILTON WAS ABLE TO REPLACE THEM WITH SYNTHETIC ORGANS.
HE GAVE YOU A NEW SKOOKUM ARM, TOO.
YOU NEED TO REST UP A FEW MORE DAYS STILL. GRACE, LEAVE THE POOR WOMAN ALONE FOR A BIT. SHE NEEDS HER REST, NOT YOU NATTERING IN HER EAR.
NO, IT'S FINE.
ALRIGHT... SUIT YOURSELF.
WHEN YOU'RE READY...DON'T PUSH YOURSELF...BUT WHEN YOU *ARE* READY, WE'LL GIVE YOU THE GRAND TOUR AND BRING YOU UP TO SPEED, OK?
BUT FOR NOW, REST. YOU NEED IT.
WAIT, I'M GOOD! I'M NOT JUST GOING TO LAY AROUND AND--
REST. THAT'S AN ORDER.
BUT--
LEELAH?
AHHHHH....
THAT *DOES* FEEL REALLY GOOD.

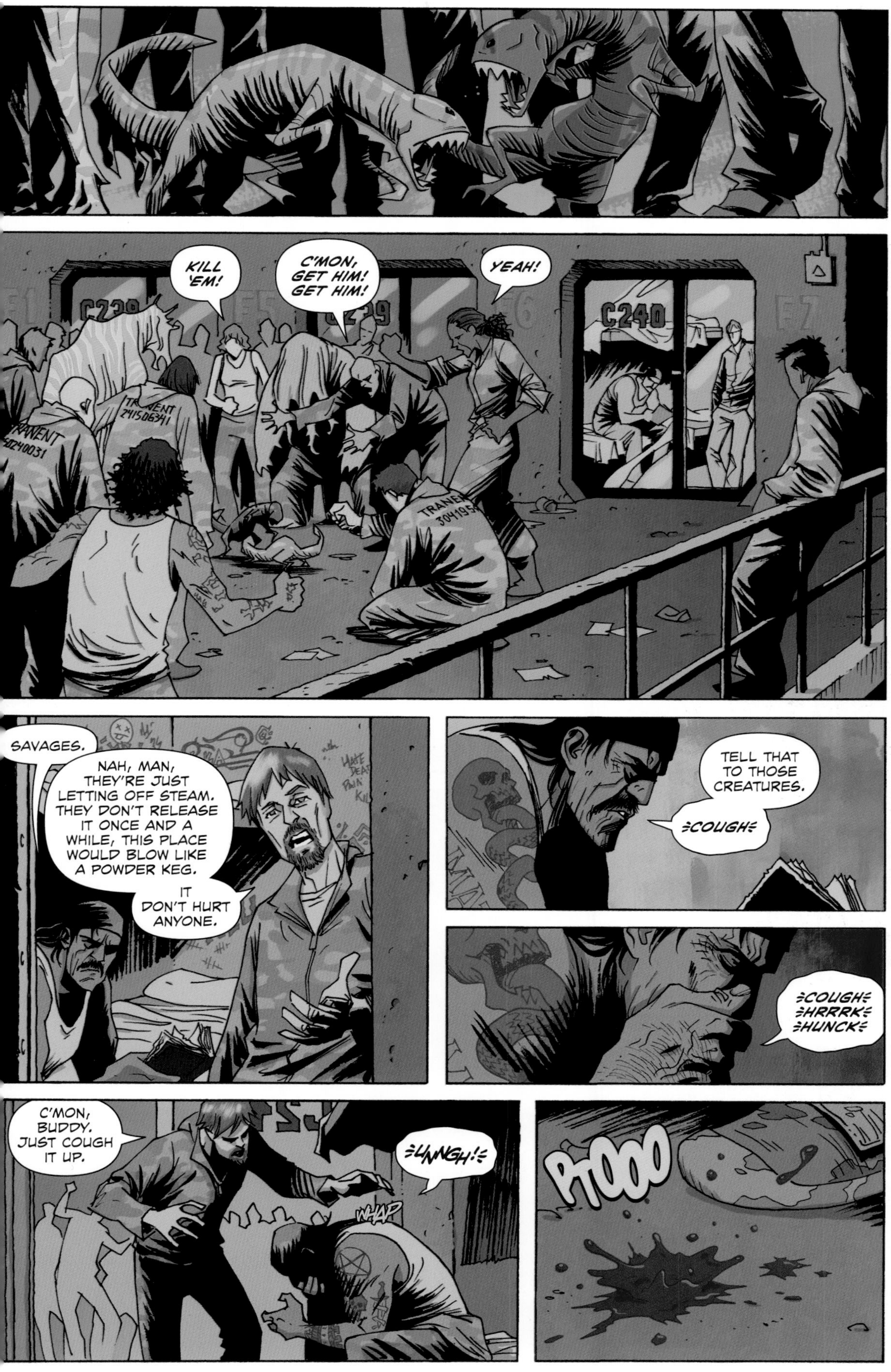
KILL 'EM!
C'MON, GET HIM! GET HIM!
YEAH!
C240
TRANENT 241506341
TRANENT 30240031
TRANENT 304195
SAVAGES.
NAH, MAN, THEY'RE JUST LETTING OFF STEAM. THEY DON'T RELEASE IT ONCE AND A WHILE, THIS PLACE WOULD BLOW LIKE A POWDER KEG.
IT DON'T HURT ANYONE.
TELL THAT TO THOSE CREATURES.
COUGH
COUGH HRRRK HUNCK
C'MON, BUDDY. JUST COUGH IT UP.
UNNGH!
WHAP
PTOOO

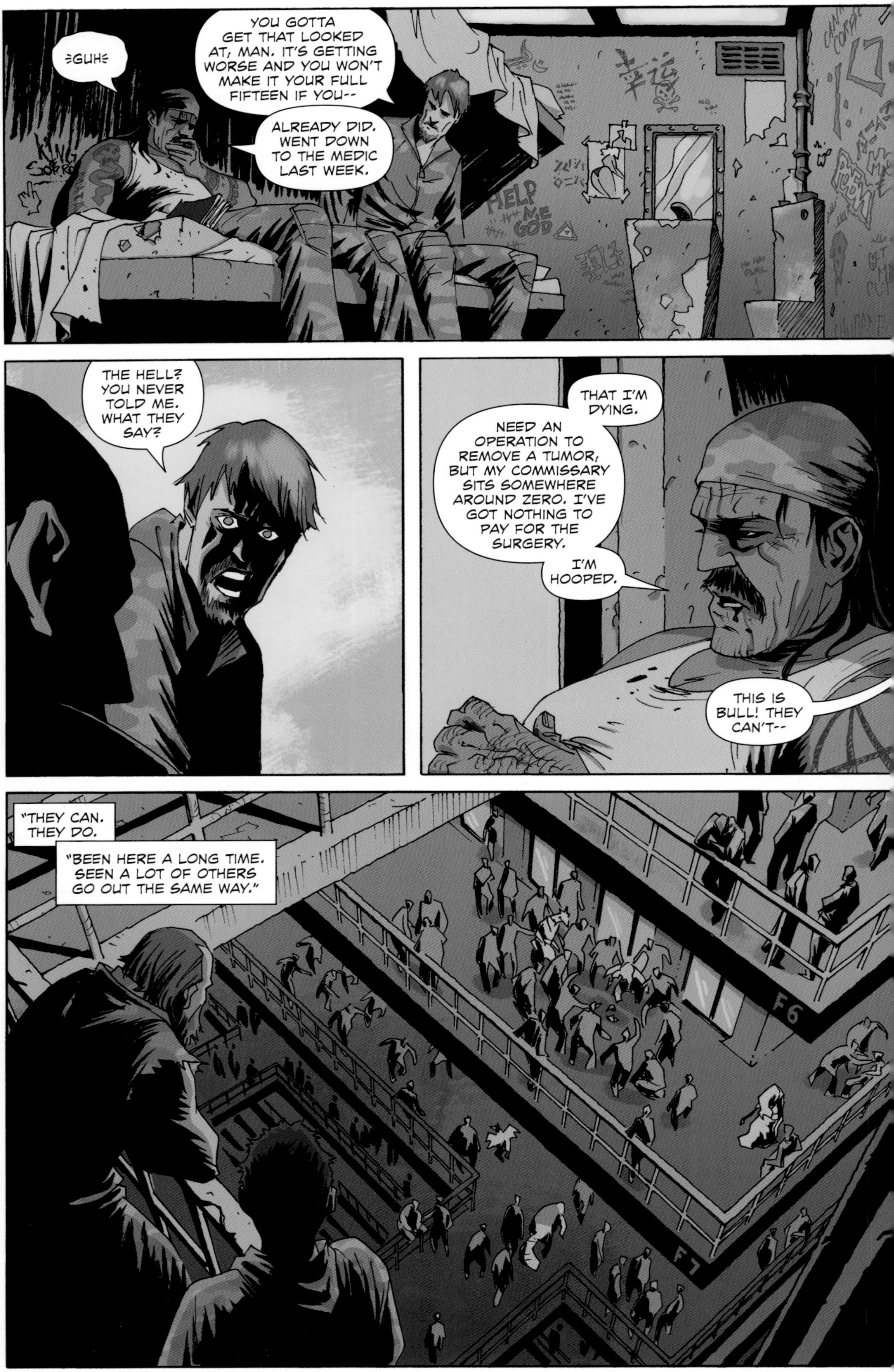

GUH
YOU GOTTA GET THAT LOOKED AT, MAN. IT'S GETTING WORSE AND YOU WON'T MAKE IT YOUR FULL FIFTEEN IF YOU--
ALREADY DID. WENT DOWN TO THE MEDIC LAST WEEK.
HELP ME GOD
THE HELL? YOU NEVER TOLD ME. WHAT THEY SAY?
THAT I'M DYING.
NEED AN OPERATION TO REMOVE A TUMOR, BUT MY COMMISSARY SITS SOMEWHERE AROUND ZERO. I'VE GOT NOTHING TO PAY FOR THE SURGERY.
I'M HOOPED.
THIS IS BULL! THEY CAN'T--
"THEY CAN. THEY DO.
"BEEN HERE A LONG TIME. SEEN A LOT OF OTHERS GO OUT THE SAME WAY."
F6

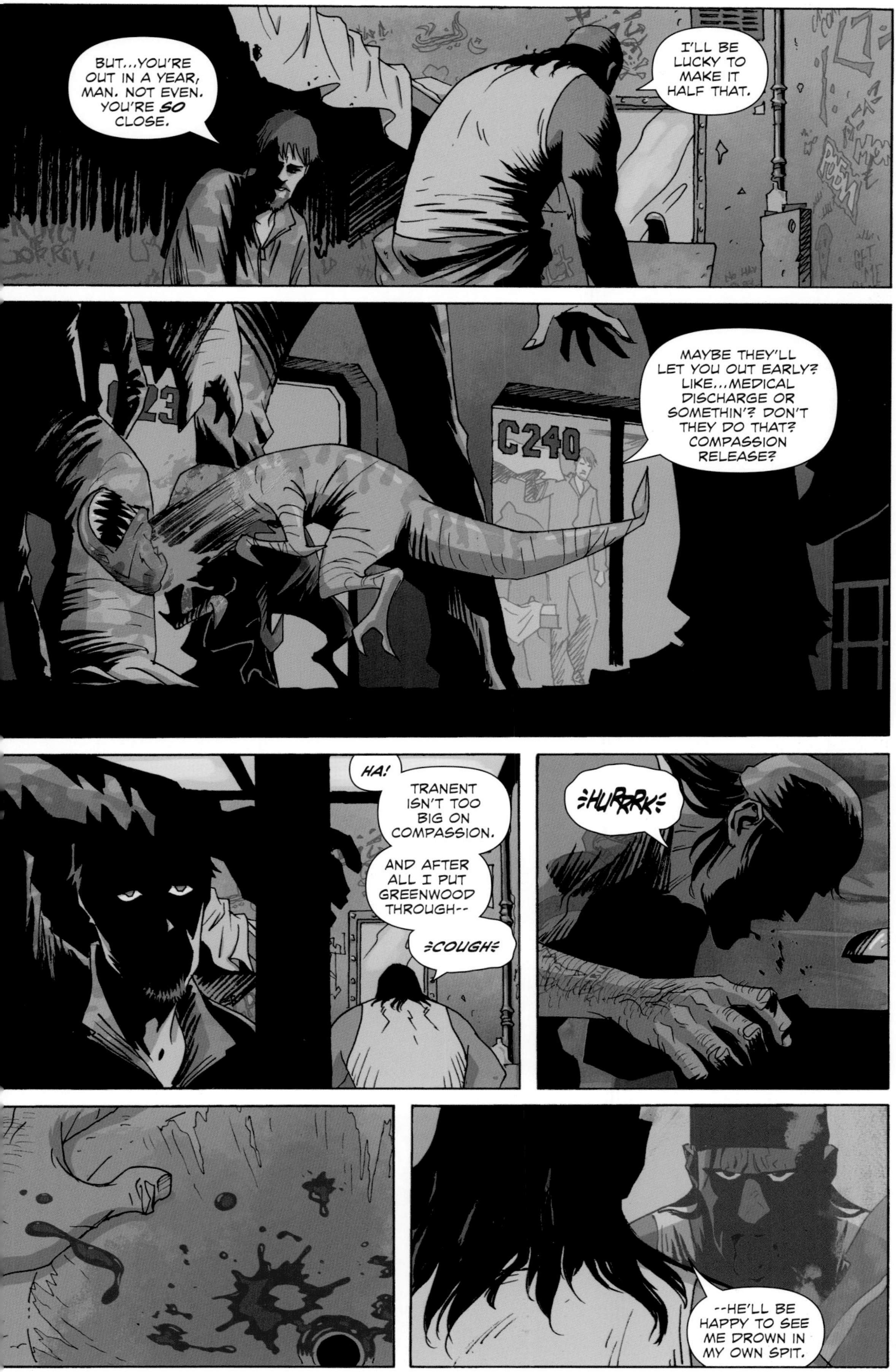
BUT...YOU'RE OUT IN A YEAR, MAN. NOT EVEN. YOU'RE *SO* CLOSE.
I'LL BE LUCKY TO MAKE IT HALF THAT.
MAYBE THEY'LL LET YOU OUT EARLY? LIKE...MEDICAL DISCHARGE OR SOMETHIN'? DON'T THEY DO THAT? COMPASSION RELEASE?
C240
HA!
TRANENT ISN'T TOO BIG ON COMPASSION.
AND AFTER ALL I PUT GREENWOOD THROUGH--
COUGH
HURRRK
--HE'LL BE HAPPY TO SEE ME DROWN IN MY OWN SPIT.

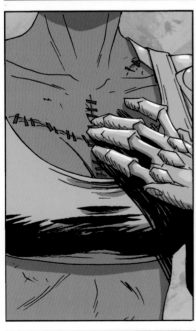

ARRRGGH!

SMASH

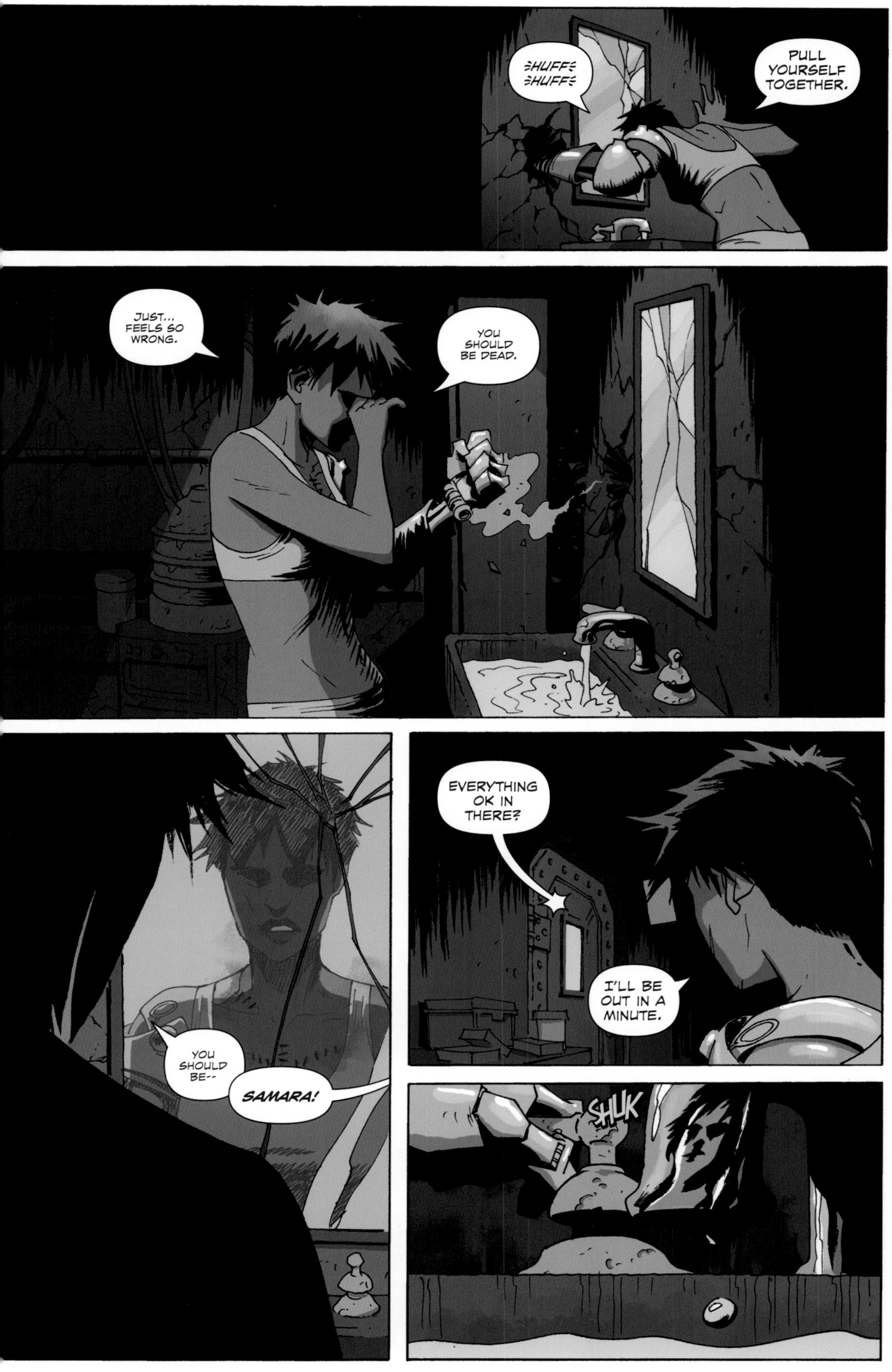

≈HUFF≈ ≈HUFF≈
PULL YOURSELF TOGETHER.
JUST... FEELS SO WRONG.
YOU SHOULD BE DEAD.
YOU SHOULD BE--
SAMARA!
EVERYTHING OK IN THERE?
I'LL BE OUT IN A MINUTE.
SHUK

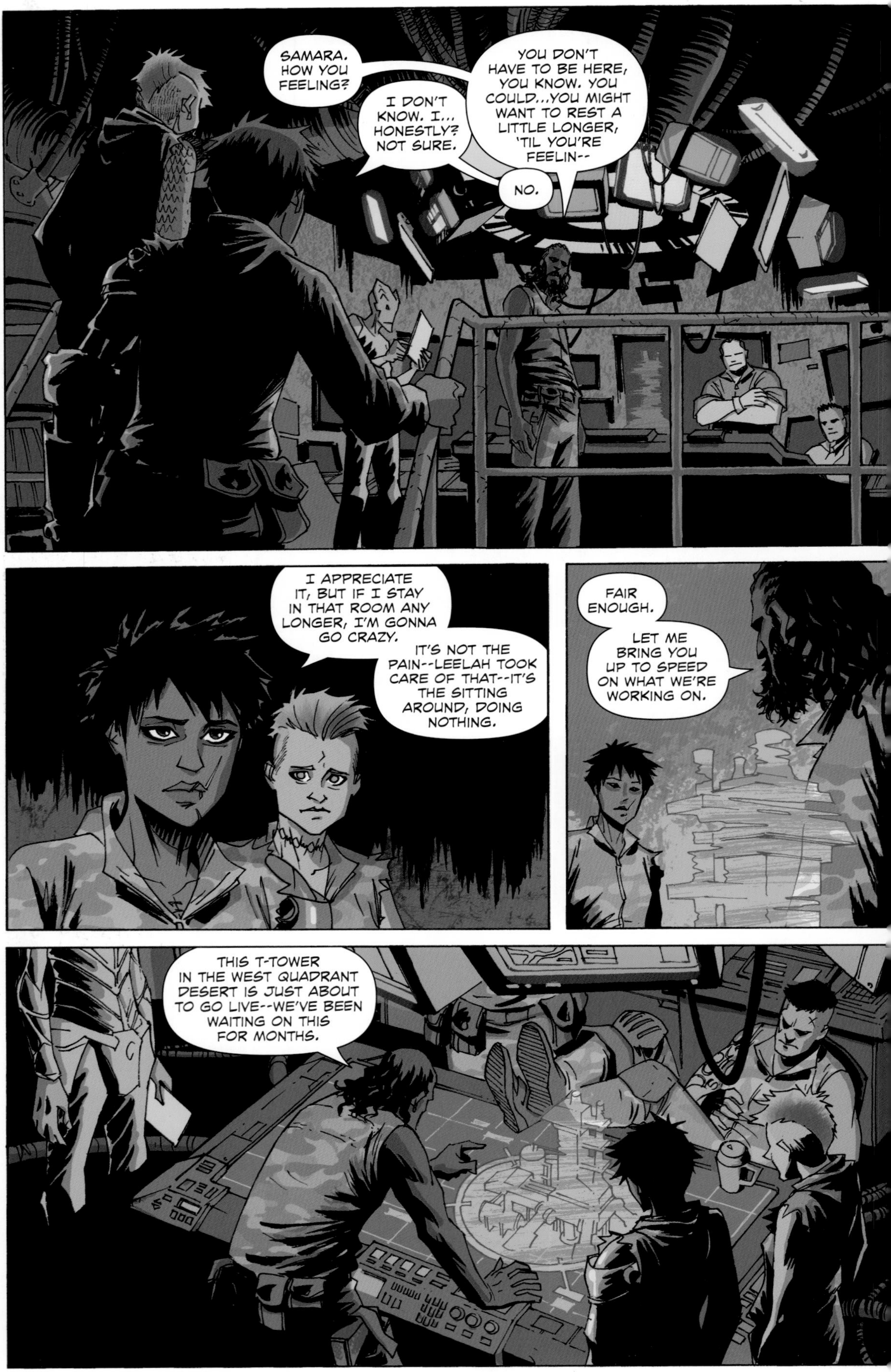
SAMARA. HOW YOU FEELING?
I DON'T KNOW. I... HONESTLY? NOT SURE.
YOU DON'T HAVE TO BE HERE, YOU KNOW. YOU COULD...YOU MIGHT WANT TO REST A LITTLE LONGER, 'TIL YOU'RE FEELIN--
NO.
I APPRECIATE IT, BUT IF I STAY IN THAT ROOM ANY LONGER, I'M GONNA GO CRAZY.
IT'S NOT THE PAIN--LEELAH TOOK CARE OF THAT--IT'S THE SITTING AROUND, DOING NOTHING.
FAIR ENOUGH.
LET ME BRING YOU UP TO SPEED ON WHAT WE'RE WORKING ON.
THIS T-TOWER IN THE WEST QUADRANT DESERT IS JUST ABOUT TO GO LIVE--WE'VE BEEN WAITING ON THIS FOR MONTHS.

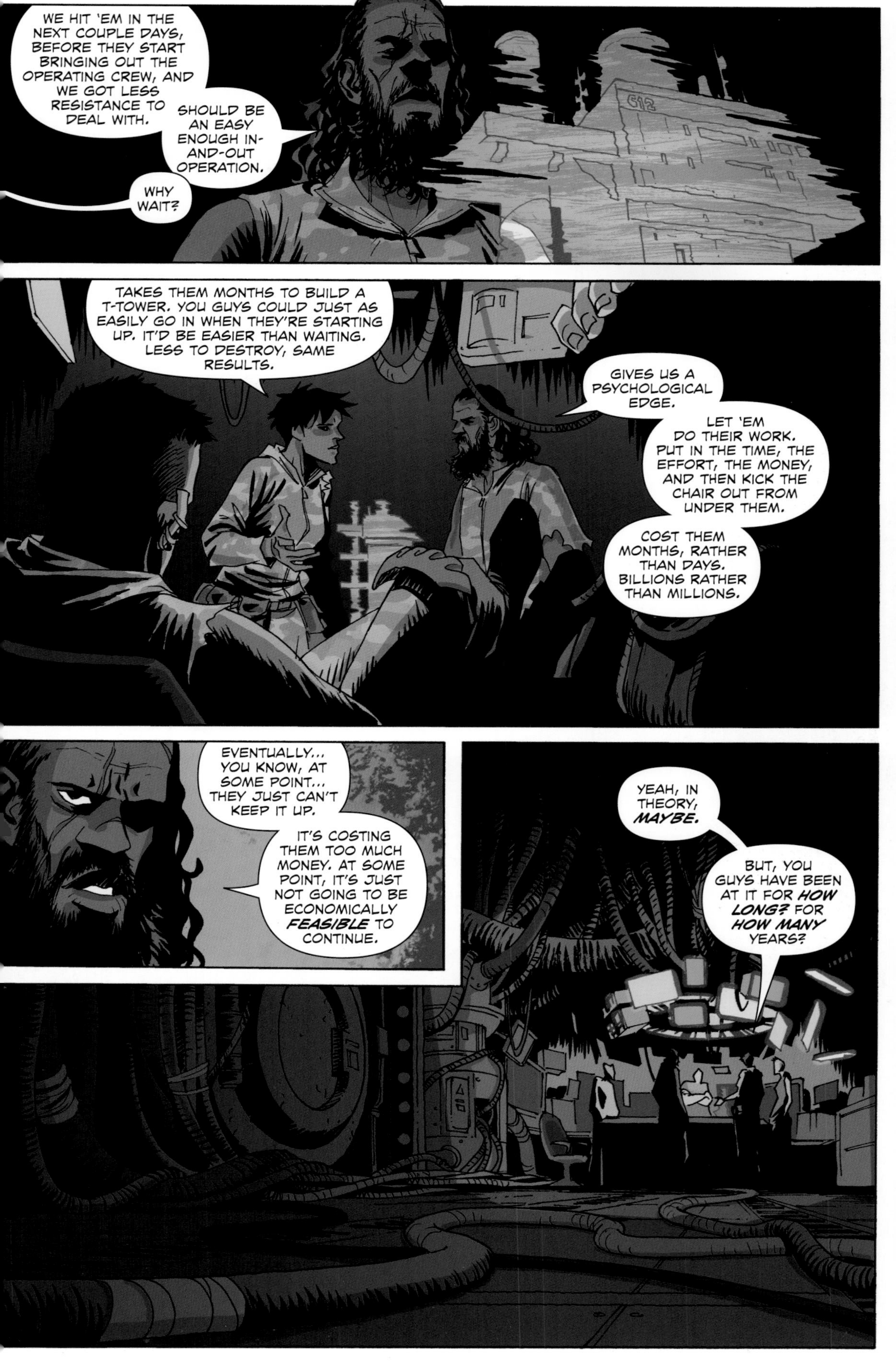
WE HIT 'EM IN THE NEXT COUPLE DAYS, BEFORE THEY START BRINGING OUT THE OPERATING CREW, AND WE GOT LESS RESISTANCE TO DEAL WITH.
SHOULD BE AN EASY ENOUGH IN-AND-OUT OPERATION.
WHY WAIT?
C12
TAKES THEM MONTHS TO BUILD A T-TOWER. YOU GUYS COULD JUST AS EASILY GO IN WHEN THEY'RE STARTING UP. IT'D BE EASIER THAN WAITING. LESS TO DESTROY, SAME RESULTS.
GIVES US A PSYCHOLOGICAL EDGE.
LET 'EM DO THEIR WORK. PUT IN THE TIME, THE EFFORT, THE MONEY, AND THEN KICK THE CHAIR OUT FROM UNDER THEM.
COST THEM MONTHS, RATHER THAN DAYS. BILLIONS RATHER THAN MILLIONS.
EVENTUALLY... YOU KNOW, AT SOME POINT... THEY JUST CAN'T KEEP IT UP.
IT'S COSTING THEM TOO MUCH MONEY. AT SOME POINT, IT'S JUST NOT GOING TO BE ECONOMICALLY *FEASIBLE* TO CONTINUE.
YEAH, IN THEORY, *MAYBE.*
BUT, YOU GUYS HAVE BEEN AT IT FOR *HOW LONG?* FOR *HOW MANY* YEARS?

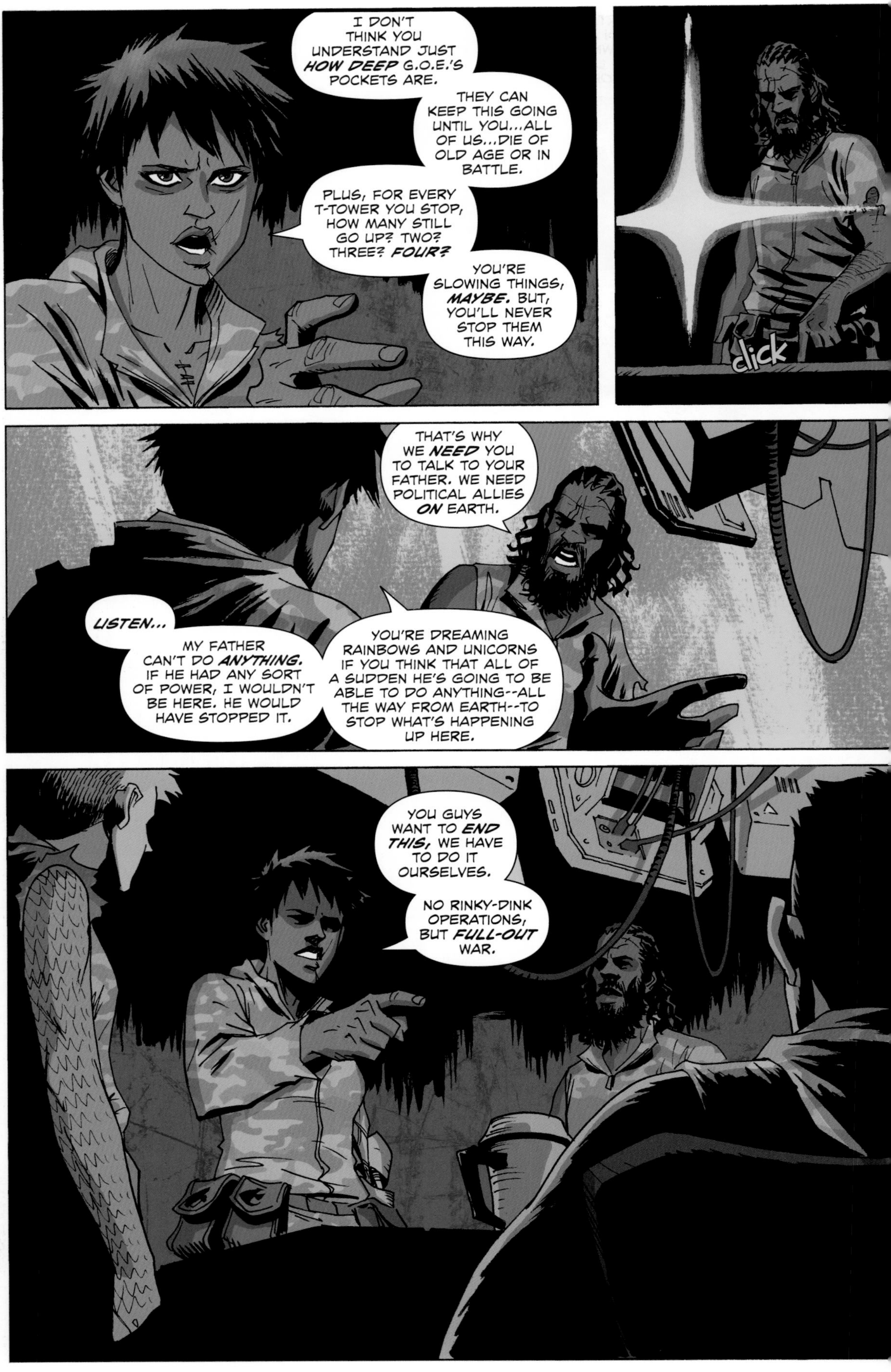
I DON'T THINK YOU UNDERSTAND JUST HOW DEEP G.O.E.'s POCKETS ARE.
THEY CAN KEEP THIS GOING UNTIL YOU...ALL OF US...DIE OF OLD AGE OR IN BATTLE.
PLUS, FOR EVERY T-TOWER YOU STOP, HOW MANY STILL GO UP? TWO? THREE? FOUR?
YOU'RE SLOWING THINGS, MAYBE. BUT, YOU'LL NEVER STOP THEM THIS WAY.
click
THAT'S WHY WE NEED YOU TO TALK TO YOUR FATHER. WE NEED POLITICAL ALLIES ON EARTH.
LISTEN...
MY FATHER CAN'T DO ANYTHING. IF HE HAD ANY SORT OF POWER, I WOULDN'T BE HERE. HE WOULD HAVE STOPPED IT.
YOU'RE DREAMING RAINBOWS AND UNICORNS IF YOU THINK THAT ALL OF A SUDDEN HE'S GOING TO BE ABLE TO DO ANYTHING--ALL THE WAY FROM EARTH--TO STOP WHAT'S HAPPENING UP HERE.
YOU GUYS WANT TO END THIS, WE HAVE TO DO IT OURSELVES.
NO RINKY-DINK OPERATIONS, BUT FULL-OUT WAR.

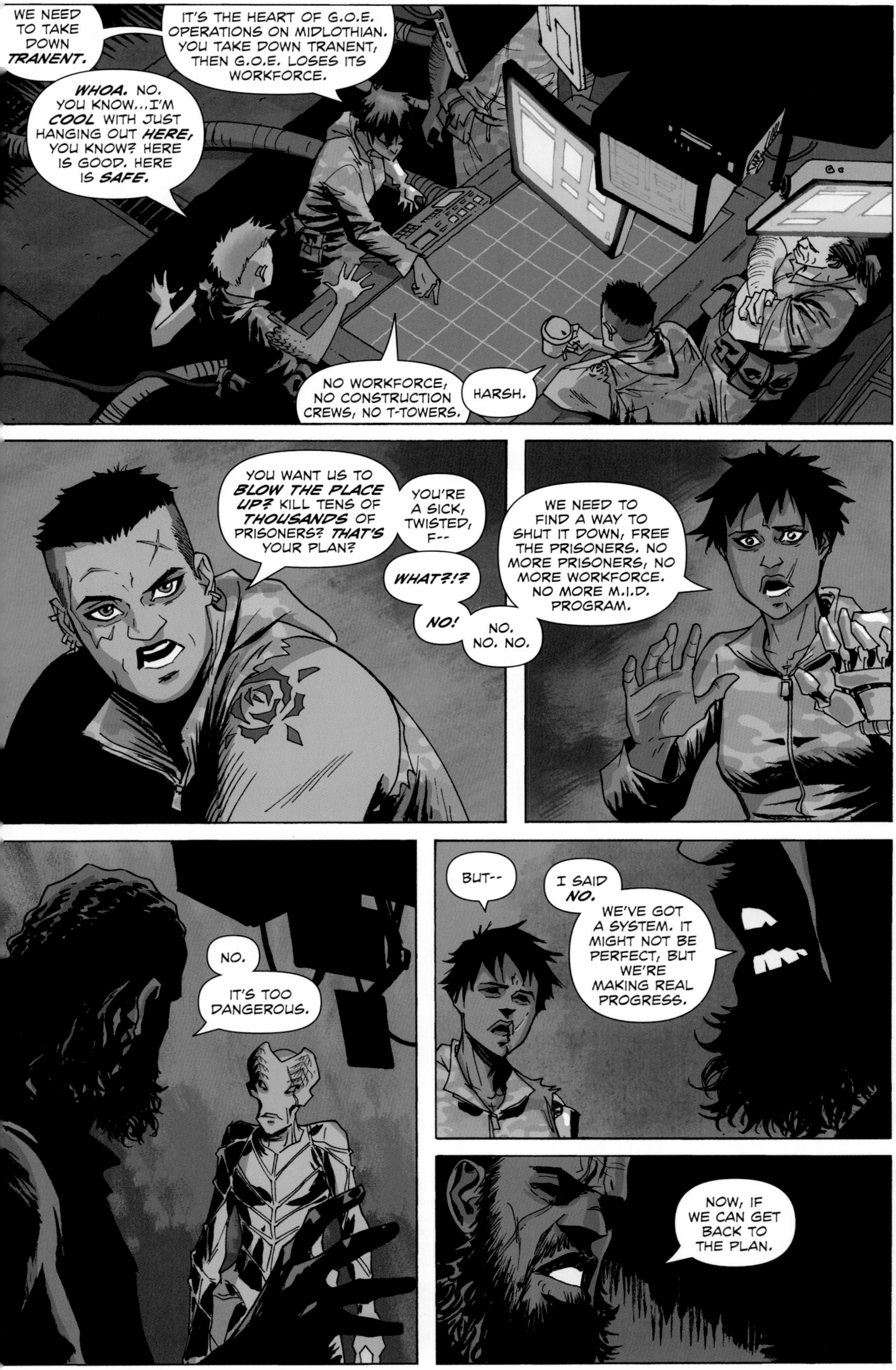
WE NEED TO TAKE DOWN TRANENT.
IT'S THE HEART OF G.O.E. OPERATIONS ON MIDLOTHIAN. YOU TAKE DOWN TRANENT, THEN G.O.E. LOSES ITS WORKFORCE.
WHOA. NO. YOU KNOW...I'M COOL WITH JUST HANGING OUT HERE, YOU KNOW? HERE IS GOOD. HERE IS SAFE.
NO WORKFORCE, NO CONSTRUCTION CREWS, NO T-TOWERS.
HARSH.
YOU WANT US TO BLOW THE PLACE UP? KILL TENS OF THOUSANDS OF PRISONERS? THAT'S YOUR PLAN?
YOU'RE A SICK, TWISTED, F--
WHAT?!?
NO!
NO. NO. NO.
WE NEED TO FIND A WAY TO SHUT IT DOWN, FREE THE PRISONERS. NO MORE PRISONERS, NO MORE WORKFORCE. NO MORE M.I.D. PROGRAM.
NO.
IT'S TOO DANGEROUS.
BUT--
I SAID NO.
WE'VE GOT A SYSTEM. IT MIGHT NOT BE PERFECT, BUT WE'RE MAKING REAL PROGRESS.
NOW, IF WE CAN GET BACK TO THE PLAN.

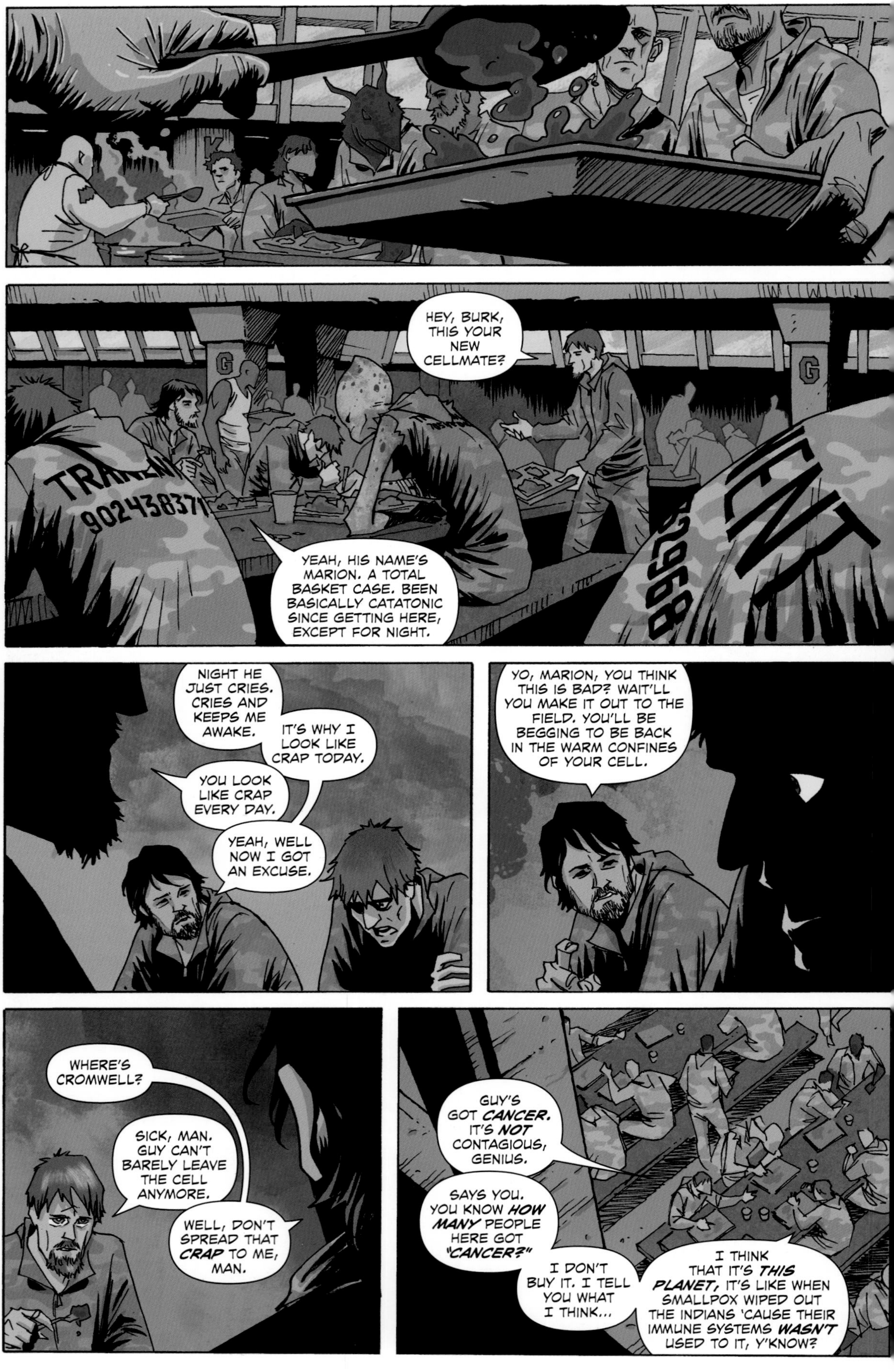
TRANE
902438371
HEY, BURK, THIS YOUR NEW CELLMATE?
YEAH, HIS NAME'S MARION. A TOTAL BASKET CASE. BEEN BASICALLY CATATONIC SINCE GETTING HERE, EXCEPT FOR NIGHT.
NIGHT HE JUST CRIES. CRIES AND KEEPS ME AWAKE.
IT'S WHY I LOOK LIKE CRAP TODAY.
YOU LOOK LIKE CRAP EVERY DAY.
YEAH, WELL NOW I GOT AN EXCUSE.
YO, MARION, YOU THINK THIS IS BAD? WAIT'LL YOU MAKE IT OUT TO THE FIELD. YOU'LL BE BEGGING TO BE BACK IN THE WARM CONFINES OF YOUR CELL.
WHERE'S CROMWELL?
SICK, MAN. GUY CAN'T BARELY LEAVE THE CELL ANYMORE.
WELL, DON'T SPREAD THAT *CRAP* TO ME, MAN.
GUY'S GOT *CANCER.* IT'S *NOT* CONTAGIOUS, GENIUS.
SAYS YOU. YOU KNOW *HOW MANY* PEOPLE HERE GOT *"CANCER?"*
I DON'T BUY IT. I TELL YOU WHAT I THINK...
I THINK THAT IT'S *THIS PLANET,* IT'S LIKE WHEN SMALLPOX WIPED OUT THE INDIANS 'CAUSE THEIR IMMUNE SYSTEMS *WASN'T* USED TO IT, Y'KNOW?

WHAT I'M SAYING IS THAT WE AIN'T USED TO THIS. OUR BODIES, I MEAN. WE AIN'T GOT THE *IMMUNITY*. WE'RE CATCHING SOME SORT OF MIDLOTHIAN *MEGA FLU* AND IT'S KILLIN' US ALL.

HELL, I BET THEY DON'T LET *NONE OF US* GO HOME, OTHERWISE WE JUST BRING IT BACK WITH US.

OR, WHO KNOWS...MAYBE THEY WILL. LET US *SPREAD* IT AROUND THE POOR SECTORS OF EARTH, WIPE 'EM *ALL* OUT.

THAT COURSE OF ACTION SOUNDS ACCEPTABLE TO ME. MY LIFE WOULD MOST DEFINITELY BE MUCH IMPROVED IF IT WERE FLUSHED OF HUMANS.

I LOVE YOU TOO, MONCK.

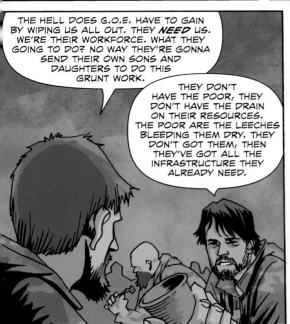

THE HELL DOES G.O.E. HAVE TO GAIN BY WIPING US ALL OUT. THEY *NEED* US. WE'RE THEIR WORKFORCE. WHAT THEY GOING TO DO? NO WAY THEY'RE GONNA SEND THEIR OWN SONS AND DAUGHTERS TO DO THIS GRUNT WORK.

THEY DON'T HAVE THE POOR, THEY DON'T HAVE THE DRAIN ON THEIR RESOURCES. THE POOR ARE THE LEECHES BLEEDING THEM DRY. THEY DON'T GOT THEM, THEN THEY'VE GOT ALL THE INFRASTRUCTURE THEY ALREADY NEED.

YOU HUMANS REALLY ARE THE WORST. YOUR KIND HAS NO HONOR.

IT'S TRUE. WE'RE AWFUL.

I JUST WANT TO GO HOME.

SHUT UP, MARION.

ATTENTION. THIS IS WARDEN GREENWOOD WITH AN IMPORTANT MESSAGE...

ATTENTION

ATTENTION

ATTENTION

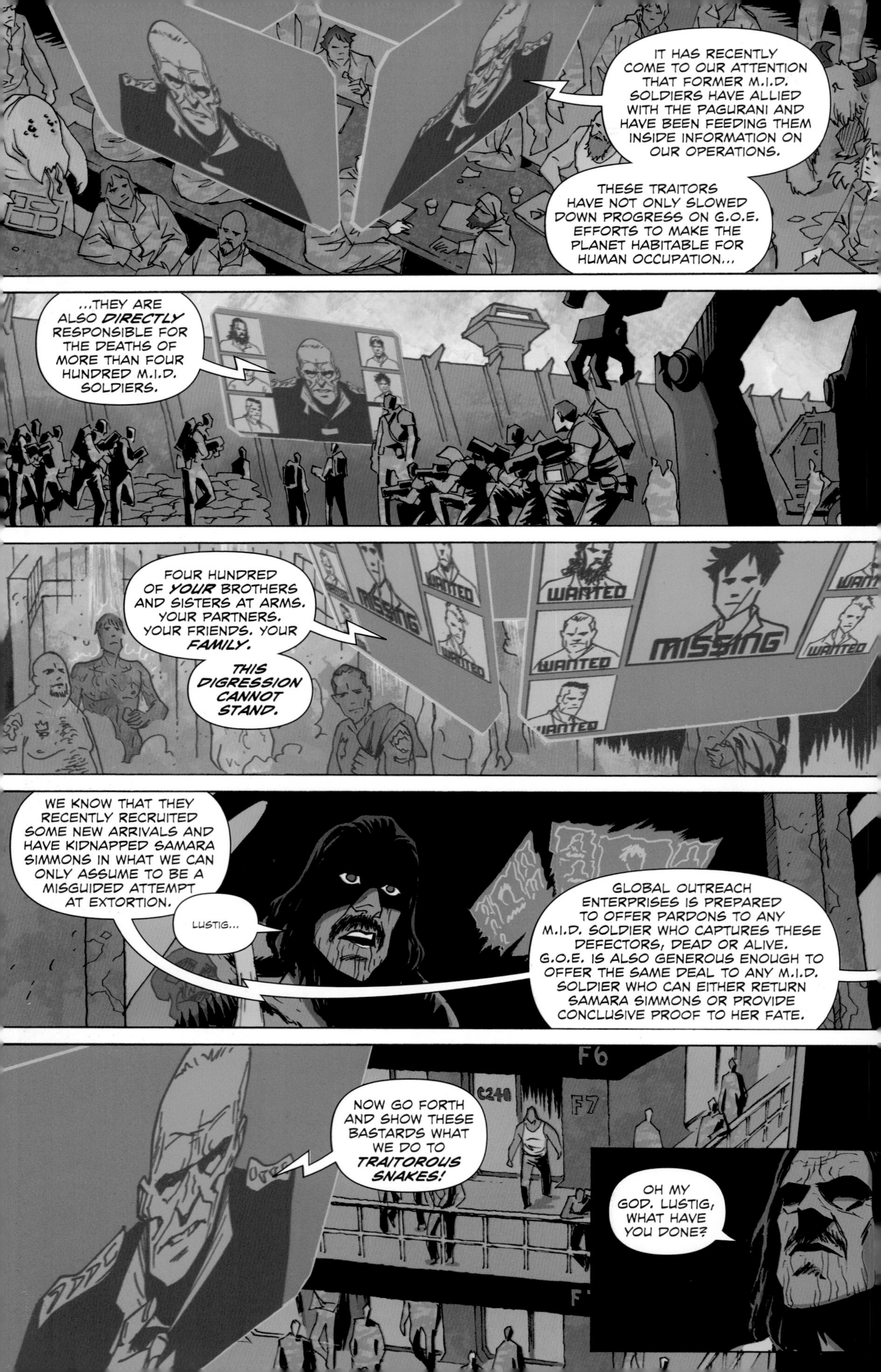
IT HAS RECENTLY COME TO OUR ATTENTION THAT FORMER M.I.D. SOLDIERS HAVE ALLIED WITH THE PAGURANI AND HAVE BEEN FEEDING THEM INSIDE INFORMATION ON OUR OPERATIONS.
THESE TRAITORS HAVE NOT ONLY SLOWED DOWN PROGRESS ON G.O.E. EFFORTS TO MAKE THE PLANET HABITABLE FOR HUMAN OCCUPATION...
...THEY ARE ALSO *DIRECTLY* RESPONSIBLE FOR THE DEATHS OF MORE THAN FOUR HUNDRED M.I.D. SOLDIERS.
FOUR HUNDRED OF *YOUR* BROTHERS AND SISTERS AT ARMS. YOUR PARTNERS. YOUR FRIENDS. YOUR *FAMILY.*
THIS DIGRESSION CANNOT STAND.
MISSING
WANTED
WANTED
WANTED
MISSING
WANTED
WANTED
WANTED
WE KNOW THAT THEY RECENTLY RECRUITED SOME NEW ARRIVALS AND HAVE KIDNAPPED SAMARA SIMMONS IN WHAT WE CAN ONLY ASSUME TO BE A MISGUIDED ATTEMPT AT EXTORTION.
LUSTIG...
GLOBAL OUTREACH ENTERPRISES IS PREPARED TO OFFER PARDONS TO ANY M.I.D. SOLDIER WHO CAPTURES THESE DEFECTORS, DEAD OR ALIVE. G.O.E. IS ALSO GENEROUS ENOUGH TO OFFER THE SAME DEAL TO ANY M.I.D. SOLDIER WHO CAN EITHER RETURN SAMARA SIMMONS OR PROVIDE CONCLUSIVE PROOF TO HER FATE.
F6
C240
F7
NOW GO FORTH AND SHOW THESE BASTARDS WHAT WE DO TO *TRAITOROUS SNAKES!*
OH MY GOD. LUSTIG, WHAT HAVE YOU DONE?

YOU'RE THINKING ABOUT IT, AREN'T YOU?

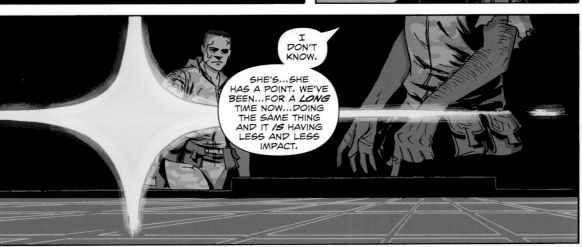

I DON'T KNOW.

SHE'S...SHE HAS A POINT. WE'VE BEEN...FOR A *LONG* TIME NOW...DOING THE SAME THING AND IT *IS* HAVING LESS AND LESS IMPACT.

MAYBE, Y'KNOW...MAYBE IT'S TIME WE TRY SOMETHING NEW. A DIFFERENT APPROACH.

WHAT DO *YOU* THINK?

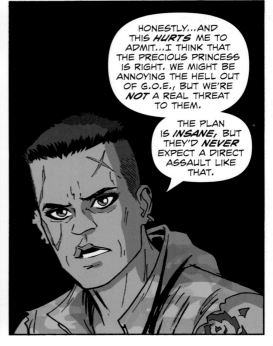

HONESTLY...AND THIS *HURTS* ME TO ADMIT...I THINK THAT THE PRECIOUS PRINCESS IS RIGHT. WE MIGHT BE ANNOYING THE HELL OUT OF G.O.E., BUT WE'RE *NOT* A REAL THREAT TO THEM.

THE PLAN IS *INSANE*, BUT THEY'D *NEVER* EXPECT A DIRECT ASSAULT LIKE THAT.

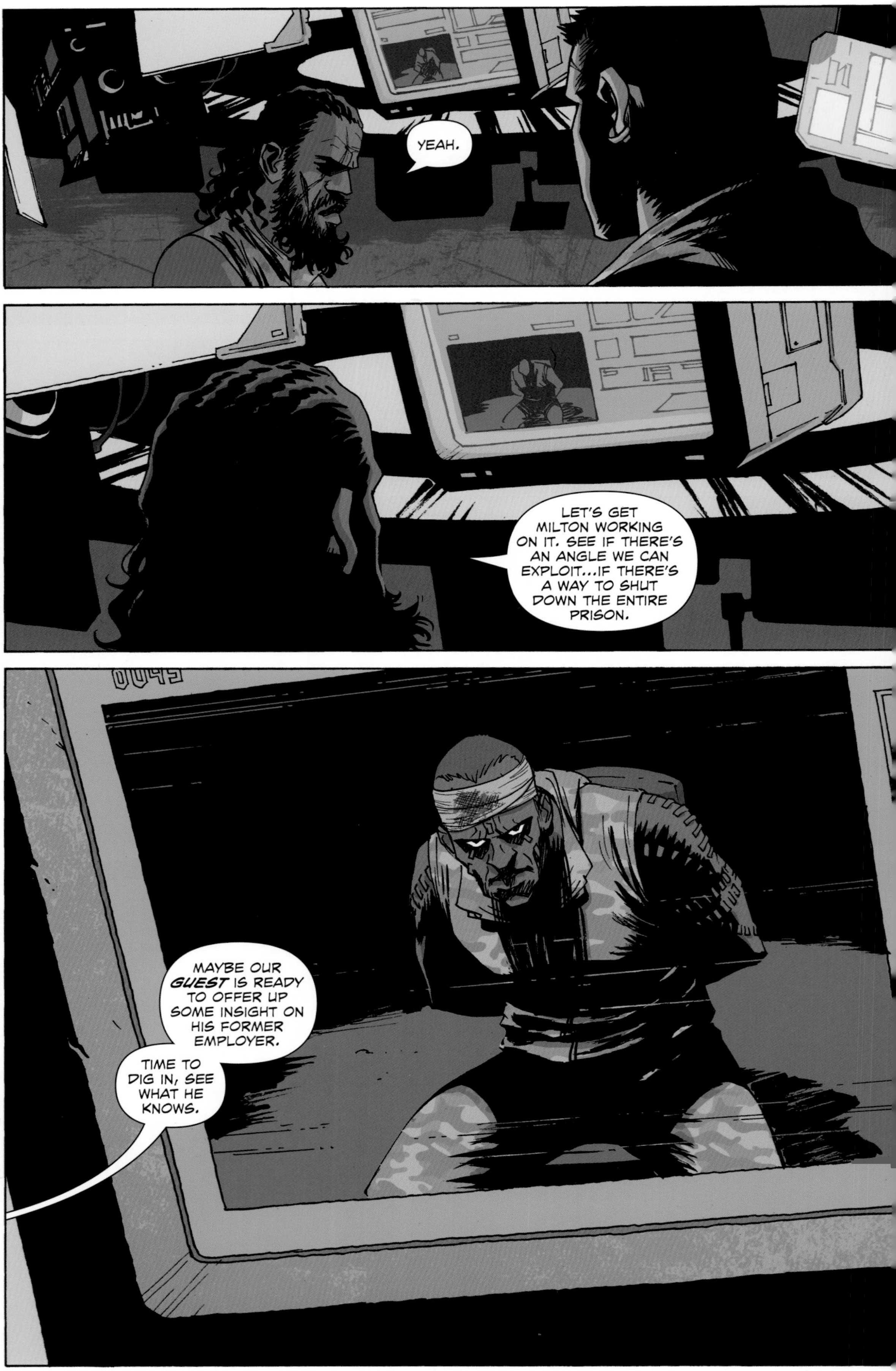
YEAH.
LET'S GET MILTON WORKING ON IT. SEE IF THERE'S AN ANGLE WE CAN EXPLOIT...IF THERE'S A WAY TO SHUT DOWN THE ENTIRE PRISON.
0045
MAYBE OUR *GUEST* IS READY TO OFFER UP SOME INSIGHT ON HIS FORMER EMPLOYER.
TIME TO DIG IN, SEE WHAT HE KNOWS.

ISSUE 005 COVER
DAMIAN COUCIERO
WITH COLORS BY **JORDAN BOYD**

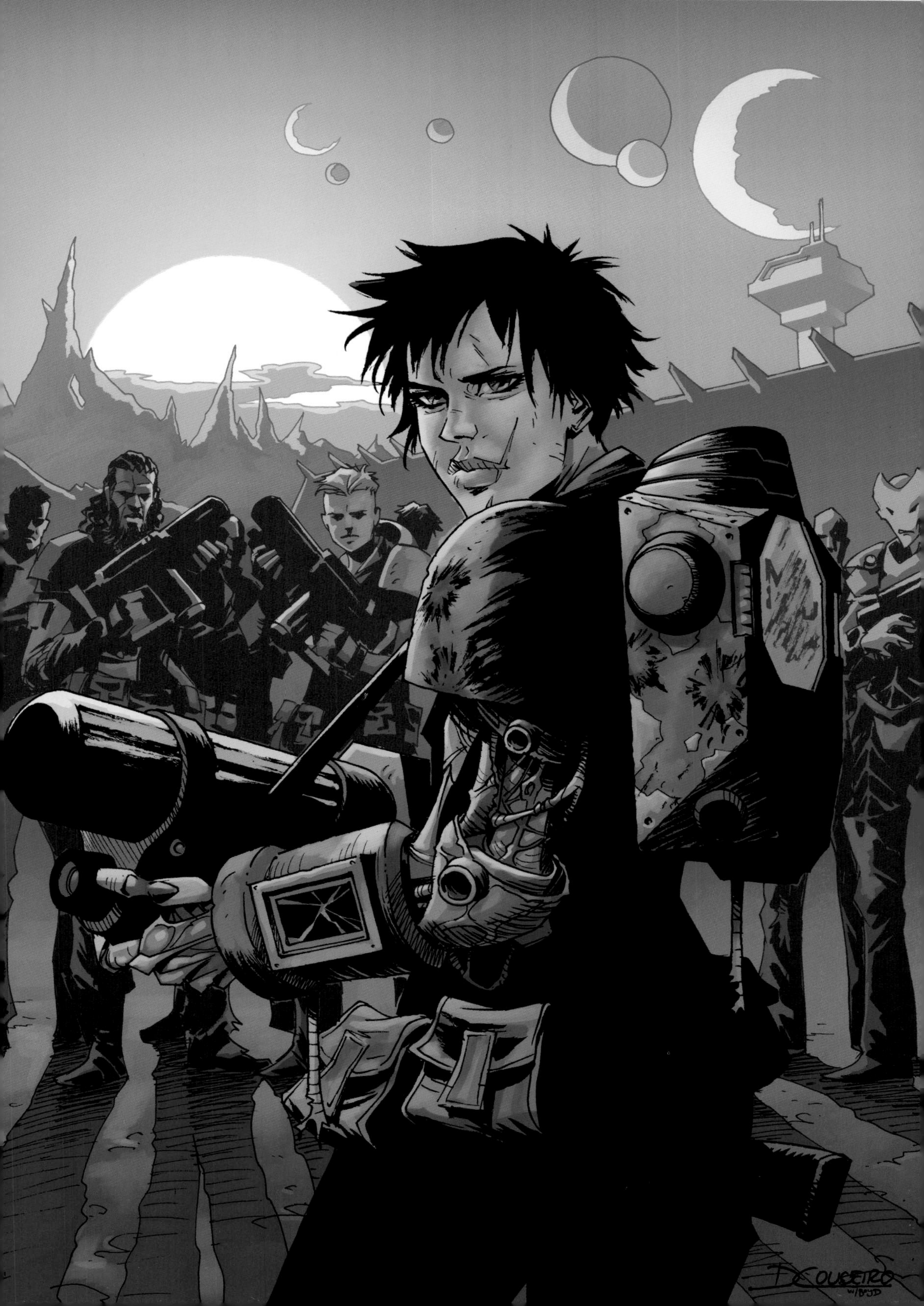

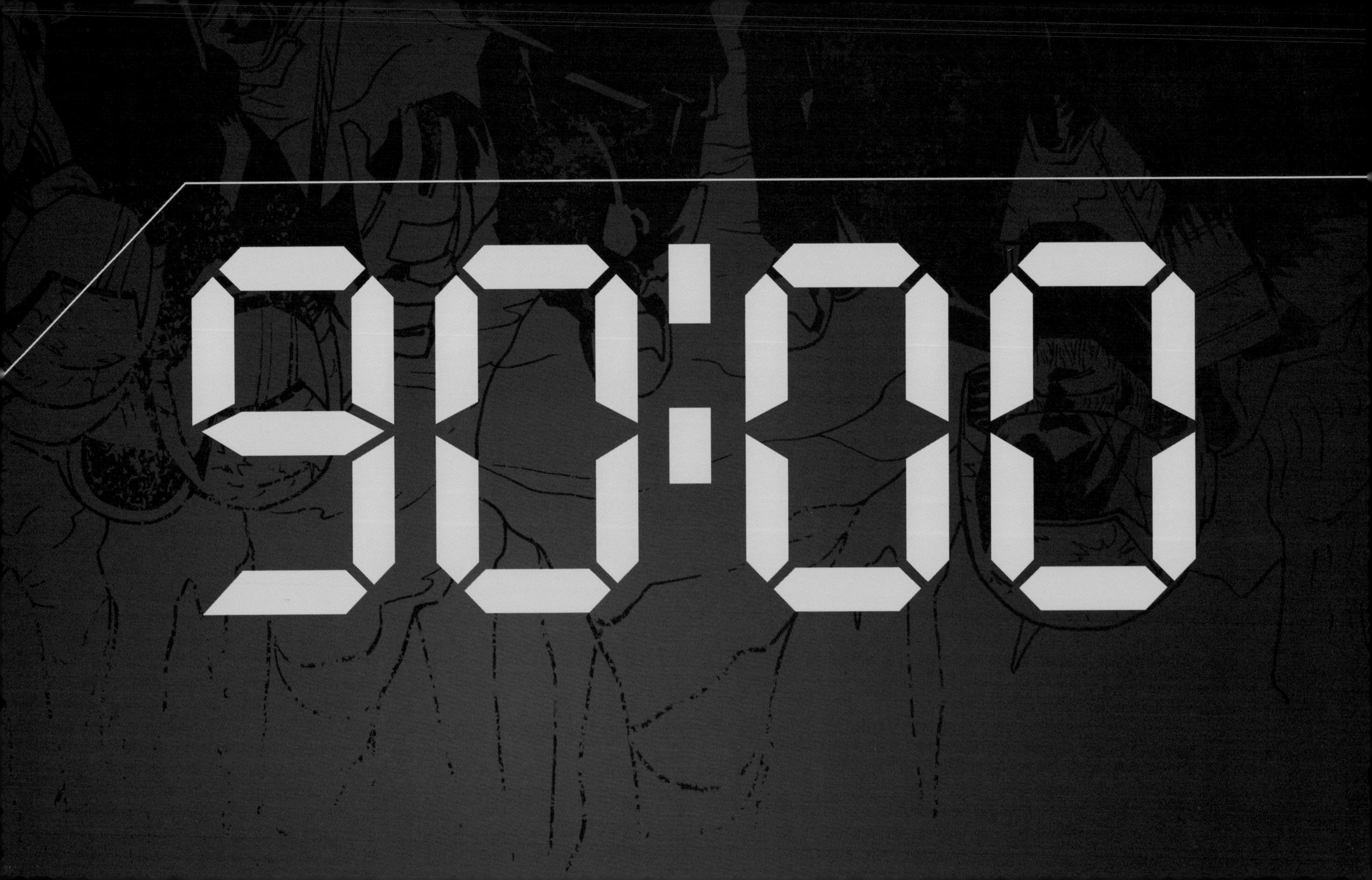
90:00

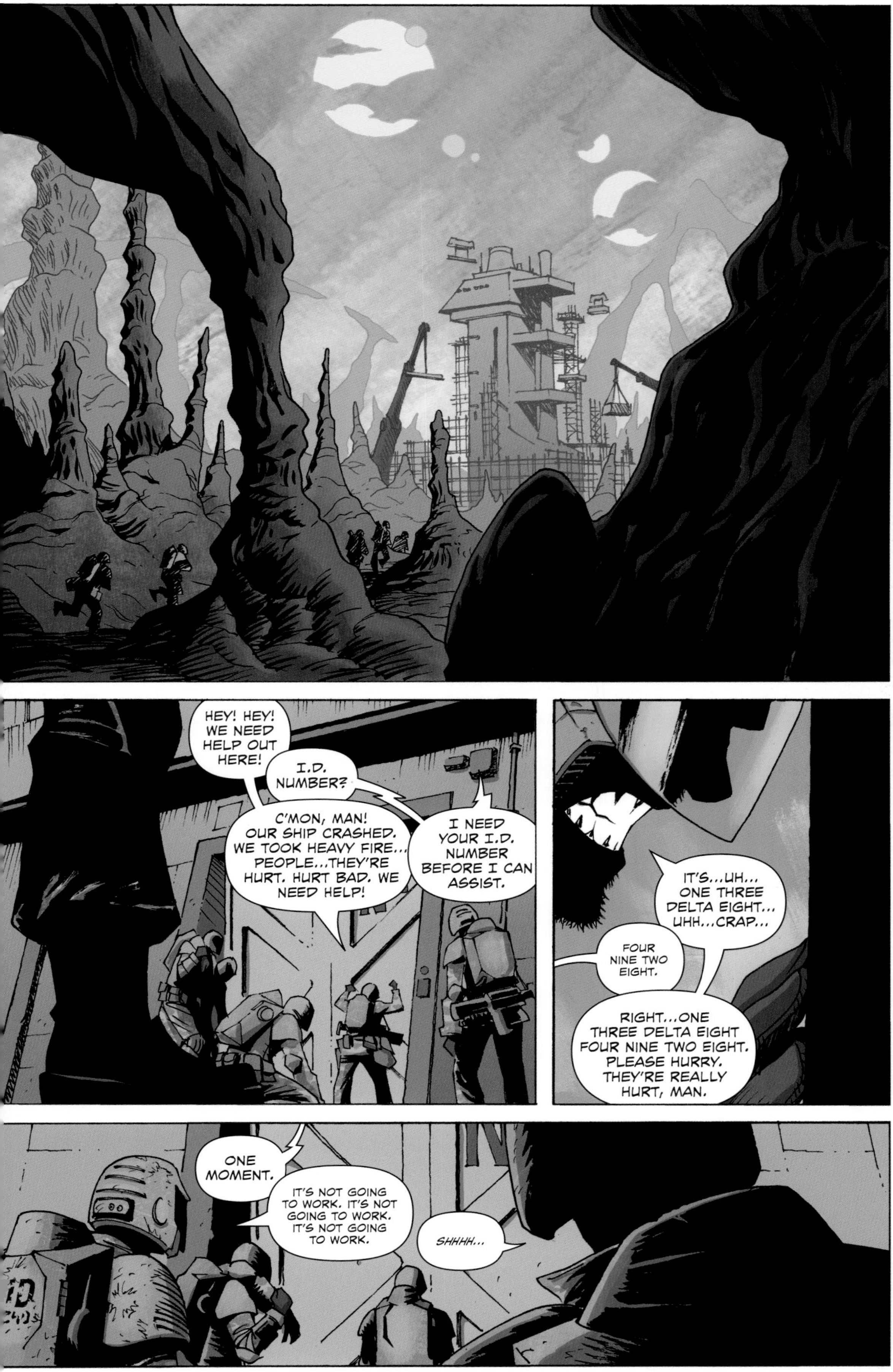
HEY! HEY! WE NEED HELP OUT HERE!
I.D. NUMBER?
C'MON, MAN! OUR SHIP CRASHED. WE TOOK HEAVY FIRE... PEOPLE...THEY'RE HURT. HURT BAD. WE NEED HELP!
I NEED YOUR I.D. NUMBER BEFORE I CAN ASSIST.
IT'S...UH... ONE THREE DELTA EIGHT... UHH...CRAP...
FOUR NINE TWO EIGHT.
RIGHT...ONE THREE DELTA EIGHT FOUR NINE TWO EIGHT. PLEASE HURRY. THEY'RE REALLY HURT, MAN.
ONE MOMENT.
IT'S NOT GOING TO WORK. IT'S NOT GOING TO WORK. IT'S NOT GOING TO WORK.
SHHHH...

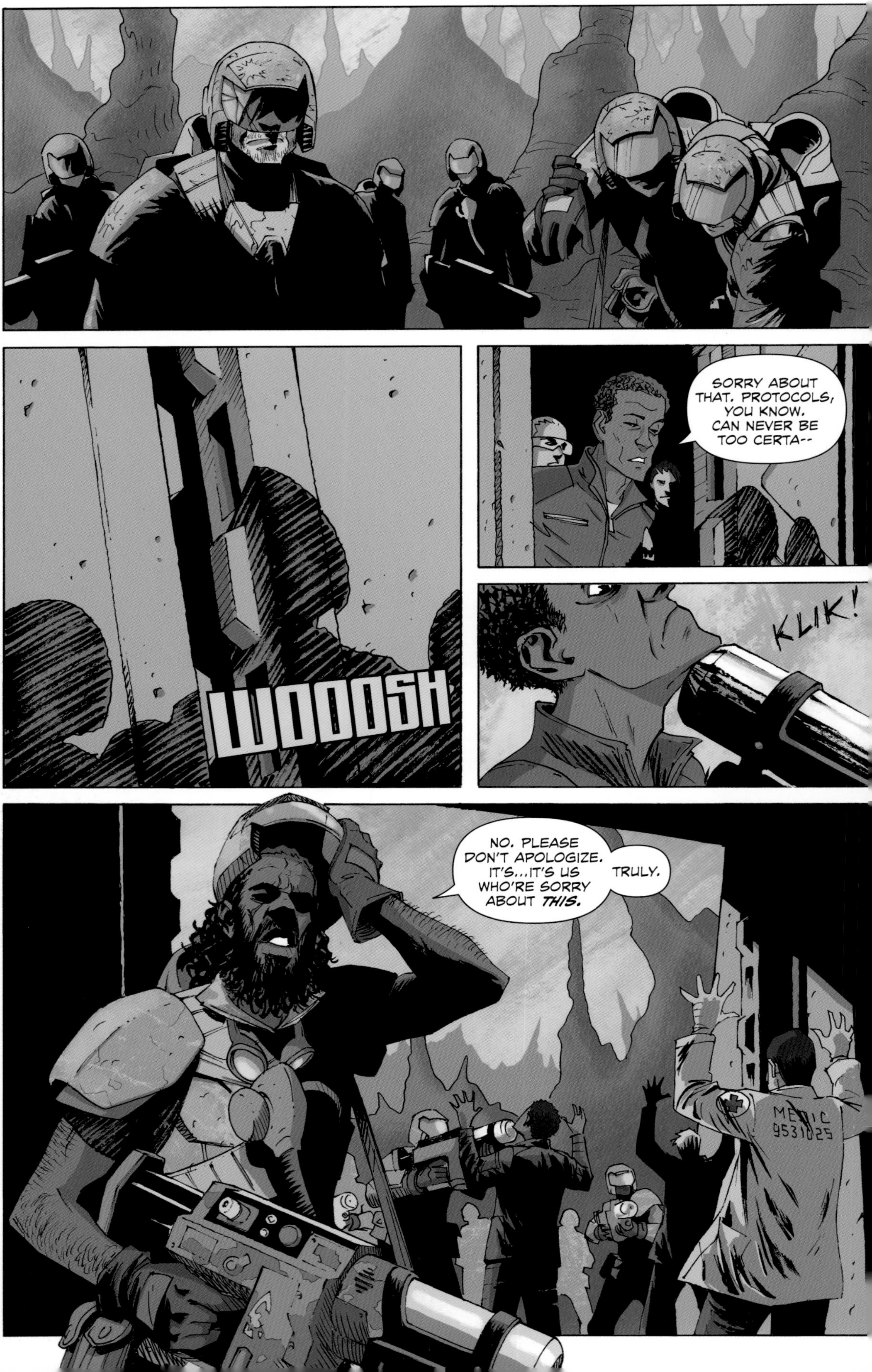
WOOOSH
SORRY ABOUT THAT. PROTOCOLS, YOU KNOW. CAN NEVER BE TOO CERTA--
KLIK!
NO. PLEASE DON'T APOLOGIZE. IT'S...IT'S US WHO'RE SORRY ABOUT *THIS.*
TRULY.
MEDIC
9531025

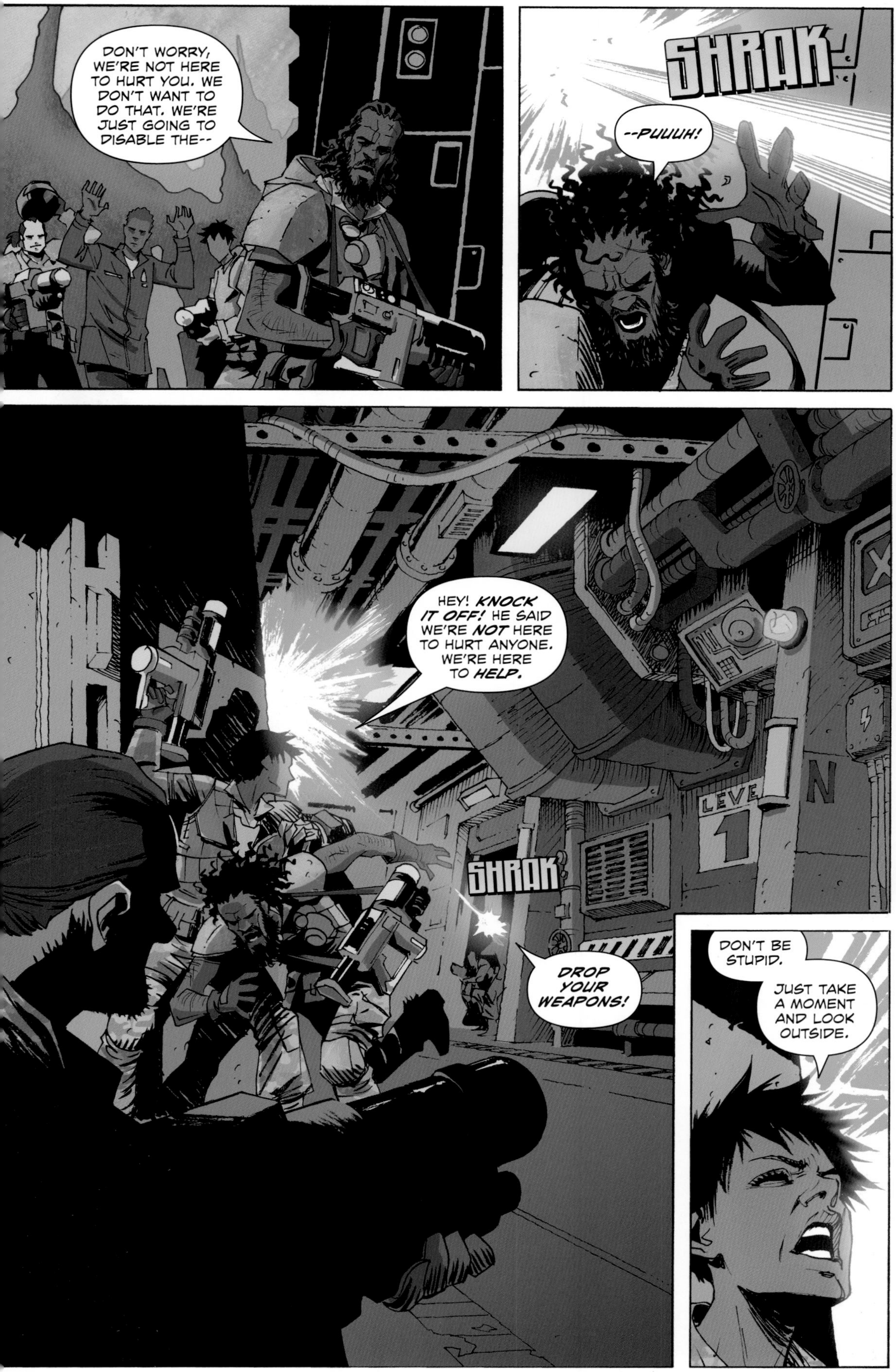
DON'T WORRY, WE'RE NOT HERE TO HURT YOU. WE DON'T WANT TO DO THAT. WE'RE JUST GOING TO DISABLE THE--
SHRAK
--PUUUH!
HEY! KNOCK IT OFF! HE SAID WE'RE NOT HERE TO HURT ANYONE. WE'RE HERE TO HELP.
LEVE
1
N
SHRAK
DROP YOUR WEAPONS!
DON'T BE STUPID.
JUST TAKE A MOMENT AND LOOK OUTSIDE.

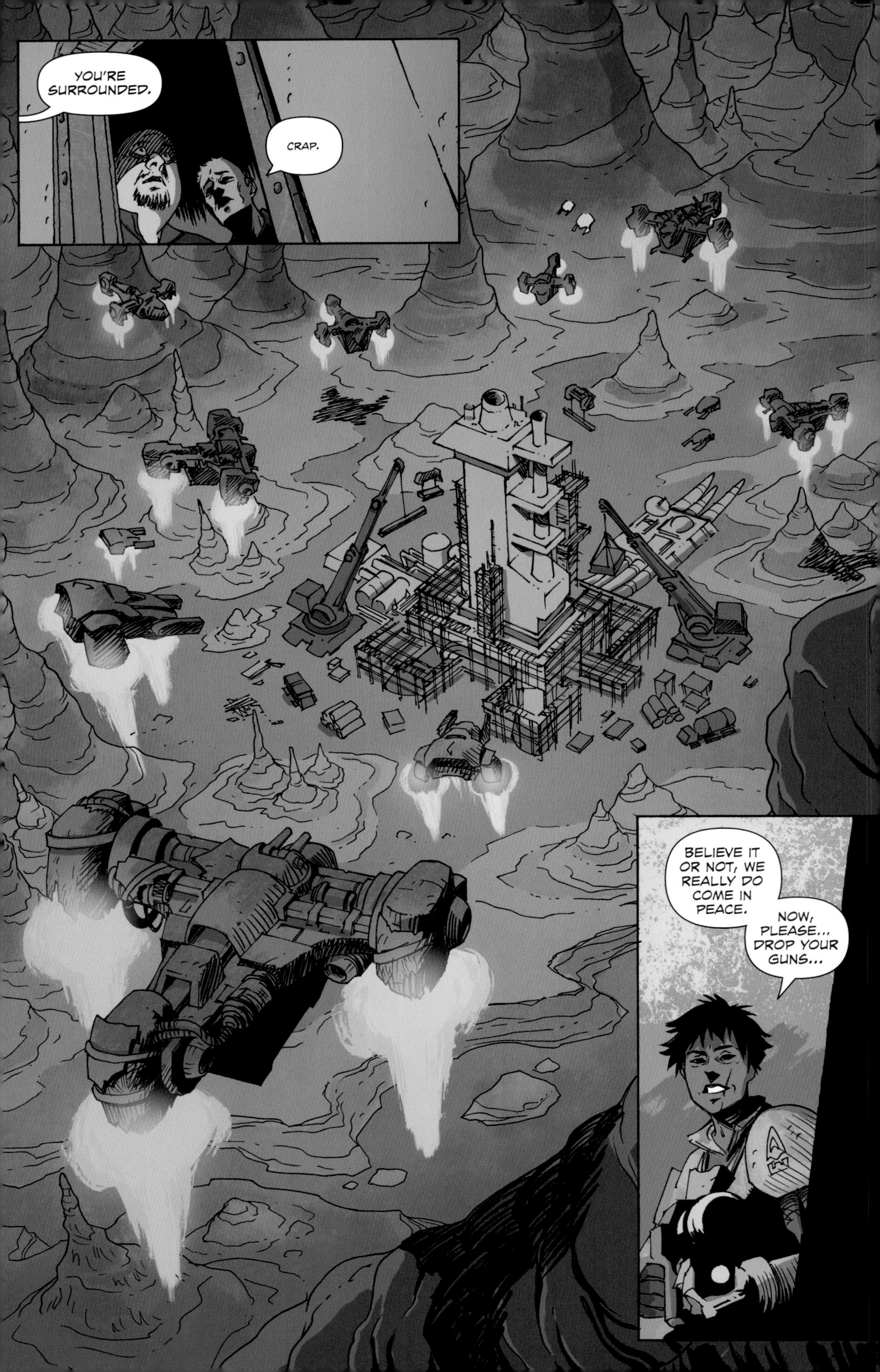

YOU'RE SURROUNDED.
CRAP.
BELIEVE IT OR NOT, WE REALLY DO COME IN PEACE.
NOW, PLEASE... DROP YOUR GUNS...

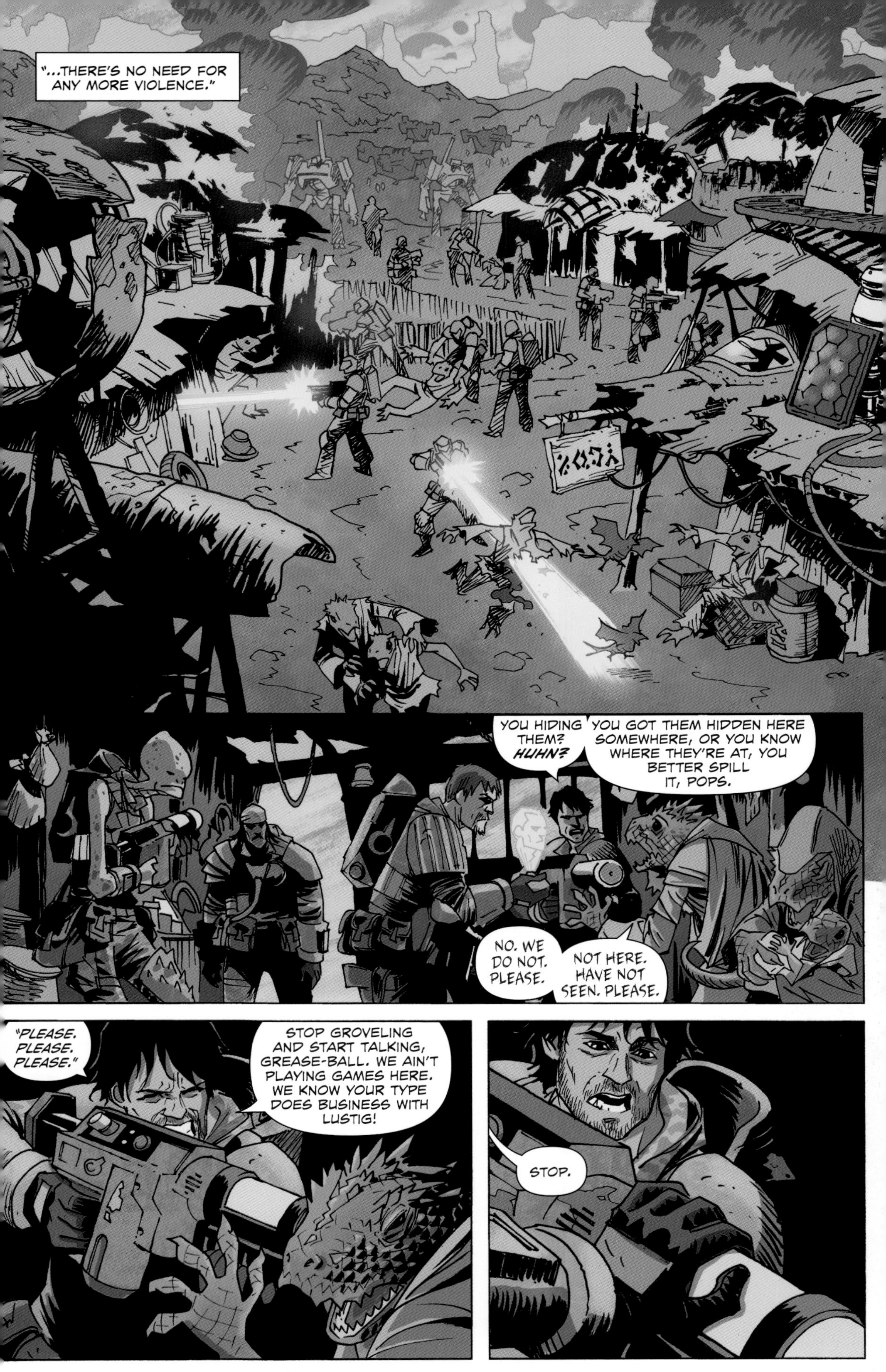
"...THERE'S NO NEED FOR ANY MORE VIOLENCE."
YOU HIDING THEM? HUHN?
YOU GOT THEM HIDDEN HERE SOMEWHERE, OR YOU KNOW WHERE THEY'RE AT, YOU BETTER SPILL IT, POPS.
NO. WE DO NOT. PLEASE.
NOT HERE. HAVE NOT SEEN. PLEASE.
"PLEASE. PLEASE. PLEASE."
STOP GROVELING AND START TALKING, GREASE-BALL. WE AIN'T PLAYING GAMES HERE. WE KNOW YOUR TYPE DOES BUSINESS WITH LUSTIG!
STOP.

THEY DON'T KNOW ANYTHING, BURK.

STICKING A GUN IN THEIR FACE ISN'T GOING TO CHANGE THAT.

HEY, MAYBE *YOU* DON'T CARE ABOUT FINDING THOSE SCUMBAGS WHO KILLED--

THEY DIDN'T KILL ANYONE.

JUST MORE G.O.E. LIES TO GET US TO COVER UP EVEN MORE G.O.E. LIES.

THE PILE'S SO HIGH, NO ONE KNOWS WHAT THE TRUTH IS ANYMORE.

LISTEN TO YOU, CROMWELL, EVEN IN THE FACE OF IT, YOU GOTTA LOOK FOR A CONSPIRACY, DON'T YOU? CAN'T EVEN SEE THE CHANCE TO SAVE YOURSELF.

WELL, NOT ME, BROTHER. I GOT A HOPE OF MAKING IT OFF THIS PLANET AND I'M GONNA TAKE IT!

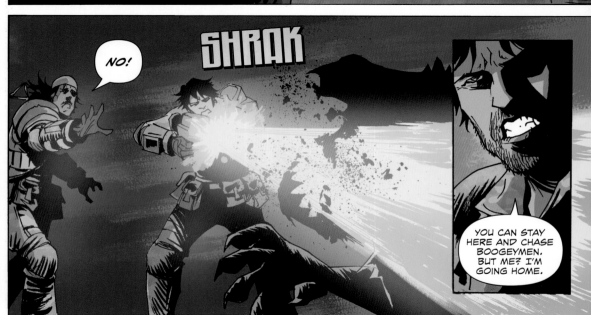

NO!

SHRAK

YOU CAN STAY HERE AND CHASE BOOGEYMEN. BUT ME? I'M GOING HOME.

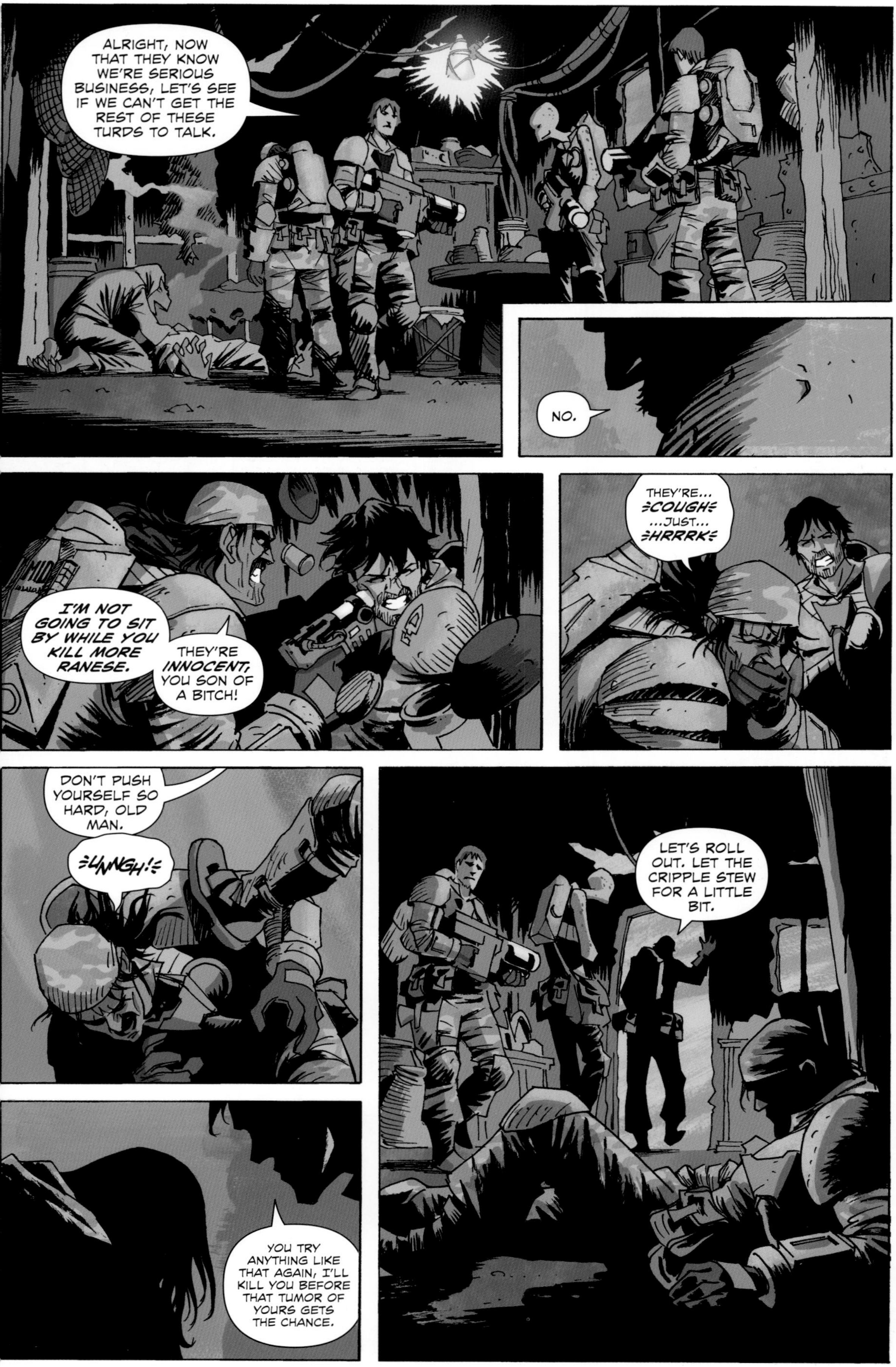
ALRIGHT, NOW THAT THEY KNOW WE'RE SERIOUS BUSINESS, LET'S SEE IF WE CAN'T GET THE REST OF THESE TURDS TO TALK.
NO.
I'M NOT GOING TO SIT BY WHILE YOU KILL MORE RANESE.
THEY'RE INNOCENT, YOU SON OF A BITCH!
THEY'RE... =COUGH= ...JUST... =HRRRK=
DON'T PUSH YOURSELF SO HARD, OLD MAN.
=UNNGH!=
YOU TRY ANYTHING LIKE THAT AGAIN, I'LL KILL YOU BEFORE THAT TUMOR OF YOURS GETS THE CHANCE.
LET'S ROLL OUT. LET THE CRIPPLE STEW FOR A LITTLE BIT.

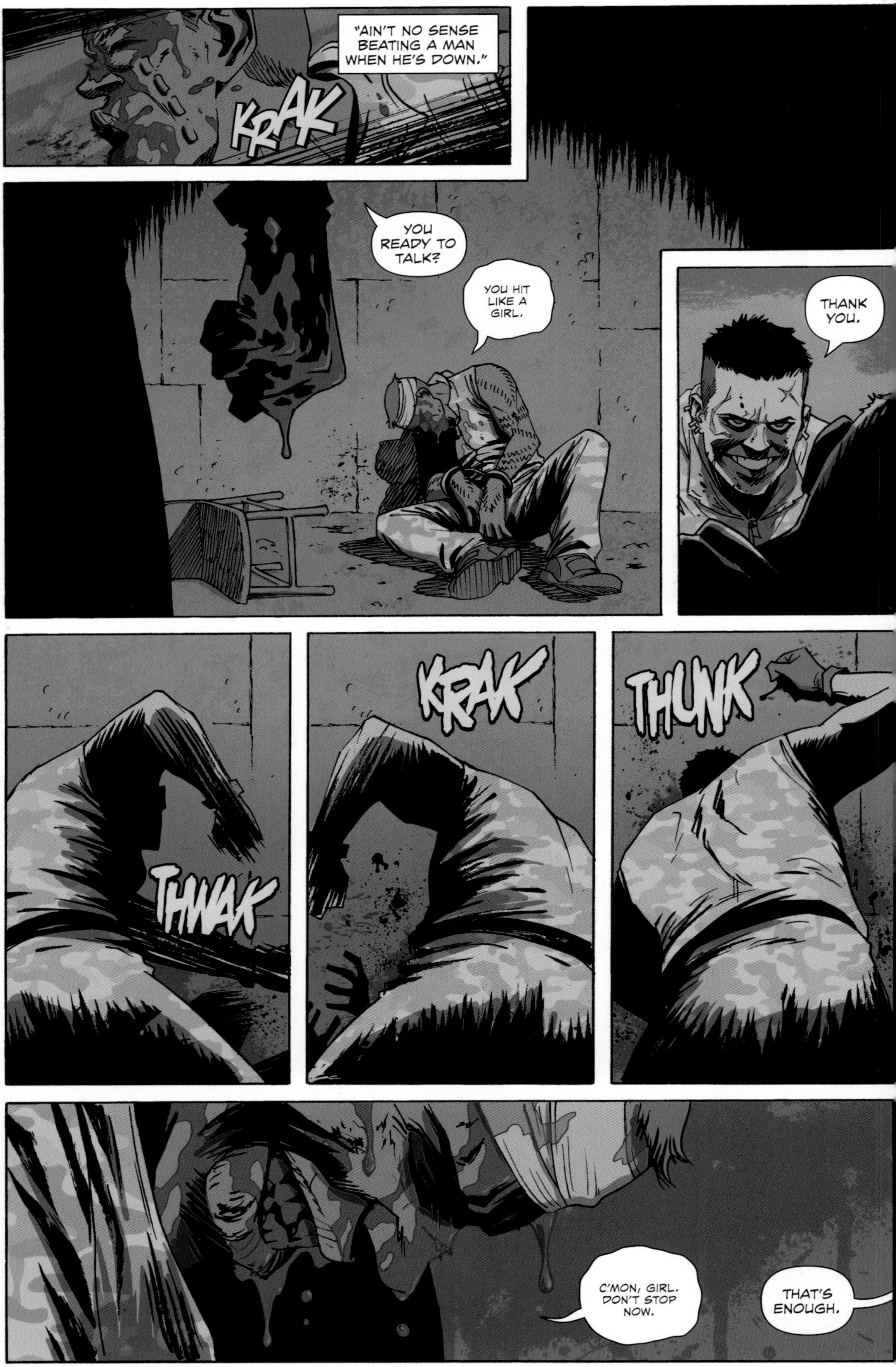
"AIN'T NO SENSE BEATING A MAN WHEN HE'S DOWN."
KRAK
YOU READY TO TALK?
YOU HIT LIKE A GIRL.
THANK YOU.
THWAK
KRAK
THUNK
C'MON, GIRL. DON'T STOP NOW.
THAT'S ENOUGH.

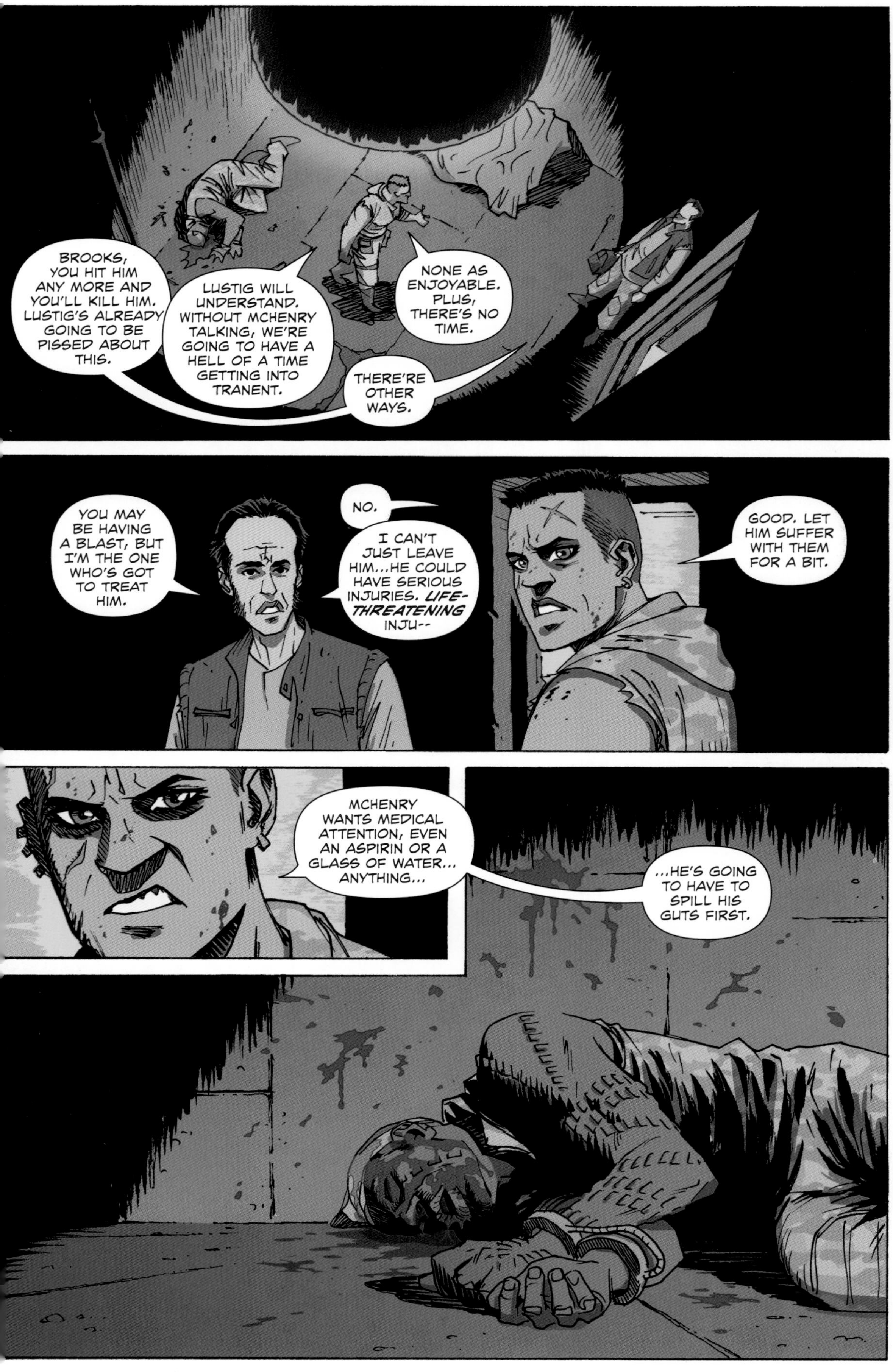
BROOKS, YOU HIT HIM ANY MORE AND YOU'LL KILL HIM. LUSTIG'S ALREADY GOING TO BE PISSED ABOUT THIS.
LUSTIG WILL UNDERSTAND. WITHOUT MCHENRY TALKING, WE'RE GOING TO HAVE A HELL OF A TIME GETTING INTO TRANENT.
NONE AS ENJOYABLE. PLUS, THERE'S NO TIME.
THERE'RE OTHER WAYS.
YOU MAY BE HAVING A BLAST, BUT I'M THE ONE WHO'S GOT TO TREAT HIM.
NO.
I CAN'T JUST LEAVE HIM...HE COULD HAVE SERIOUS INJURIES. *LIFE-THREATENING* INJU--
GOOD. LET HIM SUFFER WITH THEM FOR A BIT.
MCHENRY WANTS MEDICAL ATTENTION, EVEN AN ASPIRIN OR A GLASS OF WATER... ANYTHING...
...HE'S GOING TO HAVE TO SPILL HIS GUTS FIRST.

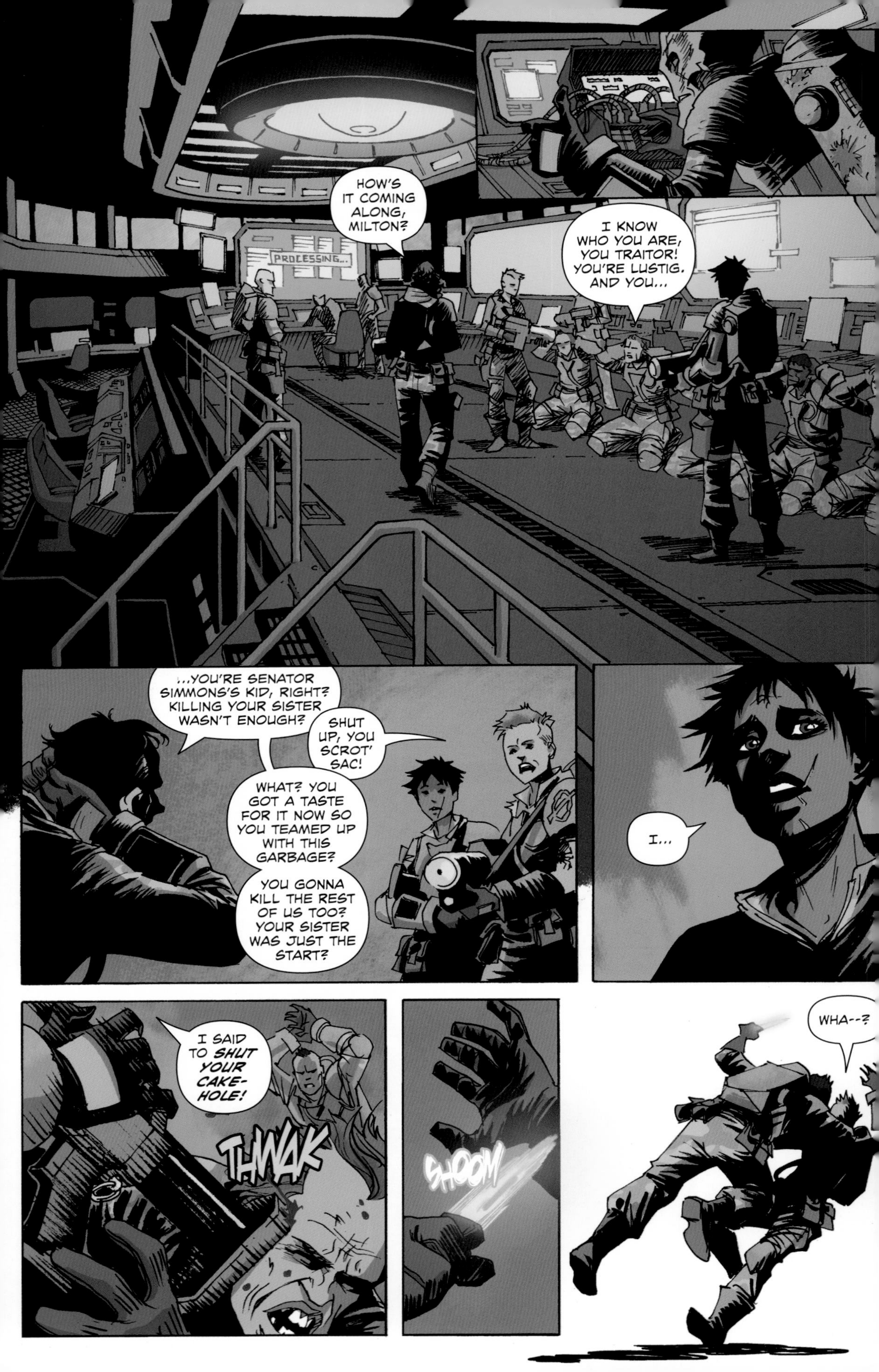
PROCESSING...
HOW'S IT COMING ALONG, MILTON?
I KNOW WHO YOU ARE, YOU TRAITOR! YOU'RE LUSTIG. AND YOU...
...YOU'RE SENATOR SIMMONS'S KID, RIGHT? KILLING YOUR SISTER WASN'T ENOUGH?
SHUT UP, YOU SCROT' SAC!
WHAT? YOU GOT A TASTE FOR IT NOW SO YOU TEAMED UP WITH THIS GARBAGE?
YOU GONNA KILL THE REST OF US TOO? YOUR SISTER WAS JUST THE START?
I...
I SAID TO SHUT YOUR CAKE-HOLE!
THWAK
SHOOM
WHA--?

ALRIGHT... ALRIGHT...

HAND OVER YOUR GUNS. JUST...JUST PUT THEM DOWN OR I SWEAR TO GOD...

LET HER GO AND PUT DOWN THE KNIFE!

I WILL KILL HER. I'M NOT PLAYING AROUND HERE.

SAMARA... PLEASE...

SAMARA...

...WHY DID YOU LET ME DIE?

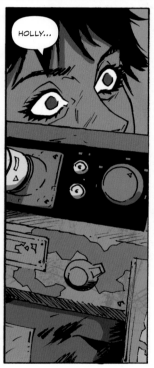
HOLLY...

SHRAK

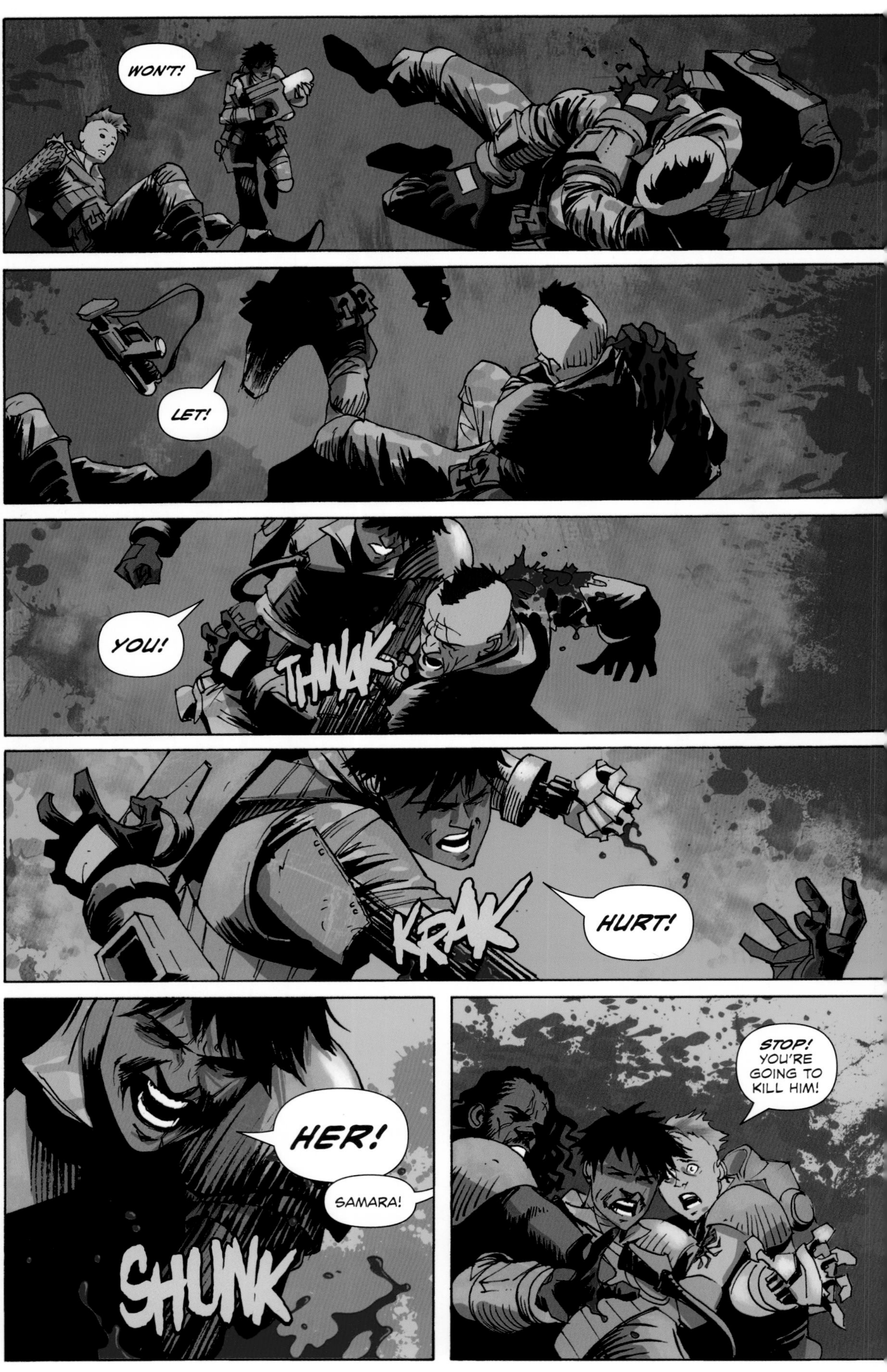

WON'T!
LET!
YOU!
THWAK
HURT!
KRAK
HER!
SAMARA!
SHUNK
STOP! YOU'RE GOING TO KILL HIM!

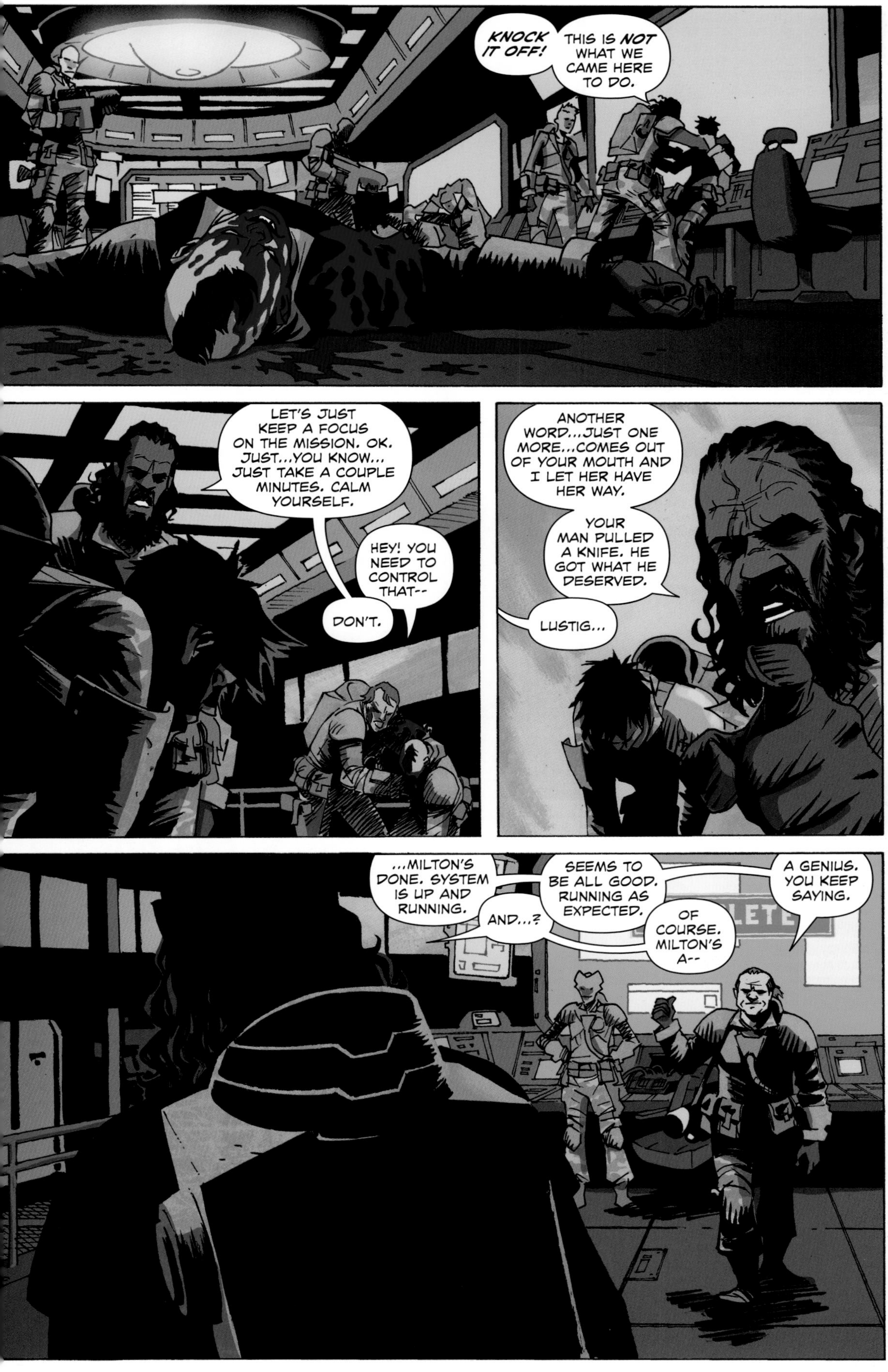
KNOCK IT OFF!
THIS IS NOT WHAT WE CAME HERE TO DO.
LET'S JUST KEEP A FOCUS ON THE MISSION. OK. JUST...YOU KNOW... JUST TAKE A COUPLE MINUTES. CALM YOURSELF.
HEY! YOU NEED TO CONTROL THAT--
DON'T.
ANOTHER WORD...JUST ONE MORE...COMES OUT OF YOUR MOUTH AND I LET HER HAVE HER WAY.
YOUR MAN PULLED A KNIFE. HE GOT WHAT HE DESERVED.
LUSTIG...
...MILTON'S DONE. SYSTEM IS UP AND RUNNING.
AND...?
SEEMS TO BE ALL GOOD. RUNNING AS EXPECTED.
OF COURSE. MILTON'S A--
A GENIUS. YOU KEEP SAYING.

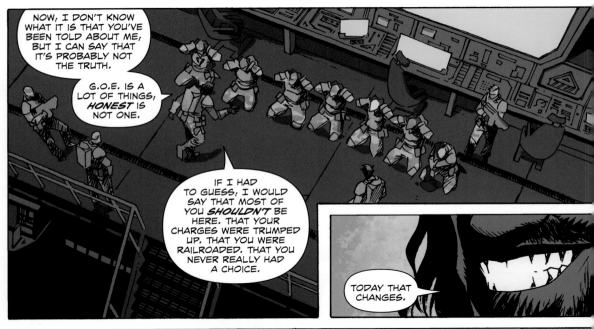

NOW, I DON'T KNOW WHAT IT IS THAT YOU'VE BEEN TOLD ABOUT ME, BUT I CAN SAY THAT IT'S PROBABLY NOT THE TRUTH.

G.O.E. IS A LOT OF THINGS, *HONEST* IS NOT ONE.

IF I HAD TO GUESS, I WOULD SAY THAT MOST OF YOU *SHOULDN'T* BE HERE. THAT YOUR CHARGES WERE TRUMPED UP. THAT YOU WERE RAILROADED. THAT YOU NEVER REALLY HAD A CHOICE.

TODAY THAT CHANGES.

WE'VE DEACTIVATED YOUR PUNCH. THAT MEANS THAT G.O.E. AND TRANENT NO LONGER HAVE YOU TETHERED. YOU AREN'T UNDER THEIR CONTROL ANYMORE.

YOU ARE NOW THE MASTERS OF YOUR OWN FATE.

YEAH, RIGHT. WHAT, YOU THINK THAT THIS MAKES US FREE? THAT WE JUST TURN OUR BACKS ON OUR OWN PLANET AND JOIN UP WITH A GROUP OF TERRORISTS?

YOU'RE CRAZY IF YOU THINK THAT'S HAPPENING.

G.O.E. ISN'T *YOUR* PLANET. THEY DON'T REPRESENT YOU OR ME. THEY ONLY REPRESENT THEMSELVES.

EVERYTHING THEY SAID TO GET YOU HERE, TO GET YOU TO DO THEIR WORK... NONE OF IT IS TRUE.

THEY'RE USING YOU!

DID YOU KNOW THAT THE AIR HERE IS TOXIC TO HUMANS? DO YOU REMEMBER THAT PART OF YOUR WELCOME SPEECH AT TRANENT?

NO. BECAUSE THEY *DON'T* TELL YOU THAT. THEY DON'T TELL YOU THAT YOU'LL DIE IN TEN YEARS...MAYBE FIFTEEN, IF YOU'RE *LUCKY*.

NO ONE MAKES IT BACK. WE'RE DISPOSABLE. WORKERS AND SOLDIERS TO BE USED AND DISCARDED ONCE WE'RE NO LONGER ANY USE. ONCE WE'RE TOO SICK TO CONTINUE.

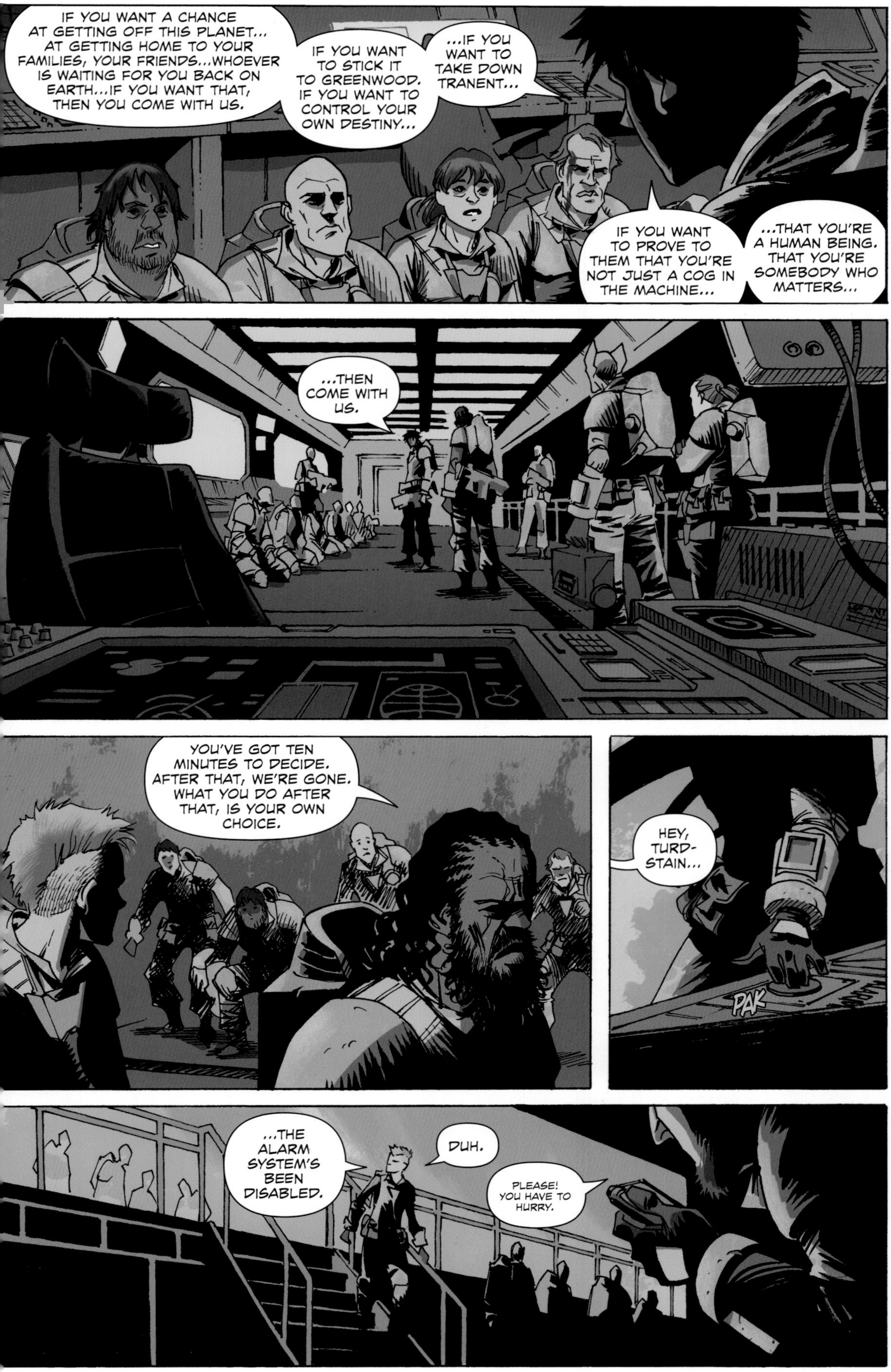
IF YOU WANT A CHANCE AT GETTING OFF THIS PLANET... AT GETTING HOME TO YOUR FAMILIES, YOUR FRIENDS...WHOEVER IS WAITING FOR YOU BACK ON EARTH...IF YOU WANT THAT, THEN YOU COME WITH US.
IF YOU WANT TO STICK IT TO GREENWOOD. IF YOU WANT TO CONTROL YOUR OWN DESTINY...
...IF YOU WANT TO TAKE DOWN TRANENT...
IF YOU WANT TO PROVE TO THEM THAT YOU'RE NOT JUST A COG IN THE MACHINE...
...THAT YOU'RE A HUMAN BEING. THAT YOU'RE SOMEBODY WHO MATTERS...
...THEN COME WITH US.
YOU'VE GOT TEN MINUTES TO DECIDE. AFTER THAT, WE'RE GONE. WHAT YOU DO AFTER THAT, IS YOUR OWN CHOICE.
HEY, TURD-STAIN...
PAK
...THE ALARM SYSTEM'S BEEN DISABLED.
DUH.
PLEASE! YOU HAVE TO HURRY.

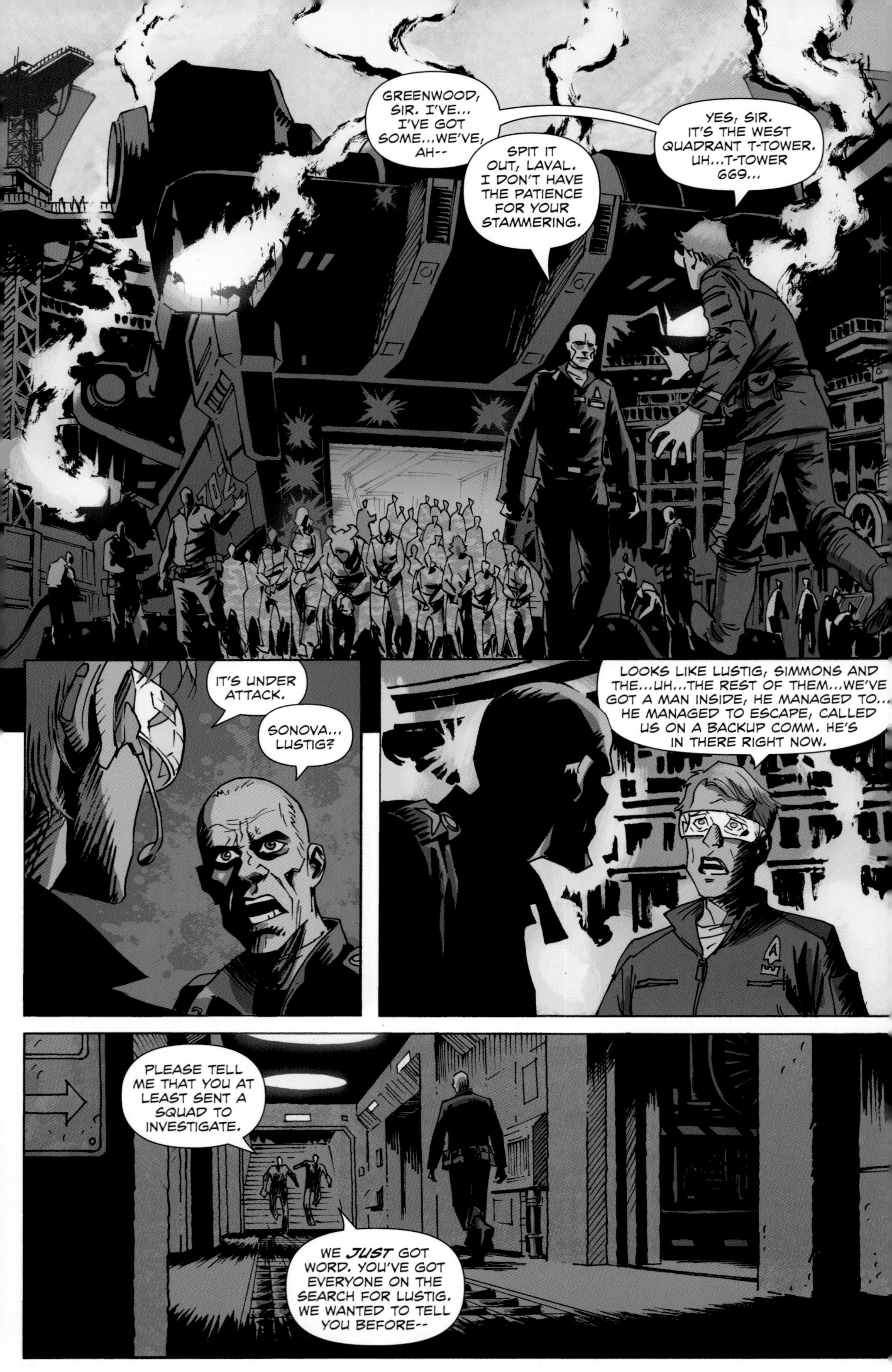
GREENWOOD, SIR. I'VE... I'VE GOT SOME...WE'VE, AH--
SPIT IT OUT, LAVAL. I DON'T HAVE THE PATIENCE FOR YOUR STAMMERING.
YES, SIR. IT'S THE WEST QUADRANT T-TOWER. UH...T-TOWER 669...
IT'S UNDER ATTACK.
SONOVA... LUSTIG?
LOOKS LIKE LUSTIG, SIMMONS AND THE...UH...THE REST OF THEM...WE'VE GOT A MAN INSIDE, HE MANAGED TO... HE MANAGED TO ESCAPE, CALLED US ON A BACKUP COMM. HE'S IN THERE RIGHT NOW.
PLEASE TELL ME THAT YOU AT LEAST SENT A SQUAD TO INVESTIGATE.
WE JUST GOT WORD. YOU'VE GOT EVERYONE ON THE SEARCH FOR LUSTIG. WE WANTED TO TELL YOU BEFORE--

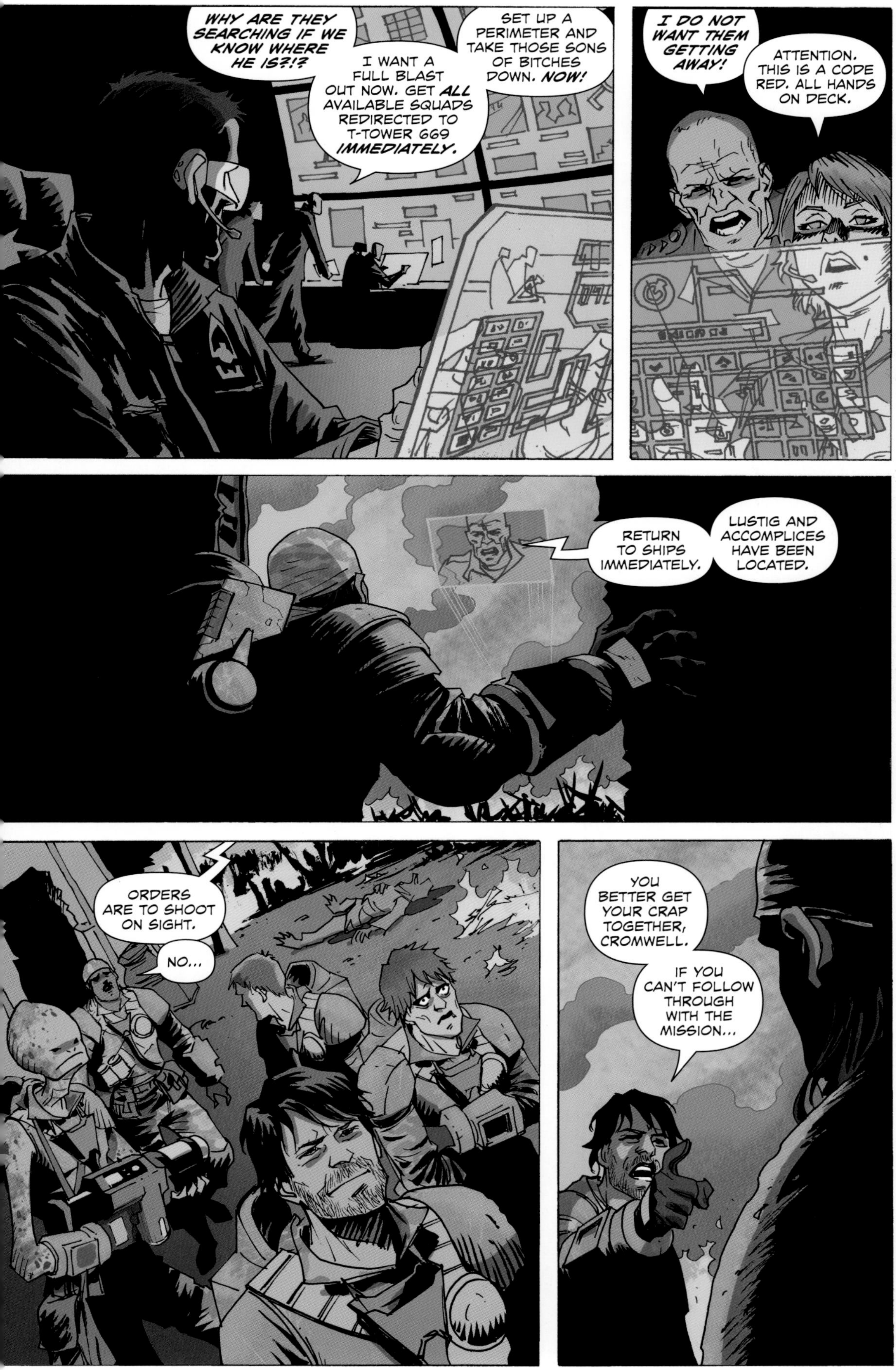
WHY ARE THEY SEARCHING IF WE KNOW WHERE HE IS?!?
I WANT A FULL BLAST OUT NOW. GET ALL AVAILABLE SQUADS REDIRECTED TO T-TOWER 669 IMMEDIATELY.
SET UP A PERIMETER AND TAKE THOSE SONS OF BITCHES DOWN. NOW!
I DO NOT WANT THEM GETTING AWAY!
ATTENTION. THIS IS A CODE RED. ALL HANDS ON DECK.
RETURN TO SHIPS IMMEDIATELY.
LUSTIG AND ACCOMPLICES HAVE BEEN LOCATED.
ORDERS ARE TO SHOOT ON SIGHT.
NO...
YOU BETTER GET YOUR CRAP TOGETHER, CROMWELL.
IF YOU CAN'T FOLLOW THROUGH WITH THE MISSION...

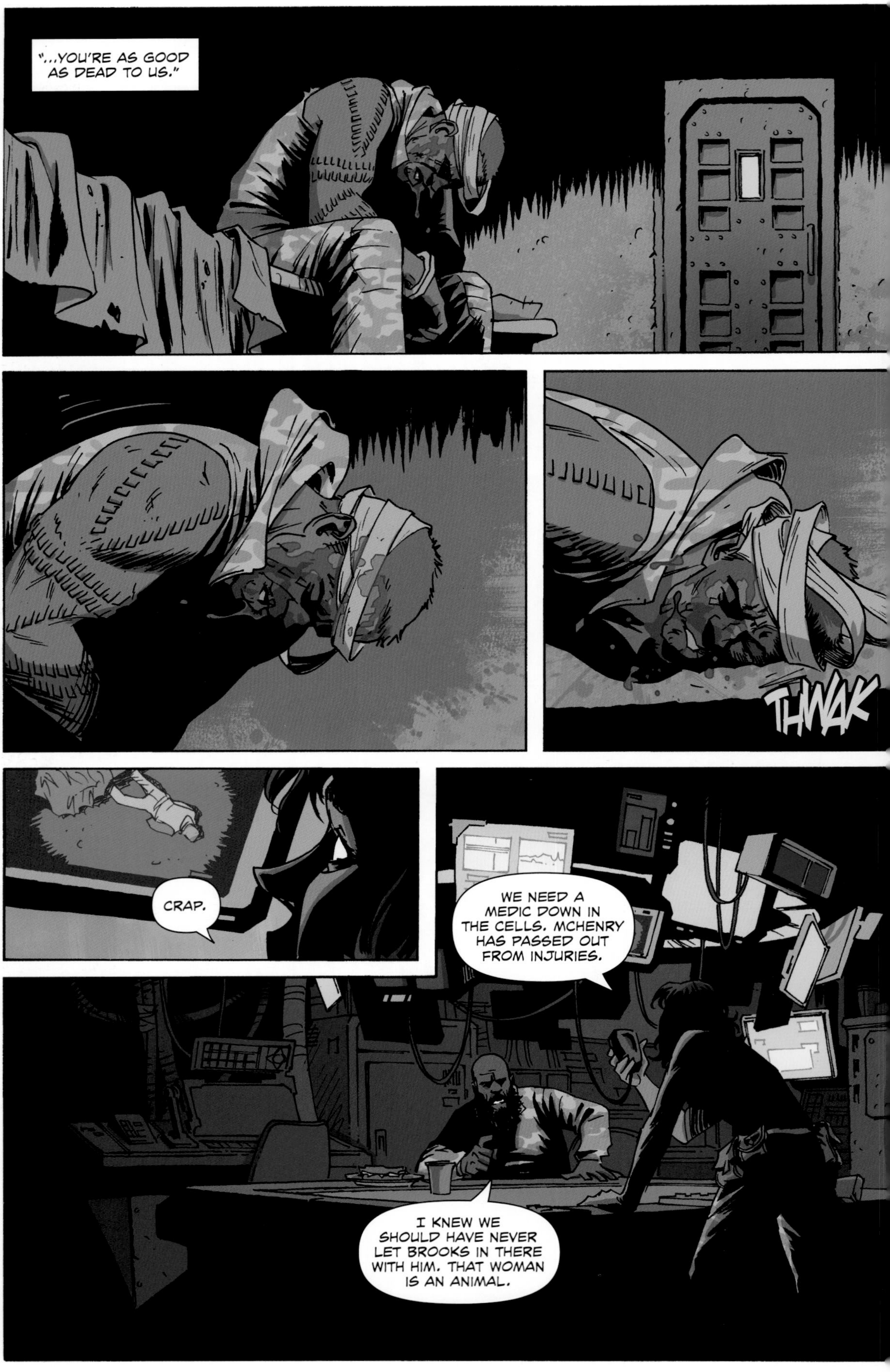
"...YOU'RE AS GOOD AS DEAD TO US."
THWAK
CRAP.
WE NEED A MEDIC DOWN IN THE CELLS. MCHENRY HAS PASSED OUT FROM INJURIES.
I KNEW WE SHOULD HAVE NEVER LET BROOKS IN THERE WITH HIM. THAT WOMAN IS AN ANIMAL.

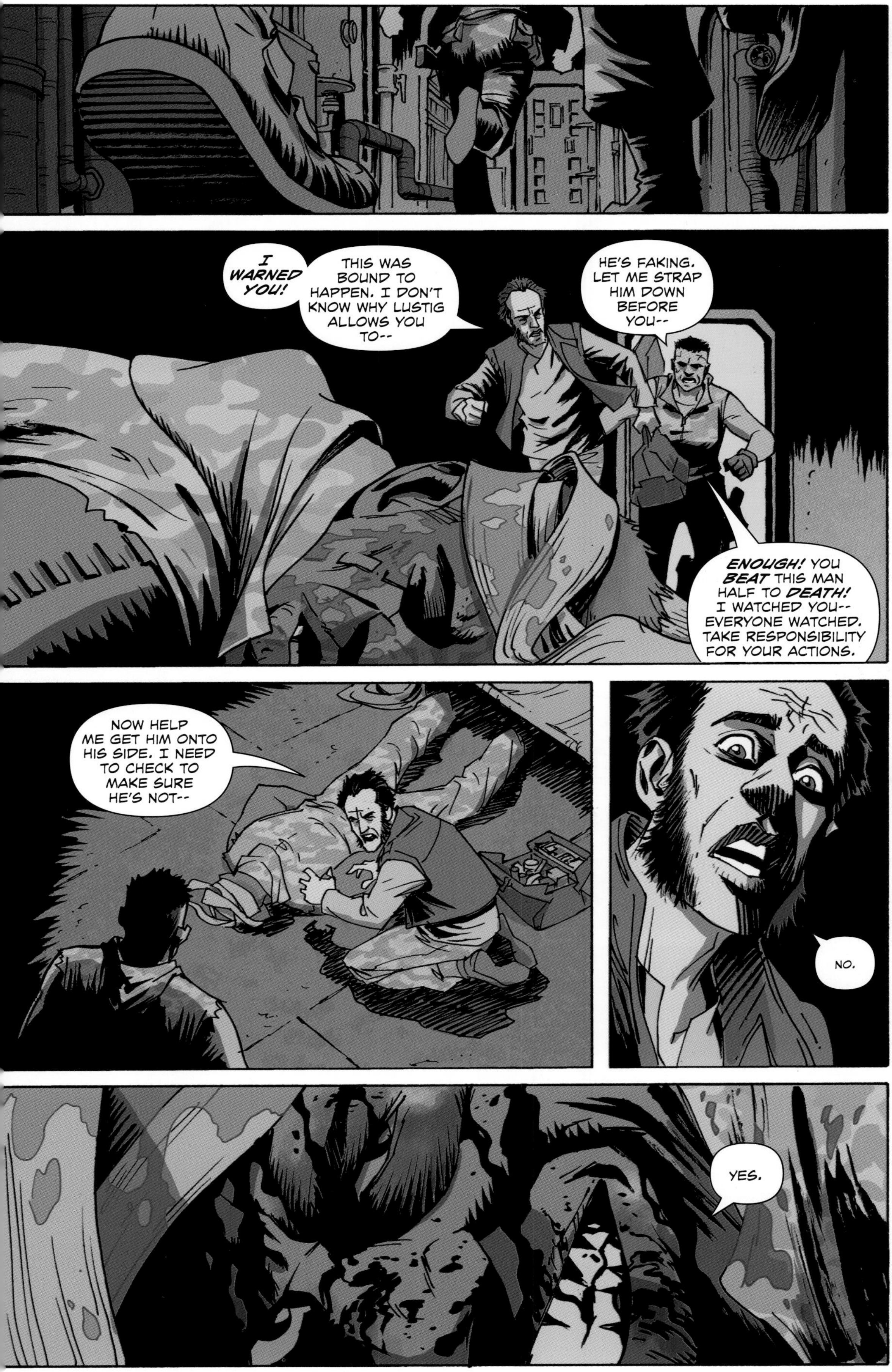
I WARNED YOU!
THIS WAS BOUND TO HAPPEN. I DON'T KNOW WHY LUSTIG ALLOWS YOU TO--
HE'S FAKING. LET ME STRAP HIM DOWN BEFORE YOU--
ENOUGH! YOU BEAT THIS MAN HALF TO DEATH! I WATCHED YOU-- EVERYONE WATCHED. TAKE RESPONSIBILITY FOR YOUR ACTIONS.
NOW HELP ME GET HIM ONTO HIS SIDE. I NEED TO CHECK TO MAKE SURE HE'S NOT--
NO.
YES.

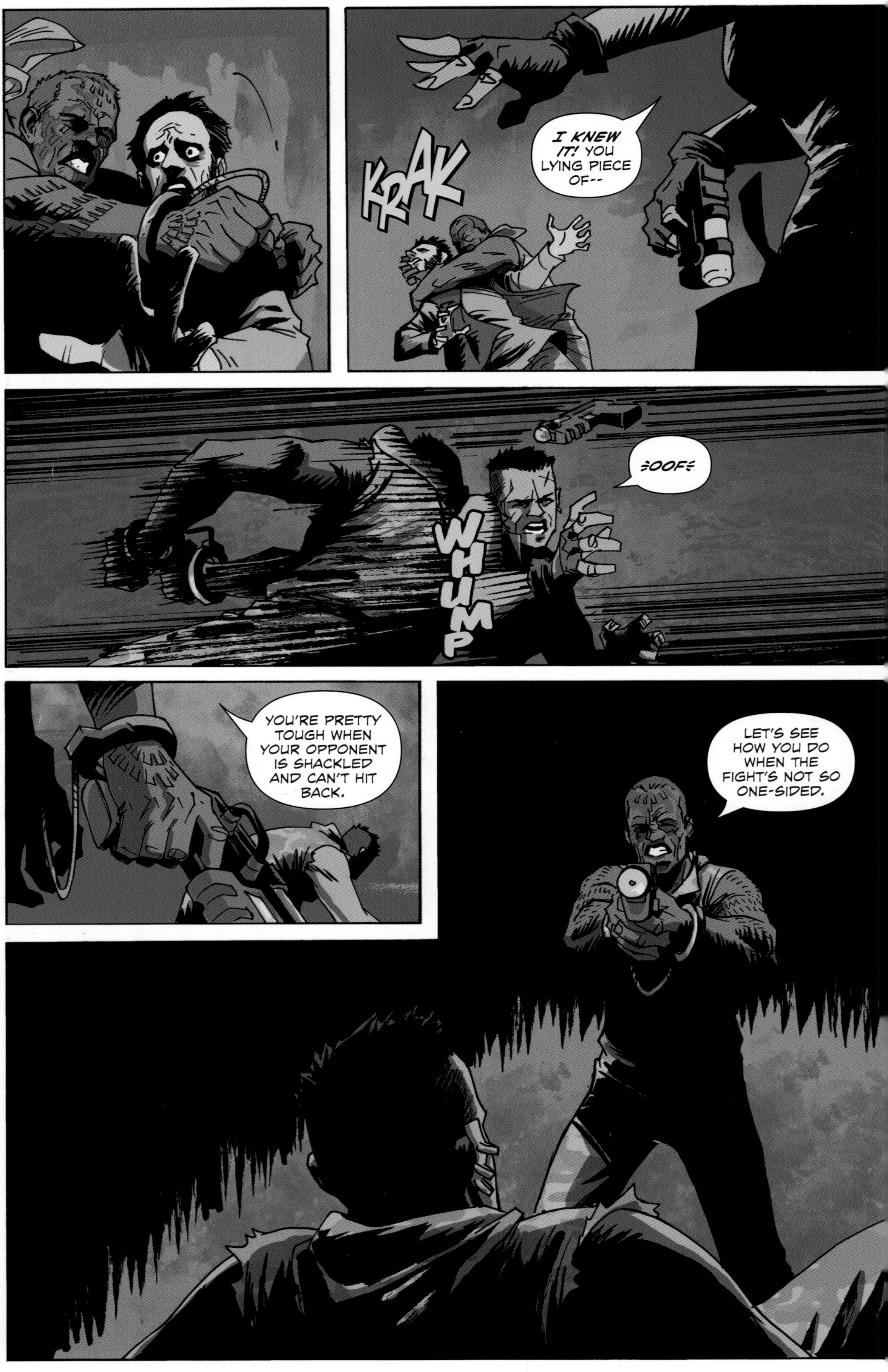
KRAK
I KNEW IT! YOU LYING PIECE OF--
≈OOF≈
WHUMP
YOU'RE PRETTY TOUGH WHEN YOUR OPPONENT IS SHACKLED AND CAN'T HIT BACK.
LET'S SEE HOW YOU DO WHEN THE FIGHT'S NOT SO ONE-SIDED.

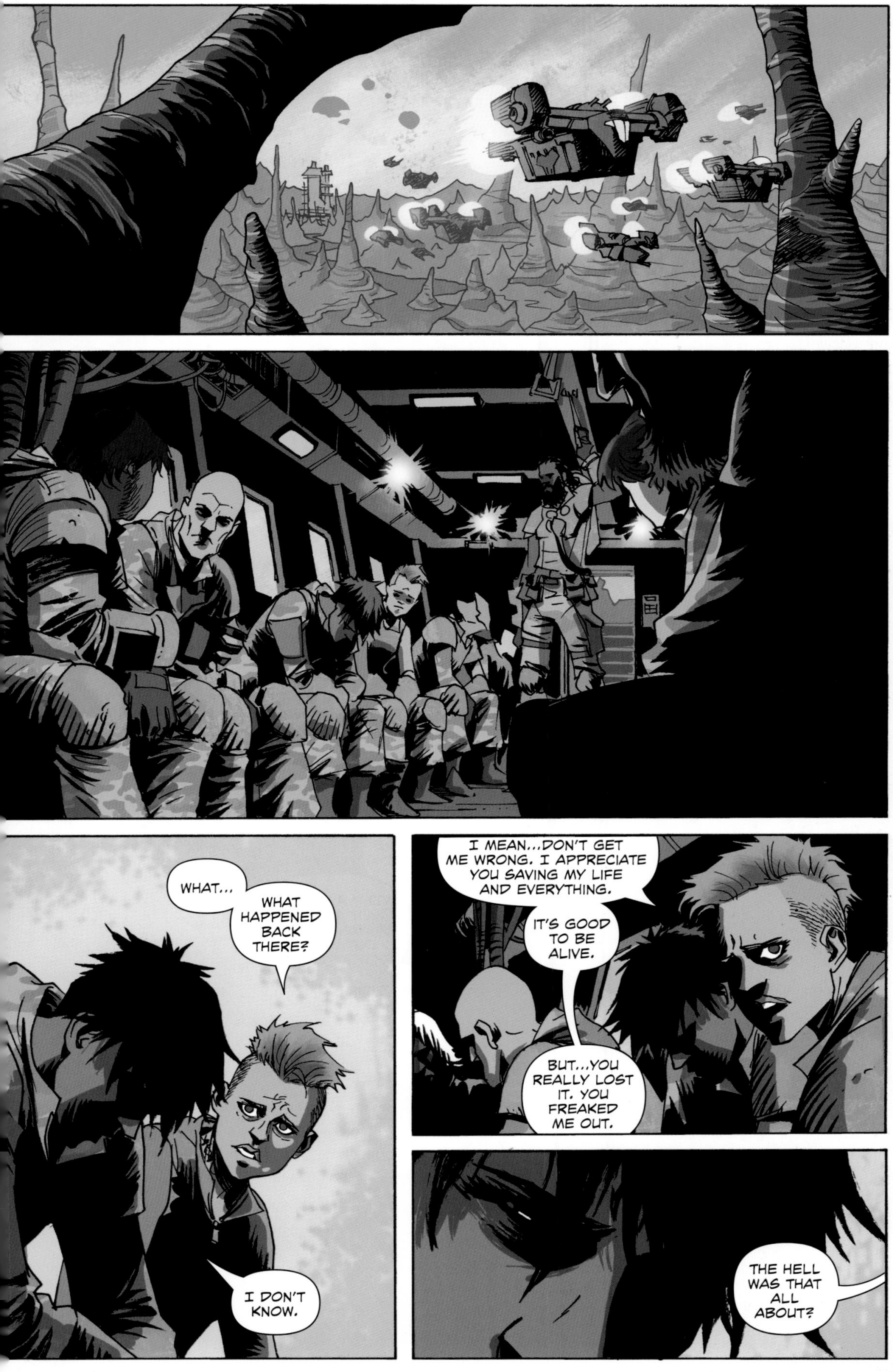
WHAT...
WHAT HAPPENED BACK THERE?
I DON'T KNOW.
I MEAN...DON'T GET ME WRONG. I APPRECIATE YOU SAVING MY LIFE AND EVERYTHING.
IT'S GOOD TO BE ALIVE.
BUT...YOU REALLY LOST IT. YOU FREAKED ME OUT.
THE HELL WAS THAT ALL ABOUT?

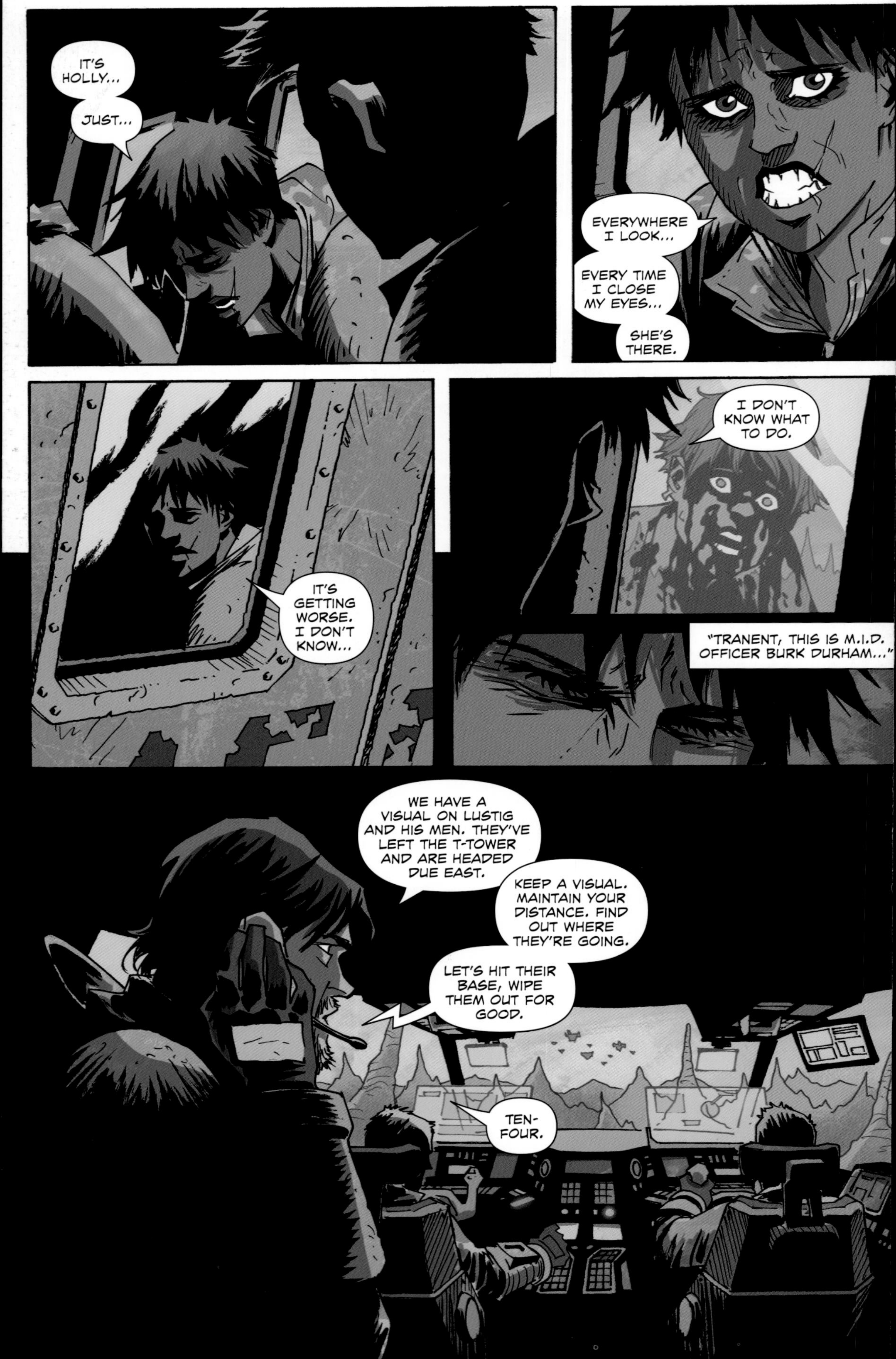
IT'S HOLLY...
JUST...
EVERYWHERE I LOOK...
EVERY TIME I CLOSE MY EYES...
SHE'S THERE.
IT'S GETTING WORSE. I DON'T KNOW...
I DON'T KNOW WHAT TO DO.
"TRANENT, THIS IS M.I.D. OFFICER BURK DURHAM..."
WE HAVE A VISUAL ON LUSTIG AND HIS MEN. THEY'VE LEFT THE T-TOWER AND ARE HEADED DUE EAST.
KEEP A VISUAL. MAINTAIN YOUR DISTANCE. FIND OUT WHERE THEY'RE GOING.
LET'S HIT THEIR BASE, WIPE THEM OUT FOR GOOD.
TEN-FOUR.

ISSUE 006 COVER
DAMIAN COUCIERO
WITH COLORS BY **JORDAN BOYD**

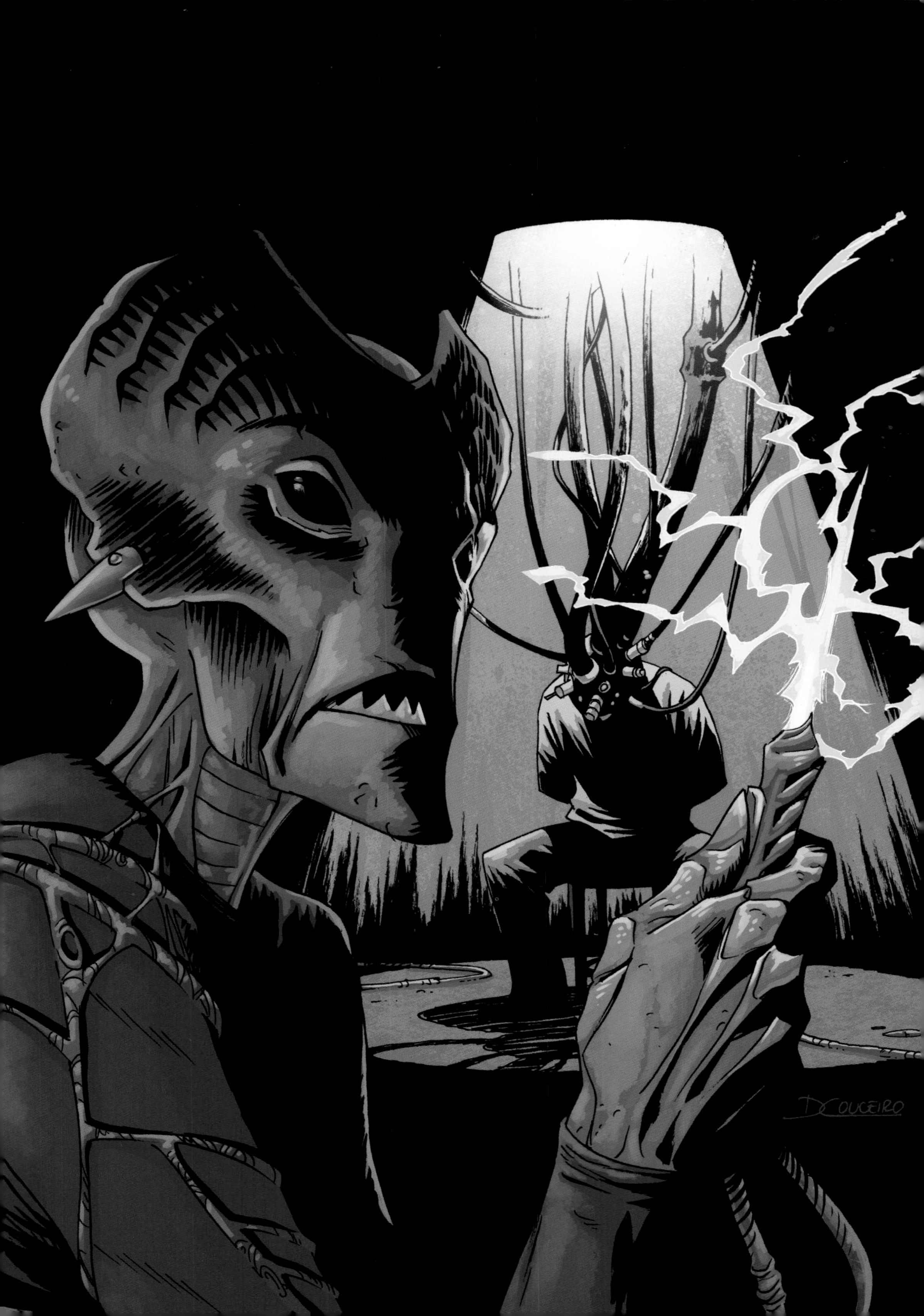

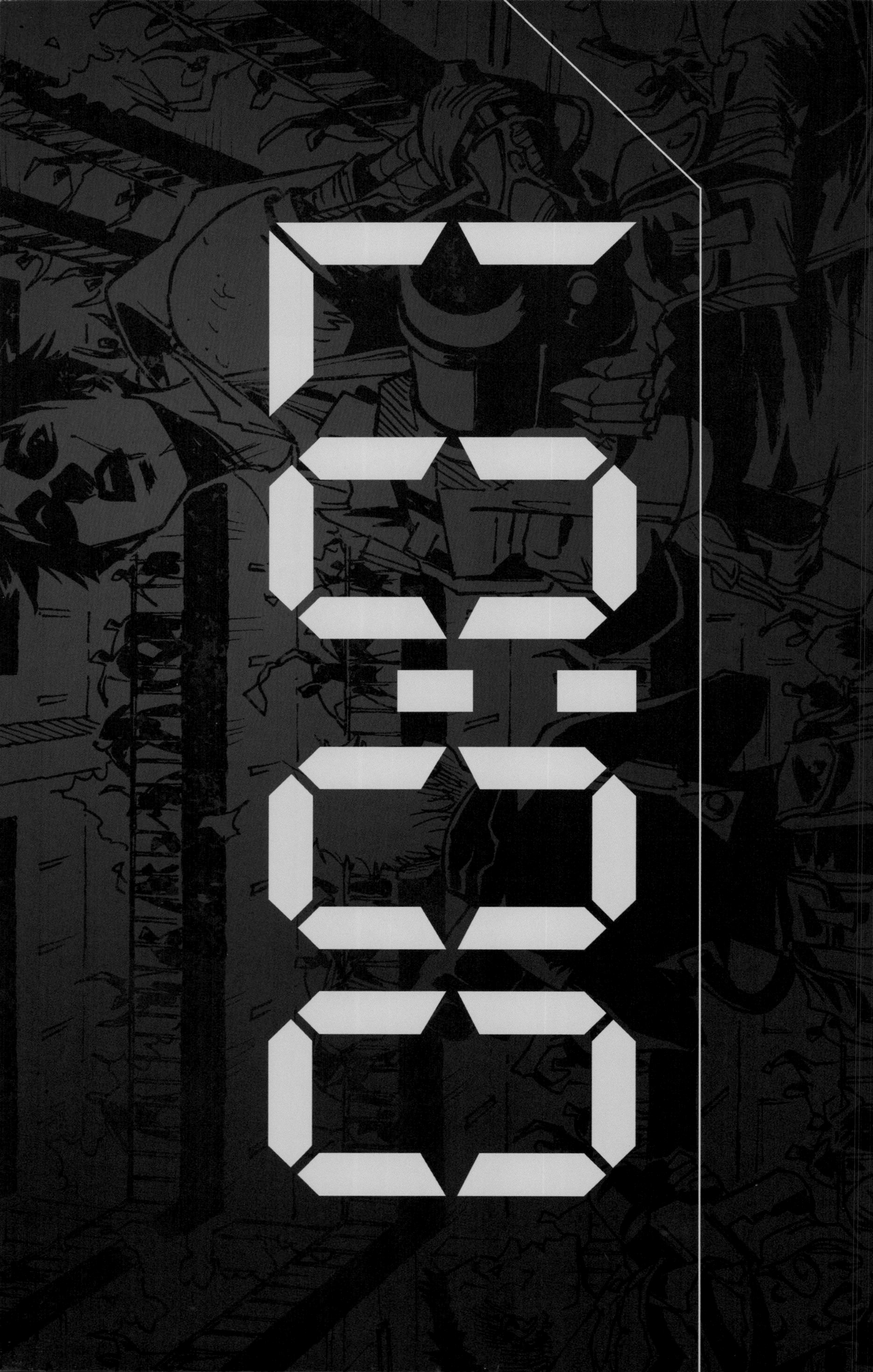
00:07

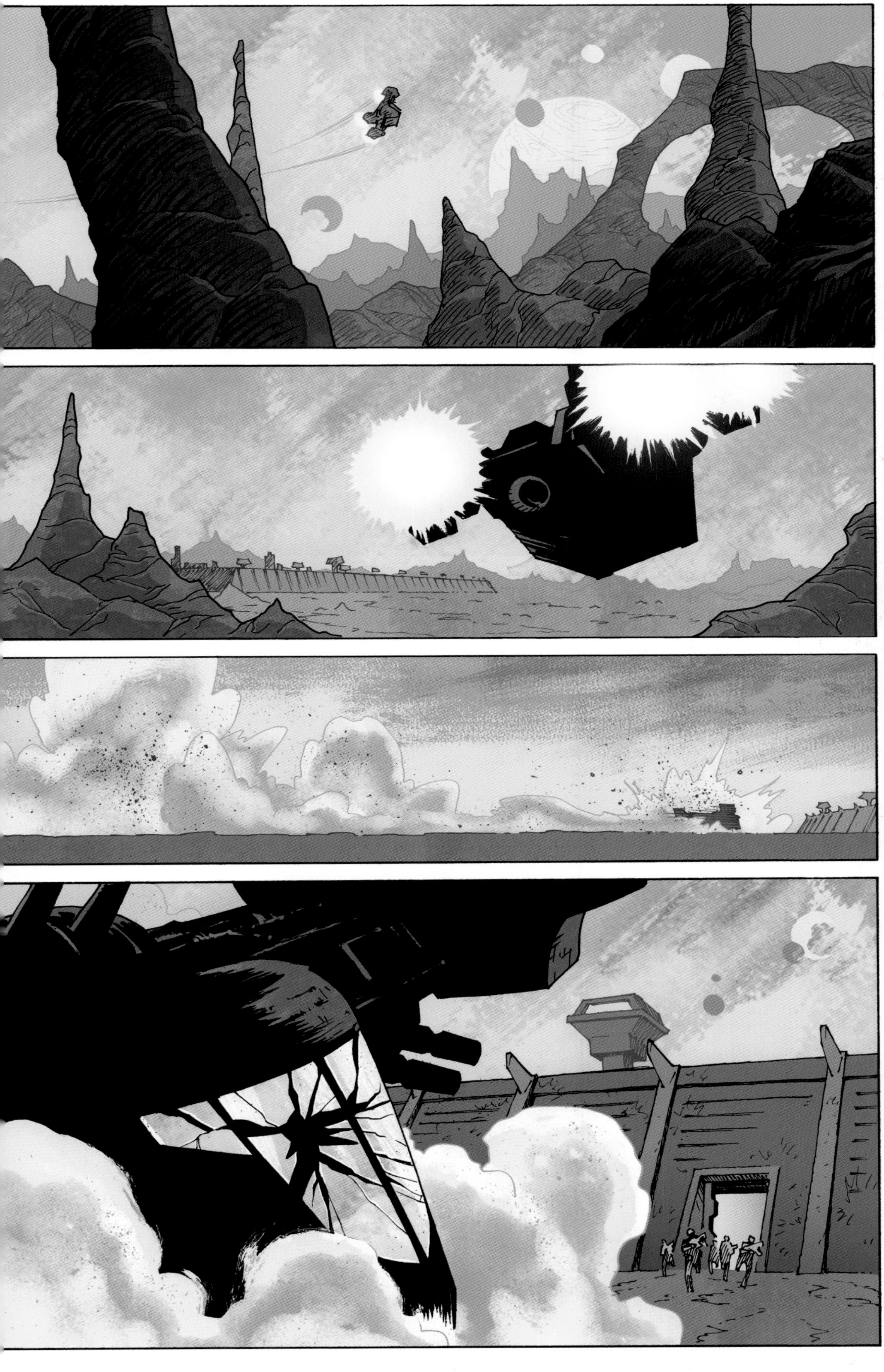

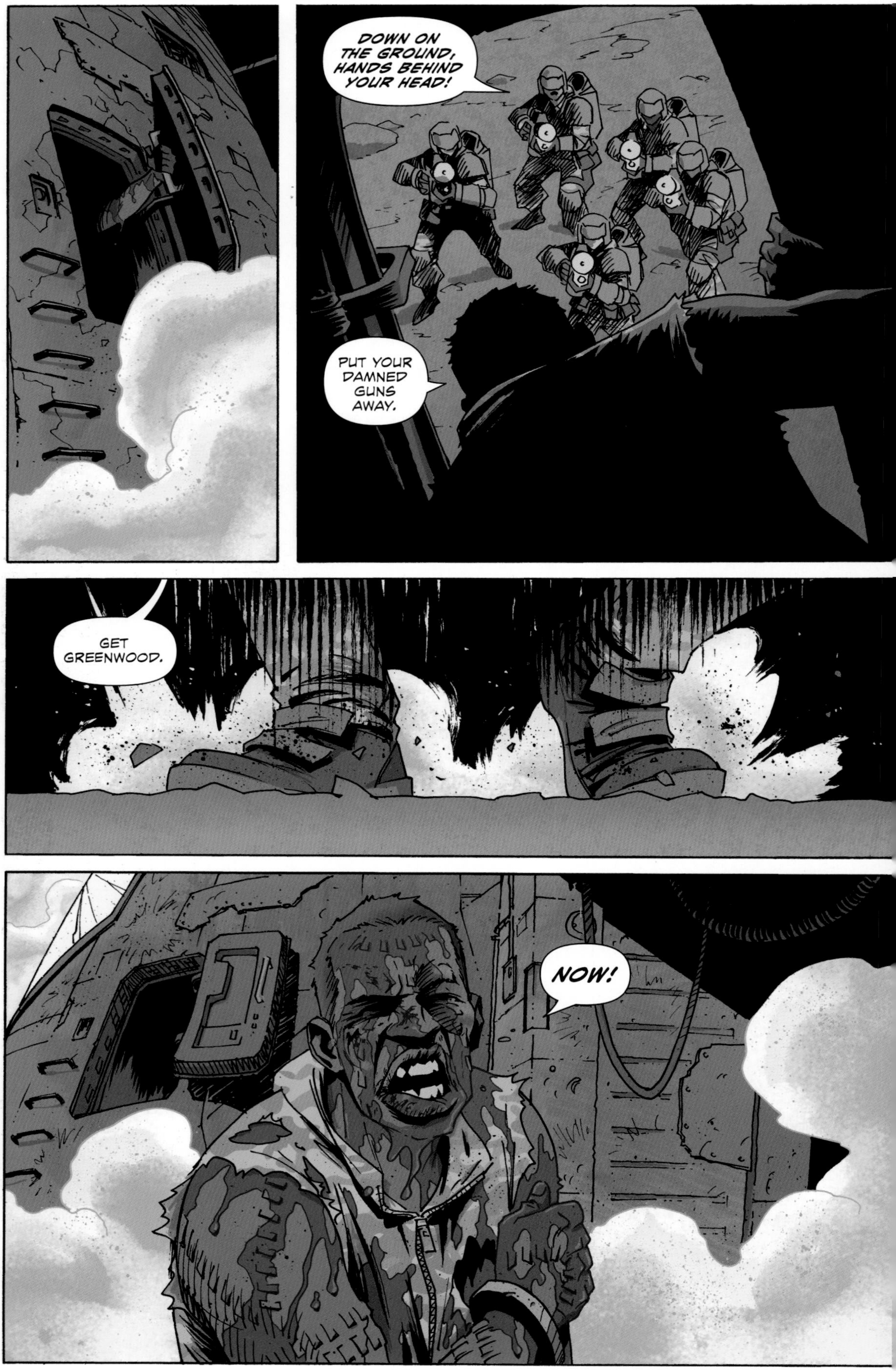
DOWN ON THE GROUND, HANDS BEHIND YOUR HEAD!
PUT YOUR DAMNED GUNS AWAY.
GET GREENWOOD.
NOW!

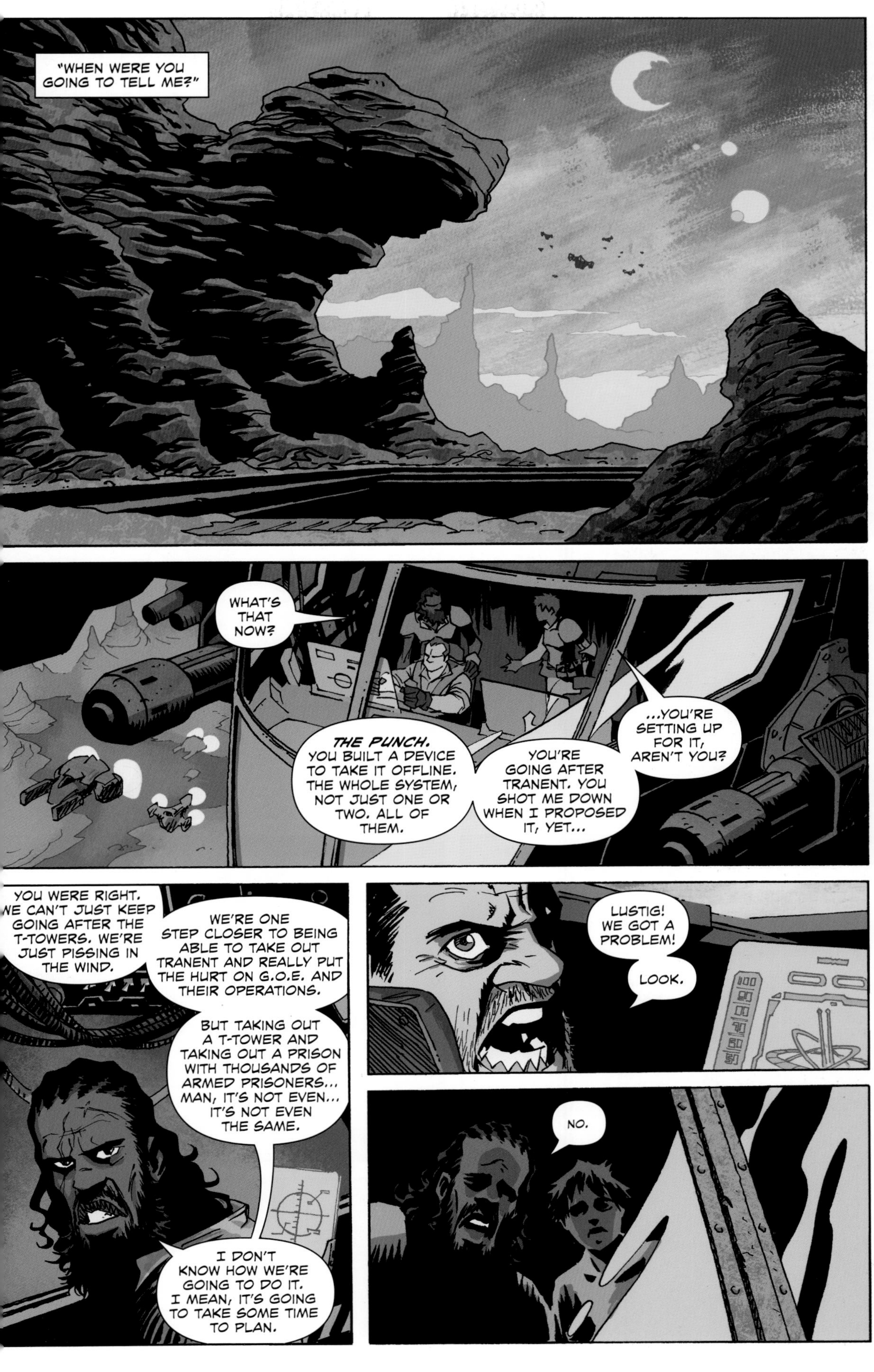
"WHEN WERE YOU GOING TO TELL ME?"
WHAT'S THAT NOW?
THE PUNCH. YOU BUILT A DEVICE TO TAKE IT OFFLINE. THE WHOLE SYSTEM, NOT JUST ONE OR TWO. ALL OF THEM.
YOU'RE GOING AFTER TRANENT. YOU SHOT ME DOWN WHEN I PROPOSED IT, YET...
...YOU'RE SETTING UP FOR IT, AREN'T YOU?
YOU WERE RIGHT. WE CAN'T JUST KEEP GOING AFTER THE T-TOWERS. WE'RE JUST PISSING IN THE WIND.
WE'RE ONE STEP CLOSER TO BEING ABLE TO TAKE OUT TRANENT AND REALLY PUT THE HURT ON G.O.E. AND THEIR OPERATIONS.
BUT TAKING OUT A T-TOWER AND TAKING OUT A PRISON WITH THOUSANDS OF ARMED PRISONERS... MAN, IT'S NOT EVEN... IT'S NOT EVEN THE SAME.
I DON'T KNOW HOW WE'RE GOING TO DO IT. I MEAN, IT'S GOING TO TAKE SOME TIME TO PLAN.
LUSTIG! WE GOT A PROBLEM!
LOOK.
NO.

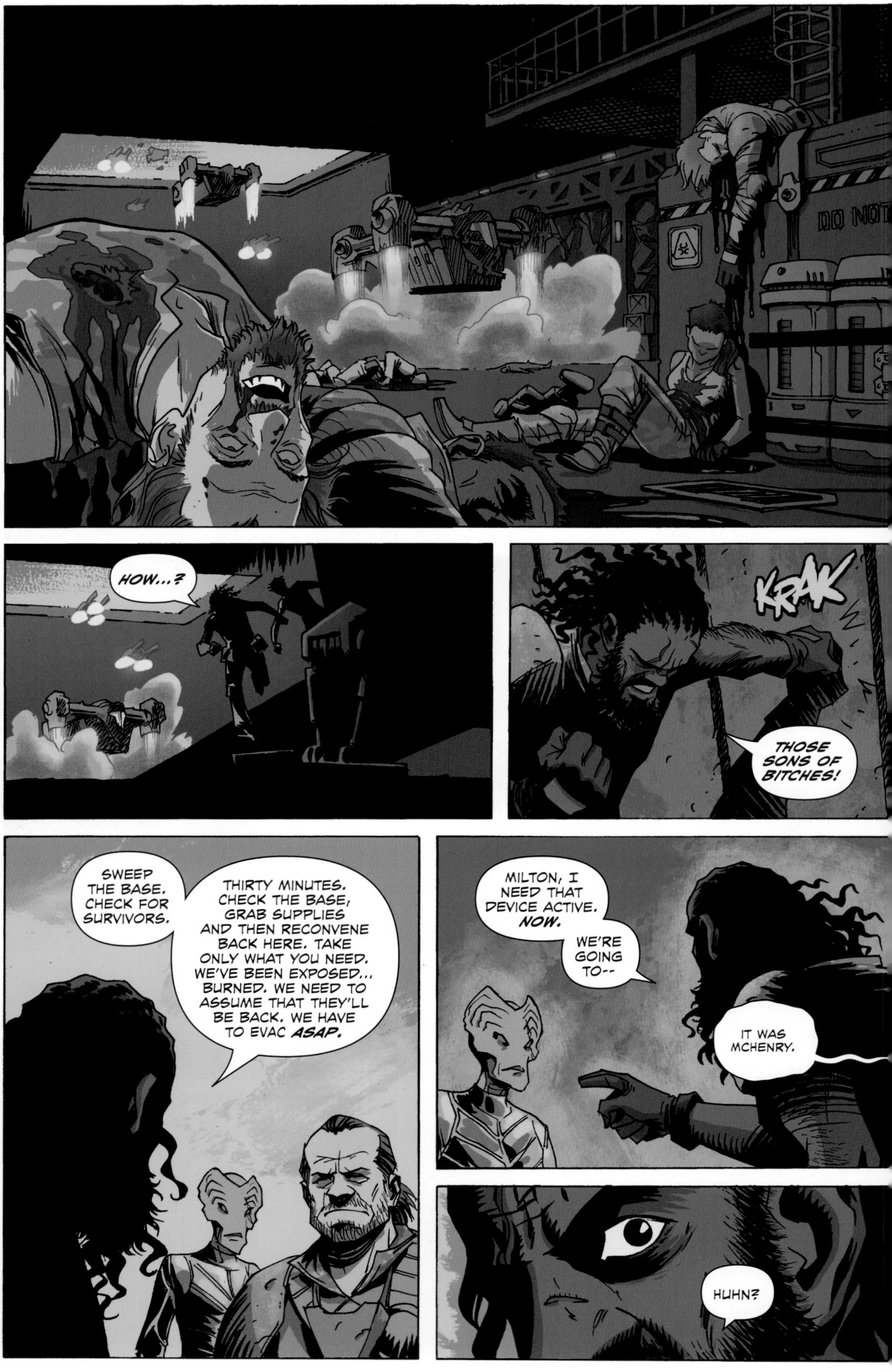
DO NOT
HOW...?
KRAK
THOSE SONS OF BITCHES!
SWEEP THE BASE. CHECK FOR SURVIVORS.
THIRTY MINUTES. CHECK THE BASE, GRAB SUPPLIES AND THEN RECONVENE BACK HERE. TAKE ONLY WHAT YOU NEED. WE'VE BEEN EXPOSED... BURNED. WE NEED TO ASSUME THAT THEY'LL BE BACK. WE HAVE TO EVAC ***ASAP.***
MILTON, I NEED THAT DEVICE ACTIVE. ***NOW.***
WE'RE GOING TO--
IT WAS MCHENRY.
HUHN?

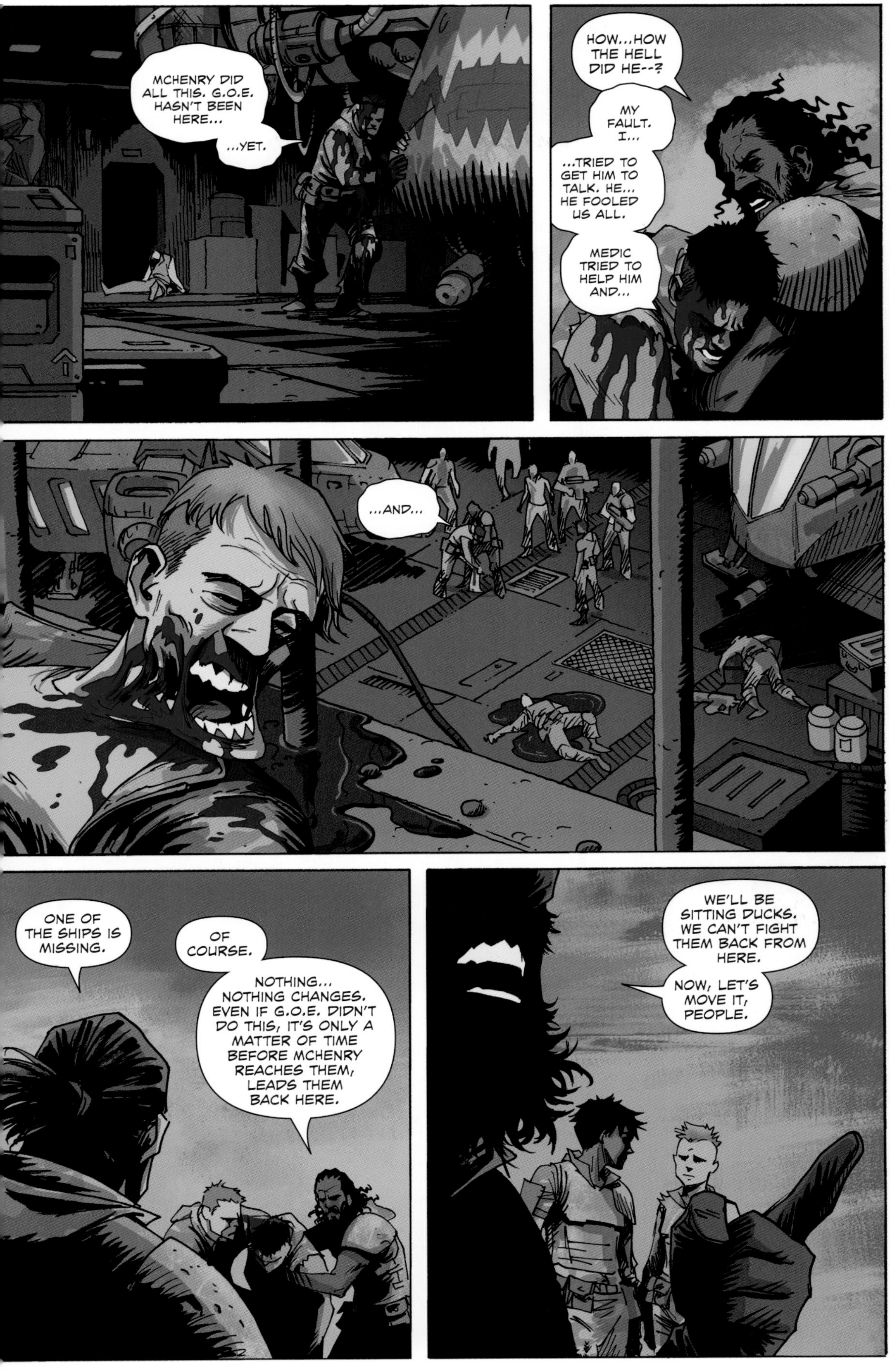
MCHENRY DID ALL THIS. G.O.E. HASN'T BEEN HERE...
...YET.
HOW...HOW THE HELL DID HE--?
MY FAULT. I...
...TRIED TO GET HIM TO TALK. HE... HE FOOLED US ALL.
MEDIC TRIED TO HELP HIM AND...
...AND...
ONE OF THE SHIPS IS MISSING.
OF COURSE.
NOTHING... NOTHING CHANGES. EVEN IF G.O.E. DIDN'T DO THIS, IT'S ONLY A MATTER OF TIME BEFORE MCHENRY REACHES THEM, LEADS THEM BACK HERE.
WE'LL BE SITTING DUCKS. WE CAN'T FIGHT THEM BACK FROM HERE.
NOW, LET'S MOVE IT, PEOPLE.

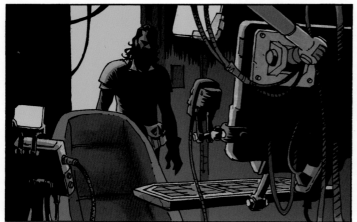

WHAT ARE YOU DOING? YOU CAN'T JUST CALL--

HE CAN'T TALK RIGHT NOW, HE'S--

PUT HIM ON.

I DON'T CARE! PUT HIM ON. *NOW.*

HOLDING...

LUSTIG, YOU'RE NOT SUPPOSED TO CONTACT ME LIKE THIS. WE NEED TO MAKE SURE THAT NO ONE IS TRACKING--

WE HAVE TO MOVE UP THE PLANS. WE NEED TO GO NOW.

I NEED MORE TIME TO ARRANGE THE PASSAGE. YOU CAN'T JUST EXPECT US TO--

WE DON'T MOVE NOW, THEN SAMARA DIES-- WE ALL DIE. YOU'LL HAVE NOTHING.

SO...YOU WANT TO SEE YOUR DAUGHTER AGAIN...

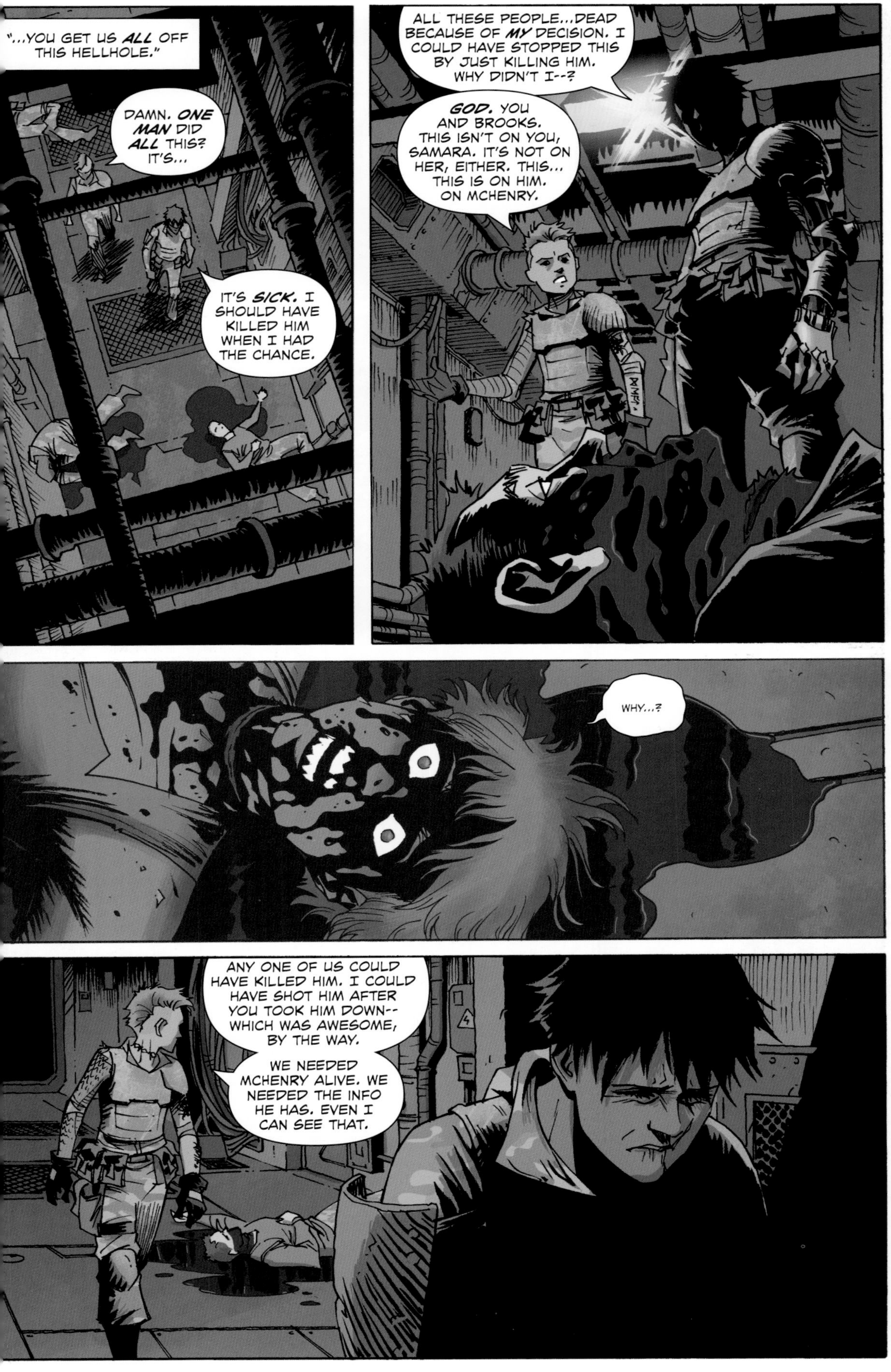
"...YOU GET US ALL OFF THIS HELLHOLE."
DAMN. ONE MAN DID ALL THIS? IT'S...
IT'S SICK. I SHOULD HAVE KILLED HIM WHEN I HAD THE CHANCE.
ALL THESE PEOPLE...DEAD BECAUSE OF MY DECISION. I COULD HAVE STOPPED THIS BY JUST KILLING HIM. WHY DIDN'T I--?
GOD. YOU AND BROOKS. THIS ISN'T ON YOU, SAMARA. IT'S NOT ON HER, EITHER. THIS... THIS IS ON HIM. ON MCHENRY.
WHY...?
ANY ONE OF US COULD HAVE KILLED HIM. I COULD HAVE SHOT HIM AFTER YOU TOOK HIM DOWN-- WHICH WAS AWESOME, BY THE WAY.
WE NEEDED MCHENRY ALIVE. WE NEEDED THE INFO HE HAS. EVEN I CAN SEE THAT.

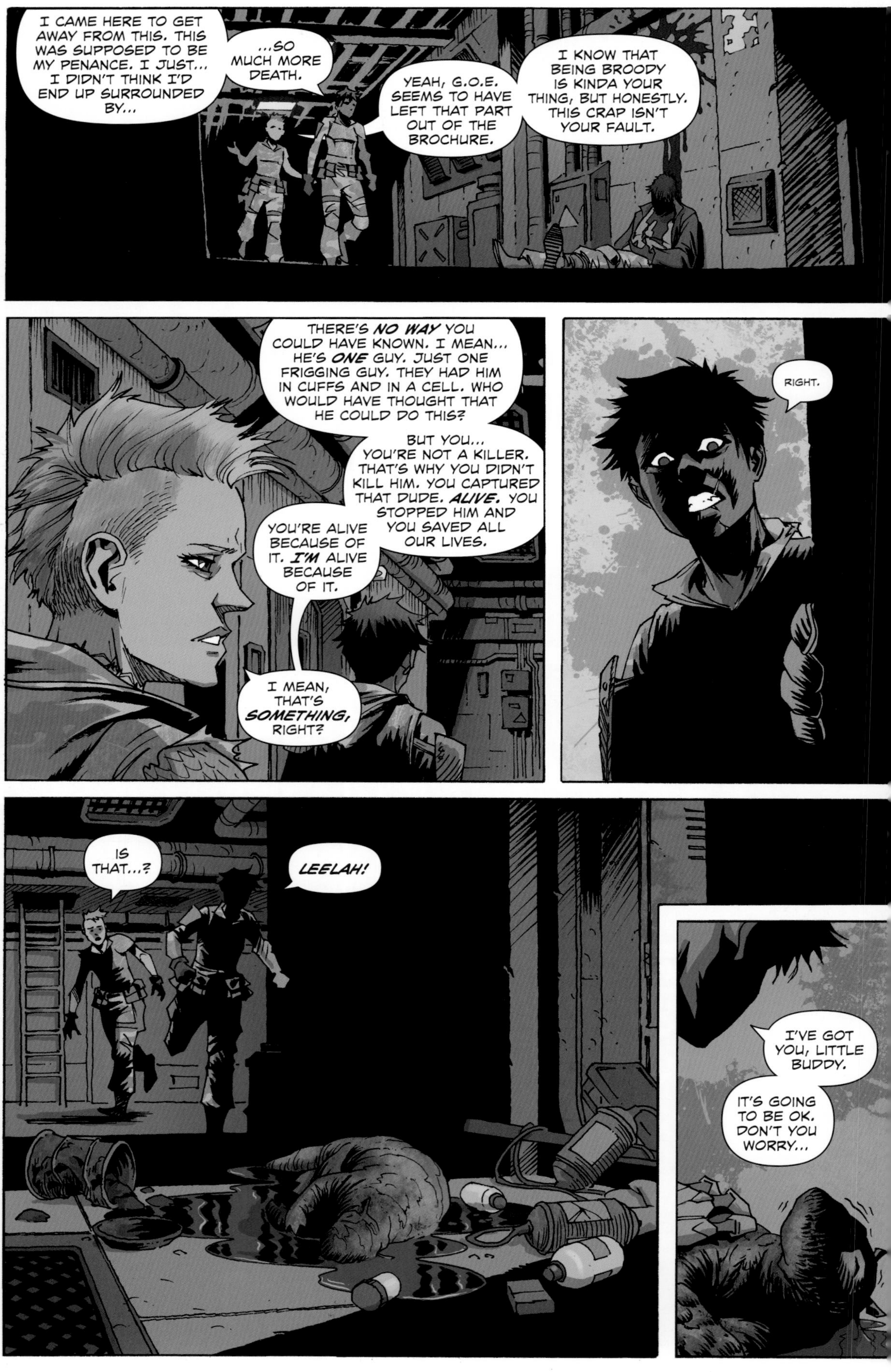
I CAME HERE TO GET AWAY FROM THIS. THIS WAS SUPPOSED TO BE MY PENANCE. I JUST... I DIDN'T THINK I'D END UP SURROUNDED BY...
...SO MUCH MORE DEATH.
YEAH, G.O.E. SEEMS TO HAVE LEFT THAT PART OUT OF THE BROCHURE.
I KNOW THAT BEING BROODY IS KINDA YOUR THING, BUT HONESTLY. THIS CRAP ISN'T YOUR FAULT.
THERE'S NO WAY YOU COULD HAVE KNOWN. I MEAN... HE'S ONE GUY. JUST ONE FRIGGING GUY. THEY HAD HIM IN CUFFS AND IN A CELL. WHO WOULD HAVE THOUGHT THAT HE COULD DO THIS?
BUT YOU... YOU'RE NOT A KILLER. THAT'S WHY YOU DIDN'T KILL HIM. YOU CAPTURED THAT DUDE. ALIVE. YOU STOPPED HIM AND YOU SAVED ALL OUR LIVES.
YOU'RE ALIVE BECAUSE OF IT. I'M ALIVE BECAUSE OF IT.
I MEAN, THAT'S SOMETHING, RIGHT?
RIGHT.
IS THAT...?
LEELAH!
I'VE GOT YOU, LITTLE BUDDY.
IT'S GOING TO BE OK. DON'T YOU WORRY...

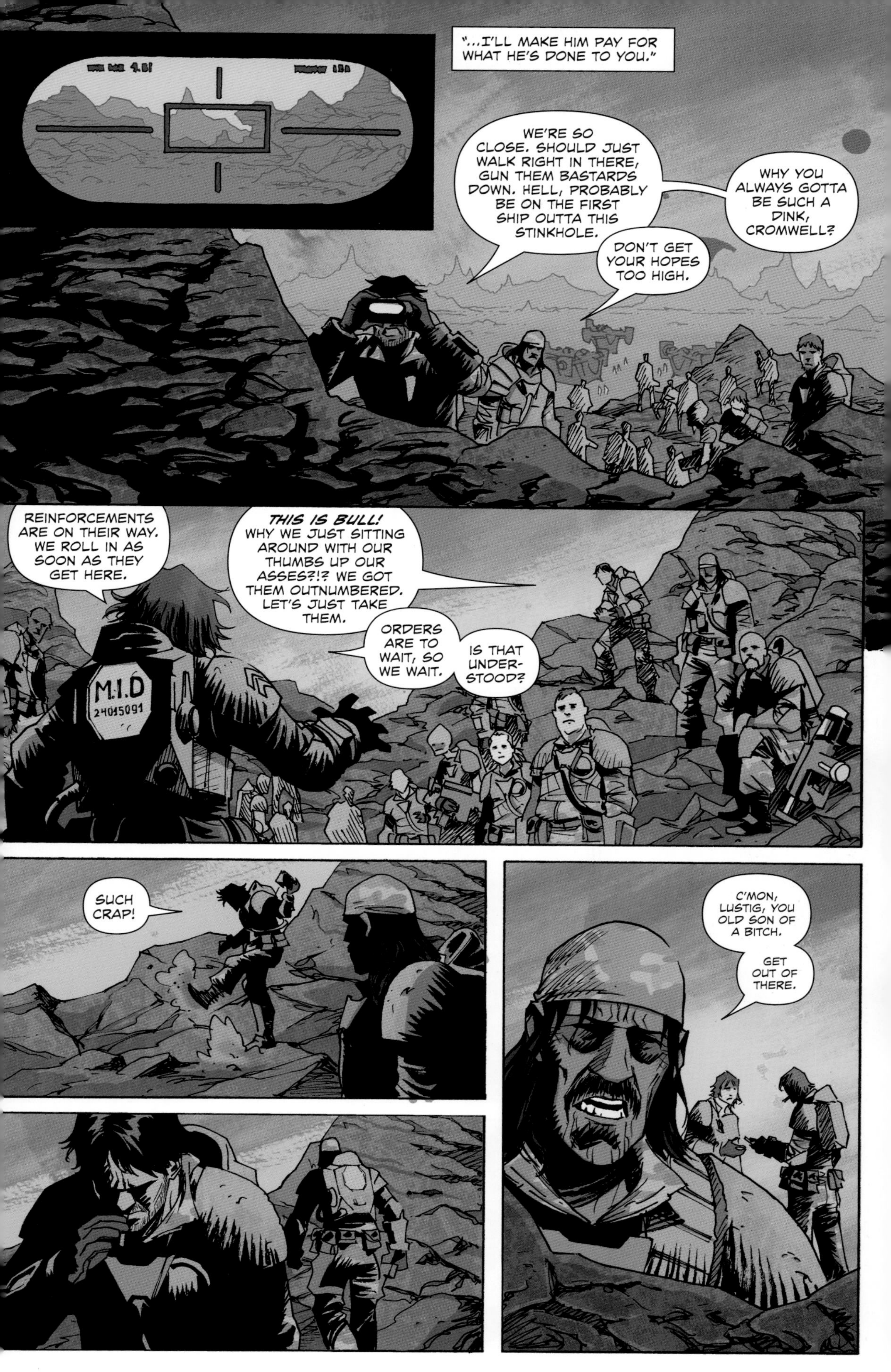
"...I'LL MAKE HIM PAY FOR WHAT HE'S DONE TO YOU."
WE'RE SO CLOSE. SHOULD JUST WALK RIGHT IN THERE, GUN THEM BASTARDS DOWN. HELL, PROBABLY BE ON THE FIRST SHIP OUTTA THIS STINKHOLE.
WHY YOU ALWAYS GOTTA BE SUCH A DINK, CROMWELL?
DON'T GET YOUR HOPES TOO HIGH.
REINFORCEMENTS ARE ON THEIR WAY. WE ROLL IN AS SOON AS THEY GET HERE.
THIS IS BULL! WHY WE JUST SITTING AROUND WITH OUR THUMBS UP OUR ASSES?!? WE GOT THEM OUTNUMBERED. LET'S JUST TAKE THEM.
ORDERS ARE TO WAIT, SO WE WAIT.
IS THAT UNDER-STOOD?
M.I.D
24015091
SUCH CRAP!
C'MON, LUSTIG, YOU OLD SON OF A BITCH.
GET OUT OF THERE.

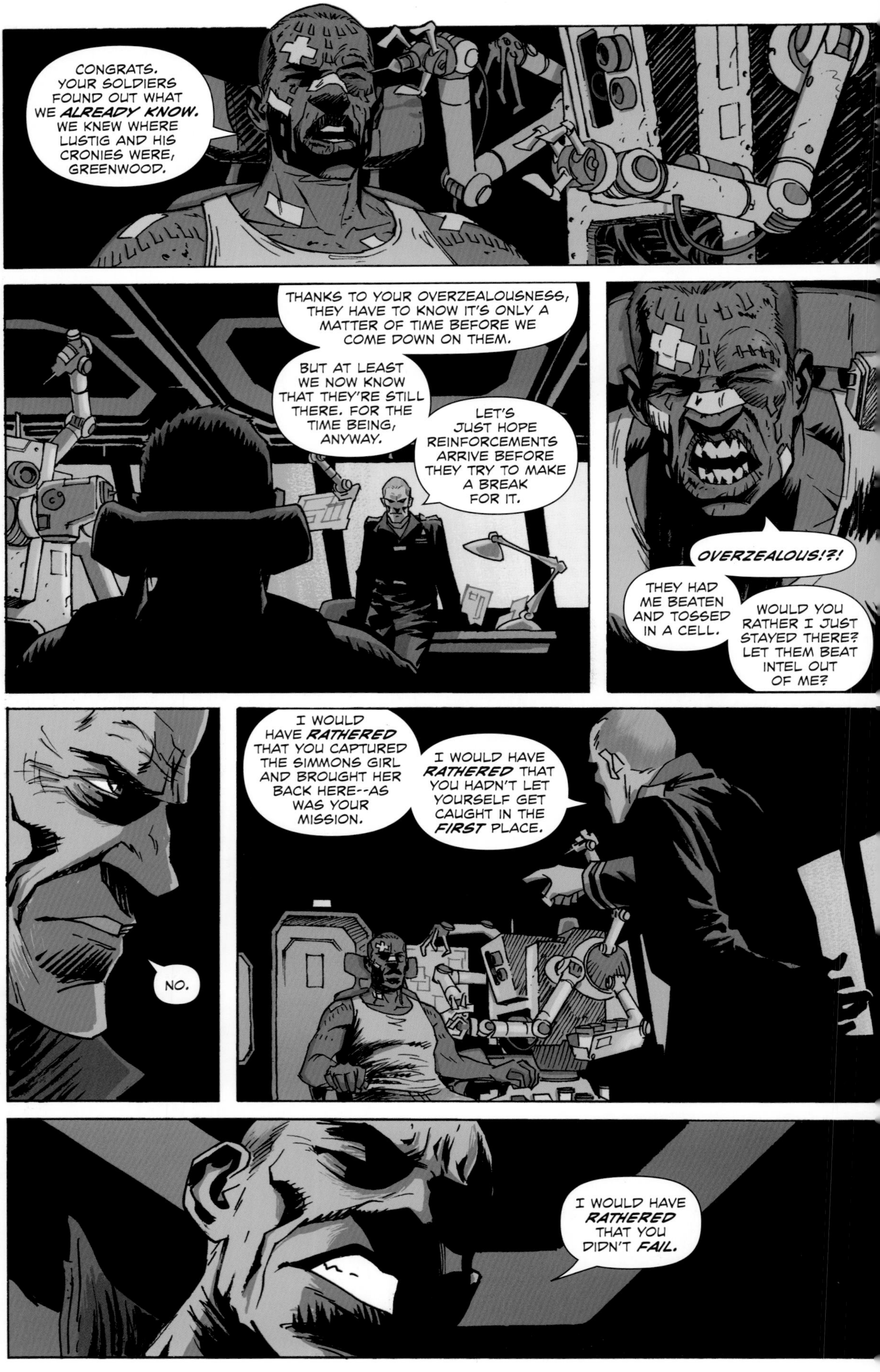
CONGRATS. YOUR SOLDIERS FOUND OUT WHAT WE ALREADY KNOW. WE KNEW WHERE LUSTIG AND HIS CRONIES WERE, GREENWOOD.
THANKS TO YOUR OVERZEALOUSNESS, THEY HAVE TO KNOW IT'S ONLY A MATTER OF TIME BEFORE WE COME DOWN ON THEM.
BUT AT LEAST WE NOW KNOW THAT THEY'RE STILL THERE. FOR THE TIME BEING, ANYWAY.
LET'S JUST HOPE REINFORCEMENTS ARRIVE BEFORE THEY TRY TO MAKE A BREAK FOR IT.
OVERZEALOUS!?!
THEY HAD ME BEATEN AND TOSSED IN A CELL.
WOULD YOU RATHER I JUST STAYED THERE? LET THEM BEAT INTEL OUT OF ME?
I WOULD HAVE RATHERED THAT YOU CAPTURED THE SIMMONS GIRL AND BROUGHT HER BACK HERE--AS WAS YOUR MISSION.
I WOULD HAVE RATHERED THAT YOU HADN'T LET YOURSELF GET CAUGHT IN THE FIRST PLACE.
NO.
I WOULD HAVE RATHERED THAT YOU DIDN'T FAIL.

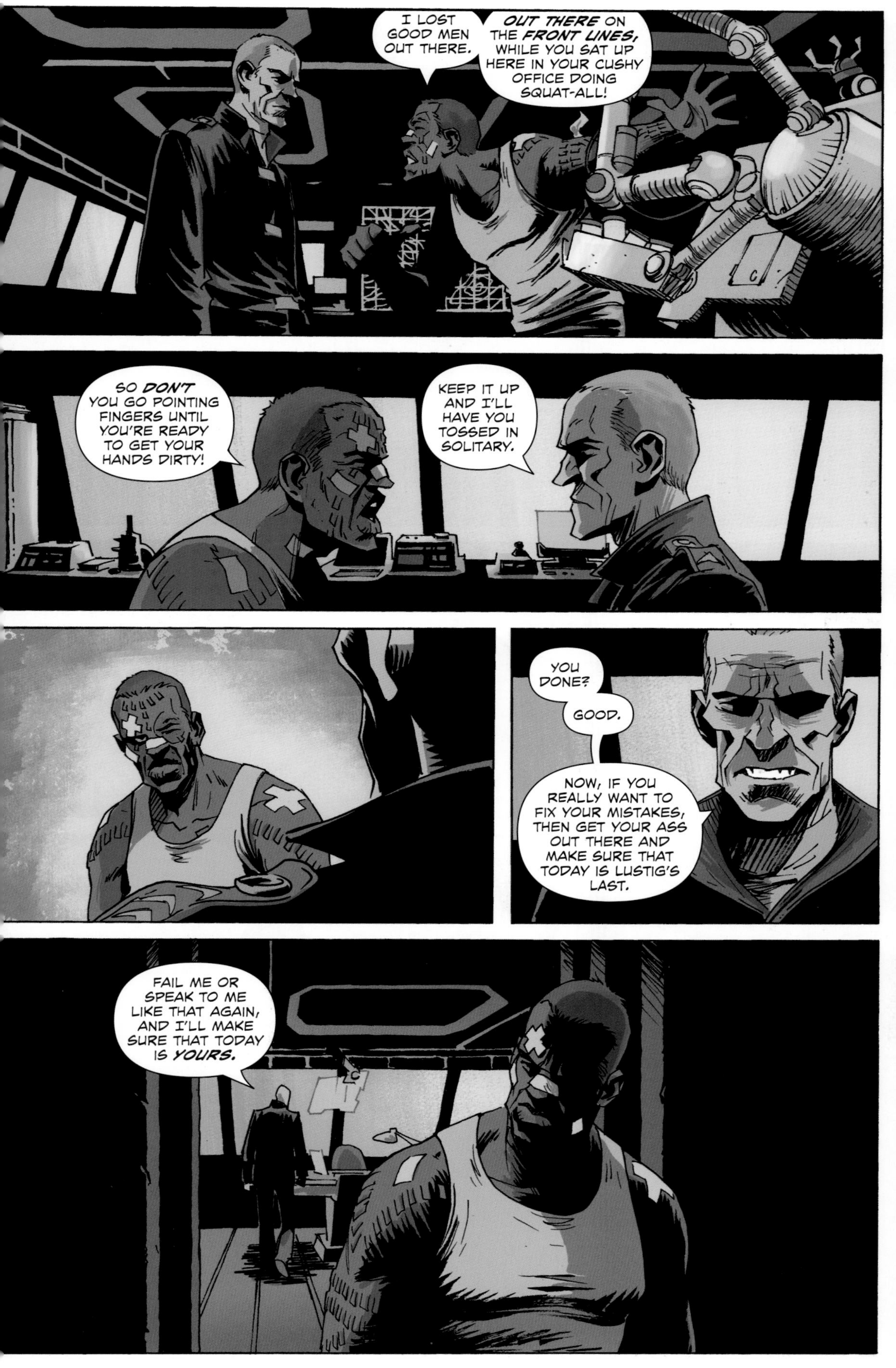
I LOST GOOD MEN OUT THERE.
OUT THERE ON THE FRONT LINES, WHILE YOU SAT UP HERE IN YOUR CUSHY OFFICE DOING SQUAT-ALL!
SO DON'T YOU GO POINTING FINGERS UNTIL YOU'RE READY TO GET YOUR HANDS DIRTY!
KEEP IT UP AND I'LL HAVE YOU TOSSED IN SOLITARY.
YOU DONE?
GOOD.
NOW, IF YOU REALLY WANT TO FIX YOUR MISTAKES, THEN GET YOUR ASS OUT THERE AND MAKE SURE THAT TODAY IS LUSTIG'S LAST.
FAIL ME OR SPEAK TO ME LIKE THAT AGAIN, AND I'LL MAKE SURE THAT TODAY IS YOURS.

GATHER AROUND, EVERYONE. WE DON'T HAVE MUCH TIME.

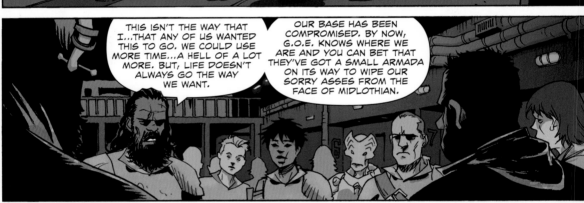

THIS ISN'T THE WAY THAT I...THAT ANY OF US WANTED THIS TO GO. WE COULD USE MORE TIME...A HELL OF A LOT MORE. BUT, LIFE DOESN'T ALWAYS GO THE WAY WE WANT.

OUR BASE HAS BEEN COMPROMISED. BY NOW, G.O.E. KNOWS WHERE WE ARE AND YOU CAN BET THAT THEY'VE GOT A SMALL ARMADA ON ITS WAY TO WIPE OUR SORRY ASSES FROM THE FACE OF MIDLOTHIAN.

WE CAN'T RUN ANYMORE. THERE'S NOWHERE FOR US TO RUN TO.

OUR ONLY HOPE IS CRAMMING THIS FIGHT DOWN THEIR THROATS. TAKING IT RIGHT TO THEM.

IF THEY'RE ON THEIR WAY HERE, THAT MEANS THEIR DEFENSES AT TRANENT WILL BE COMPROMISED, THEY'LL ALL BE HEADED HERE. THIS IS THE TIME TO STRIKE.

RIGHT NOW THERE ARE FOUR TRANSPORT SHIPS AT TRANENT. ENOUGH TO GET US--ALL OF US--BACK HOME TO EARTH. BACK TO OUR FAMILIES, OUR FRIENDS, WHOEVER IT IS YOU GOT WAITING FOR YOU.

BUT IT'S WORTH A SHOT TO END THIS. TO GET US HOME AND TO SPREAD THE TRUTH ABOUT G.O.E. AND WHAT'S REALLY HAPPENING ON MIDLOTHIAN.

BUT I'M NOT GOING TO TRY TO FOOL YOU ALL INTO THINKING WE'RE ALL GOING TO MAKE IT. HELL, I'M NOT GOING TO PROMISE THAT ANY OF US WILL MAKE IT.

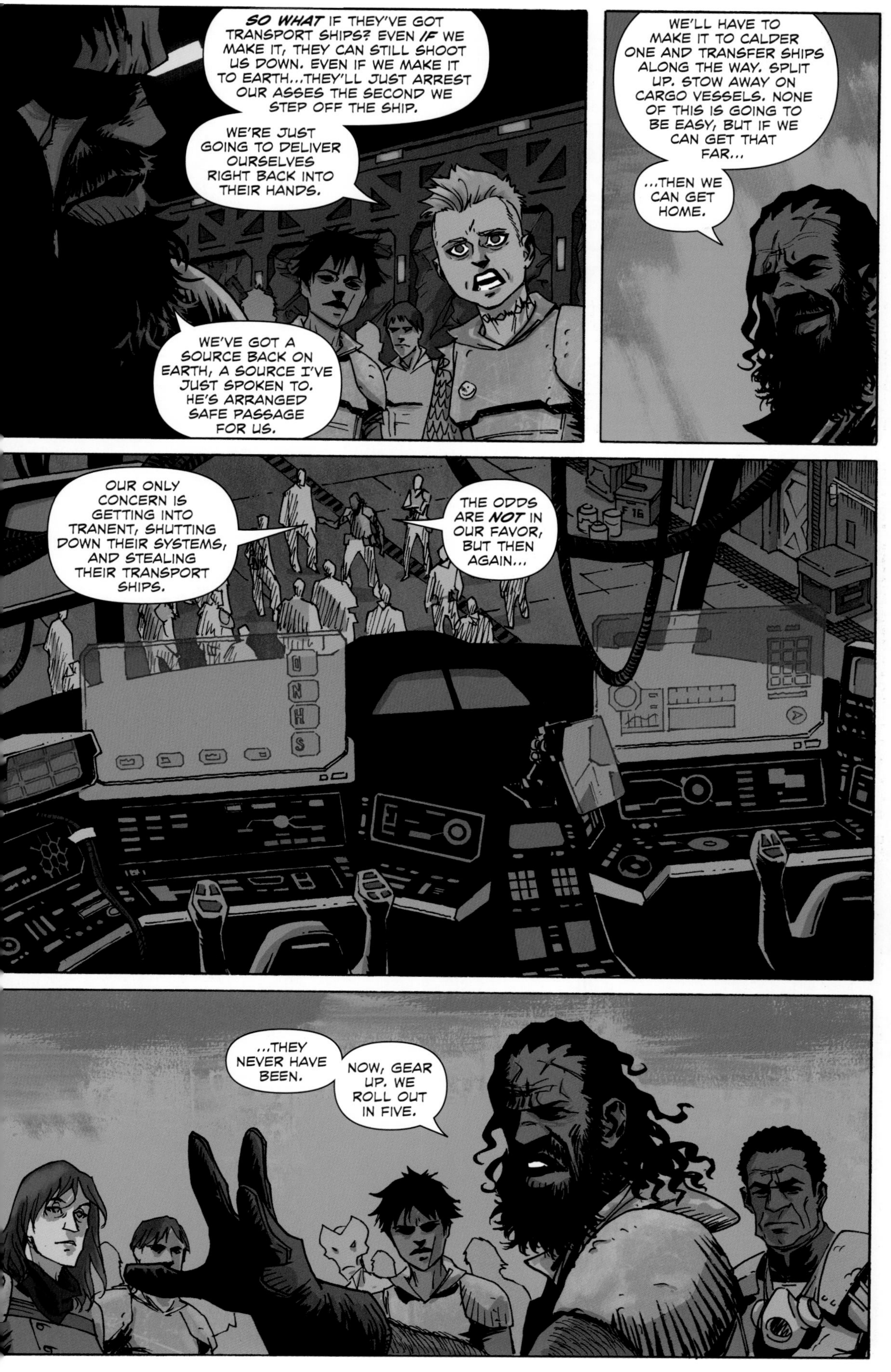
SO WHAT IF THEY'VE GOT TRANSPORT SHIPS? EVEN IF WE MAKE IT, THEY CAN STILL SHOOT US DOWN. EVEN IF WE MAKE IT TO EARTH...THEY'LL JUST ARREST OUR ASSES THE SECOND WE STEP OFF THE SHIP.
WE'RE JUST GOING TO DELIVER OURSELVES RIGHT BACK INTO THEIR HANDS.
WE'VE GOT A SOURCE BACK ON EARTH, A SOURCE I'VE JUST SPOKEN TO. HE'S ARRANGED SAFE PASSAGE FOR US.
WE'LL HAVE TO MAKE IT TO CALDER ONE AND TRANSFER SHIPS ALONG THE WAY. SPLIT UP. STOW AWAY ON CARGO VESSELS. NONE OF THIS IS GOING TO BE EASY, BUT IF WE CAN GET THAT FAR...
...THEN WE CAN GET HOME.
OUR ONLY CONCERN IS GETTING INTO TRANENT, SHUTTING DOWN THEIR SYSTEMS, AND STEALING THEIR TRANSPORT SHIPS.
THE ODDS ARE NOT IN OUR FAVOR, BUT THEN AGAIN...
...THEY NEVER HAVE BEEN.
NOW, GEAR UP. WE ROLL OUT IN FIVE.

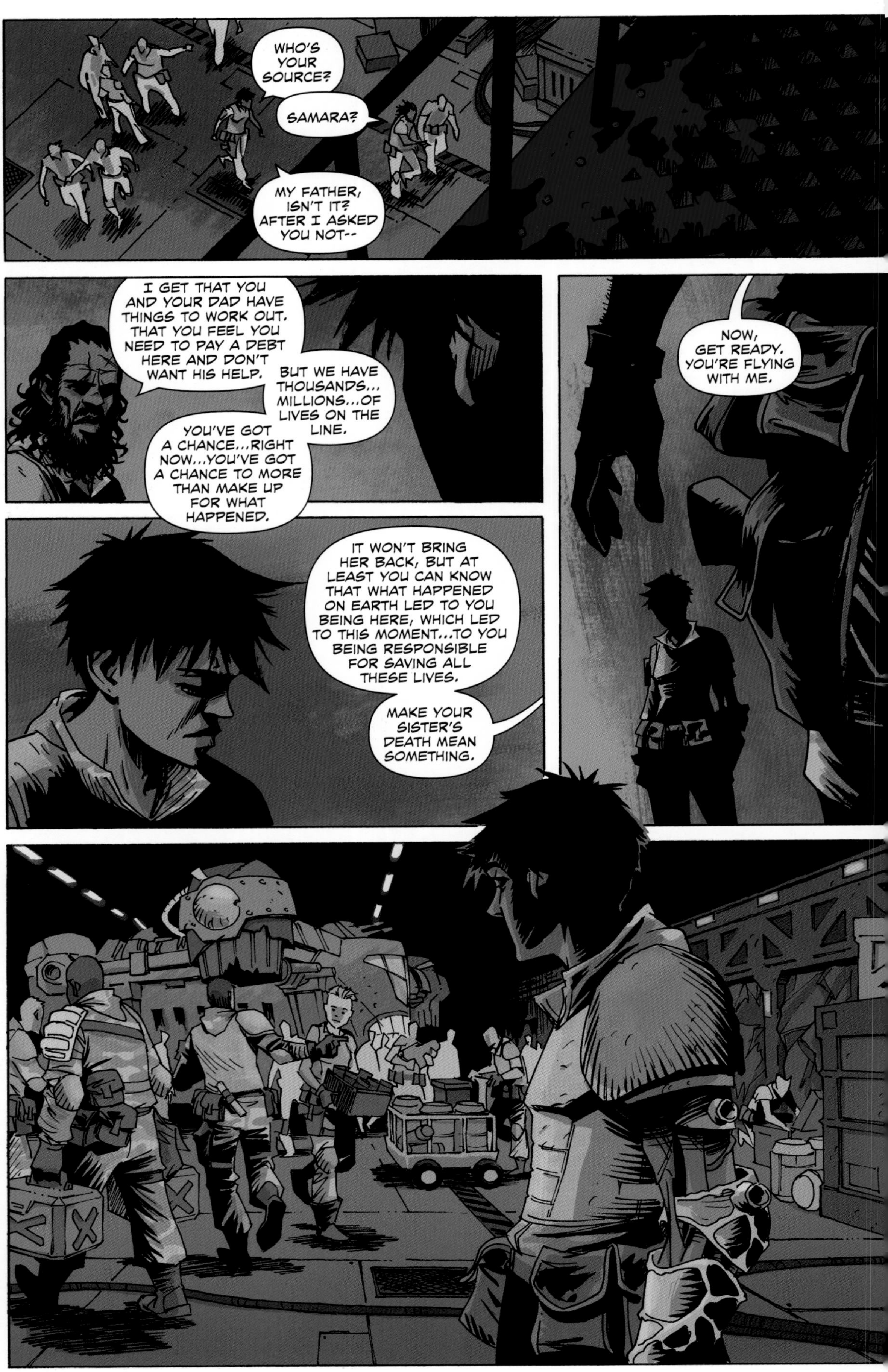
WHO'S YOUR SOURCE?
SAMARA?
MY FATHER, ISN'T IT? AFTER I ASKED YOU NOT--
I GET THAT YOU AND YOUR DAD HAVE THINGS TO WORK OUT. THAT YOU FEEL YOU NEED TO PAY A DEBT HERE AND DON'T WANT HIS HELP.
BUT WE HAVE THOUSANDS... MILLIONS...OF LIVES ON THE LINE.
YOU'VE GOT A CHANCE...RIGHT NOW...YOU'VE GOT A CHANCE TO MORE THAN MAKE UP FOR WHAT HAPPENED.
NOW, GET READY. YOU'RE FLYING WITH ME.
IT WON'T BRING HER BACK, BUT AT LEAST YOU CAN KNOW THAT WHAT HAPPENED ON EARTH LED TO YOU BEING HERE, WHICH LED TO THIS MOMENT...TO YOU BEING RESPONSIBLE FOR SAVING ALL THESE LIVES.
MAKE YOUR SISTER'S DEATH MEAN SOMETHING.

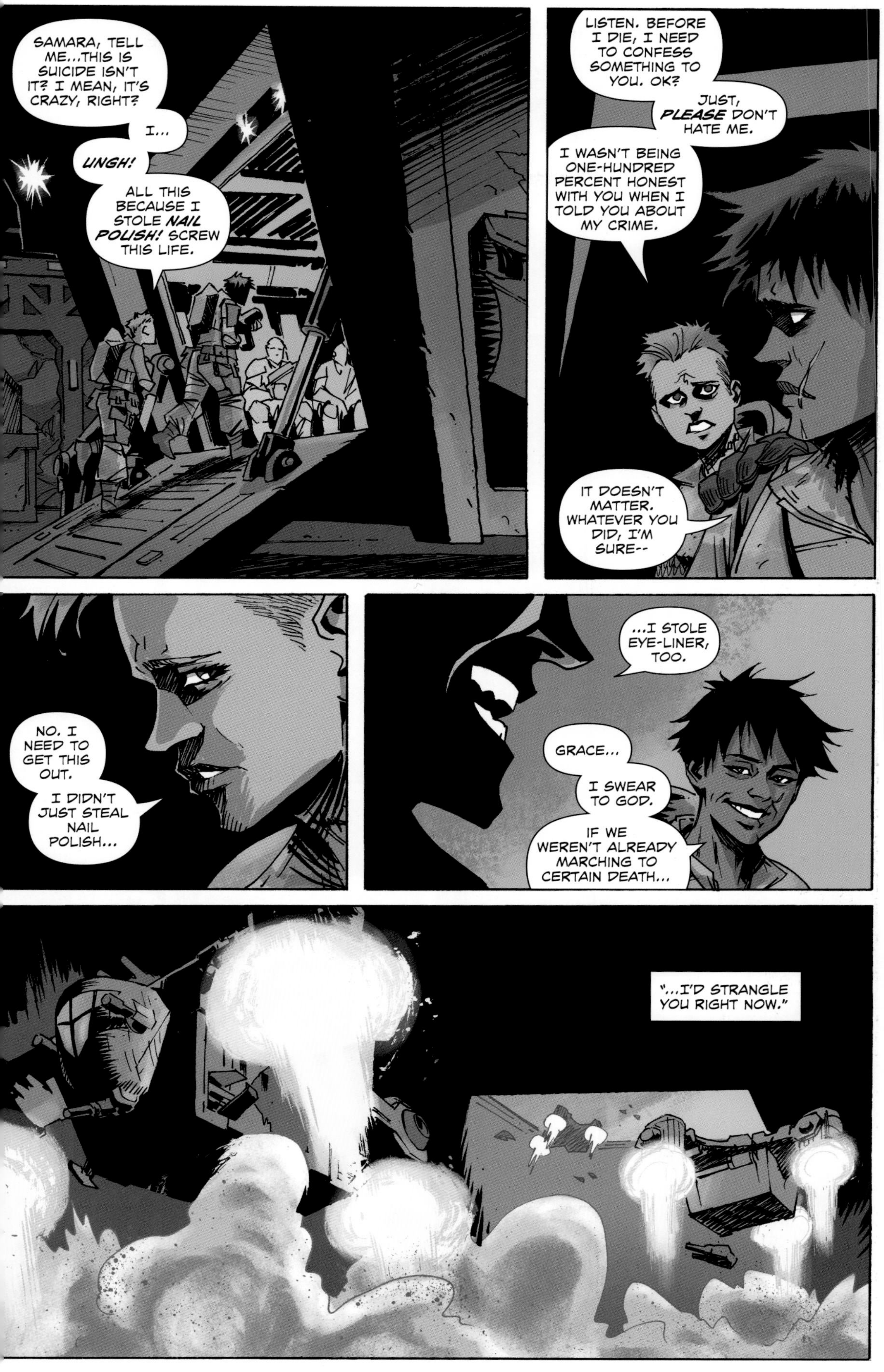
SAMARA, TELL ME...THIS IS SUICIDE ISN'T IT? I MEAN, IT'S CRAZY, RIGHT?
I...
UNGH!
ALL THIS BECAUSE I STOLE NAIL POLISH! SCREW THIS LIFE.
LISTEN. BEFORE I DIE, I NEED TO CONFESS SOMETHING TO YOU. OK?
JUST, PLEASE DON'T HATE ME.
I WASN'T BEING ONE-HUNDRED PERCENT HONEST WITH YOU WHEN I TOLD YOU ABOUT MY CRIME.
IT DOESN'T MATTER. WHATEVER YOU DID, I'M SURE--
NO. I NEED TO GET THIS OUT.
I DIDN'T JUST STEAL NAIL POLISH...
...I STOLE EYE-LINER, TOO.
GRACE...
I SWEAR TO GOD.
IF WE WEREN'T ALREADY MARCHING TO CERTAIN DEATH...
"...I'D STRANGLE YOU RIGHT NOW."

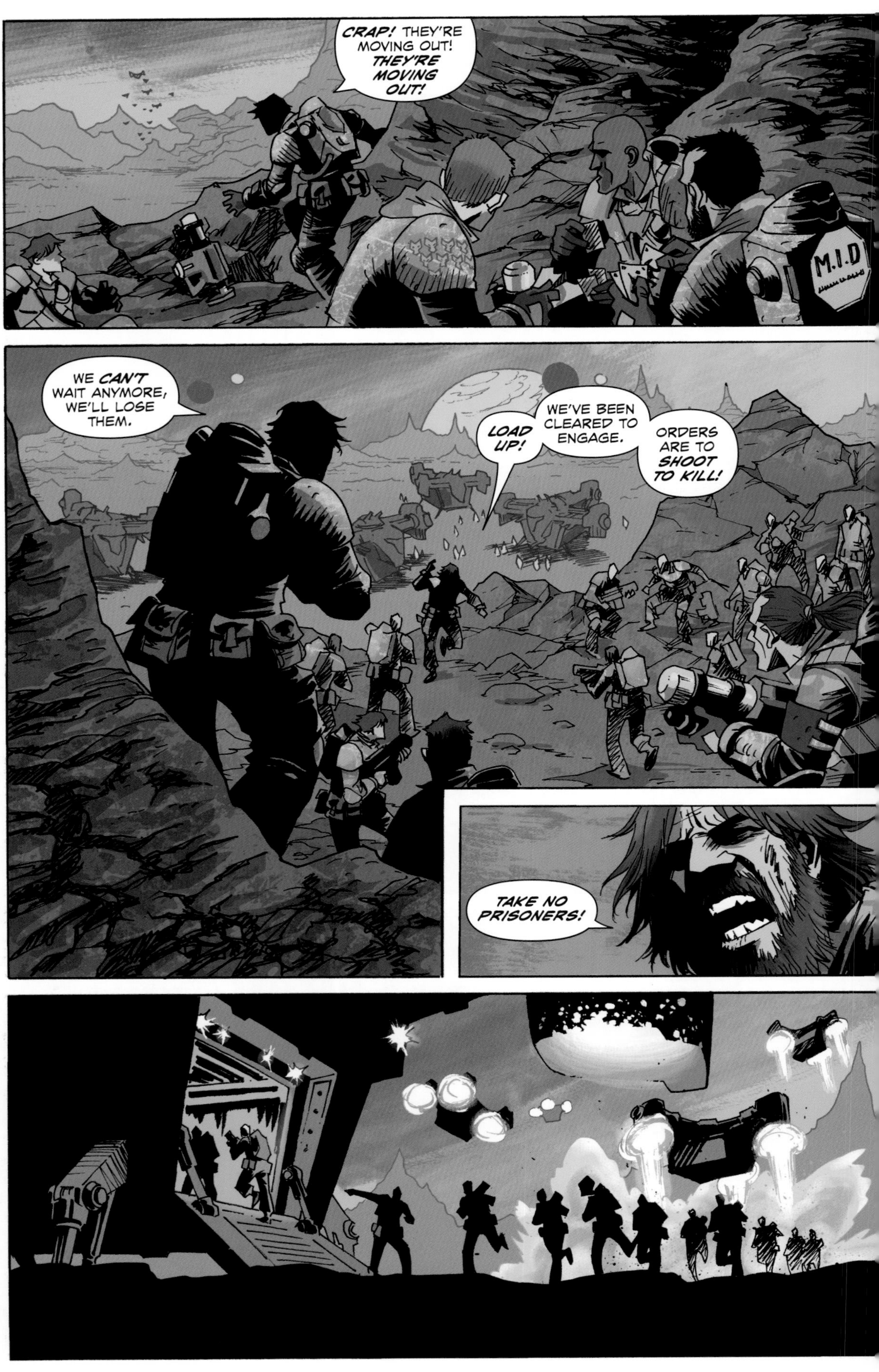
CRAP! THEY'RE MOVING OUT! THEY'RE MOVING OUT!
M.I.D
WE CAN'T WAIT ANYMORE, WE'LL LOSE THEM.
LOAD UP!
WE'VE BEEN CLEARED TO ENGAGE.
ORDERS ARE TO SHOOT TO KILL!
TAKE NO PRISONERS!

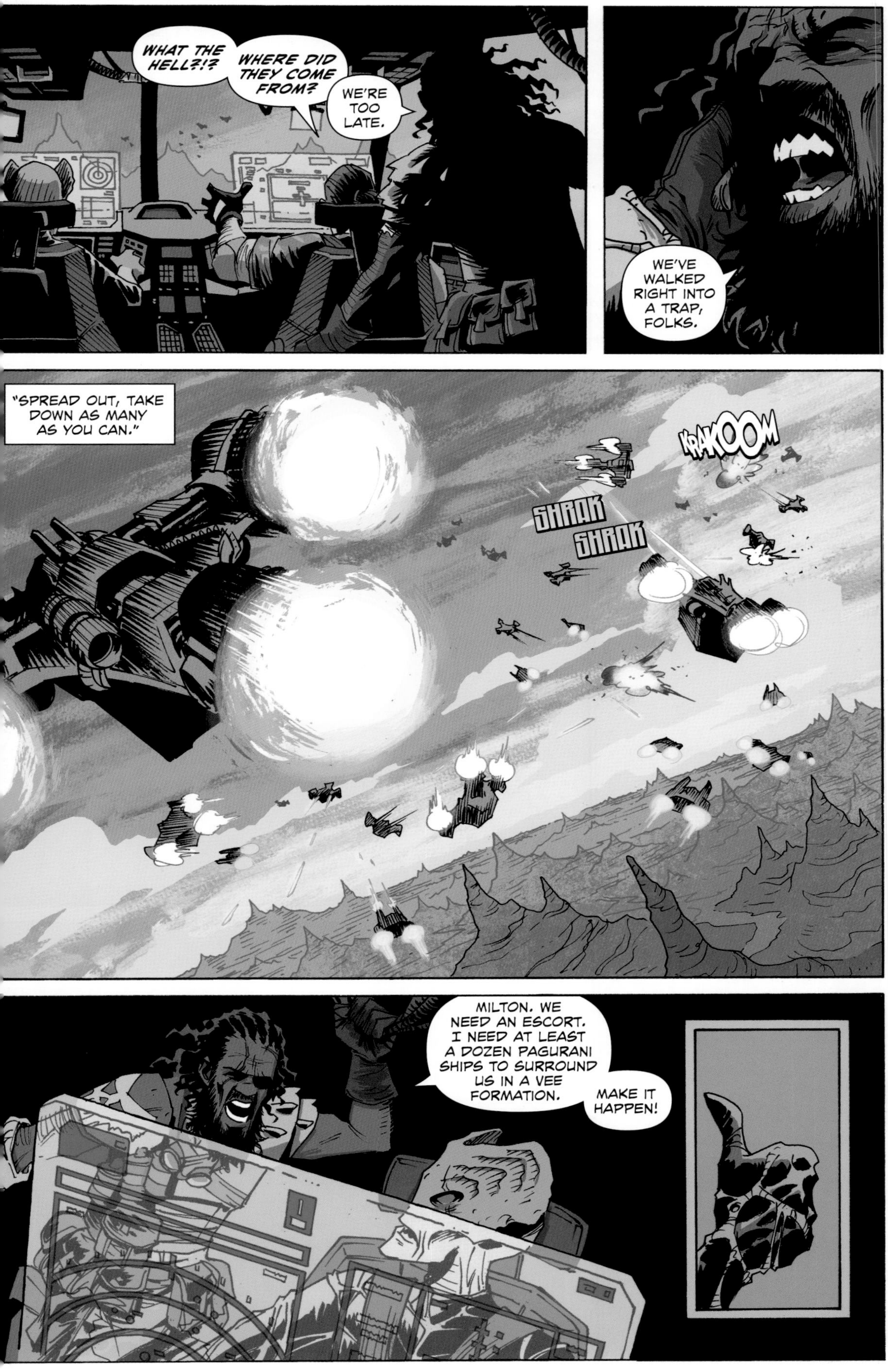
WHAT THE HELL?!?
WHERE DID THEY COME FROM?
WE'RE TOO LATE.
WE'VE WALKED RIGHT INTO A TRAP, FOLKS.
"SPREAD OUT, TAKE DOWN AS MANY AS YOU CAN."
KRAKOOM
SHRAK
SHRAK
MILTON. WE NEED AN ESCORT. I NEED AT LEAST A DOZEN PAGURANI SHIPS TO SURROUND US IN A VEE FORMATION.
MAKE IT HAPPEN!

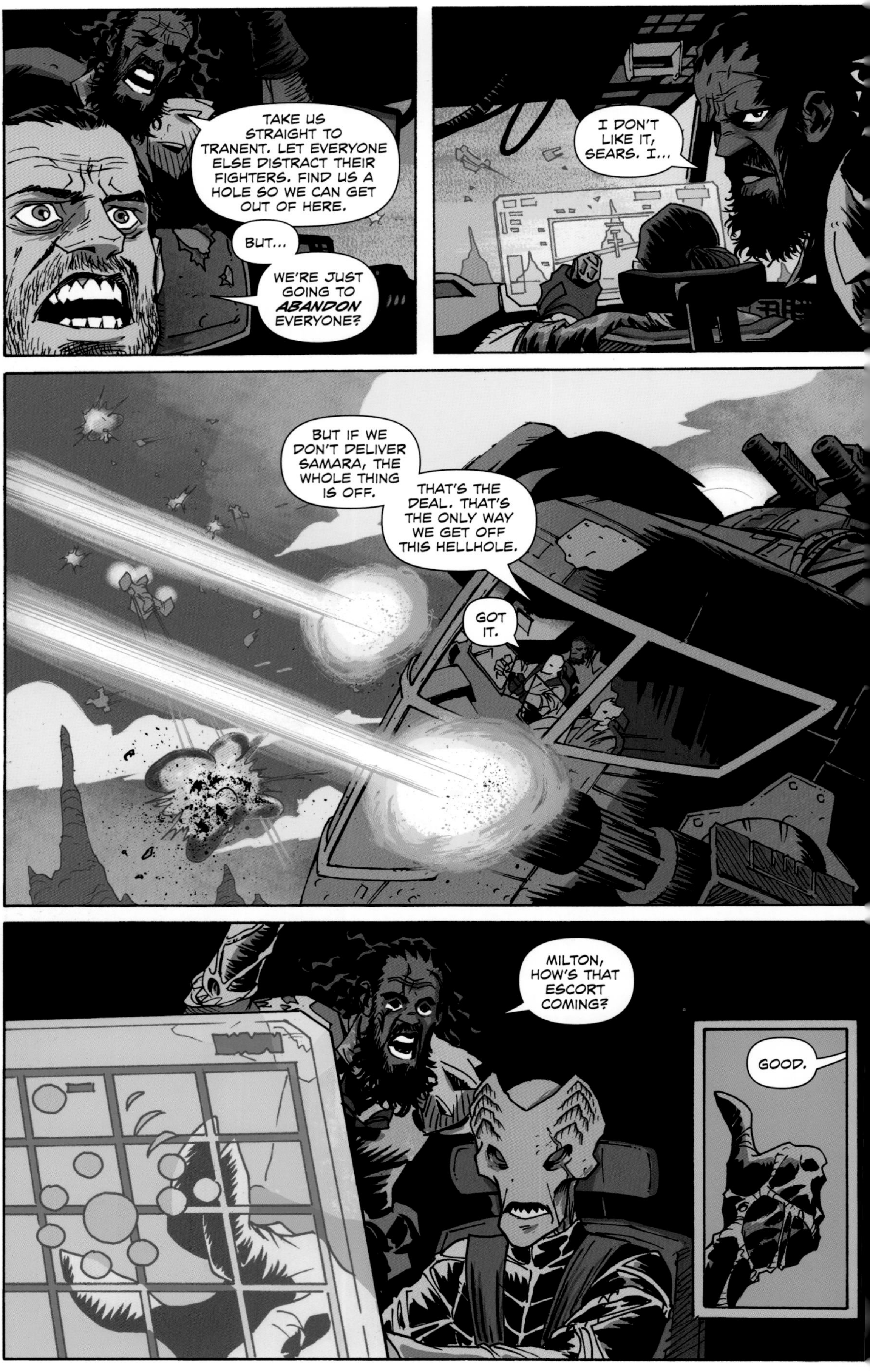
TAKE US STRAIGHT TO TRANENT. LET EVERYONE ELSE DISTRACT THEIR FIGHTERS. FIND US A HOLE SO WE CAN GET OUT OF HERE.
BUT...
WE'RE JUST GOING TO *ABANDON* EVERYONE?
I DON'T LIKE IT, SEARS. I...
BUT IF WE DON'T DELIVER SAMARA, THE WHOLE THING IS OFF.
THAT'S THE DEAL. THAT'S THE ONLY WAY WE GET OFF THIS HELLHOLE.
GOT IT.
MILTON, HOW'S THAT ESCORT COMING?
GOOD.

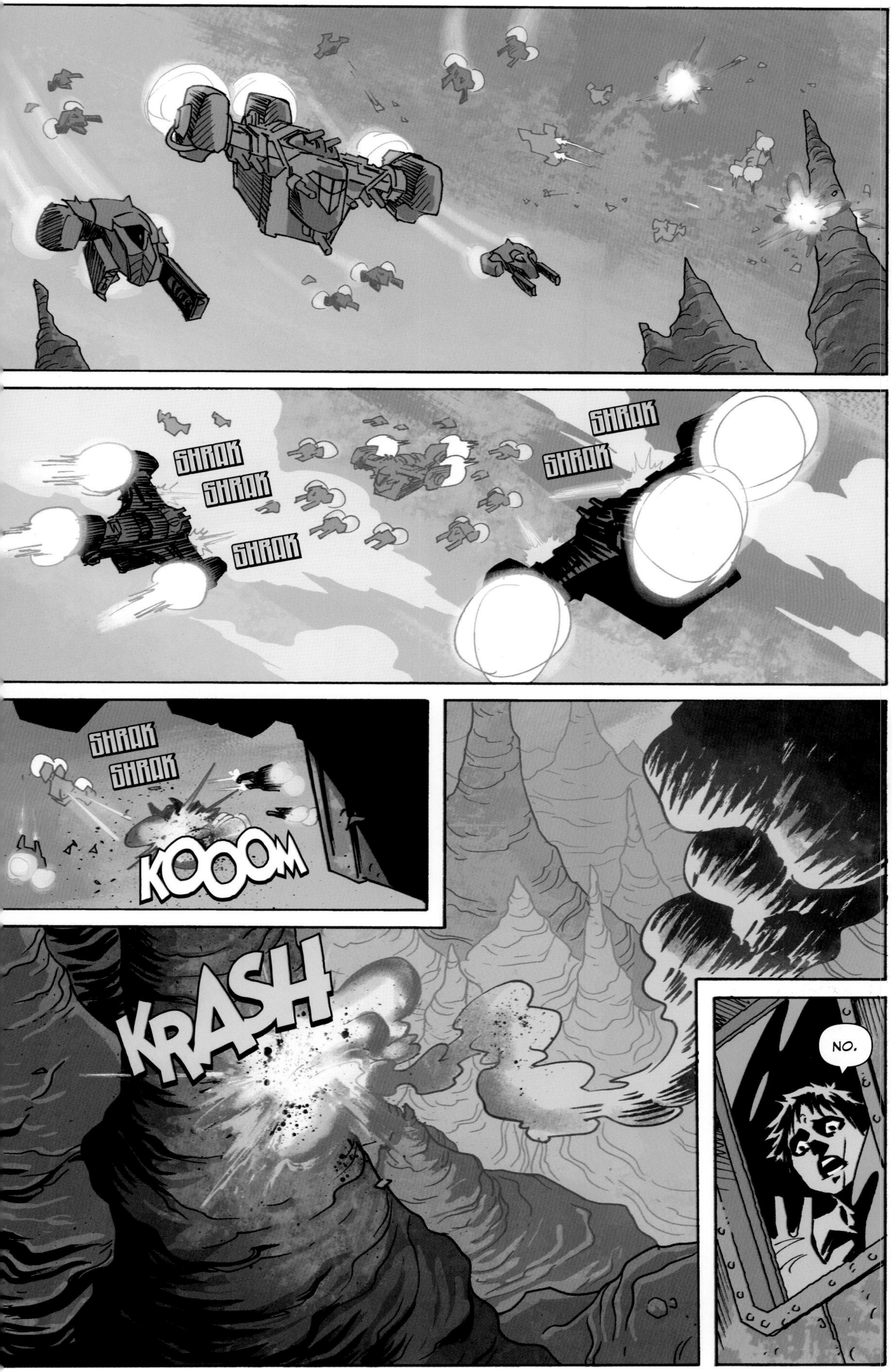
SHRAK
SHRAK
SHRAK
SHRAK
SHRAK
SHRAK
SHRAK
KOOOM
KRASH
NO.

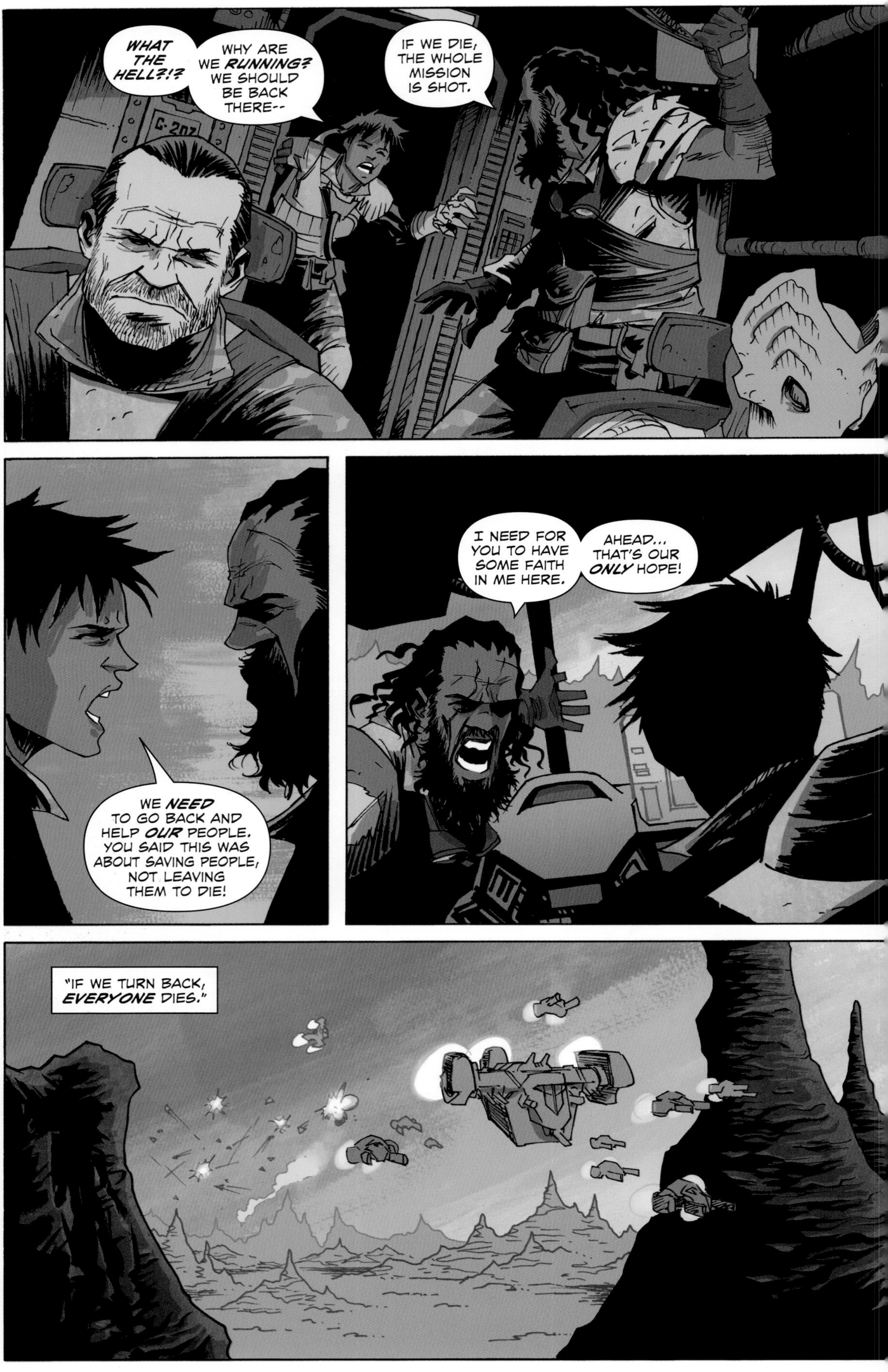
WHAT THE HELL?!?
WHY ARE WE RUNNING? WE SHOULD BE BACK THERE--
IF WE DIE, THE WHOLE MISSION IS SHOT.
WE NEED TO GO BACK AND HELP OUR PEOPLE. YOU SAID THIS WAS ABOUT SAVING PEOPLE, NOT LEAVING THEM TO DIE!
I NEED FOR YOU TO HAVE SOME FAITH IN ME HERE.
AHEAD... THAT'S OUR ONLY HOPE!
"IF WE TURN BACK, EVERYONE DIES."

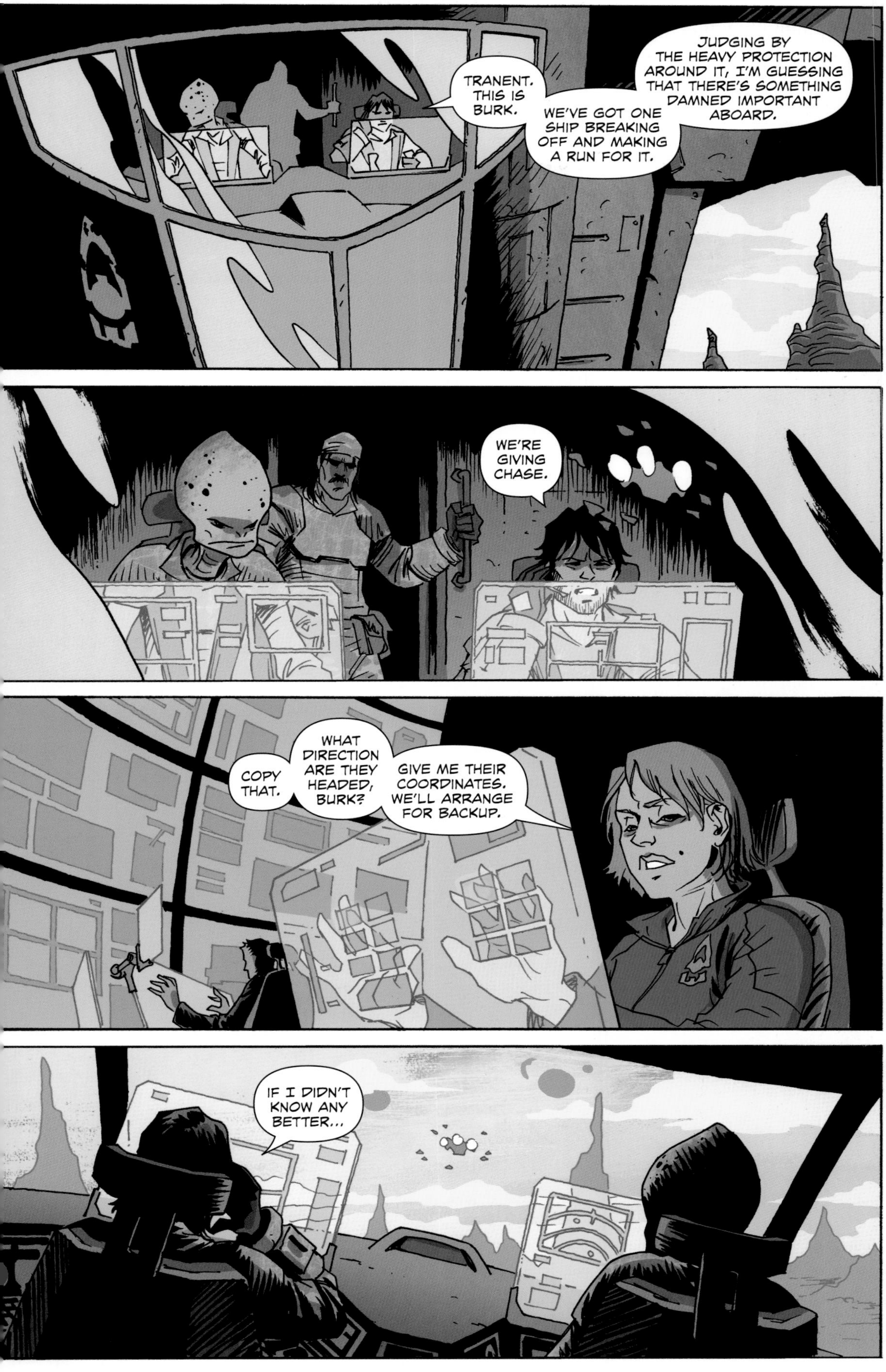
TRANENT. THIS IS BURK.
WE'VE GOT ONE SHIP BREAKING OFF AND MAKING A RUN FOR IT.
JUDGING BY THE HEAVY PROTECTION AROUND IT, I'M GUESSING THAT THERE'S SOMETHING DAMNED IMPORTANT ABOARD.
WE'RE GIVING CHASE.
COPY THAT.
WHAT DIRECTION ARE THEY HEADED, BURK?
GIVE ME THEIR COORDINATES. WE'LL ARRANGE FOR BACKUP.
IF I DIDN'T KNOW ANY BETTER...

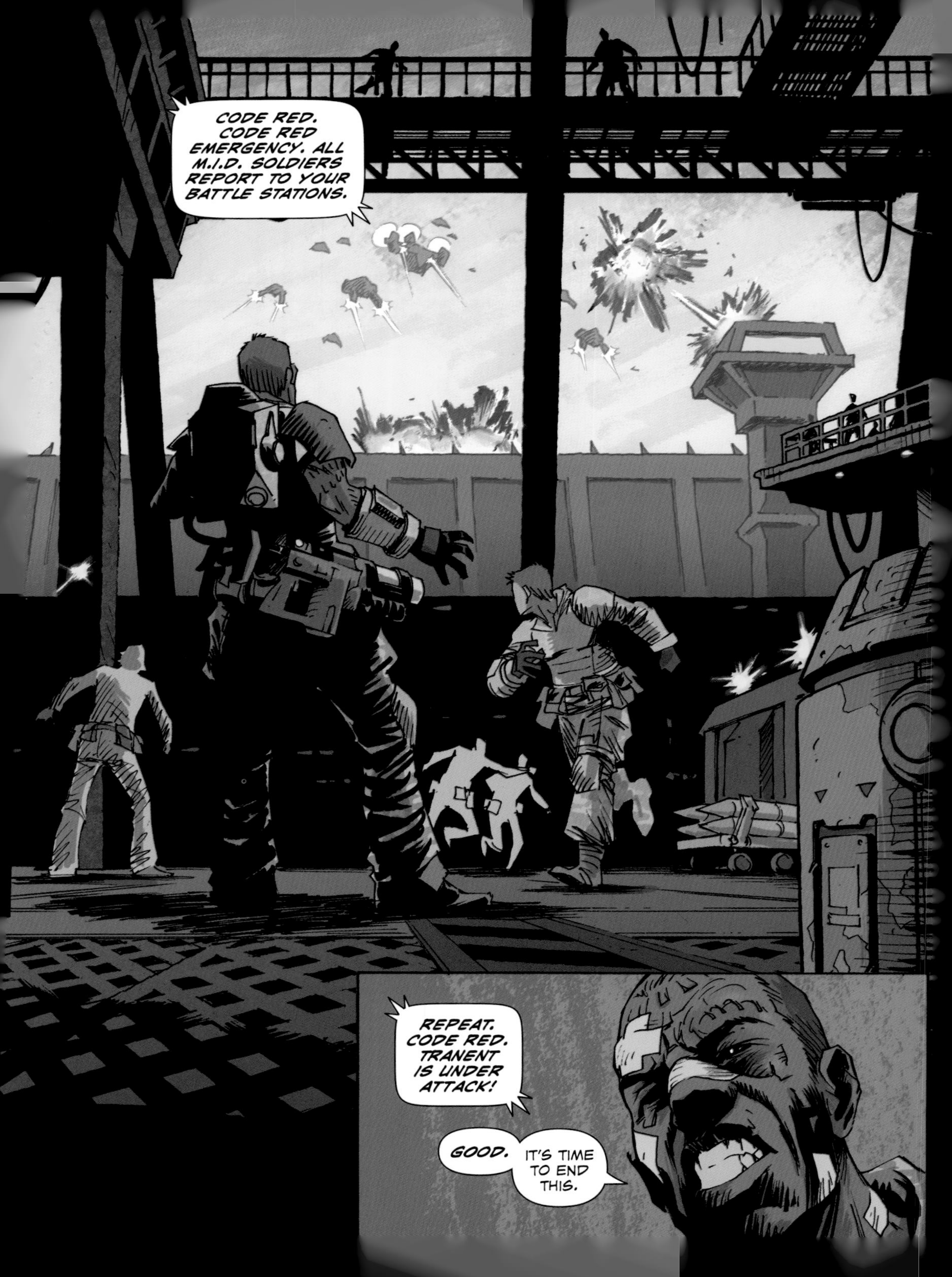
CODE RED. CODE RED EMERGENCY. ALL M.I.D. SOLDIERS REPORT TO YOUR BATTLE STATIONS.
REPEAT. CODE RED. TRANENT IS UNDER ATTACK!
GOOD.
IT'S TIME TO END THIS.

ISSUE 007 COVER

DAMIAN COUCIERO

WITH COLORS BY **JORDAN BOYD**

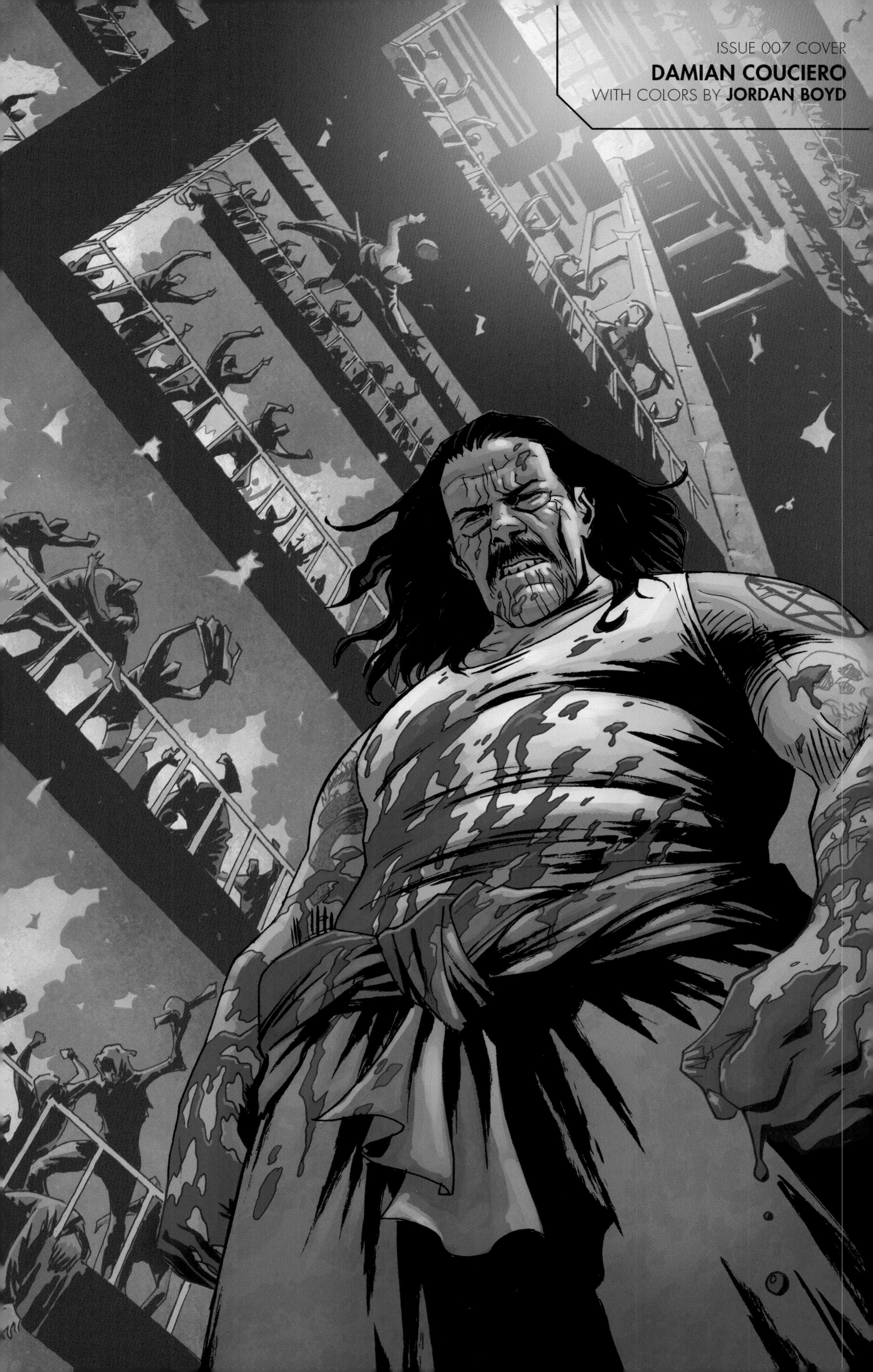

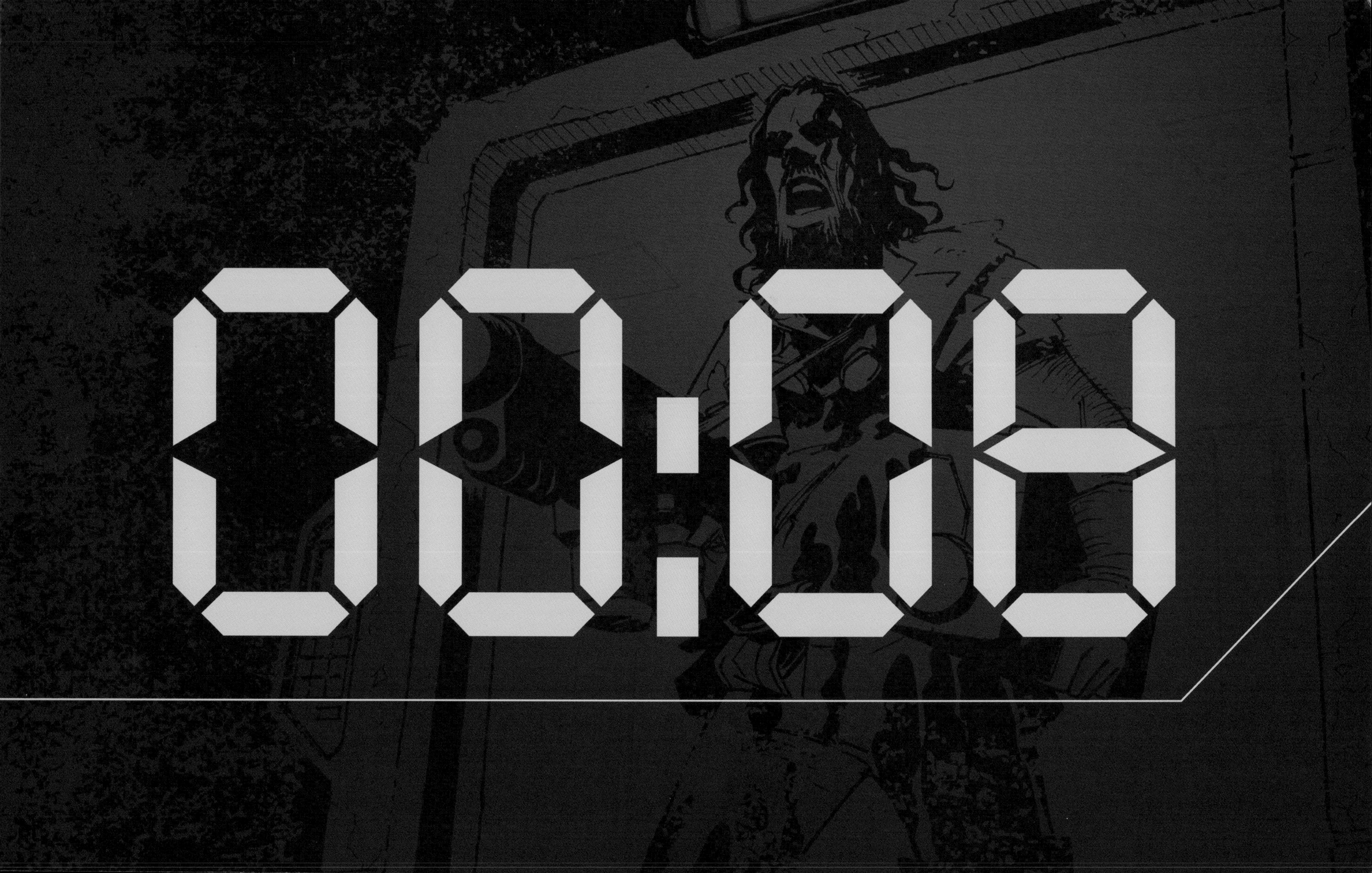
00:08

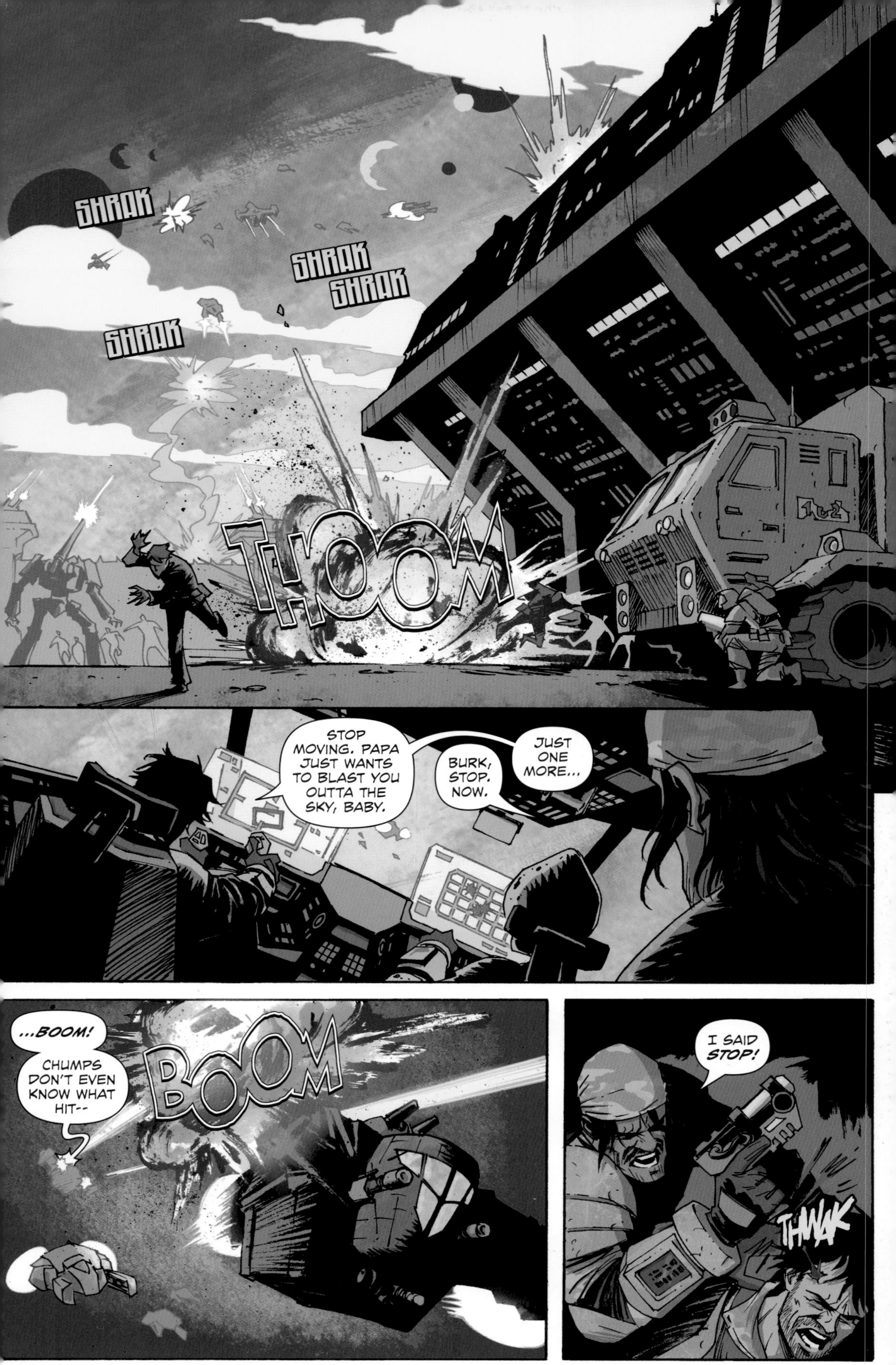
SHRAK
SHRAK
SHRAK
SHRAK
THOOM
STOP MOVING. PAPA JUST WANTS TO BLAST YOU OUTTA THE SKY, BABY.
JUST ONE MORE...
BURK, STOP. NOW.
...BOOM!
CHUMPS DON'T EVEN KNOW WHAT HIT--
BOOM
I SAID STOP!
THWAK

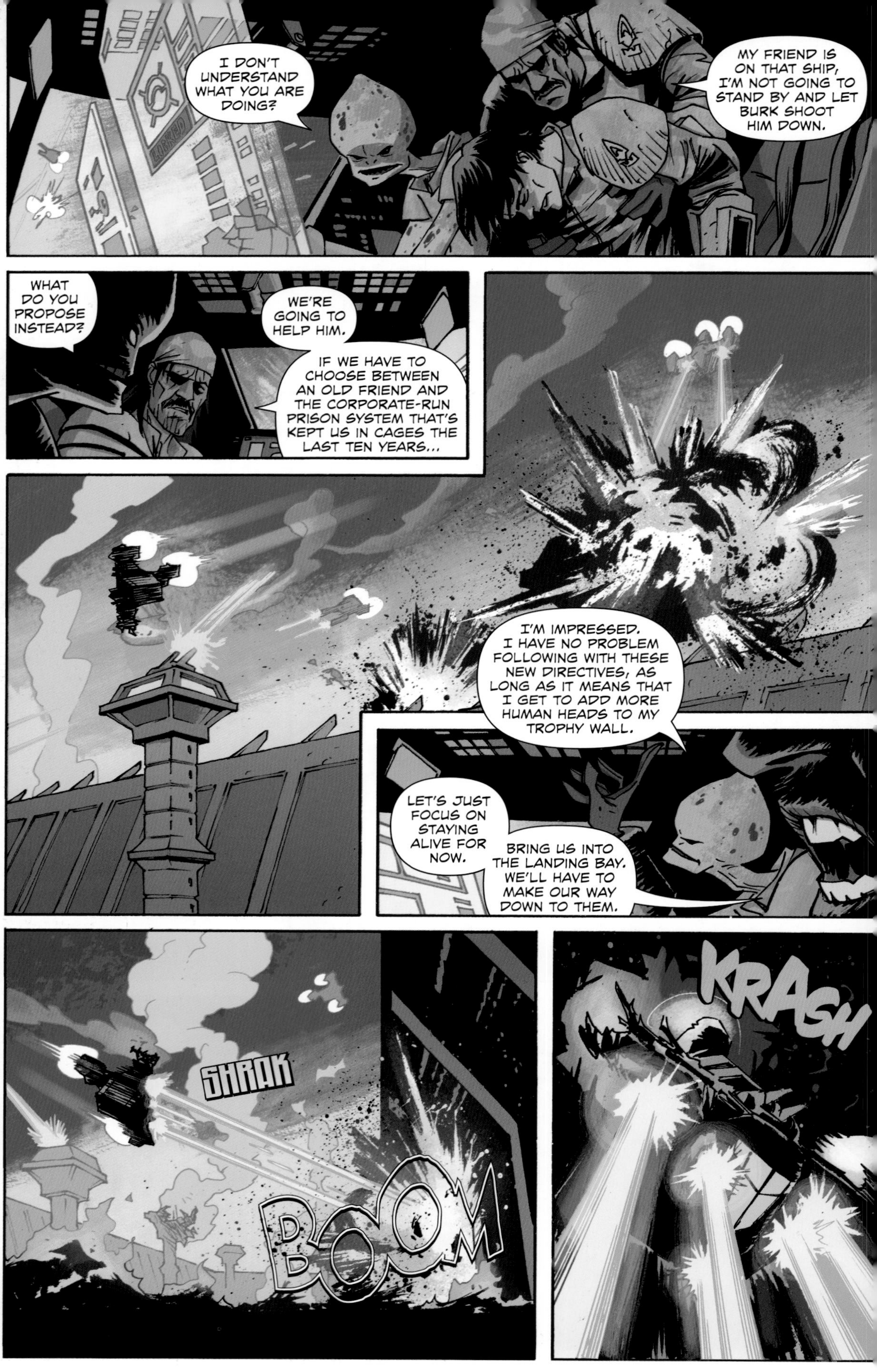

I DON'T UNDERSTAND WHAT YOU ARE DOING?
MY FRIEND IS ON THAT SHIP, I'M NOT GOING TO STAND BY AND LET BURK SHOOT HIM DOWN.
WHAT DO YOU PROPOSE INSTEAD?
WE'RE GOING TO HELP HIM.
IF WE HAVE TO CHOOSE BETWEEN AN OLD FRIEND AND THE CORPORATE-RUN PRISON SYSTEM THAT'S KEPT US IN CAGES THE LAST TEN YEARS...
I'M IMPRESSED. I HAVE NO PROBLEM FOLLOWING WITH THESE NEW DIRECTIVES, AS LONG AS IT MEANS THAT I GET TO ADD MORE HUMAN HEADS TO MY TROPHY WALL.
LET'S JUST FOCUS ON STAYING ALIVE FOR NOW.
BRING US INTO THE LANDING BAY. WE'LL HAVE TO MAKE OUR WAY DOWN TO THEM.
SHRAK
BOOM
KRASH

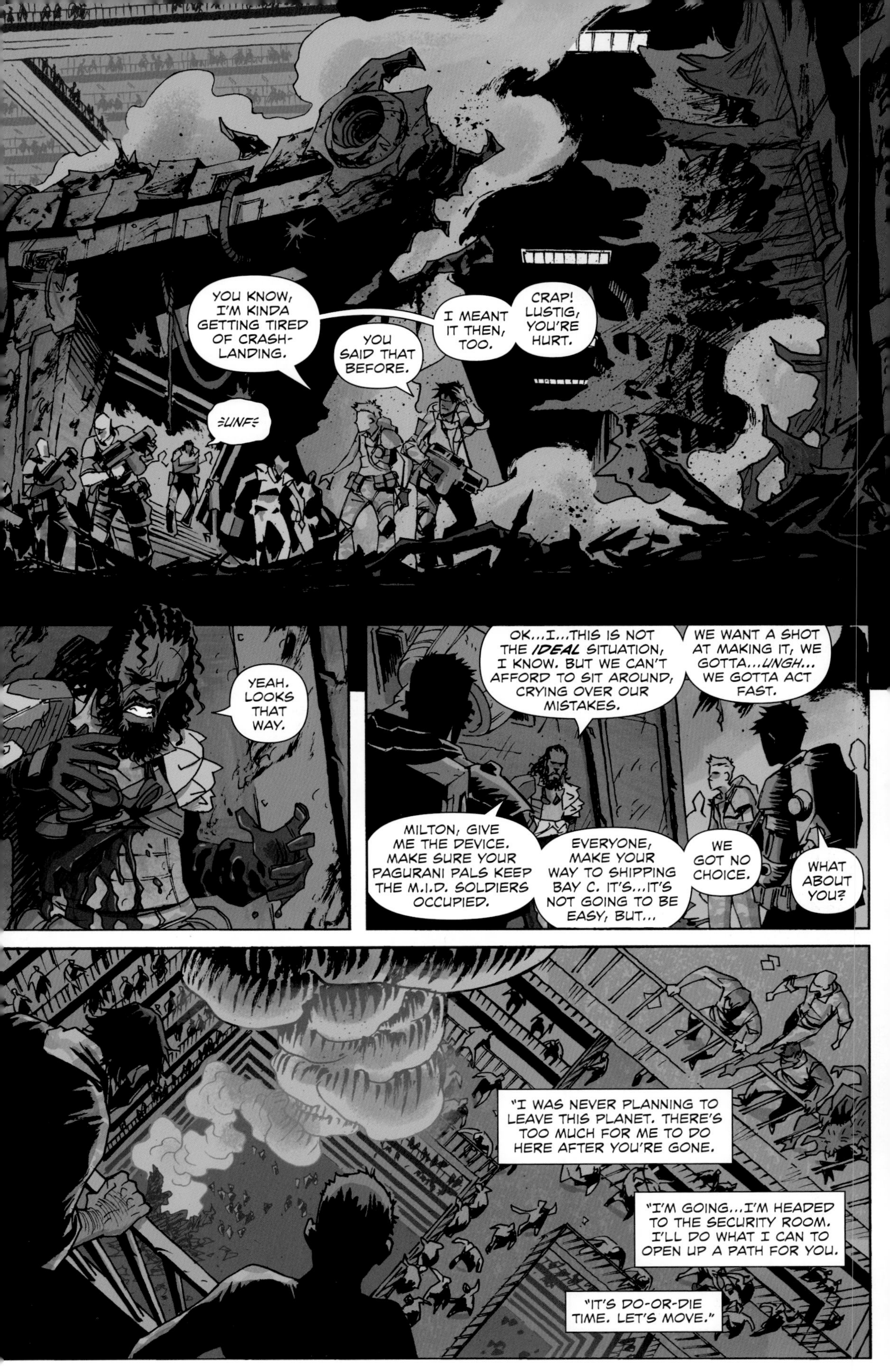
YOU KNOW, I'M KINDA GETTING TIRED OF CRASH-LANDING.
I MEANT IT THEN, TOO.
YOU SAID THAT BEFORE.
CRAP! LUSTIG, YOU'RE HURT.
UNF
YEAH. LOOKS THAT WAY.
OK...I...THIS IS NOT THE IDEAL SITUATION, I KNOW. BUT WE CAN'T AFFORD TO SIT AROUND, CRYING OVER OUR MISTAKES.
WE WANT A SHOT AT MAKING IT, WE GOTTA...UNGH... WE GOTTA ACT FAST.
MILTON, GIVE ME THE DEVICE. MAKE SURE YOUR PAGURANI PALS KEEP THE M.I.D. SOLDIERS OCCUPIED.
EVERYONE, MAKE YOUR WAY TO SHIPPING BAY C. IT'S...IT'S NOT GOING TO BE EASY, BUT...
WE GOT NO CHOICE.
WHAT ABOUT YOU?
"I WAS NEVER PLANNING TO LEAVE THIS PLANET. THERE'S TOO MUCH FOR ME TO DO HERE AFTER YOU'RE GONE.
"I'M GOING...I'M HEADED TO THE SECURITY ROOM. I'LL DO WHAT I CAN TO OPEN UP A PATH FOR YOU.
"IT'S DO-OR-DIE TIME. LET'S MOVE."

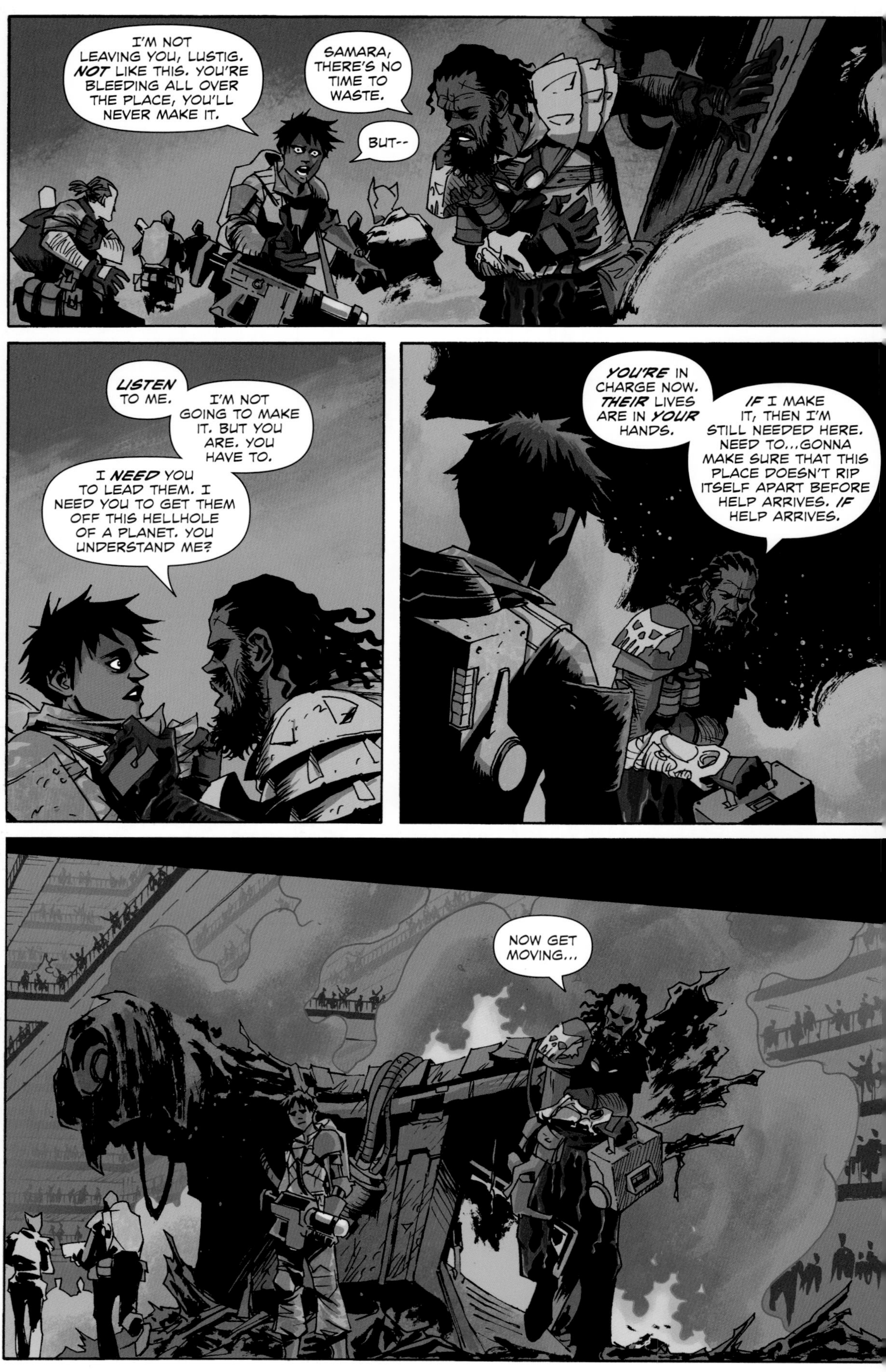
I'M NOT LEAVING YOU, LUSTIG. NOT LIKE THIS. YOU'RE BLEEDING ALL OVER THE PLACE, YOU'LL NEVER MAKE IT.
SAMARA, THERE'S NO TIME TO WASTE.
BUT--
LISTEN TO ME.
I'M NOT GOING TO MAKE IT. BUT YOU ARE. YOU HAVE TO.
I NEED YOU TO LEAD THEM. I NEED YOU TO GET THEM OFF THIS HELLHOLE OF A PLANET. YOU UNDERSTAND ME?
YOU'RE IN CHARGE NOW. THEIR LIVES ARE IN YOUR HANDS.
IF I MAKE IT, THEN I'M STILL NEEDED HERE. NEED TO...GONNA MAKE SURE THAT THIS PLACE DOESN'T RIP ITSELF APART BEFORE HELP ARRIVES. IF HELP ARRIVES.
NOW GET MOVING...

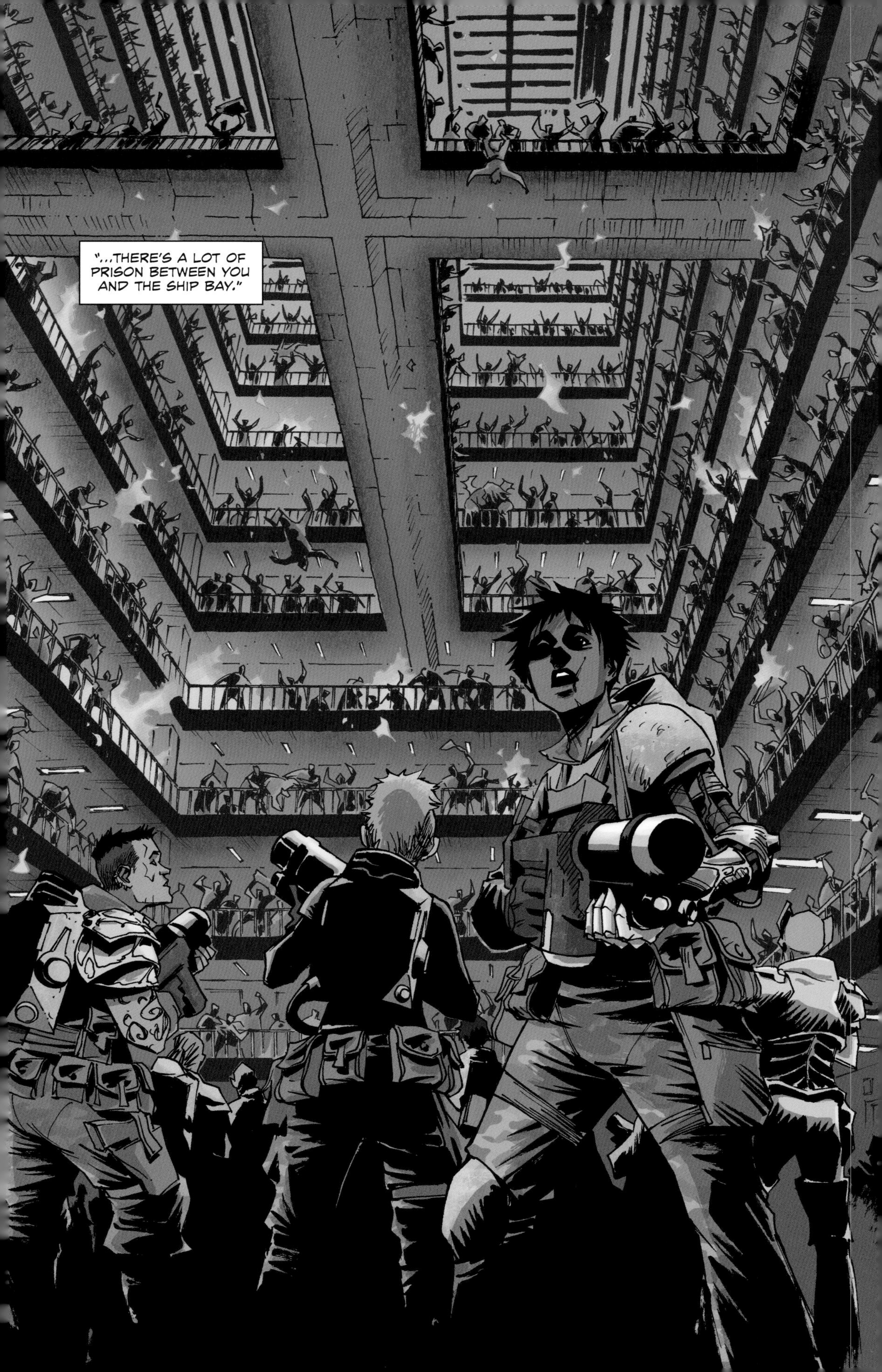
"...THERE'S A LOT OF PRISON BETWEEN YOU AND THE SHIP BAY."

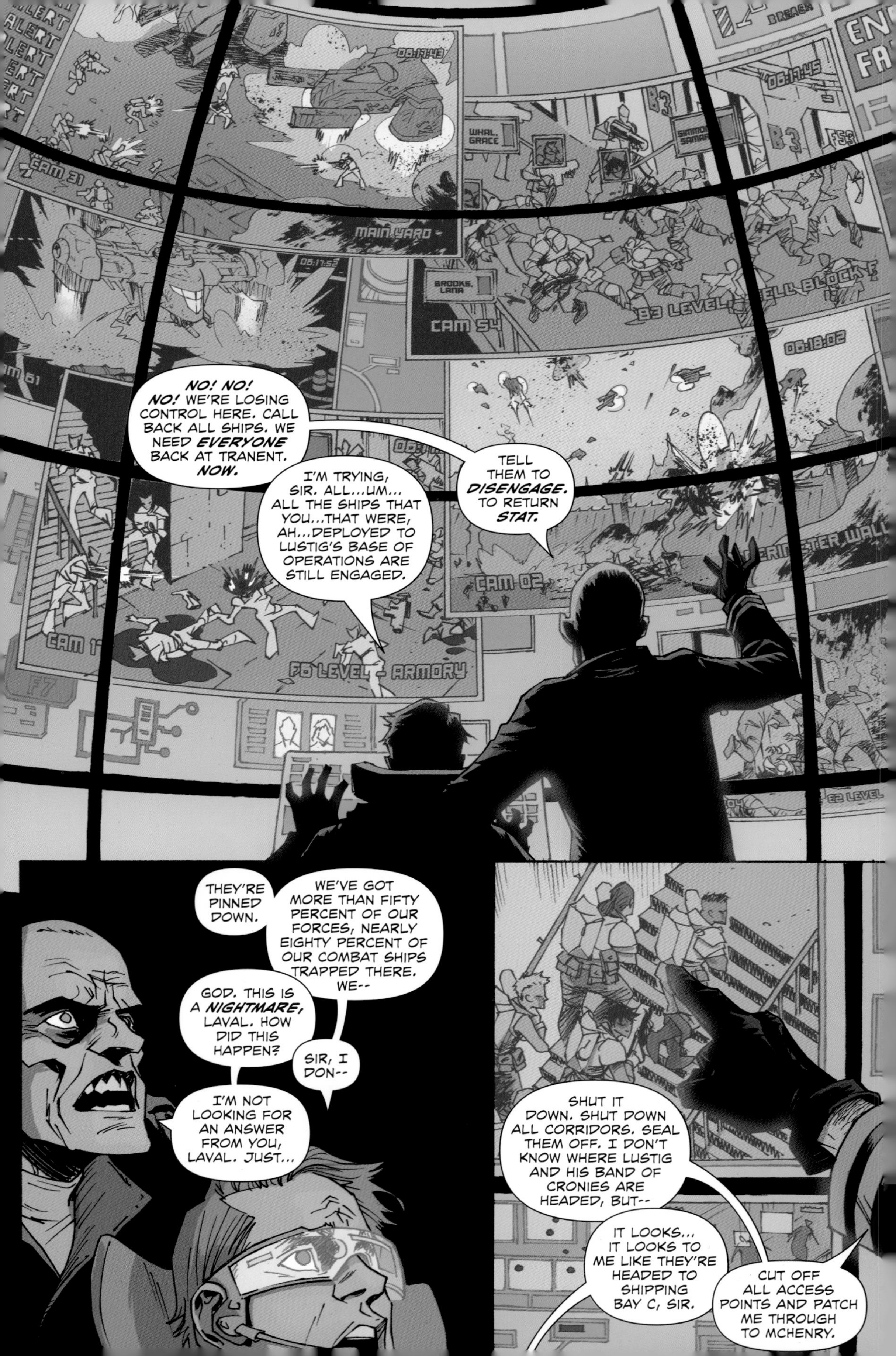

CAM 31
MAIN YARD
CAM 54
B3 LEVEL
CAM 02
F6 LEVEL - ARMORY
NO! NO! NO! WE'RE LOSING CONTROL HERE. CALL BACK ALL SHIPS. WE NEED EVERYONE BACK AT TRANENT. NOW.
I'M TRYING, SIR. ALL...UM... ALL THE SHIPS THAT YOU...THAT WERE, AH...DEPLOYED TO LUSTIG'S BASE OF OPERATIONS ARE STILL ENGAGED.
TELL THEM TO DISENGAGE. TO RETURN STAT.
THEY'RE PINNED DOWN.
WE'VE GOT MORE THAN FIFTY PERCENT OF OUR FORCES, NEARLY EIGHTY PERCENT OF OUR COMBAT SHIPS TRAPPED THERE. WE--
GOD. THIS IS A NIGHTMARE, LAVAL. HOW DID THIS HAPPEN?
SIR, I DON--
I'M NOT LOOKING FOR AN ANSWER FROM YOU, LAVAL. JUST...
SHUT IT DOWN. SHUT DOWN ALL CORRIDORS. SEAL THEM OFF. I DON'T KNOW WHERE LUSTIG AND HIS BAND OF CRONIES ARE HEADED, BUT--
IT LOOKS... IT LOOKS TO ME LIKE THEY'RE HEADED TO SHIPPING BAY C, SIR.
CUT OFF ALL ACCESS POINTS AND PATCH ME THROUGH TO MCHENRY.

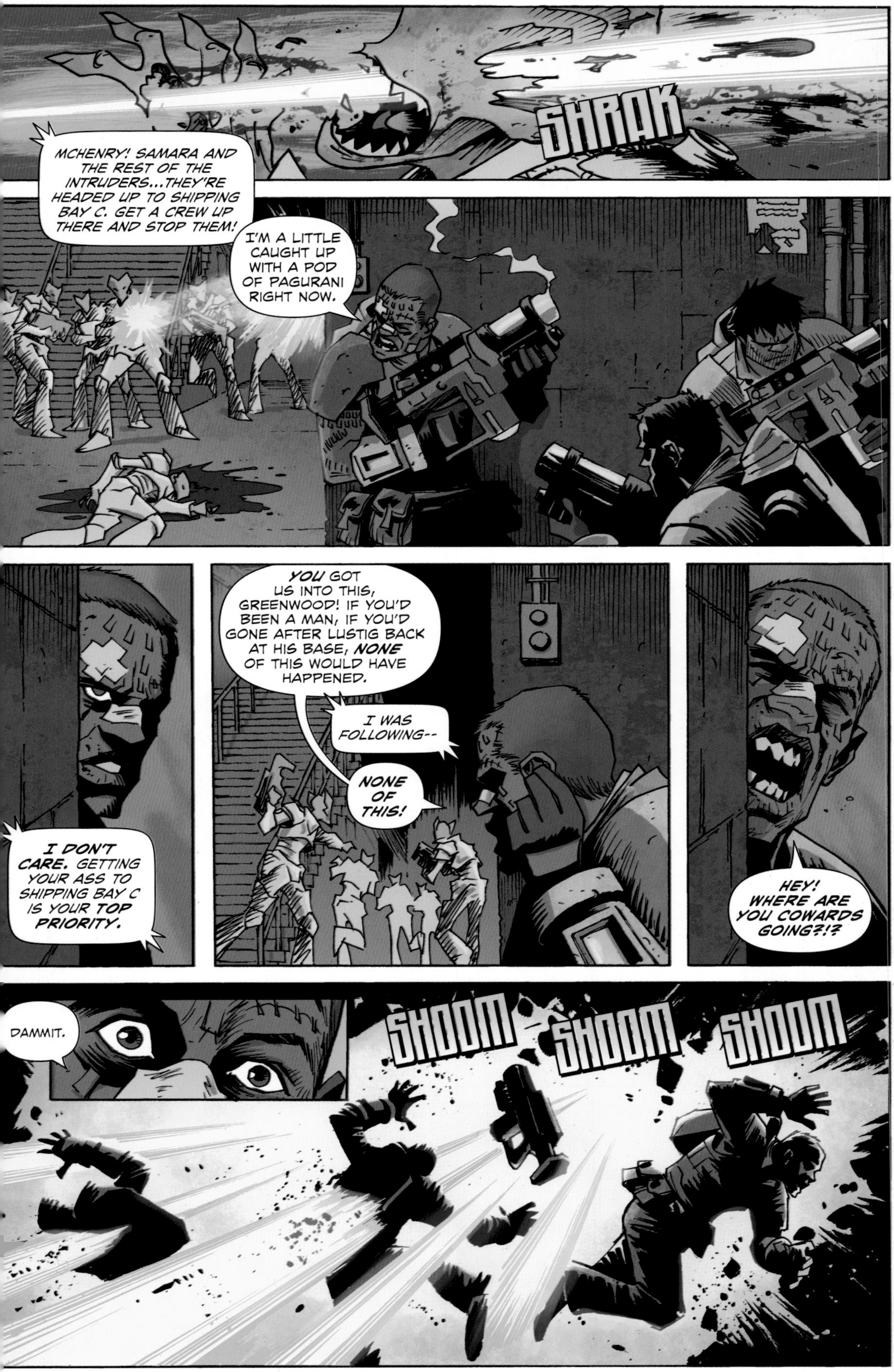
SHRAK
MCHENRY! SAMARA AND THE REST OF THE INTRUDERS...THEY'RE HEADED UP TO SHIPPING BAY C. GET A CREW UP THERE AND STOP THEM!
I'M A LITTLE CAUGHT UP WITH A POD OF PAGURANI RIGHT NOW.
I DON'T CARE. GETTING YOUR ASS TO SHIPPING BAY C IS YOUR TOP PRIORITY.
YOU GOT US INTO THIS, GREENWOOD! IF YOU'D BEEN A MAN, IF YOU'D GONE AFTER LUSTIG BACK AT HIS BASE, NONE OF THIS WOULD HAVE HAPPENED.
I WAS FOLLOWING--
NONE OF THIS!
HEY! WHERE ARE YOU COWARDS GOING?!?
DAMMIT.
SHOOM SHOOM SHOOM

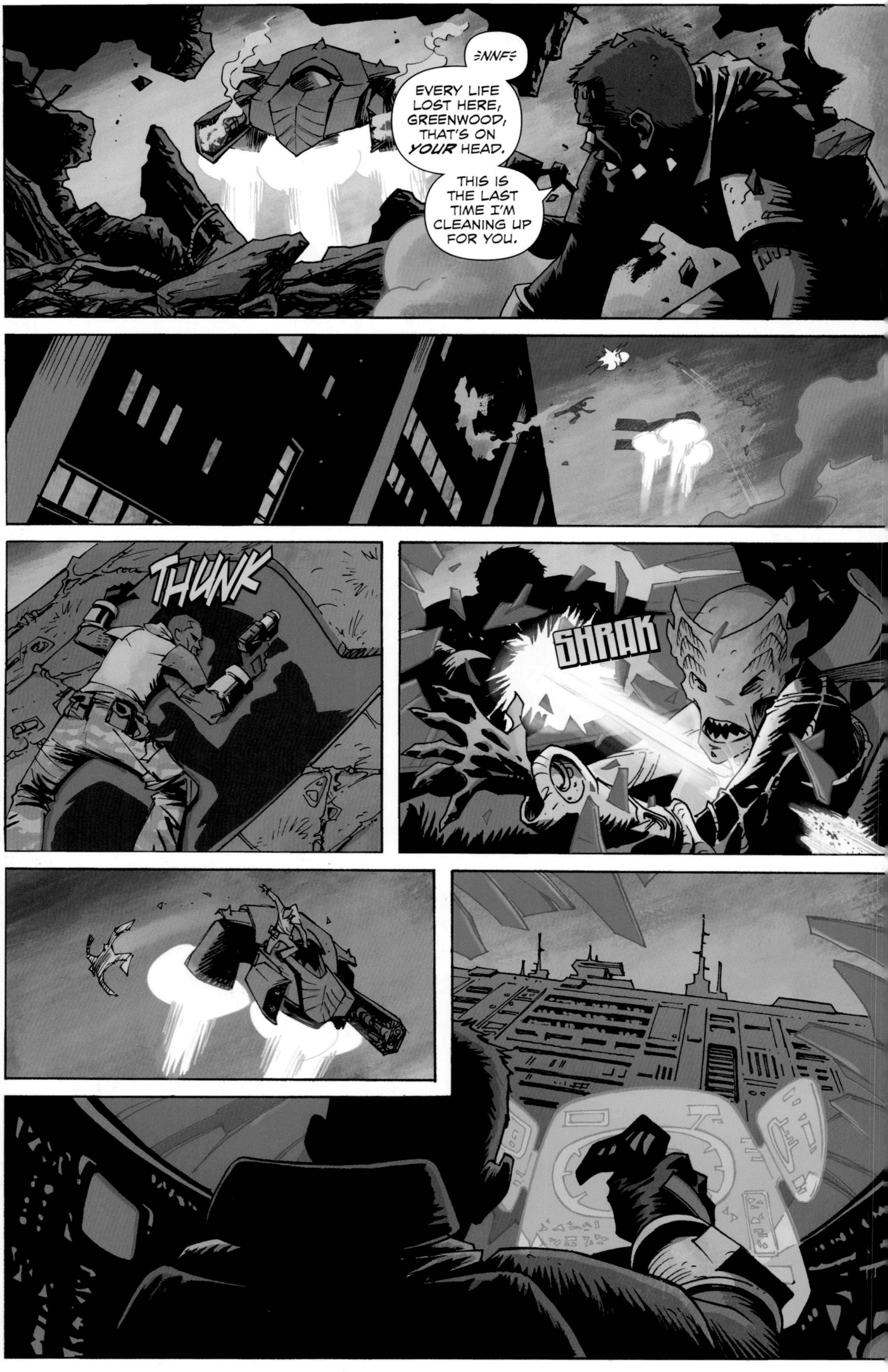

NNF
EVERY LIFE LOST HERE, GREENWOOD, THAT'S ON YOUR HEAD.
THIS IS THE LAST TIME I'M CLEANING UP FOR YOU.
THUNK
SHRAK

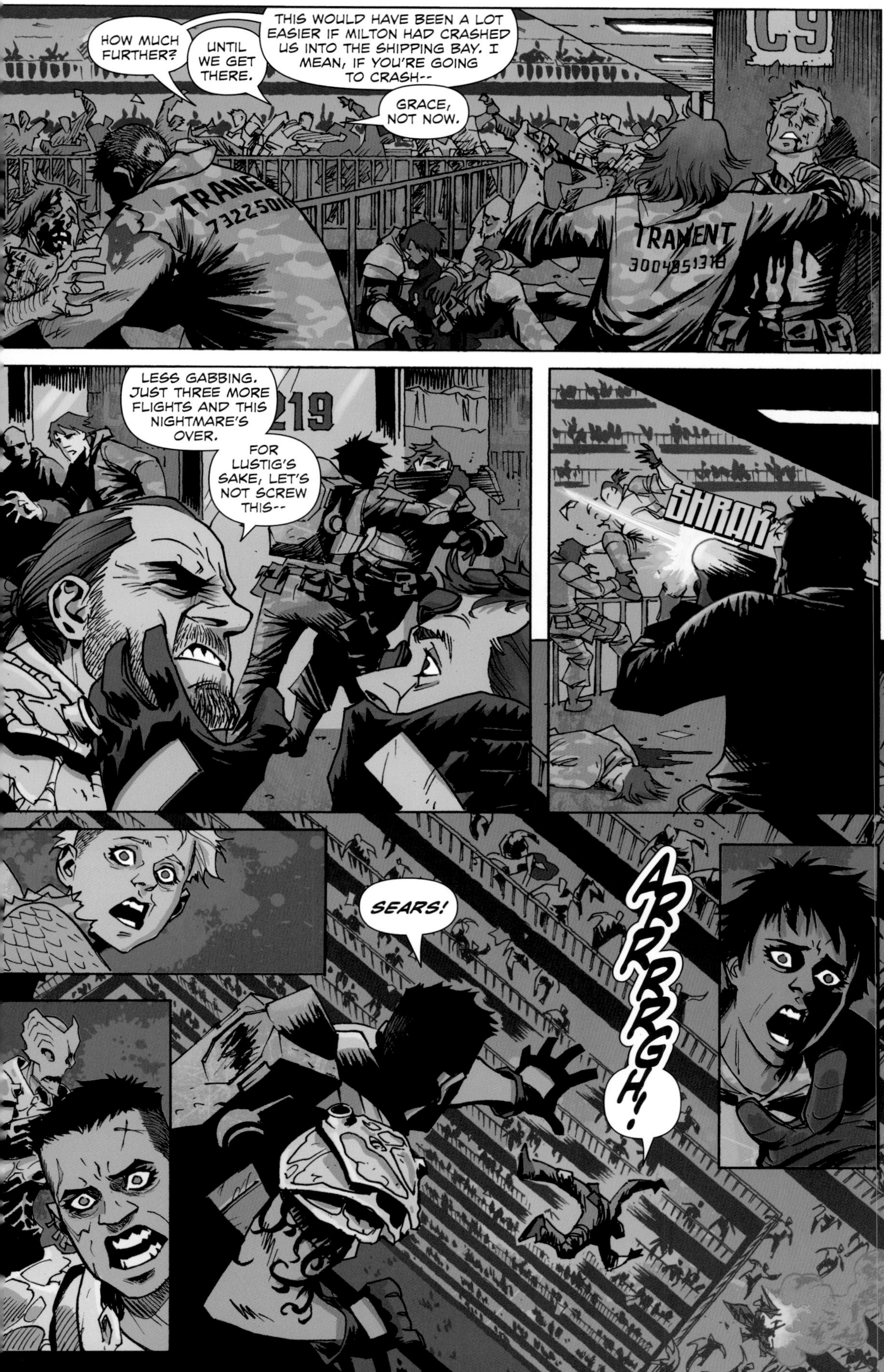
HOW MUCH FURTHER?
UNTIL WE GET THERE.
THIS WOULD HAVE BEEN A LOT EASIER IF MILTON HAD CRASHED US INTO THE SHIPPING BAY. I MEAN, IF YOU'RE GOING TO CRASH--
GRACE, NOT NOW.
C9
TRANE
7322501
TRAMENT
30048513118
LESS GABBING. JUST THREE MORE FLIGHTS AND THIS NIGHTMARE'S OVER.
219
FOR LUSTIG'S SAKE, LET'S NOT SCREW THIS--
SHRAK
SEARS!
ARRRRGH!

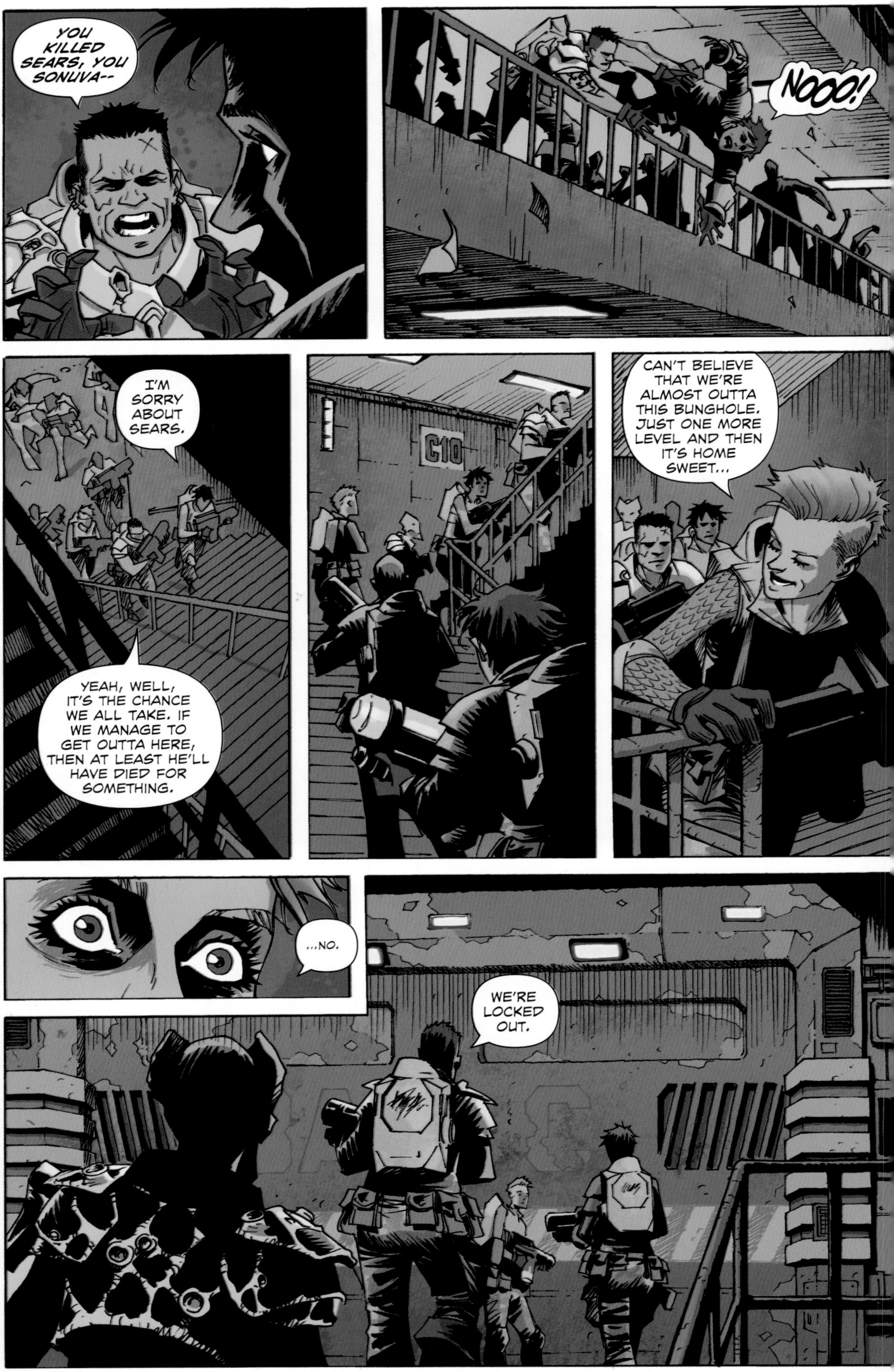
YOU KILLED SEARS, YOU SONUVA--
NOOO!
I'M SORRY ABOUT SEARS.
YEAH, WELL, IT'S THE CHANCE WE ALL TAKE. IF WE MANAGE TO GET OUTTA HERE, THEN AT LEAST HE'LL HAVE DIED FOR SOMETHING.
C10
CAN'T BELIEVE THAT WE'RE ALMOST OUTTA THIS BUNGHOLE. JUST ONE MORE LEVEL AND THEN IT'S HOME SWEET...
...NO.
WE'RE LOCKED OUT.

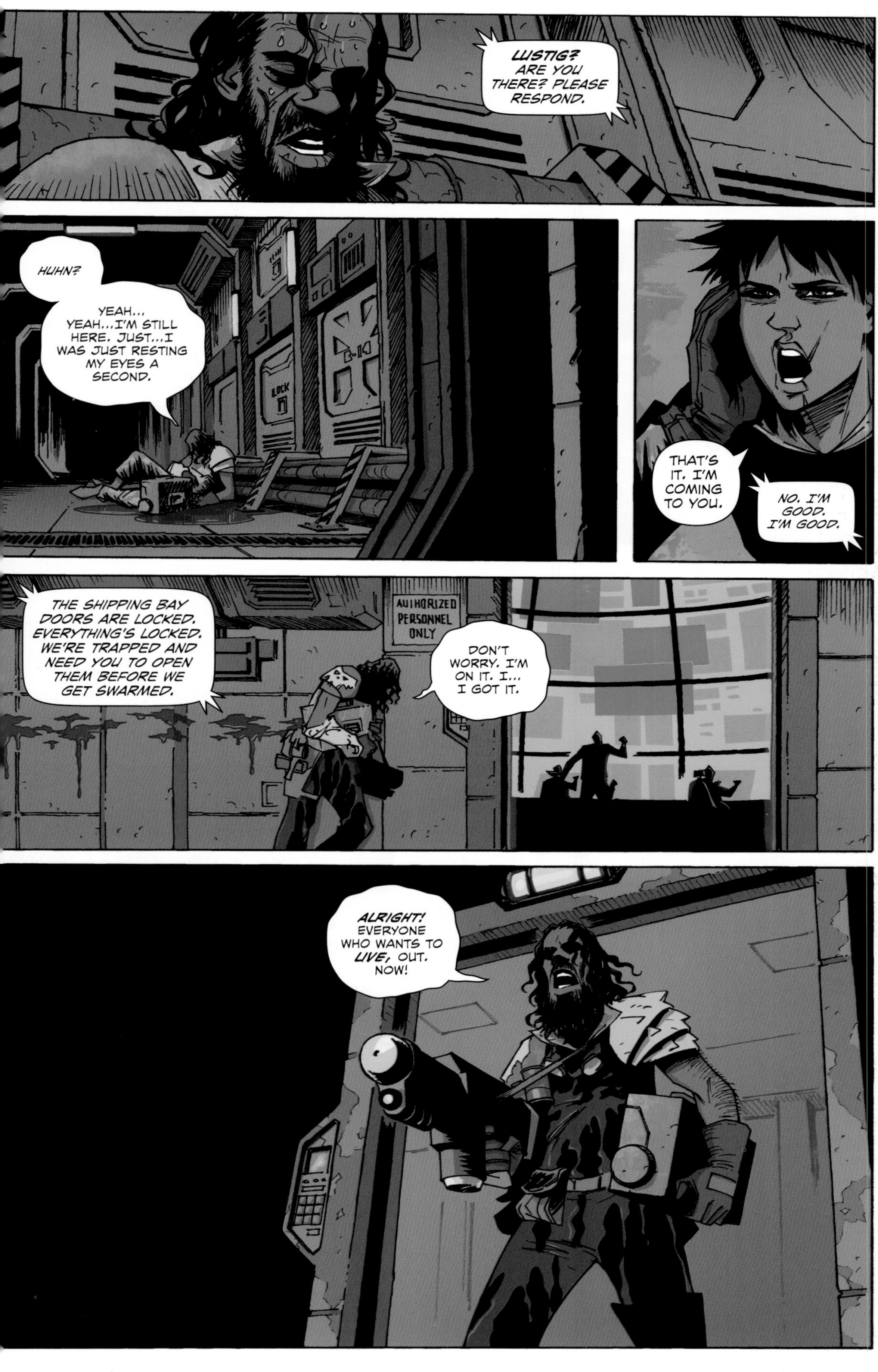

LUSTIG? ARE YOU THERE? PLEASE RESPOND.
HUHN?
YEAH... YEAH...I'M STILL HERE. JUST...I WAS JUST RESTING MY EYES A SECOND.
THAT'S IT. I'M COMING TO YOU.
NO. I'M GOOD. I'M GOOD.
THE SHIPPING BAY DOORS ARE LOCKED. EVERYTHING'S LOCKED. WE'RE TRAPPED AND NEED YOU TO OPEN THEM BEFORE WE GET SWARMED.
AUTHORIZED PERSONNEL ONLY
DON'T WORRY. I'M ON IT. I... I GOT IT.
ALRIGHT! EVERYONE WHO WANTS TO LIVE, OUT. NOW!

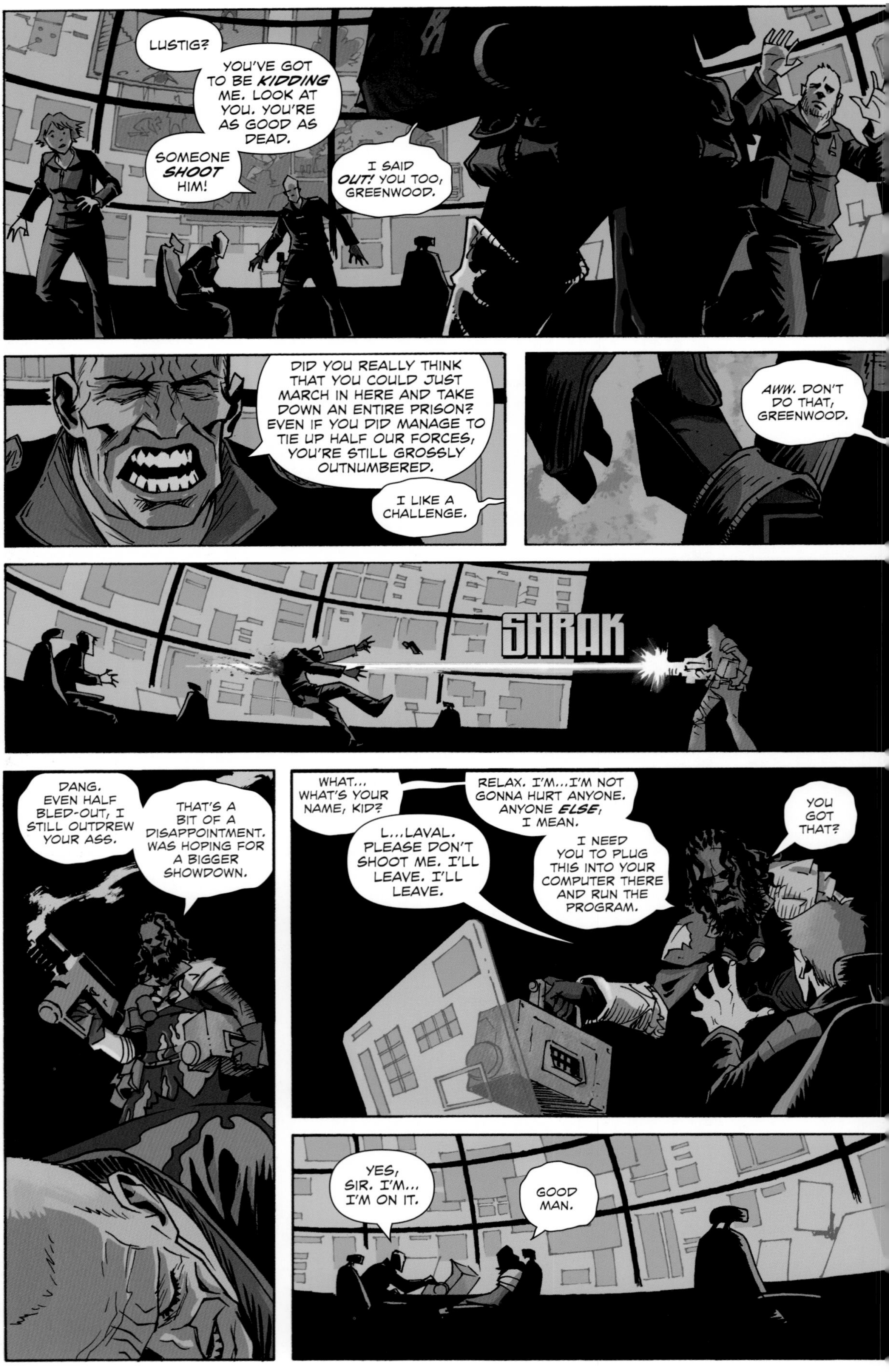
LUSTIG?
YOU'VE GOT TO BE KIDDING ME. LOOK AT YOU. YOU'RE AS GOOD AS DEAD.
SOMEONE SHOOT HIM!
I SAID OUT! YOU TOO, GREENWOOD.
DID YOU REALLY THINK THAT YOU COULD JUST MARCH IN HERE AND TAKE DOWN AN ENTIRE PRISON? EVEN IF YOU DID MANAGE TO TIE UP HALF OUR FORCES, YOU'RE STILL GROSSLY OUTNUMBERED.
I LIKE A CHALLENGE.
AWW. DON'T DO THAT, GREENWOOD.
SHRAK
DANG. EVEN HALF BLED-OUT, I STILL OUTDREW YOUR ASS.
THAT'S A BIT OF A DISAPPOINTMENT. WAS HOPING FOR A BIGGER SHOWDOWN.
WHAT... WHAT'S YOUR NAME, KID?
L...LAVAL. PLEASE DON'T SHOOT ME. I'LL LEAVE. I'LL LEAVE.
RELAX. I'M...I'M NOT GONNA HURT ANYONE. ANYONE ELSE, I MEAN.
I NEED YOU TO PLUG THIS INTO YOUR COMPUTER THERE AND RUN THE PROGRAM.
YOU GOT THAT?
YES, SIR. I'M... I'M ON IT.
GOOD MAN.

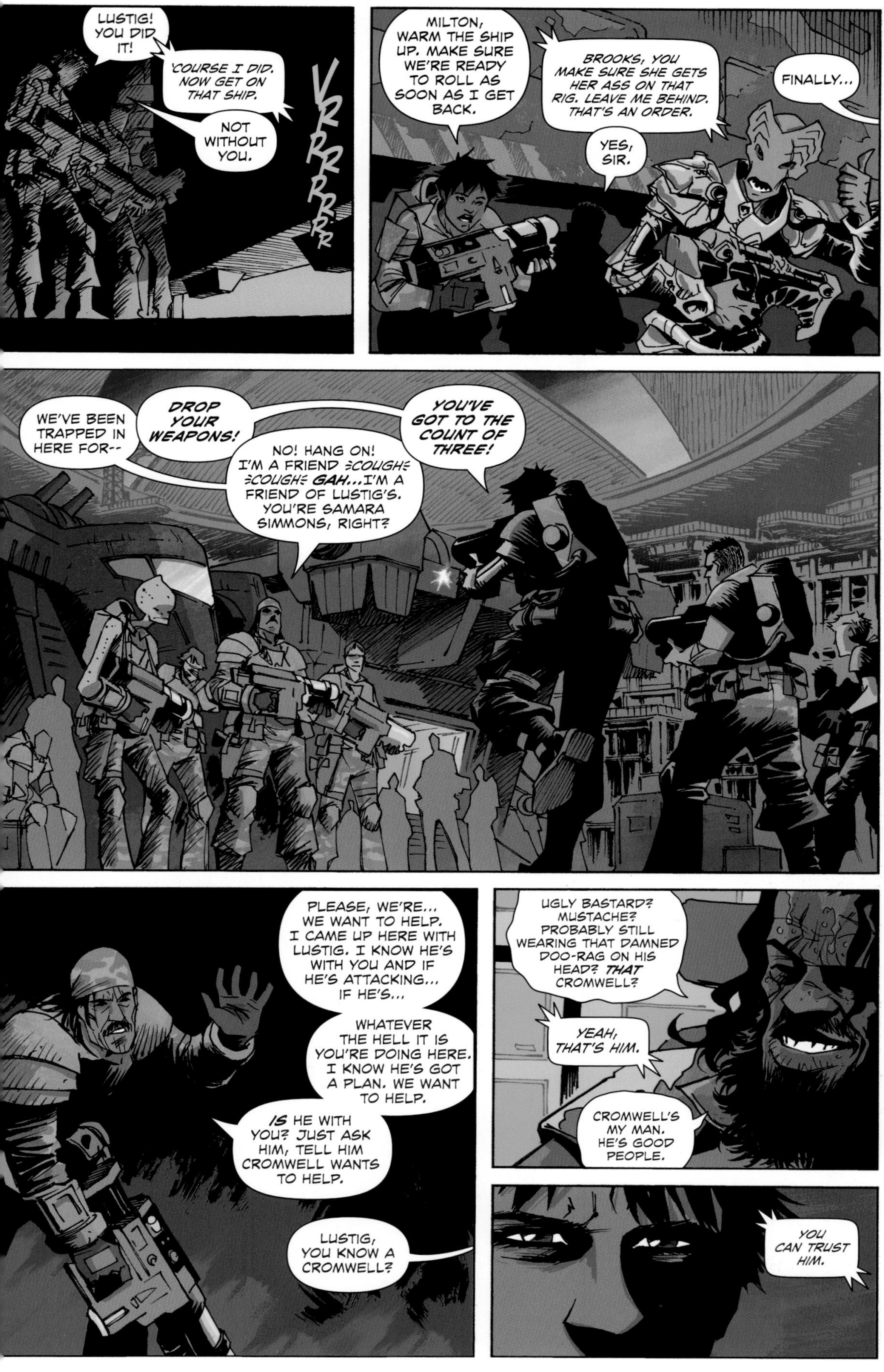
LUSTIG! YOU DID IT!
'COURSE I DID. NOW GET ON THAT SHIP.
NOT WITHOUT YOU.
VRRRRRRR
MILTON, WARM THE SHIP UP. MAKE SURE WE'RE READY TO ROLL AS SOON AS I GET BACK.
BROOKS, YOU MAKE SURE SHE GETS HER ASS ON THAT RIG. LEAVE ME BEHIND. THAT'S AN ORDER.
YES, SIR.
FINALLY...
WE'VE BEEN TRAPPED IN HERE FOR--
DROP YOUR WEAPONS!
YOU'VE GOT TO THE COUNT OF THREE!
NO! HANG ON! I'M A FRIEND *COUGH* *COUGH* GAH...I'M A FRIEND OF LUSTIG'S. YOU'RE SAMARA SIMMONS, RIGHT?
PLEASE, WE'RE... WE WANT TO HELP. I CAME UP HERE WITH LUSTIG. I KNOW HE'S WITH YOU AND IF HE'S ATTACKING... IF HE'S...
WHATEVER THE HELL IT IS YOU'RE DOING HERE. I KNOW HE'S GOT A PLAN. WE WANT TO HELP.
IS HE WITH YOU? JUST ASK HIM, TELL HIM CROMWELL WANTS TO HELP.
LUSTIG, YOU KNOW A CROMWELL?
UGLY BASTARD? MUSTACHE? PROBABLY STILL WEARING THAT DAMNED DOO-RAG ON HIS HEAD? THAT CROMWELL?
YEAH, THAT'S HIM.
CROMWELL'S MY MAN. HE'S GOOD PEOPLE.
YOU CAN TRUST HIM.

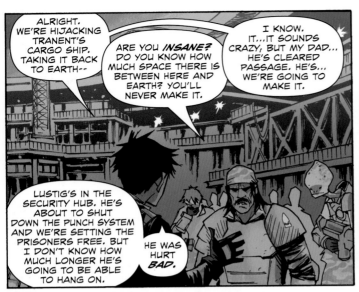

ALRIGHT. WE'RE HIJACKING TRANENT'S CARGO SHIP. TAKING IT BACK TO EARTH--

ARE YOU *INSANE?* DO YOU KNOW HOW MUCH SPACE THERE IS BETWEEN HERE AND EARTH? YOU'LL NEVER MAKE IT.

I KNOW. IT...IT SOUNDS CRAZY, BUT MY DAD... HE'S CLEARED PASSAGE. HE'S..., WE'RE GOING TO MAKE IT.

HE WANTS TO STAY BEHIND, TO KEEP THINGS FROM GETTING TOO OUT OF HAND--

YOU'RE *SETTING AN ENTIRE PRISON FREE.* THINGS ARE GOING TO GET WELL BEYOND OUT OF HAND.

HEY, *BACK OFF!* WE WERE AMBUSHED! WE THOUGHT WE HAD MORE TIME TO PLAN.

LUSTIG'S IN THE SECURITY HUB. HE'S ABOUT TO SHUT DOWN THE PUNCH SYSTEM AND WE'RE SETTING THE PRISONERS FREE. BUT I DON'T KNOW HOW MUCH LONGER HE'S GOING TO BE ABLE TO HANG ON.

HE WAS HURT *BAD.*

DEAL.

I SUGGEST YOU MAKE A STOP ALONG THE WAY AND DROP THE BIG-HEADED ALIEN OFF.

HE DON'T LIKE PEOPLE MUCH.

ALRIGHT. I'M NOT GOING ANYWHERE, I'M SICK AND WOULDN'T SURVIVE THE TRIP.

I'LL GO FIND LUSTIG...HELP HIM TRY AND KEEP SOME SEMBLANCE OF SANITY HERE AFTER YOU'RE GONE.

BUT I WANT YOU TO TAKE MY CREW WITH YOU. YOU GOT PASSAGE OUT OF HERE, YOU'RE GOING TO NEED PEOPLE.

DEAL?

ALRIGHT, EVERYONE. GET YOUR ASSES ON THAT SHIP.

WE'RE ALMOST OUT--

SHRAK

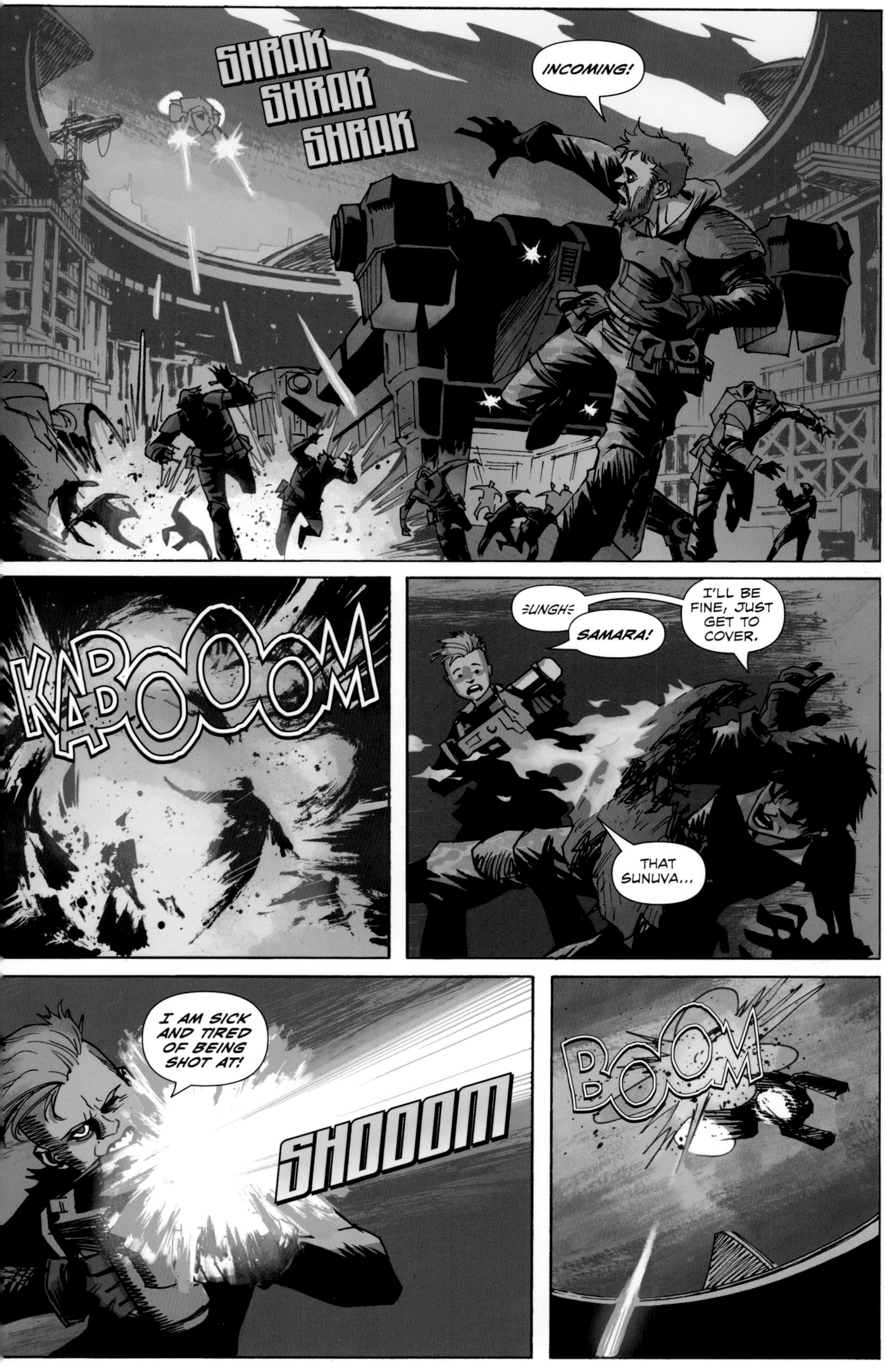
SHRAK
SHRAK
SHRAK
INCOMING!
KABOOOOM
UNGH
SAMARA!
I'LL BE FINE, JUST GET TO COVER.
THAT SUNUVA...
I AM SICK AND TIRED OF BEING SHOT AT!
SHOOOM
BOOOM

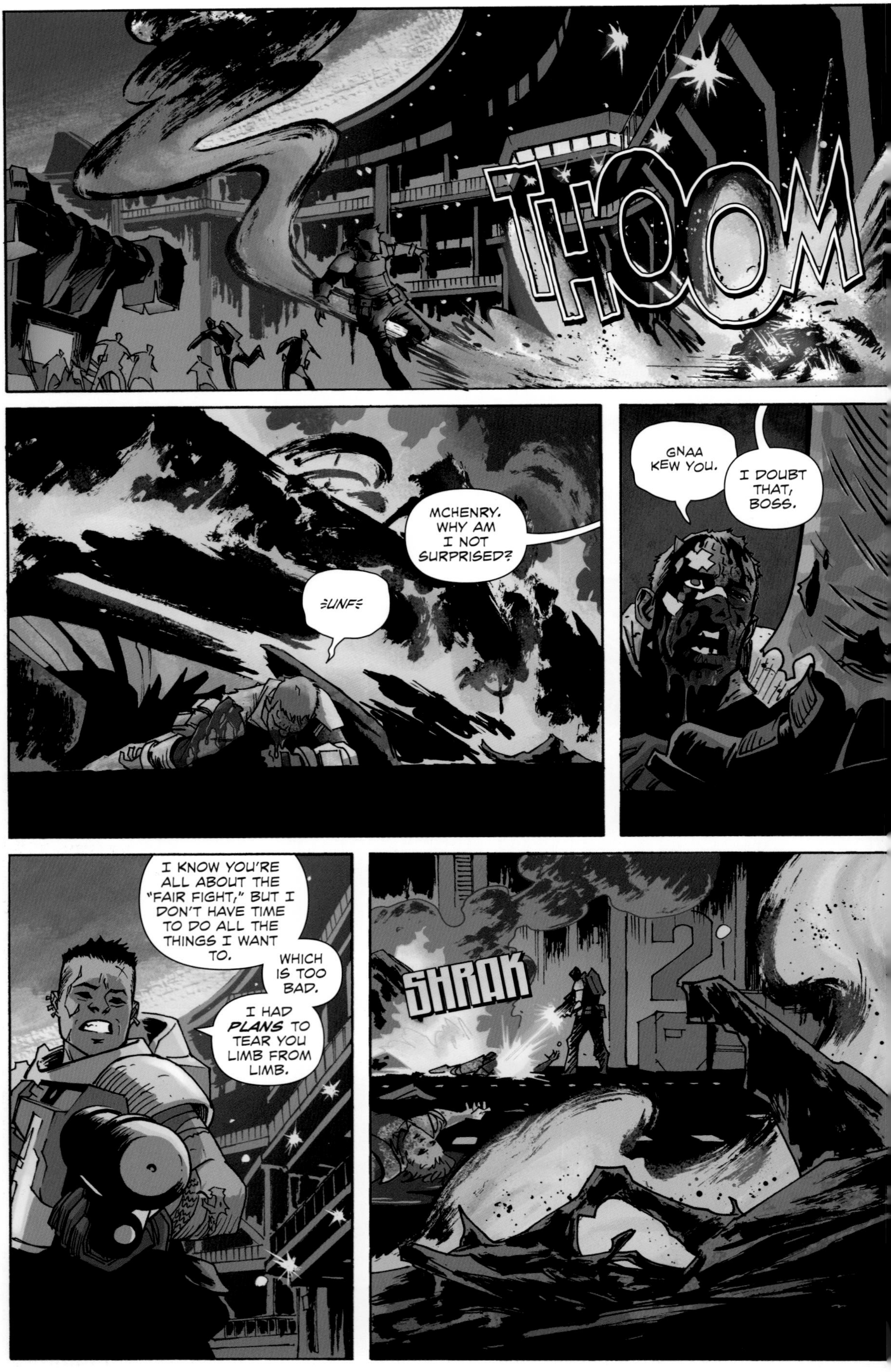
THOOM
MCHENRY. WHY AM I NOT SURPRISED?
=UNF=
GNAA KEW YOU.
I DOUBT THAT, BOSS.
I KNOW YOU'RE ALL ABOUT THE "FAIR FIGHT," BUT I DON'T HAVE TIME TO DO ALL THE THINGS I WANT TO.
WHICH IS TOO BAD.
I HAD PLANS TO TEAR YOU LIMB FROM LIMB.
SHRAK

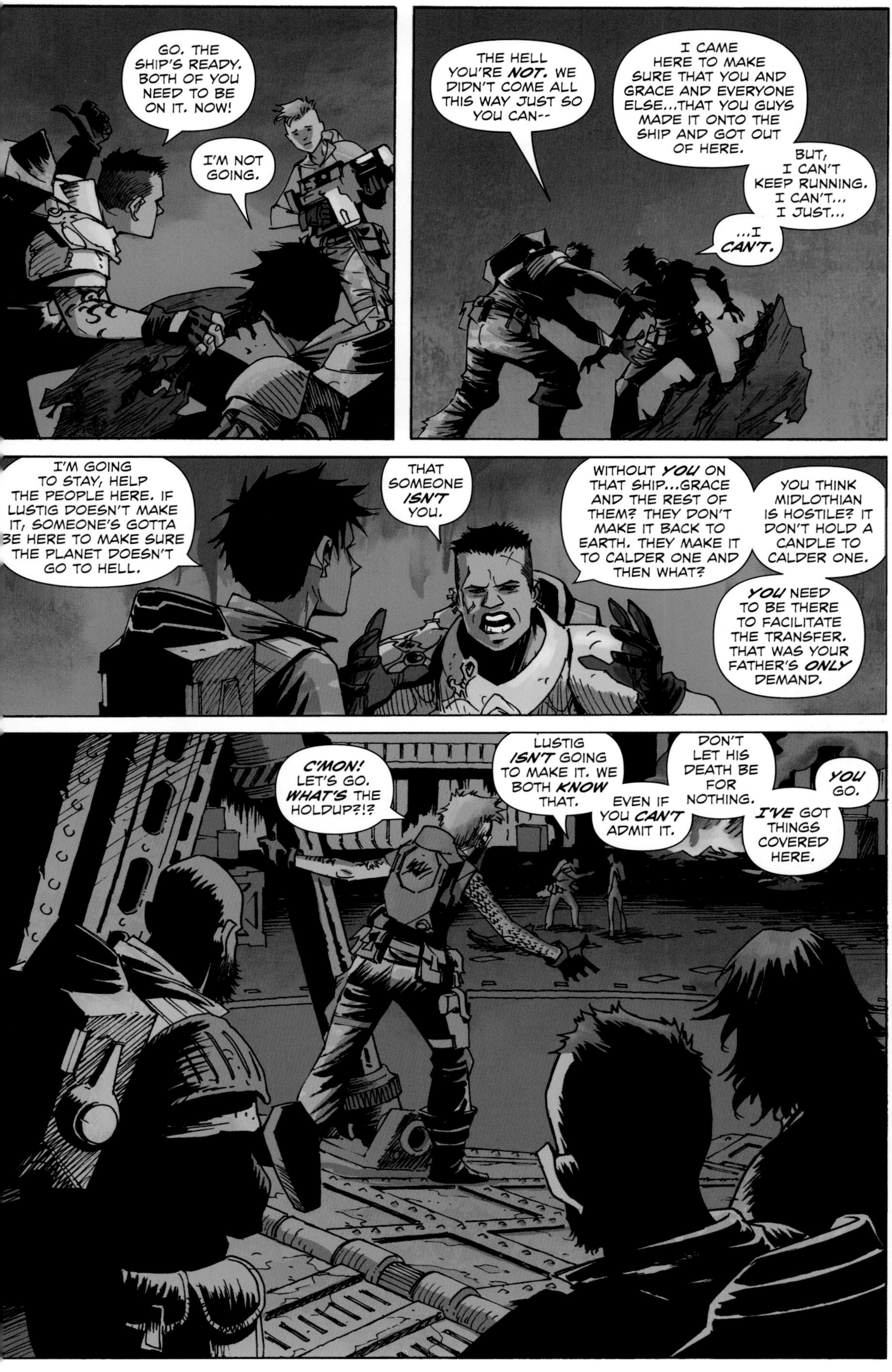
GO. THE SHIP'S READY. BOTH OF YOU NEED TO BE ON IT. NOW!
I'M NOT GOING.
THE HELL YOU'RE NOT. WE DIDN'T COME ALL THIS WAY JUST SO YOU CAN--
I CAME HERE TO MAKE SURE THAT YOU AND GRACE AND EVERYONE ELSE...THAT YOU GUYS MADE IT ONTO THE SHIP AND GOT OUT OF HERE.
BUT, I CAN'T KEEP RUNNING. I CAN'T... I JUST...
...I CAN'T.
I'M GOING TO STAY, HELP THE PEOPLE HERE. IF LUSTIG DOESN'T MAKE IT, SOMEONE'S GOTTA BE HERE TO MAKE SURE THE PLANET DOESN'T GO TO HELL.
THAT SOMEONE ISN'T YOU.
WITHOUT YOU ON THAT SHIP...GRACE AND THE REST OF THEM? THEY DON'T MAKE IT BACK TO EARTH. THEY MAKE IT TO CALDER ONE AND THEN WHAT?
YOU THINK MIDLOTHIAN IS HOSTILE? IT DON'T HOLD A CANDLE TO CALDER ONE.
YOU NEED TO BE THERE TO FACILITATE THE TRANSFER. THAT WAS YOUR FATHER'S ONLY DEMAND.
C'MON! LET'S GO. WHAT'S THE HOLDUP?!?
LUSTIG ISN'T GOING TO MAKE IT. WE BOTH KNOW THAT.
EVEN IF YOU CAN'T ADMIT IT.
DON'T LET HIS DEATH BE FOR NOTHING.
YOU GO.
I'VE GOT THINGS COVERED HERE.

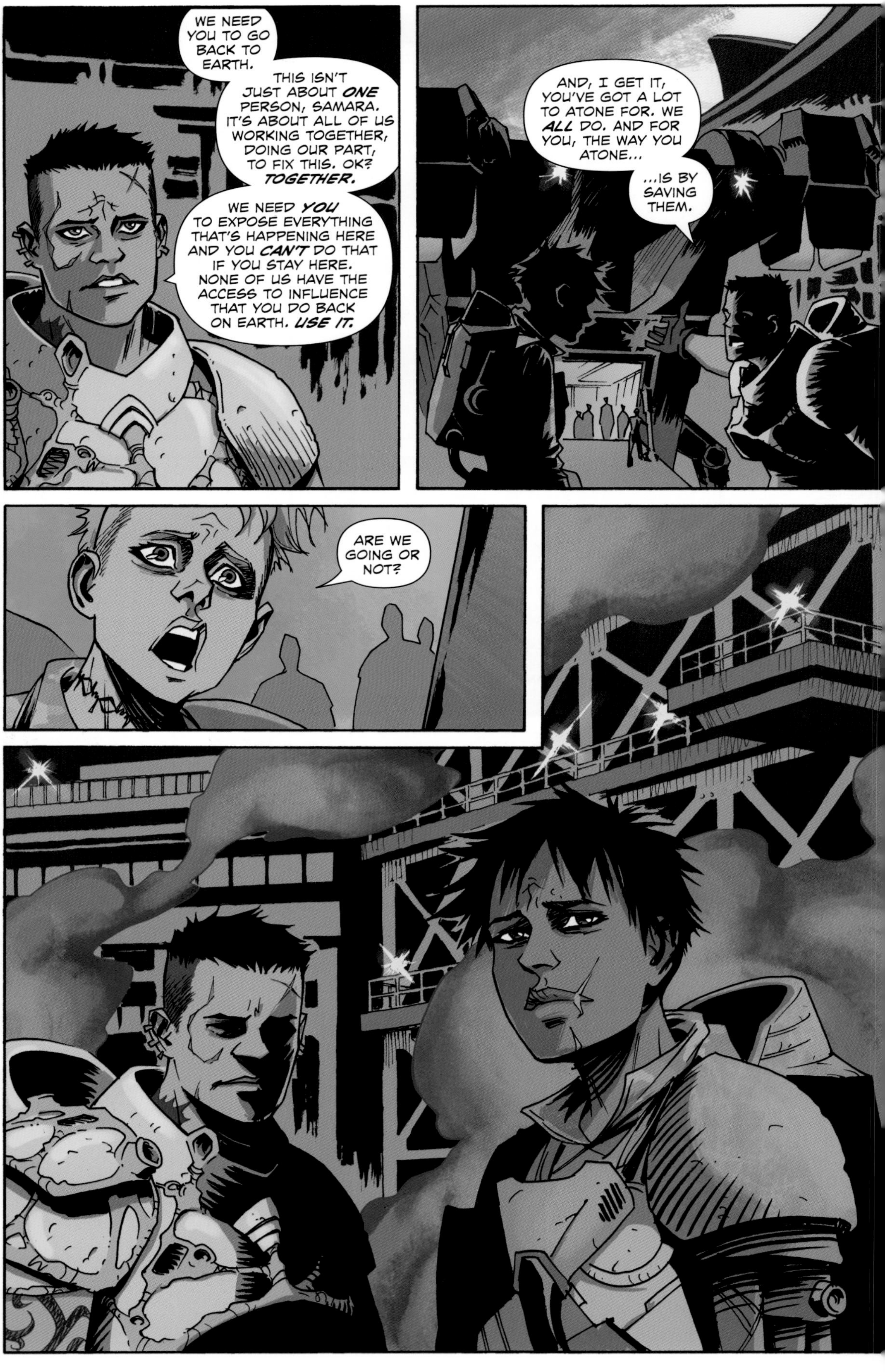
WE NEED YOU TO GO BACK TO EARTH.
THIS ISN'T JUST ABOUT *ONE* PERSON, SAMARA. IT'S ABOUT ALL OF US WORKING TOGETHER, DOING OUR PART, TO FIX THIS. OK? *TOGETHER.*
WE NEED *YOU* TO EXPOSE EVERYTHING THAT'S HAPPENING HERE AND YOU *CAN'T* DO THAT IF YOU STAY HERE. NONE OF US HAVE THE ACCESS TO INFLUENCE THAT YOU DO BACK ON EARTH. *USE IT.*
AND, I GET IT, YOU'VE GOT A LOT TO ATONE FOR. WE *ALL* DO. AND FOR YOU, THE WAY YOU ATONE...
...IS BY SAVING THEM.
ARE WE GOING OR NOT?

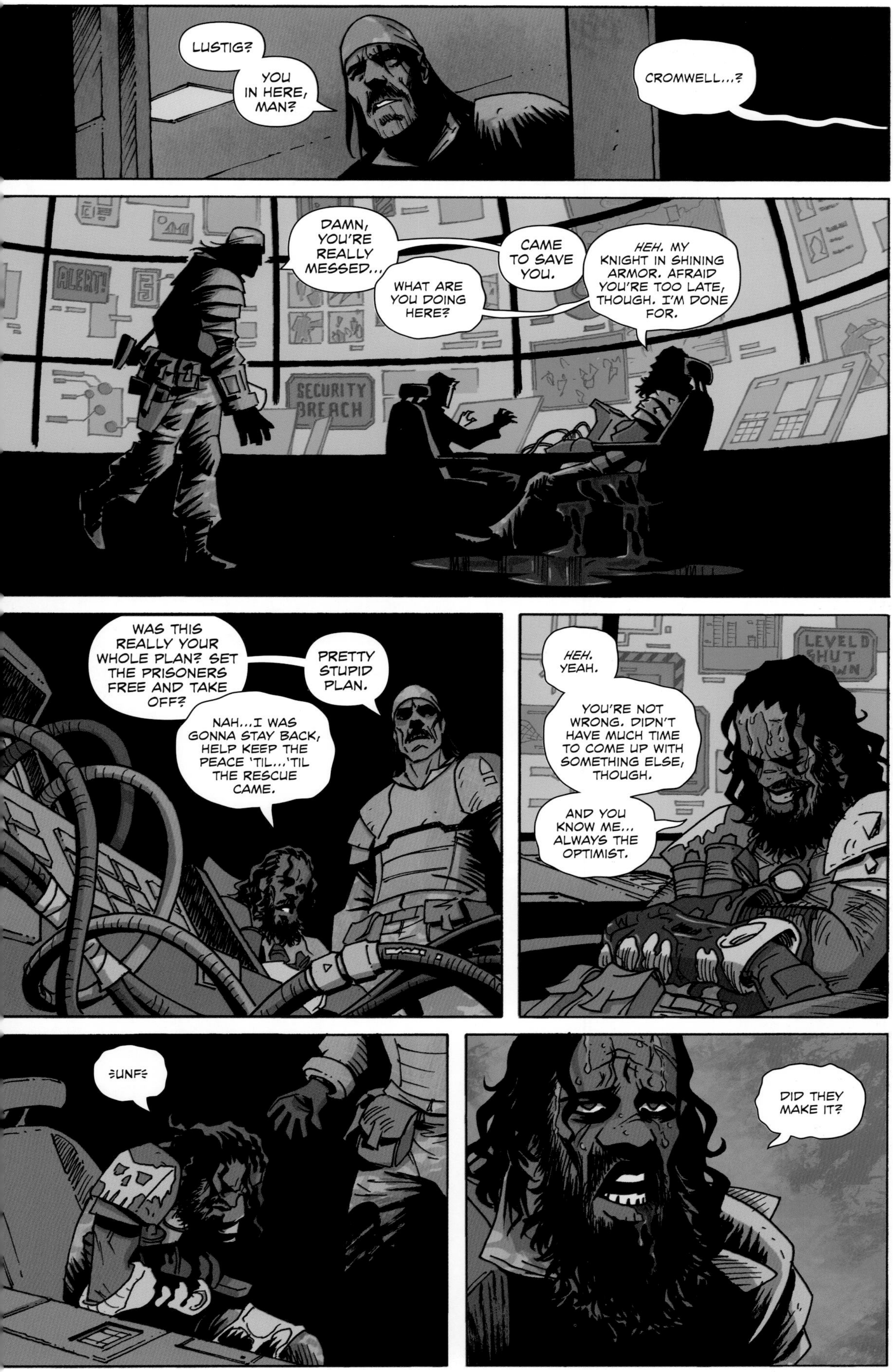
LUSTIG?
YOU IN HERE, MAN?
CROMWELL...?
DAMN, YOU'RE REALLY MESSED...
WHAT ARE YOU DOING HERE?
CAME TO SAVE YOU.
HEH. MY KNIGHT IN SHINING ARMOR. AFRAID YOU'RE TOO LATE, THOUGH. I'M DONE FOR.
ALERT!
SECURITY BREACH
WAS THIS REALLY YOUR WHOLE PLAN? SET THE PRISONERS FREE AND TAKE OFF?
PRETTY STUPID PLAN.
NAH...I WAS GONNA STAY BACK, HELP KEEP THE PEACE 'TIL...'TIL THE RESCUE CAME.
LEVEL D SHUT DOWN
HEH. YEAH.
YOU'RE NOT WRONG. DIDN'T HAVE MUCH TIME TO COME UP WITH SOMETHING ELSE, THOUGH.
AND YOU KNOW ME... ALWAYS THE OPTIMIST.
=UNF=
DID THEY MAKE IT?

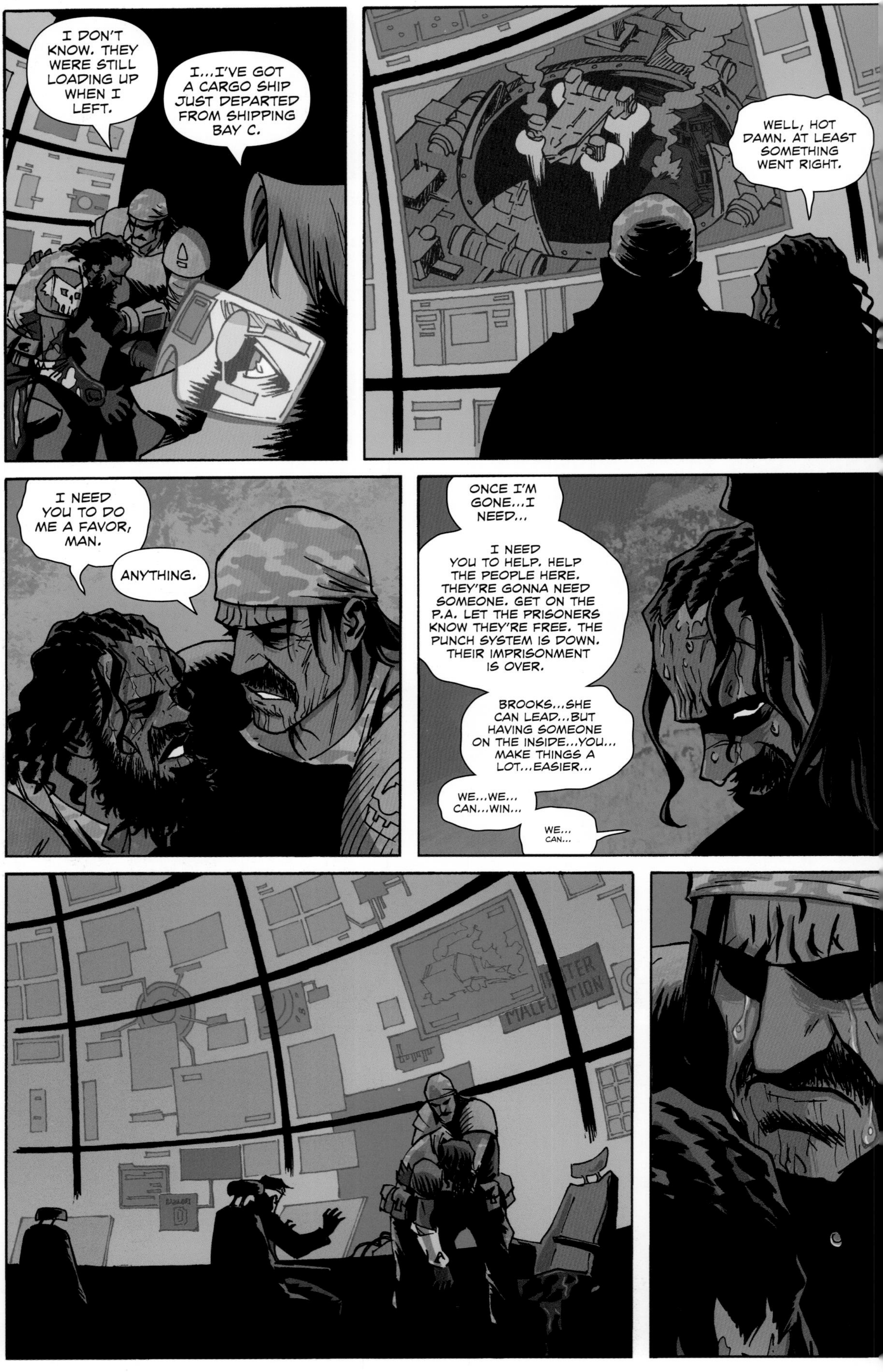
I DON'T KNOW. THEY WERE STILL LOADING UP WHEN I LEFT.
I...I'VE GOT A CARGO SHIP JUST DEPARTED FROM SHIPPING BAY C.
WELL, HOT DAMN. AT LEAST SOMETHING WENT RIGHT.
I NEED YOU TO DO ME A FAVOR, MAN.
ANYTHING.
ONCE I'M GONE...I NEED...
I NEED YOU TO HELP. HELP THE PEOPLE HERE. THEY'RE GONNA NEED SOMEONE. GET ON THE P.A. LET THE PRISONERS KNOW THEY'RE FREE. THE PUNCH SYSTEM IS DOWN. THEIR IMPRISONMENT IS OVER.
BROOKS...SHE CAN LEAD...BUT HAVING SOMEONE ON THE INSIDE...YOU... MAKE THINGS A LOT...EASIER...
WE...WE... CAN...WIN...
WE... CAN...

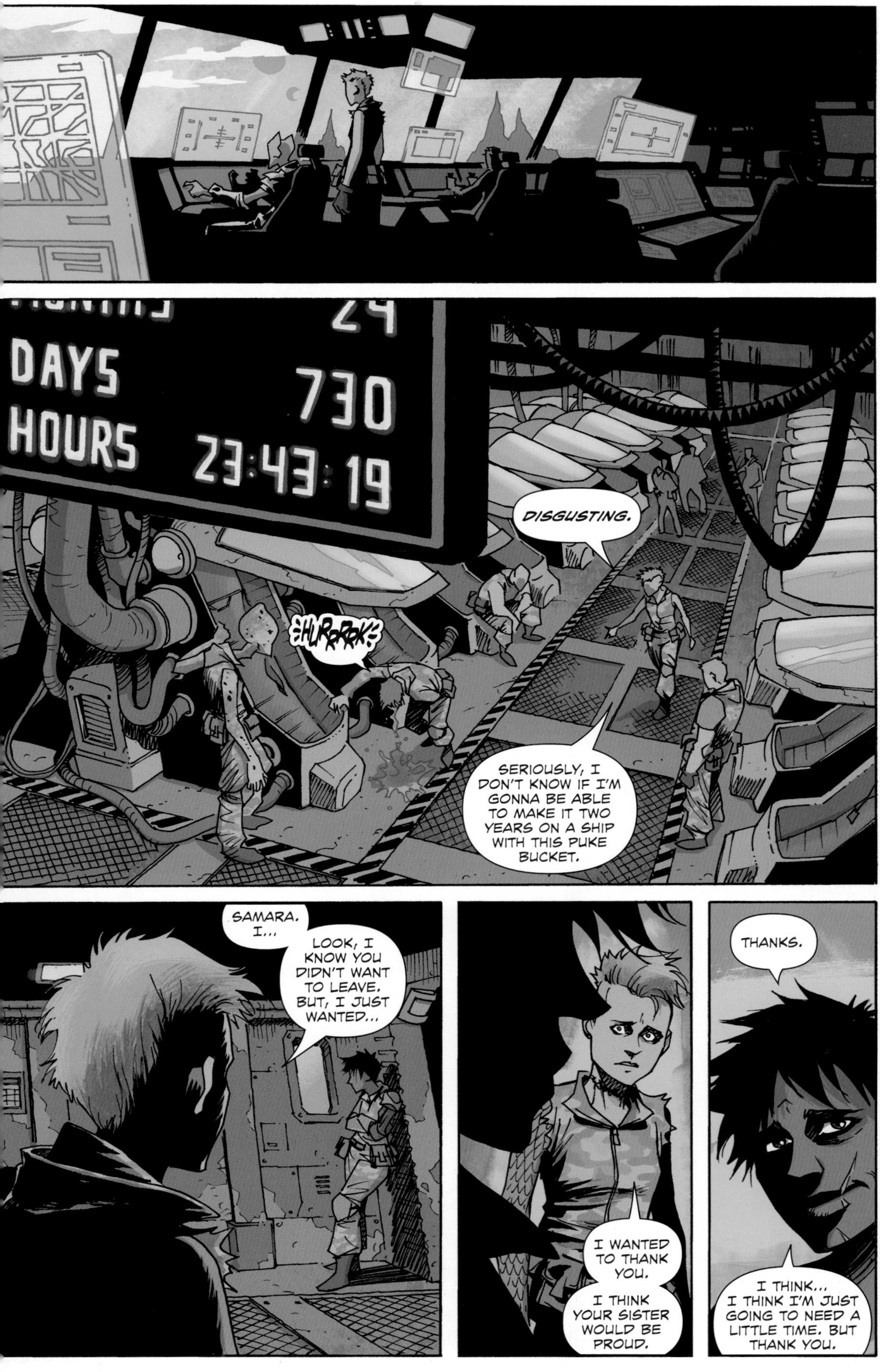

DAYS 730
HOURS 23:43:19
DISGUSTING.
HURRRRK!
SERIOUSLY, I DON'T KNOW IF I'M GONNA BE ABLE TO MAKE IT TWO YEARS ON A SHIP WITH THIS PUKE BUCKET.
SAMARA. I...
LOOK, I KNOW YOU DIDN'T WANT TO LEAVE. BUT, I JUST WANTED...
I WANTED TO THANK YOU.
I THINK YOUR SISTER WOULD BE PROUD.
THANKS.
I THINK... I THINK I'M JUST GOING TO NEED A LITTLE TIME. BUT THANK YOU.

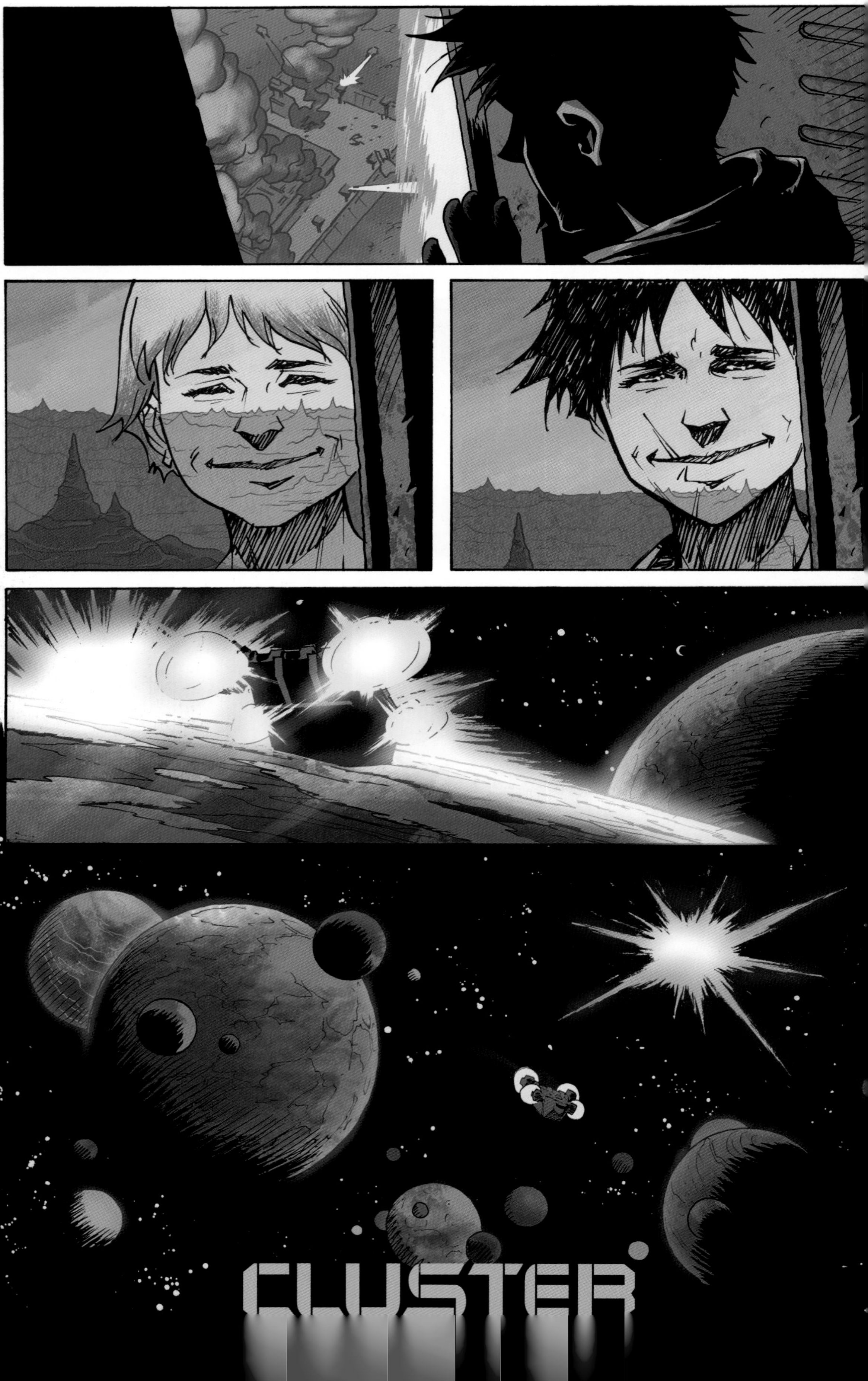
CLUSTER

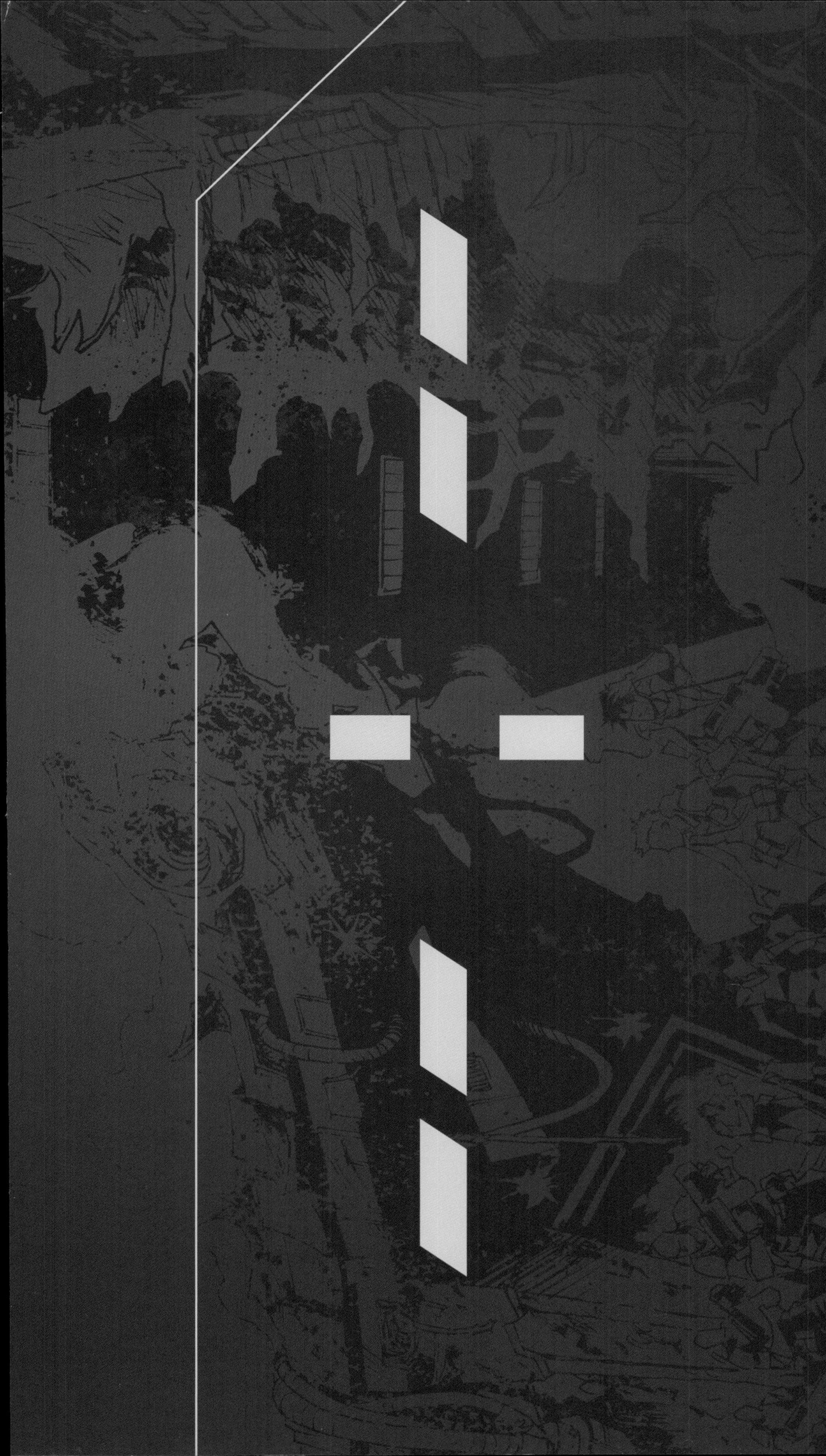

ISSUE 008 COVER
DYLAN BURNETT

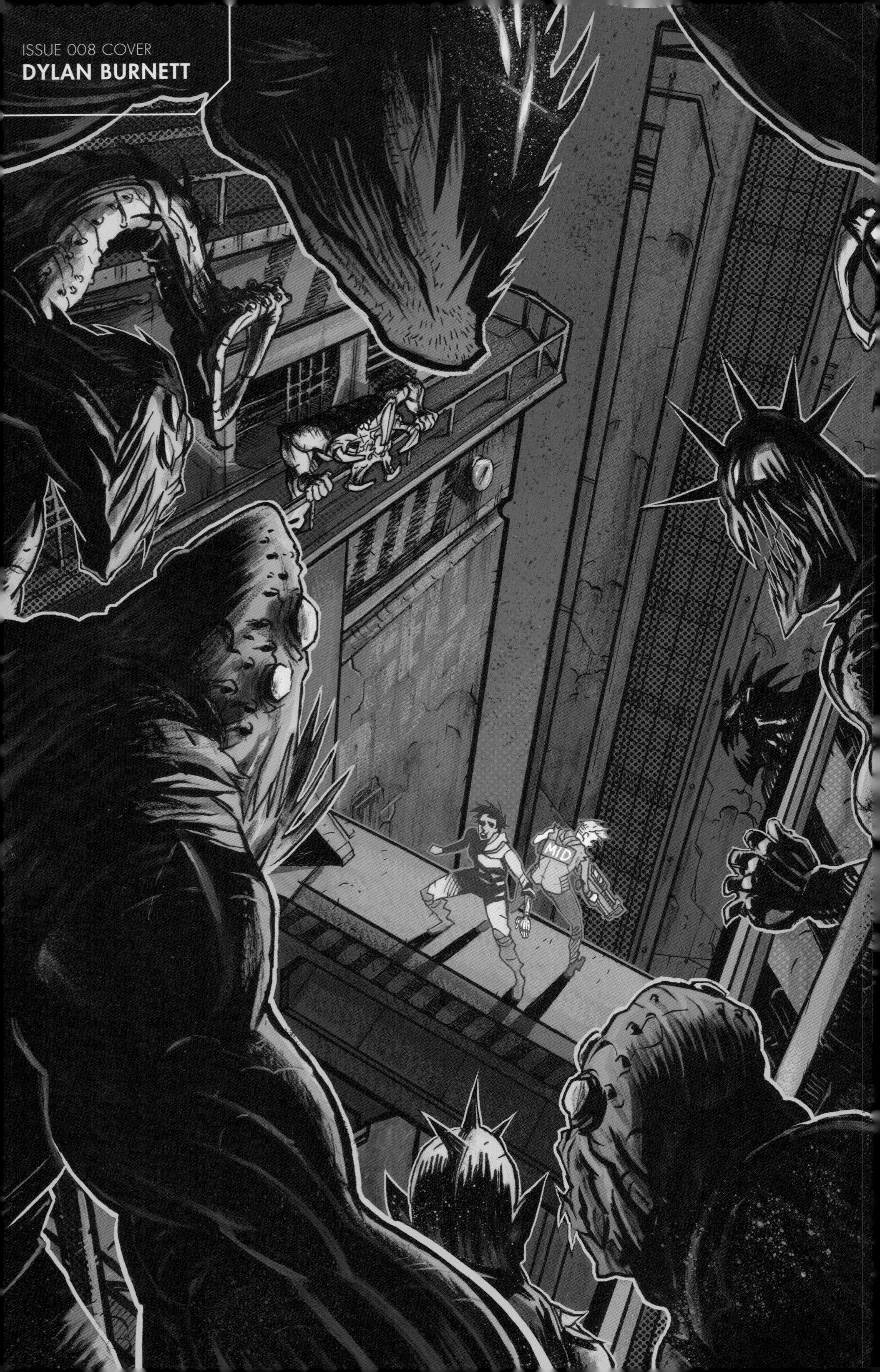
MID

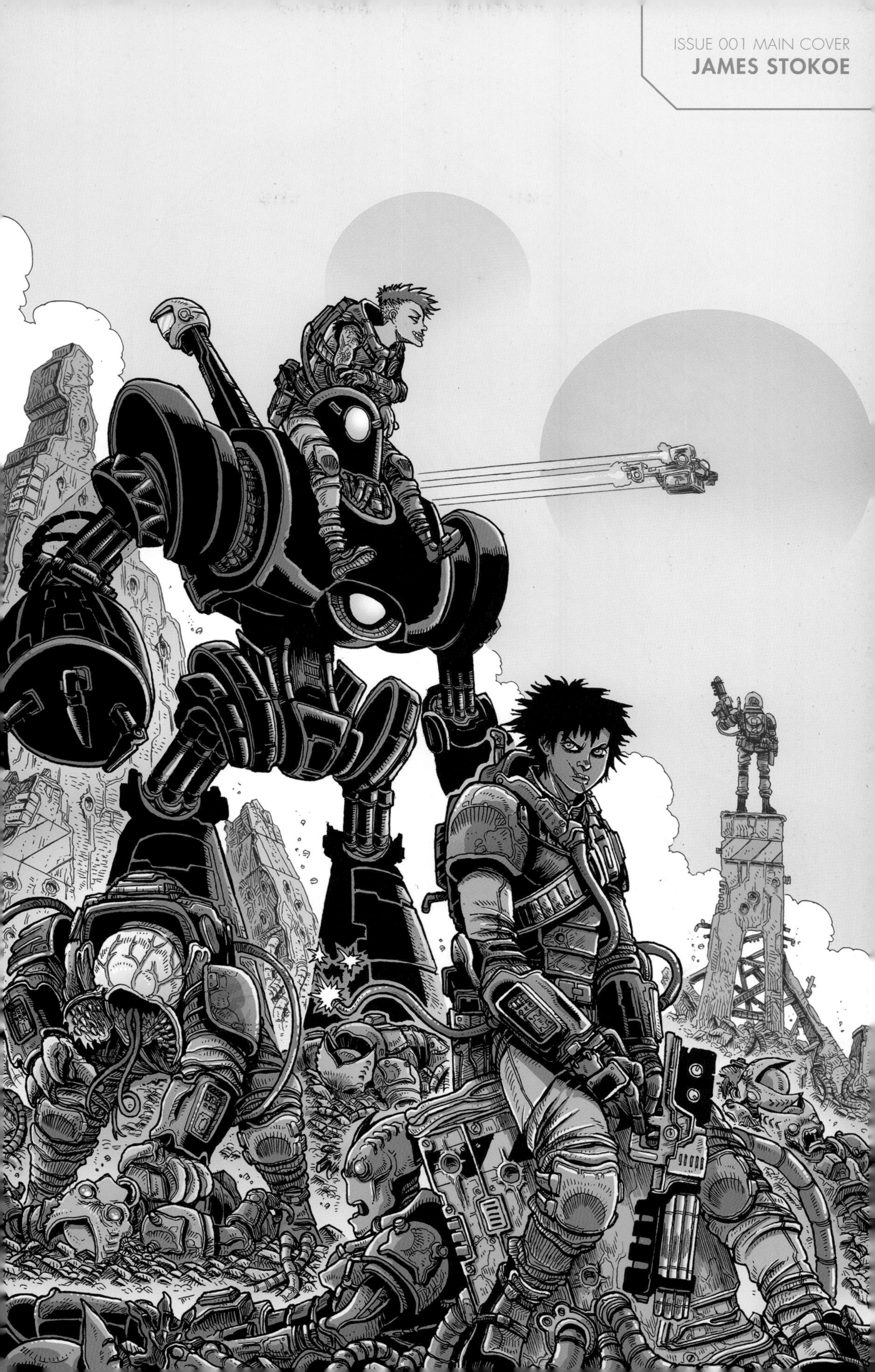

ISSUE 001 MAIN COVER
JAMES STOKOE

ISSUE 001 JACKPOT
VARIANT COVER
SIMON ROY

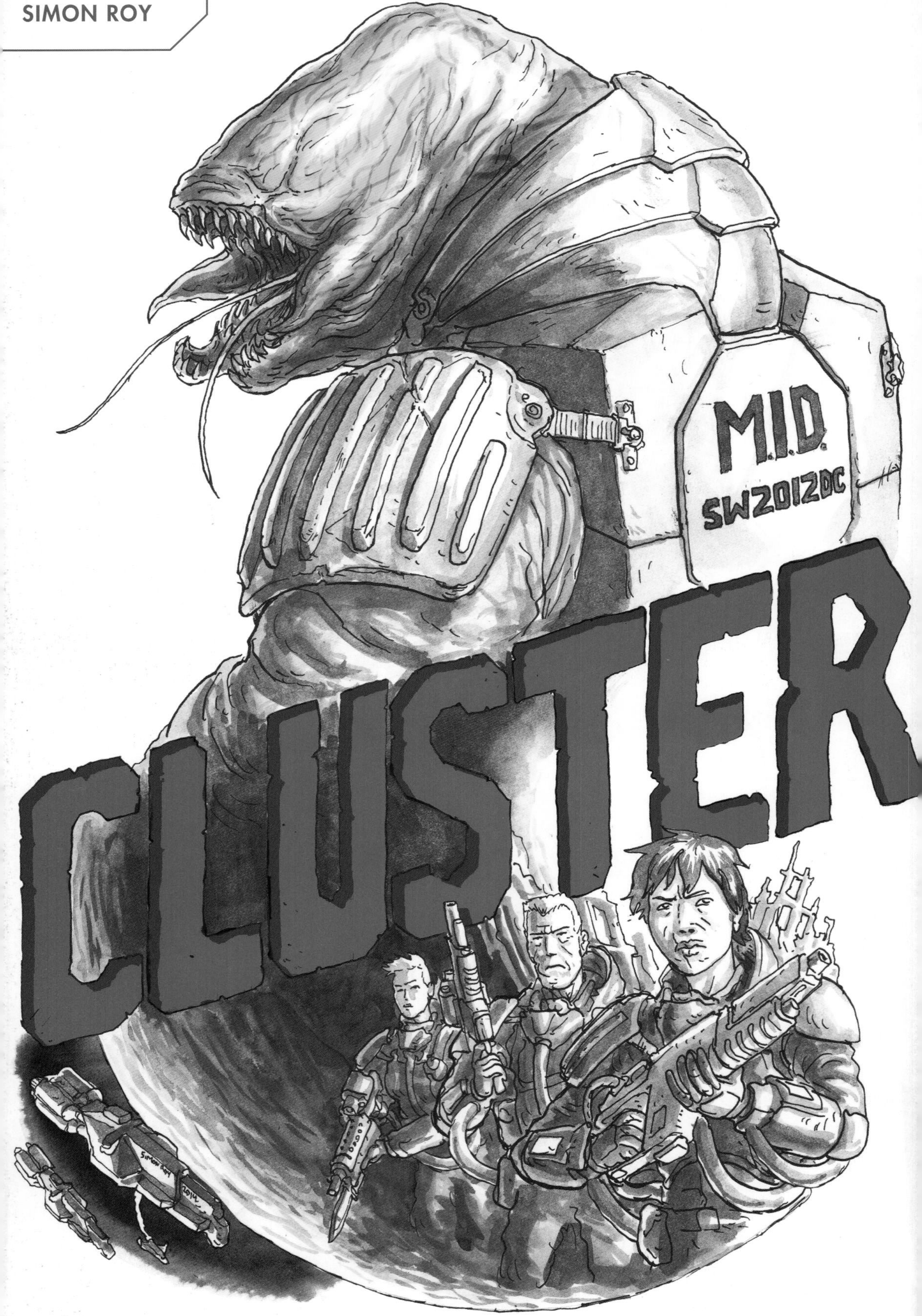
M.I.D.
SW2012DC
CLUSTER
SIMON ROY 2014

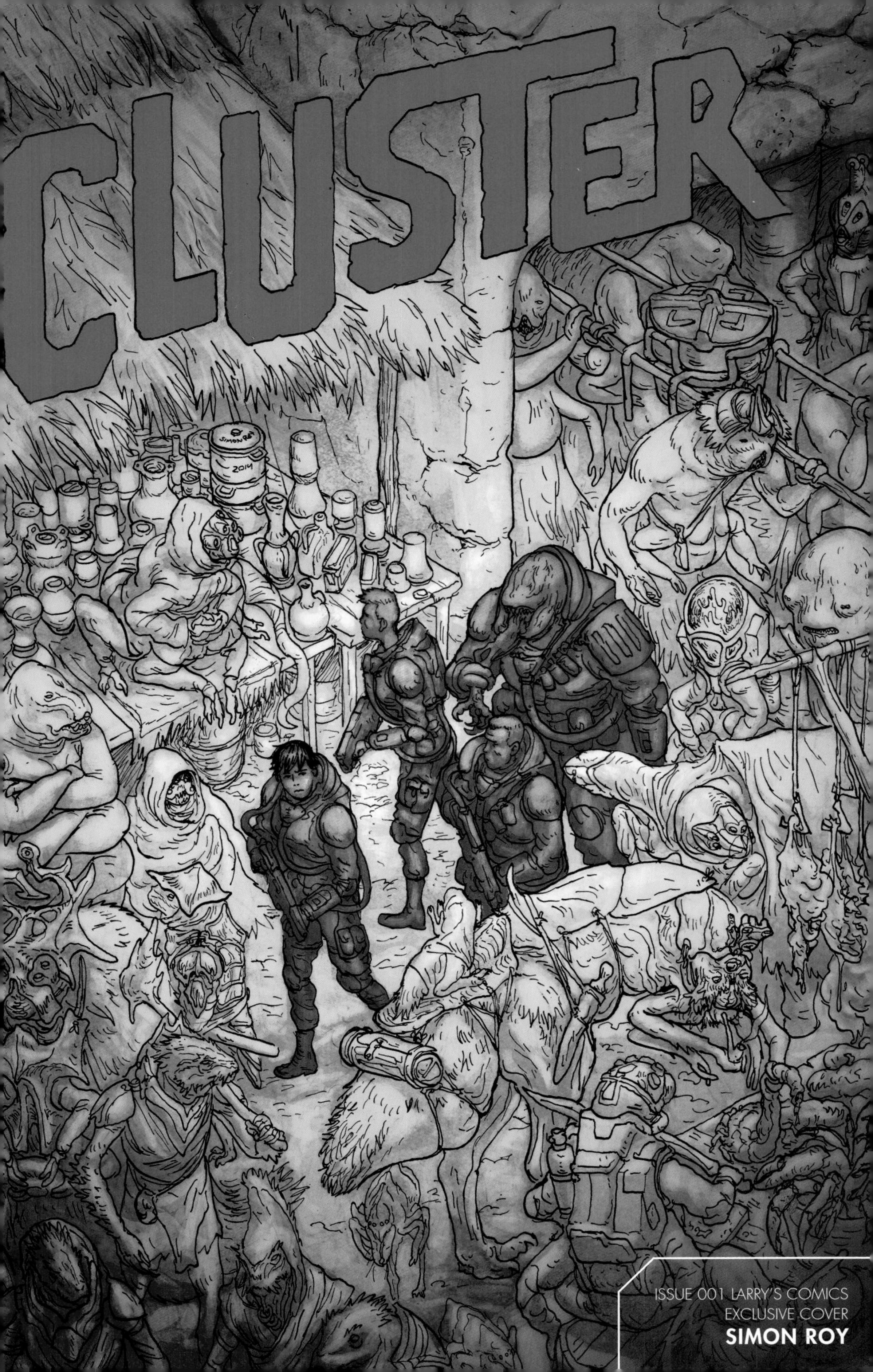
CLUSTER
SIMON ROY
2014
ISSUE 001 LARRY'S COMICS
EXCLUSIVE COVER
SIMON ROY

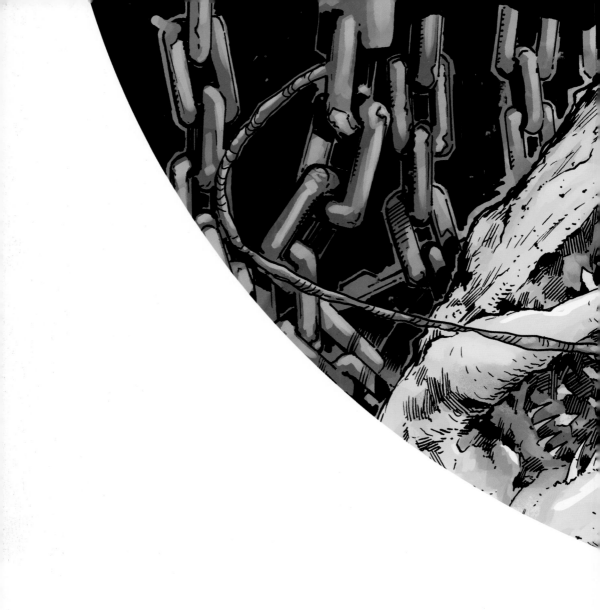

ISSUE 001 BOOM! TEN YEARS
VARIANT COVER
TREVOR HAIRSINE
WITH COLORS BY **JORDAN BOYD**

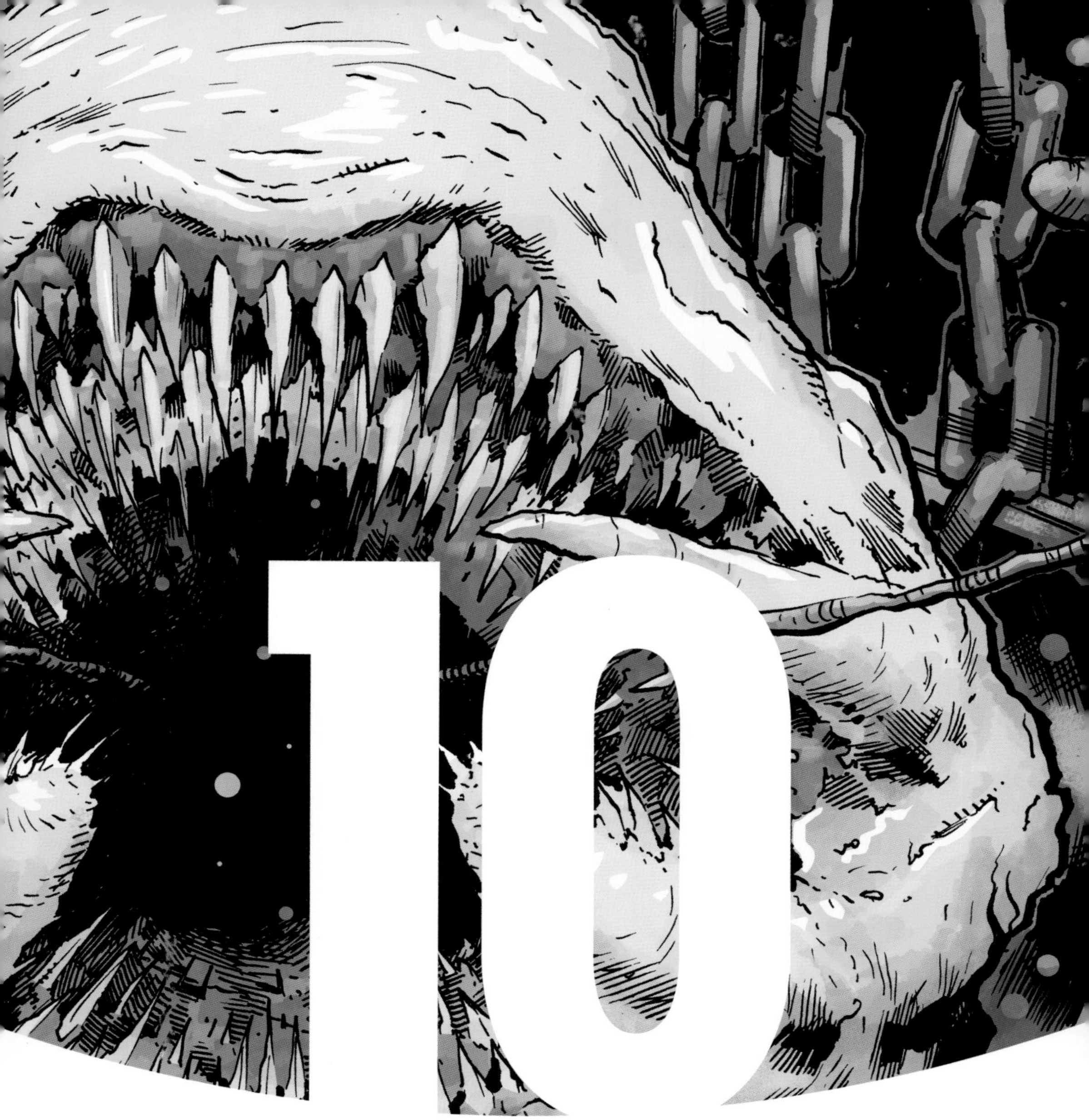
10

ISSUE 001SECOND PRINT COVER
DAMIAN COUCIERO
WITH COLORS BY **JORDAN BOYD**

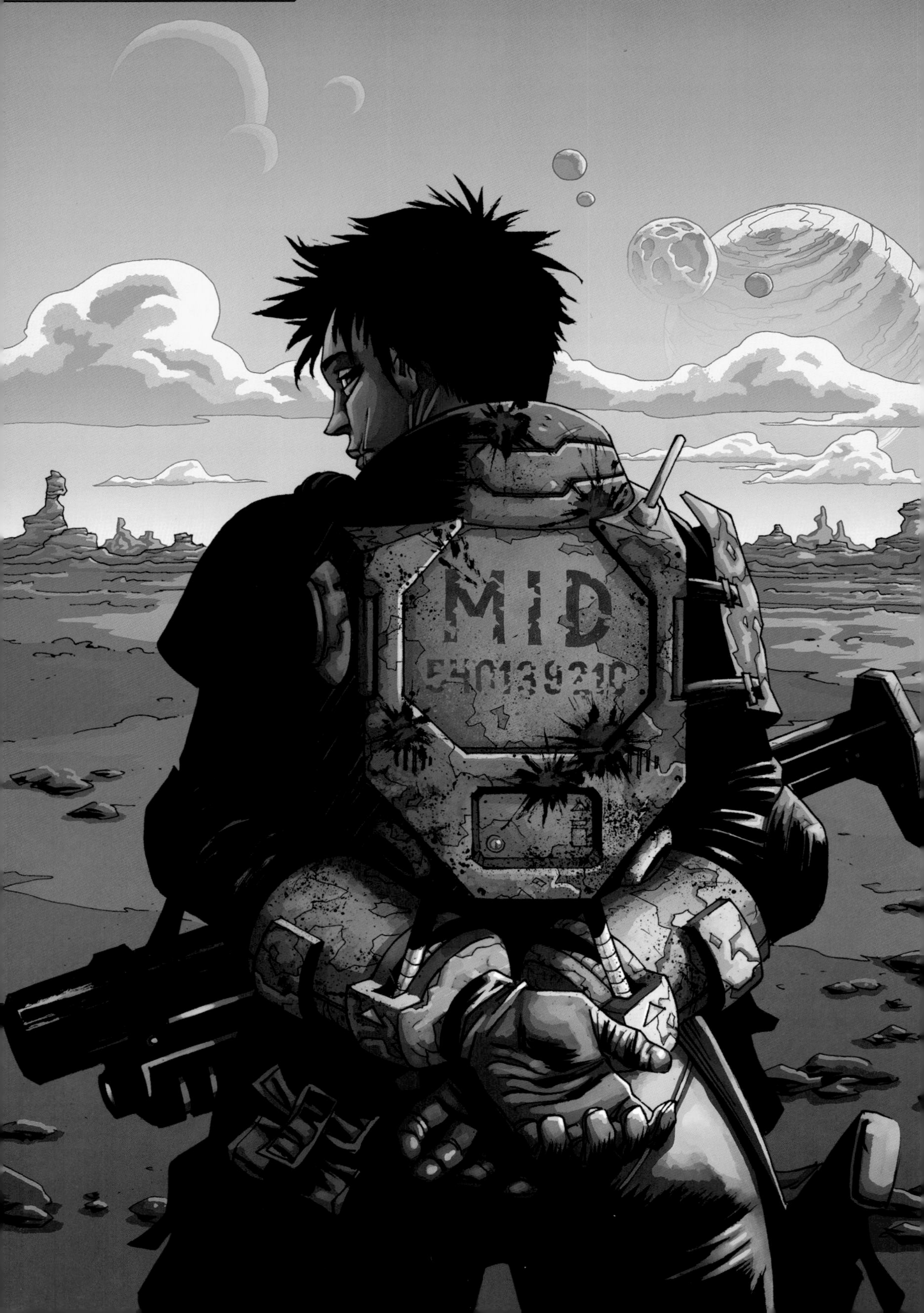
MID

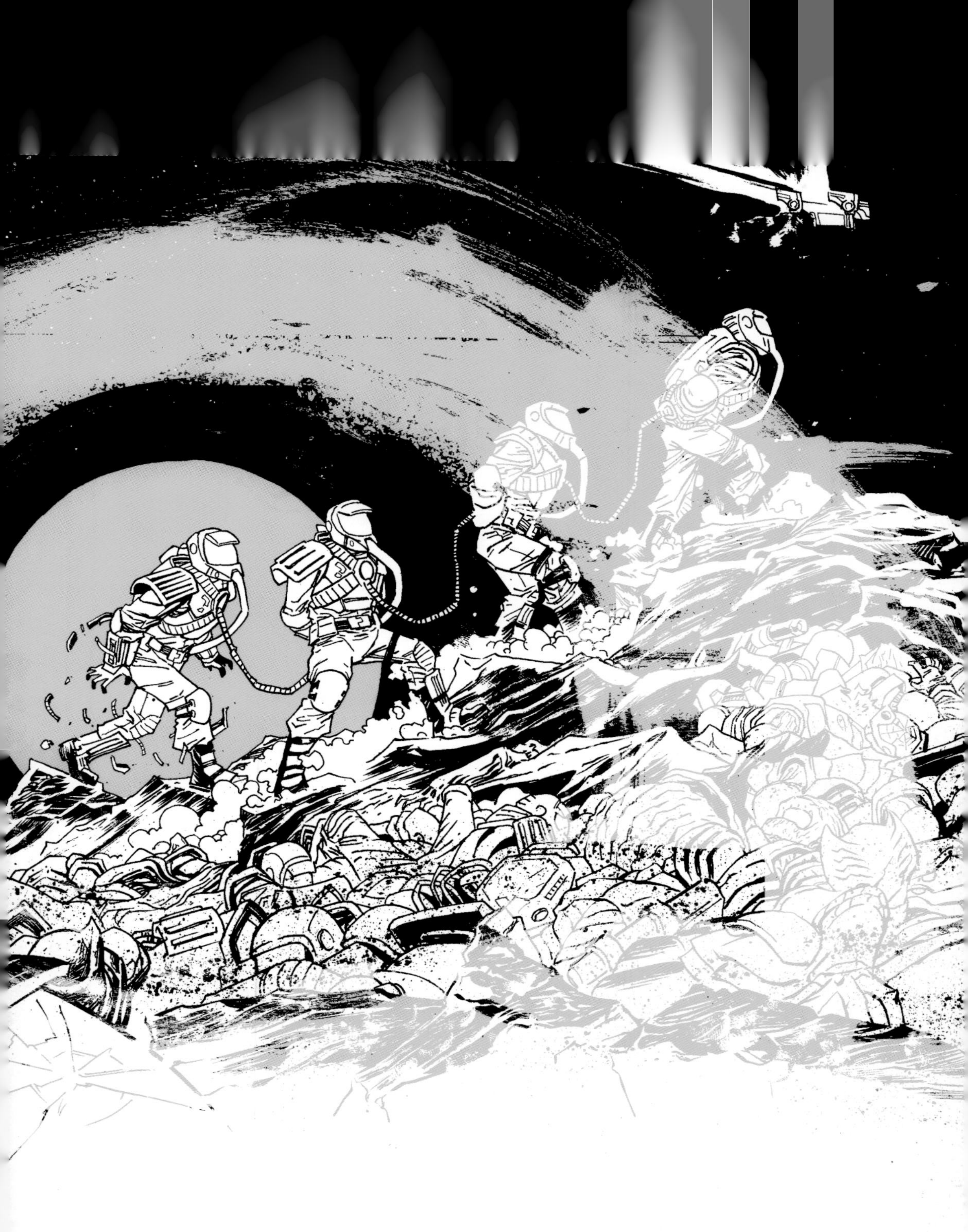

ISSUE 001 VARIANT COVER
DECLAN SHALVEY
WITH COLORS BY **JORDIE BELLAIRE**

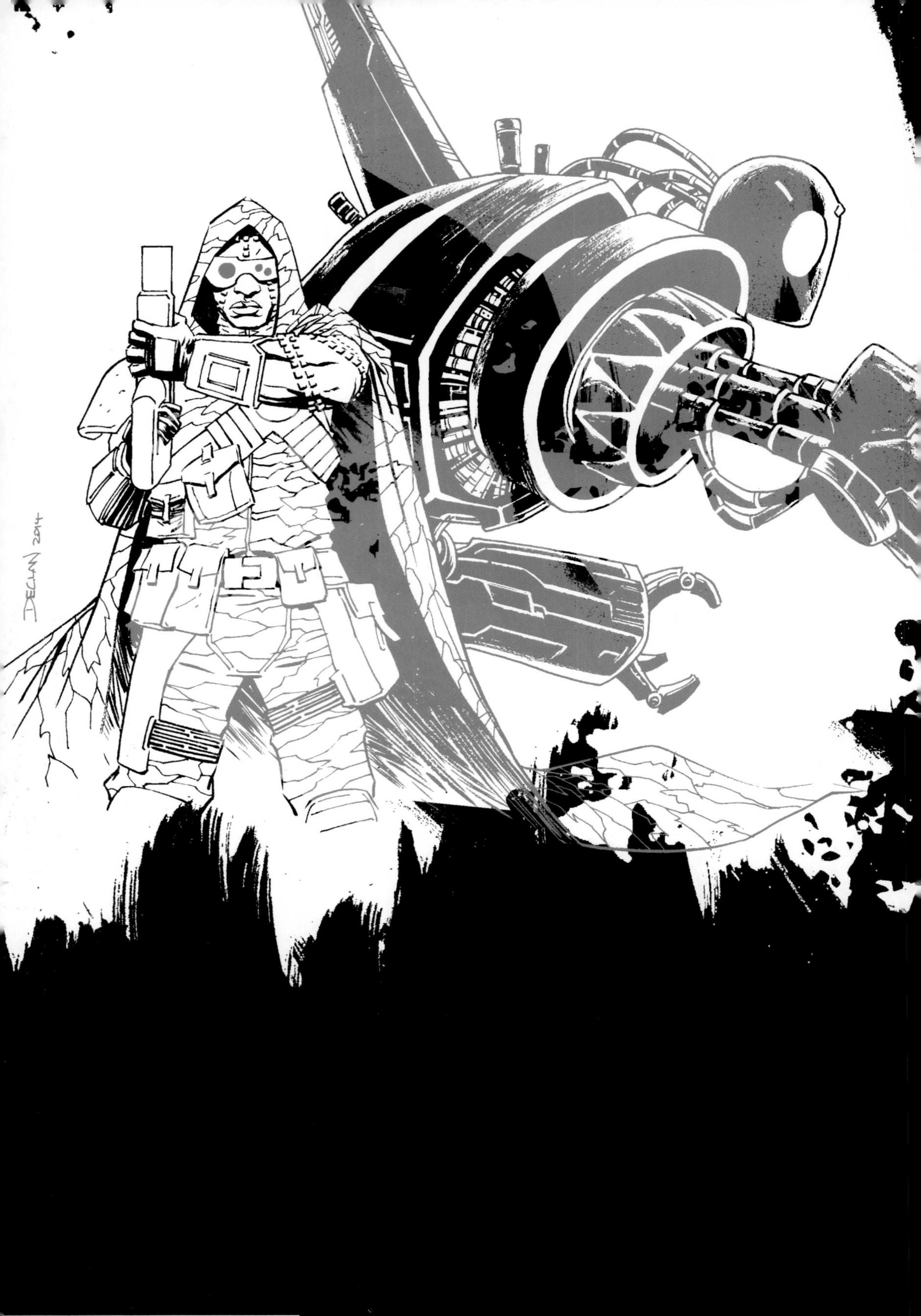
DECLAN 2014

ISSUE 002 VARIANT COVER

DECLAN SHALVEY

WITH COLORS BY **JORDIE BELLAIRE**

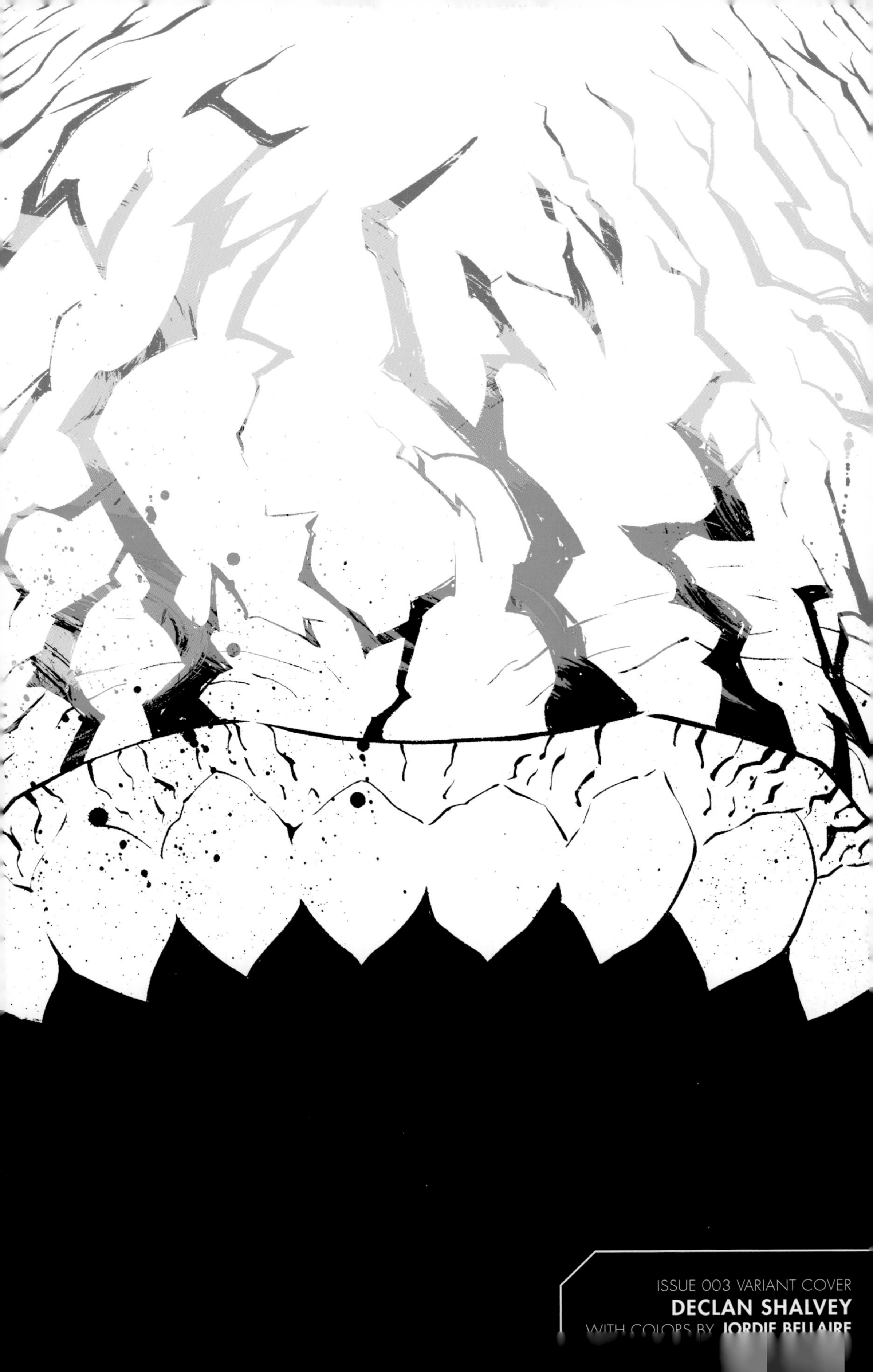

ISSUE 003 VARIANT COVER
DECLAN SHALVEY
WITH COLORS BY **JORDIE BELLAIRE**

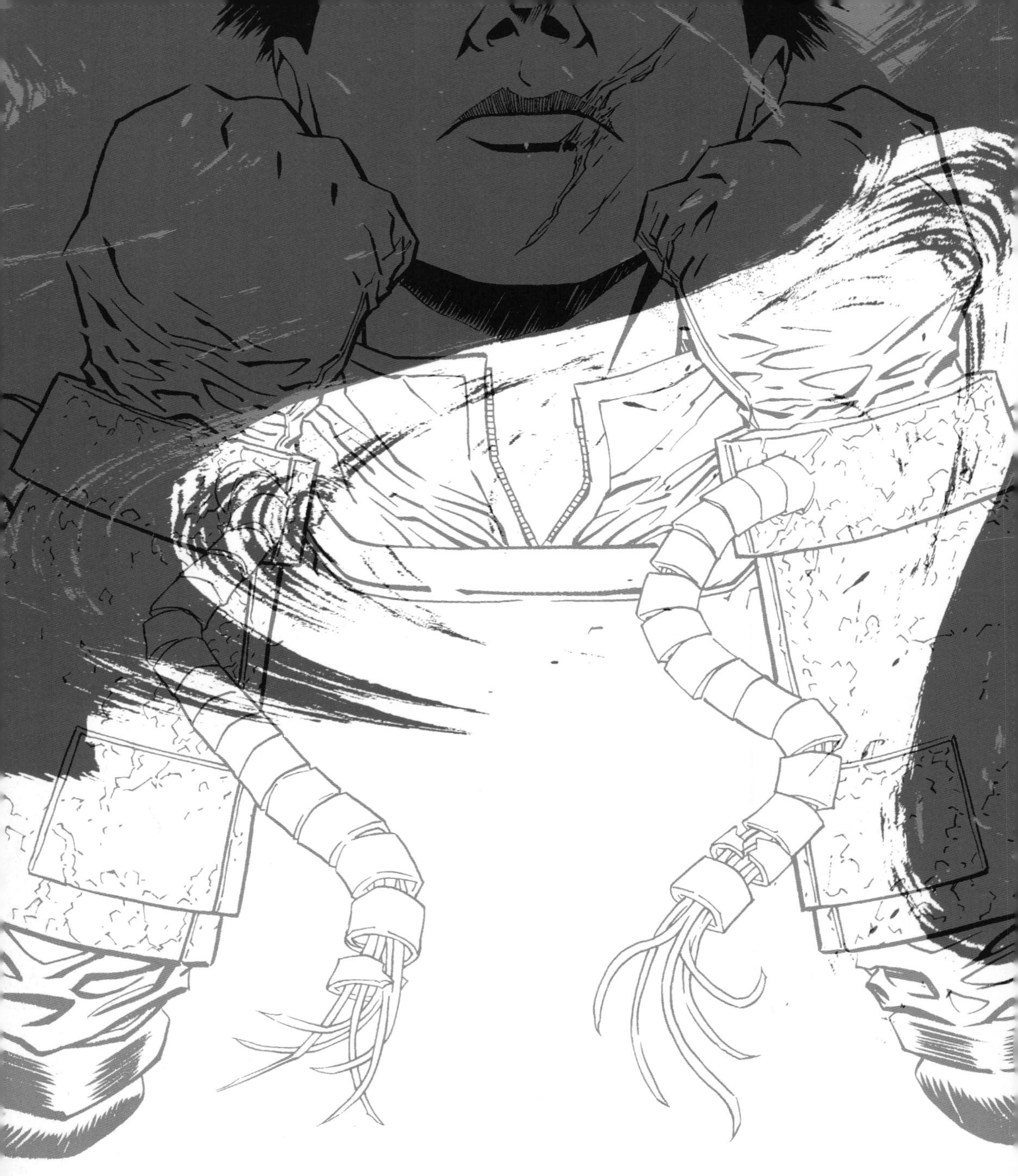
DECLAN 2015

ISSUE 004 VARIANT COVER
DECLAN SHALVEY
WITH COLORS BY **JORDIE BELLAIRE**

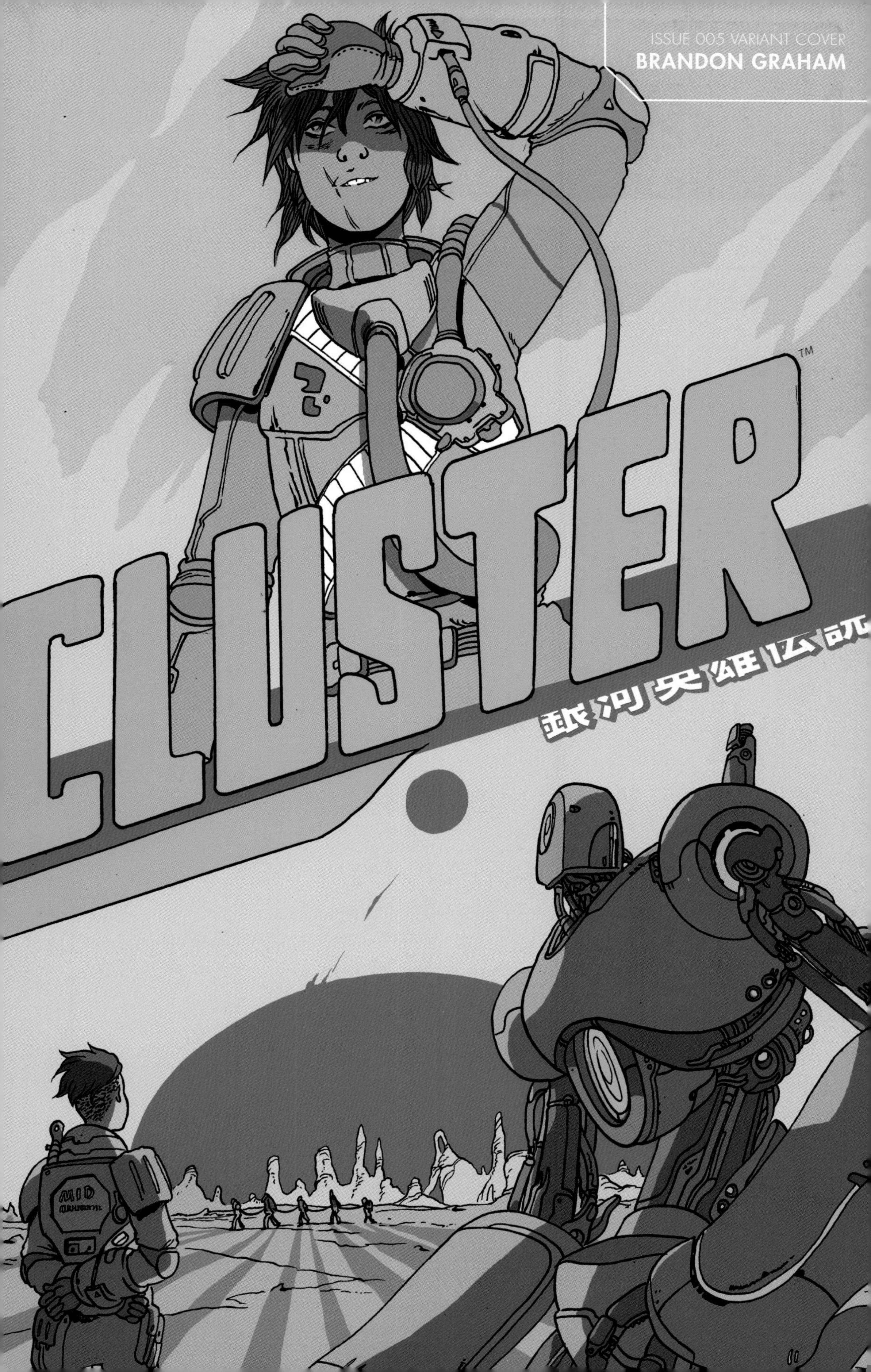

ISSUE 005 VARIANT COVER
BRANDON GRAHAM
CLUSTER™
MID